T0366307

HOW TO PREVENT RECESSION

HOW TO PREVENT RECESSION

USING ANCIENT WISDOM
&
MANAGEMENT IDEAS

Foreword by His Holiness The Dalai Lama

S A T Y A   S A U R A B H   K H O S L A

AFTER PREDICTING THE 2008 RECESSION, AUTHOR SHARES WAY TO PREVENT ONE.

PARTRIDGE
A Penguin Random House Company

To order additional copies of this book, contact
Toll Free 800 101 2657 (Singapore)
Toll Free 1 800 81 7340 (Malaysia)
orders.singapore@partridgepublishing.com

www.partridgepublishing.com/singapore

**This book is dedicated to blossoming
the excellence hidden in man...**

Ancient Indians had a way of bringing out this excellence. They also had a different concept of **capitalism, profit** and **competition**. This led to balance and prosperity for thousands of years. Balance emerged when their education helped man discipline the mind. Their spirituality merged with other faiths. It led to good economics and Best Management Practices. The 'perfect fit' of management of life and business with values led to prosperity. The global financial crisis occurred as many sought to take as much debt as they possibly could. Ancient wisdom, instead, taught how to repay eternal debts.

This book is meant for all seekers of wisdom. It broadens ideas of management to apply them to the business of living life. Its ideas have enabled man's transformation towards excellence for thousands of years – leading to prosperity and values in society.

The cover uses symbols of Boolean algebra (which deals with Truth Values). It depicts that if ancient wisdom and management are both true, then, contents here are true.

All religions have three aspects:

1. *A common message of: adhere to Truth, follow morality with Love and Peace.*
2. *Differences in philosophy, beliefs: about existence of a creator and His nature.*
3. *Cultural aspects of religions: customs differ and can even change with time.*

This book uses the first aspect and interprets the second to benefit man and society.

Foreword

Today human society on the whole has far more material resources at its disposal than ever before. At the same time, we are beset by problems, some created by our own action; overpopulation, dwindling natural resources, widening gap between rich and poor, and an environmental crisis that threatens existence on this small planet that is our only home. One of the main causes for these is the excessive unethical malpractices, including insatiable greed of individuals and corporate houses, existing within sections of our society.

If we look further we can find that today's education system unfortunately has failed to incorporate fundamental values of love and compassion that can provide a wholesome development of the individual. While material development is necessary for human comfort they can not provide us inner happiness, which can help confront some of the challenges mentioned above.

I have been highlighting this need by promoting the concept of what I term "universal responsibility". The world has become so interdependent that a problem in one part of the world becomes a problem of everybody. In reality our interests and others' interests are very much interconnected and our centuries old held concept of "us" and "them" being independent of each other is outdated. Therefore, we should develop a sense of concern for the whole of humanity, the whole world.

Fortunately, more and more people are coming to recognize the importance of promotion of inner development. Until comparatively recently, few people gave much thought to the effects of human activity on our planet.

Accordingly, I welcome this book, *How To Prevent Recession: Using Ancient Wisdom and Management Ideas,* by Satya Saurabh Khosla as it tries to address this very issue. I am particularly encouraged that, just as I myself have relied on the ancient Indian thoughts in my effort to promote awareness about the importance of compassion, this book dwells on the fourfold ancient concept of Chatush Purusharthas to help modern society and business leaders tackle modern world problems, especially in business management. The central message of the concept is that one should moderate the two and live a balanced life of material and mental happiness simultaneously. This is a very profound concept put in a very simple and beautiful format.

March 31, 2015

In Latin Preface meant 'spoken before'

*Many ideas of this book have been spoken before – by wise people
in ancient times. These ideas are reworded in today's idiom here.
The Preface gives a glimpse of how and why this has been done
– to rignite wise ideas that benefit society. The acknowledgements
towards those who participated in this process is given at the end of
the book. Thus the Preface and acknowledgements are like a pair of
hands enclosing the contents of the book – lest the flame of eternal
wisdom be blown by gusts of greed – leading soceity to another recession.*

Preface

How to make life fulfilling for man in society? Education has been answering this question from time immemorial. In different periods of time, man's concerns have been changing. In the present age, the concern is for earning money. So, a recession affects many and gives an opportunity to seek answers from the experience of previous educators. This book is one such attempt. It seeks answers from ancient Indian tradition. Texts of this tradition have been recorded at different times to fulfill concerns of that time and age. Their purpose is to discuss the vagaries of the mind and guide man how to reshape it. How does its method of education and way of fulfilling concerns apply to society today – to prevent recession? What technique or way of learning can our education system incorporate to fulfill this task? The book seeks an answer by enabling transformation of man through education.

It discovers that ancient Indian education sought to achieve two objectives. Firstly, it sought to create in man an Awareness of the potential of goodness and excellence that was within him. Practices, habits that led to it are given. Secondly, it taught him how to use this potential within 'limits' so that it is used to maximise society's welfare through which his personal welfare is looked after. These 'limits' were called *Purusharthas* and were goals of life.

This book demonstrates how Awareness can be created and goals be used for purpose of creating wealth in today's context. As management study is used for this purpose, it applies ideas of this tradition to study of management. As this study is ever-evolving – those concepts were chosen which armed students in 1980's and '90's with ideas with which they, as senior managers, faced the recession of 2008. How could the same ideas be taught with a slight change in focus – using technique of ancient Indian tradition? Can recession be prevented if these ideas are applied to management thought? If so, can all disciplines use the four *Purusharthas* or ideas similar to their interpretation in management thought as – Co-operation, focused Concern, Competitive Response and Compatibility Advantage? How can present academic theory promote 'Co-operation' and develop a 'Focus' on excellence with a 'Concern' for society? How to change the understanding of meaning of 'Competitive' and mould 'Response' of managers so that it is 'Compatible' with needs of society and nature – enabling all to enjoy the 'Advantage' of such a way of 'C'ing or seeing life? In this manner the 4C Approach to management interprets and applies the four *Purusharthas*.

Recession can be prevented by ethics driven, goal oriented action. Ancient Indians used four goals of life or *Purusharthas* to integrate the goal of ethics in daily behaviour of man. Ideas from *Vedanta* and about God enabled it. *Salaat* or devotion in Islam is a basis of life for many. However, Buddhism, without using idea of a God, reaches the same conclusions! Thus ancient education, across religions, makes student follow Truth and Morality. With this Best Management Practice, he discovers excellence in all dimensions (or the Soul principle) – by practicing Unity of Thought, Word and Deed. This leads to detachment from fruit of action – in 'experience' of ancient Indians. Then, best management practices for life emerge in man's behaviour. His work in the firm is a sub set of life. Thus, best management practices emerge within each firm, too. This creates 'balance' in cluster, industry, society, nation etc. How such a practice can apply to man's behaviour is explained at the end of Chapter 1. How it applies to everchanging management theory and how the Source has applied it to benefit society is explained in Chapter 7.

Only after inculcating this idea were skills for a particular trade, vocation, field of application taught. The student sought excellence by following four fold path of this tradition (4C Approach of this book). That this path merges with eight fold path of Buddhism, basic ideas of Jesus (Love) and Islam (Peace, Surrender) led to 'balance' within man and society…and also with nature! Buddhism's *Samyak Drishti*, for example, is the ability to 'C' this. *Zaakat* in Islam is same as Compassion of Buddhism or 'Help Ever, Hurt Never'. These ideas are eternal. **The book's idea is to state, not propogate them**.

The merger of four *Purusharthas* of management (4Cs) with ideas of ancient Indian tradition that led to balance (Invisible Truth, *Dharma*, *Yoga*, Meditation, *Moksha*) is demonstrated. It helps an understanding that 'balance' is a three – fold concept: First, 'balance' is essential within man. Education creates it through practice of truth, morality and 'unity of thought, word and deed'. Lack of balance in man leads to lack of balance in society and lack of balance with nature. Lack of balance in society brings social conflict, crime, recession, non – inclusive growth etc. Lack of balance with nature creates global warming. It is also caused by over exploitation of natural resources, urban pressures on forests and hills and consequences of same. All the three states of balance exist simultaneously. One balance leads to the other – when education transforms man. Man and society are, thus, inextricably interlinked!

One question, however, seeks an answer: 'Goal' is visualised by some as a distant object. How can it be a 'limit' for man? The answer is simple: a river flows to its goal within the limits of its banks; the ocean's vastness achieves its goal through the limit of its shores. If these limits are crossed the balance between man and nature is disturbed. A soccer match gets its meaning through the 'limit' of two goals at the edge of a field. To reach a goal a path with limits is useful. Hence for any play, 'lila' or activity to achieve its meaning, 'limits' are important – so, too, for man. Limits allow man to achieve the purpose of the activity.

Another question needs an answer. How can this book be rewritten from a religion's point of view? Let us take the example of Buddhism, here. Buddha's search began with the question 'what is the cause of misery?' Only earlier chapter about Awareness needs rewriting to answer this question (instead of the question 'What is man?'). Similarly, Chapter 6 has to be rewritten interpreting all texts to prove interconnectedness of man and society. It is even simpler in Buddhism for Buddha saw a dead body and began His search. Hence, seeing misery in society transformed Him. Similarly, seeing misery of recession in society can transform students of Buddhism.

The author seeks that word 'Man' be read as gender neutral in this book. Man can be a pun on the Hindi word 'Mun' where 'a' – if sounded as 'u' – means mind of a human being. The idea of education is to train the mind – for life. Therefore, ideas here are about 'Man Management'. 'Managing' the mind helps man and firm to prevent social problems. Common goals and strategy for man and firm creates unity in action at home, work – for the benefit of society. Ancient techniques can help direct thoughts of man, plans of firm. Just as four *Purusharthas* give meaning to man's actions – making them fit for society, 4C's give meaning to a firm. This leads society to express and enjoy true culture (*samskara*) – for ancient Indians state: *Samyak Kriti iti samskara.*

How to take contents of the Foreword forward?

The purpose of Contents of exchange of ideas should be to remove discontent. If that can not be removed, it can, at least, be transformed into a quest. The quest for excellence is the highest among all quests. When applied to life, it leads to questioning the purpose of life itself and the Truth about it. When applied to society, it removes conflict among men and nations. When applied to business it should remove recession. How? A discontent with many ideas that lead to success but do not give satisfaction or enable excellence within man or society led to a quest reflected in the Contents here.

CONTENTS

*Chapter 1 helps Truth of appropriate (optimum) Strategy emerge from 'within' man;
Chapters 2 to 5 outline this Strategy – this creates balance in all activities of man.*

Part A: <u>**Ancient Wisdom**</u> – Values are the basis for the Strategy of life – Values create **Awareness of potential of Excellence 'within' man**
EDUCATION MAKES MAN THE MASTER OF HIS MIND – THIS CREATES BALANCE IN MAN
Awakening man's Awareness of Excellence 'within': Strategy of Management for Man & firm is same. Porter's ingredients of Strategy apply to Strategy for living life – Merging ideas of Strategy. Values are the basis for the ancient Indian strategy for life

Part B: <u>**Management Ideas**</u> – Strategy of firm emerges from values – Ethics set 'Limits' through Goals of Life (4C Approach to Management)
EDUCATION MAKES MAN'S ACTIONS CREATE BALANCE IN SOCIETY:
Man should perform a role in society within limits to achieve goals. Four *Purusharthas* are goals of human behaviour. They shape social values and define Limits for man – Interpretation and application of these in Management practice as **4C's of Management**

To read between the lines, watch this space before sections and Chapters:

If the content of an effort results in transformation in a desired direction, the effort is considered fruitful. How can a book on recession achieve a transformation within man? Before the beginning of some sections and Chapters an endeavour to delineate steps that can lead to inner transformation may be given – on the even numbered left hand page.

These pages can give a quick review of some ideas of the book.

If this book were a novel, the synopsis would give the outline of the plot. Inadvertently, misguided actions of a few plotted the recession. Of course, they felt they were innocent – after all, they were only protecting their self interest. This is where the plot thickens. Can self interest that harms society be of interest to society? After all, did not the perpetrators suffer, too? If failure or misuse of systems, laws and management ideas can be plotted, can their skilful use, too, not be plotted? This is the plot of this book as a novel idea that brings ethics into education and such education to workplaces. Of course, the plot begins with life. If life is transformed by ethics, then the deeper and real plot of a novel idea is revealed...

SYNOPSIS

Many believe that success in business is because of a strategy. Therefore, it may be important to understand 'what is strategy'? The way of achieving a goal is called strategy. Then, should the way of achieving goals of life not be called a 'Strategy of living life'?

Success is a goal of life for many. But, success depends on many factors. Many of them are outside the control of man. Sometimes success, earning wealth and fame etc. does not satisfy man. In some cases it leads to greed. When greed is not restrained it leads to many social problems, including recession. Managers felt they were succeeding in 2008, too – yet society experienced a recession. Excellence is also possible through man's conscious effort, reforming habits, control of mind and refining of character. The desire of excellence, too, is never ending. The only difference is that it seeks to bring out the best 'within' man, for himself and society, without greed. This is called Self Actualisation in management/psychology and is a goal of life in ancient Indian tradition. Awareness about it was created as the basis of action in life – which includes man's actions in firm.

Creating awareness of the potential of excellence 'within' man was the task of education in ancient India. It helped overcome greed and, thus, prevented recession. This book details how this awareness is created and used to impart skills of management that lead to balance 'within' man and in society. Such a 'balance' prevents recession.

How to prevent Recession?

An answer to this question is discovered in the synopsis here through many questions and realisations. Some of these are:
- How to use academic research for curing recession?
- Preventing recession will need self confidence. How to develop it?
- How can we prevent recession?
- How to best use all traditions and faiths to bring out the best in man?
- What is the need for this book?
- Strategy must teach that society benefits with enlightened self interest – not selfishness
- How did ancient Indians use idea of Divinity to uplift humanity?
- Reform of society begins with man
- Reform of society leads to 'balance'
- Ancient Indian tradition's approach to education
- What is role of education for 'balance' in society – Ancient Indian way?
- Why do problems exist in society today?
- What creates 'balance' in society?
- Which ideas made ancient Indian tradition last?
- Integrating ancient Indian tradition with education, including management education
- Test the Truth of this book's hypothesis: apply it to education and life.

2008:
All managers thought they were successful at that time.
Their companies made record profit and they received record bonus
Yet society discovered later that their actions led to the recession
The failure of their success never hurt society harder...

How to Prevent Recession?

The word 'recession' had been forgotten. Human memory is short and 1929 was many years ago. The 2008 recession came at a time when nobody thought anything could go wrong. Some were tempted to think that 'there is no harm if I buy assets a little more than what I can afford – it will only help the economy grow – after all asset prices are increasing'. All those who thought like this may or may not have caused the recession – but some of them were affected by it.

Economists gave this growth a name – 'Goldilocks' growth. This is a story we have heard as children. Goldilocks got all she wanted despite the danger of losing her way and entering a bear's house. She ate their porridge, broke a chair, slept but left as a friend of the bear family. The growth economists talk of was like the porridge she ate – neither too hot nor too cold. It was just right. Goldilocks growth, too, is not too hot to cause inflation nor too cold to cause recession. Everybody gets what they want. With low unemployment, low interest rates allow taking loans and almost everybody's income grows – along with stock markets and asset prices. It seemed like that in the first decade of the new millennium …till something went wrong as 2008 approached. Around 16th October, 2007 the stock market gave a small downtick…such a minor growl of the Bear move. Nobody noticed it. As the down movement continued, everybody thought it was a 'healthy' correction till it cascaded. 2008 recognised this 'healthy correction' as a recession.

What caused this Bear market? A simple answer confronts us: Greed. How to prevent it from happening again? Some say that greed is ingrained in man's nature. Others feel that anger, too, is. If man can learn to control anger, why not greed? Thus the question: 'What should man learn to restrain greed?'

After the recession, thinkers like Michael Porter and Rosabeth Kanter from Harvard Business School made contributions. Raj Sisodia of Babson College, USA translated ideas of Conscious Capitalism into action with a 'movement' along with a firm's CEO. Michael Porter suggests the need for **Shared Value**. He states that theory about it is still emerging (This book identifies, in its Introduction, **four Shared Values** that lead to four goals of life. These help man, business and lead to balance in society, too). Either way, all seem to agree that greed is restrained when profit is not the only or No. 1 priority of business.

If profit is not the only or No. 1 priority of business....what is?

Recently, some company CEOs gave examples of how they and others are moving away from profit being the No.1 priority of business. The USA Commerce Secretary agreed with this idea of Clinton Foundaton, a former USA President's Foundation. What impact would this approach have on business? What should be the shape of strategy?

To answer this question, the book compares Profit to the speed of a car. If a car is programmed to go at top speed only – there is great likelihood of a crash. The global economic crisis occurred when maximising personal and firm's profit was the 'mantra'. It was like a car programmed to travel at top speed only, forgetting brakes.

How were financial crises averted in ancient India? What was their strategy?
The book uses Harvard Professor Michael Porter's ingredient of strategy: Optimisation Effort. It states that profit should be an Optimisation Effort not a Maximisation Effort! It takes the example of a car's speed, once again. If a car is programmed to optimise its speed, it will take many variables into account like: bumpiness of a terrain (to avoid jerks for passengers), fuel efficiency may be a criteria, or, it may foresee risk of a crash and reduce speed etc. Which criteria to apply when is the program that education teaches. This judgment comes from 'within' a manager when he is in the driving seat.

How to develop this judgment in man? Ancient Indian tradition trains students for life, not just corporate work. It transforms them by imparting discrimination: influencing a change in attitude from maximum speed to 'optimum' speed! Society, then, enjoyed prosperity with practice of righteous restraint – imparted through four goals of life. Fig 0.27 in Introduction will show them as four wheels of a car. How do these translate into goals for firm's life – in management thought? The book answers this question. Chapter 1 reveals Truth 'within' man and Chapters 2 to 5 give balance – while driving the car of life, even to work. It gives a theory of competition that is based on excellence emerging from 'within' man. Success can be due to many factors – some outside the control of man – but pursuit of excellence makes success by unfair means unacceptable. Such an approach made ancient Indian civilisation contribute significantly to global GDP for thousands of years. When ancient wisdom is merged with modern management ideas, prosperity, guided by righteous self restraint or *Dharma*, prevents recession and other social problems. The book demonstrates how – its 101 Diagrams unite ancient wisdom with Porter's work in strategy of firm and competitive advantage of nations – then apply the thought to McGraths idea of transient advantage (to demonstrate its applicability across seemingly divergent ideas).

How to use academic research for curing recession?

Many articles in journals prove a simple point – that research done in 1999 is not applicable in 2013. Then: 'How do we know that what is taught in 2015 will be relevant in 2025'? Also, many believe that management books must use case studies to demonstrate good practices. When sum total of practices lead to a recession, who can guide? Theory – not case studies – must guide, then – for the failure of society is a case study. Can debates or blames cure a recession? Restraining greed is the bitter pill needed – it comes through re-education. Can ancient wisdom help to restrain greed? If so, can academic theory be integrated with its techniques? Such integration should be able to face the test of resolving seemingly opposing concerns of researchers – enabling solutions that benefit society. Porter's concern is addressed by four **shared values** that integrate society, restrain greed.

Ancient wisdom was used for thousands of years and may apply in 2025 also. Its ideas of strategy are likely to be sustainable – but adaptable to new situations in an ever changing world. If its ideas restrain greed, its study of strategy will prevent recession. Then, its ideas of strategy should have enabled a civilisation to survive. Such ideas are discovered and merged with work of Porter till 1999 in Chapter 1 to 5, here. Finally, they are applied to McGrath's 2013 idea of non sustainable advantage in strategy in Chapter 7(a). What behaviour of firms can address concerns about society (that arise after reading the work of Thomas Piketty of Paris School of economics)? Chapter 4 gives a possible solution. Such a study of strategy can help man, businesses and society prevent recession. But, first, two questions need answers that do not change every few years:
(1) Preventing recession will need self confidence. How to develop it?
(2) How can we prevent recession?

A steady answer needs ideas that are steady, over time. They may belong to spirituality or anything not so susceptible to change. After all, management study uses the best of all resources. It, then, uses its problem-solving skills to adapt them to today's reality. So, how to use the best of all traditions to solve problems of society? This book merges many ideas with management ideas to identify sustainable ideas of strategy. Any method or plan of achieving a goal is called strategy. Ancient Indian tradition uses goals of life – which is life's strategy. For, goals lead to strategy. Its goals restrained greed. Strategy that adds meaning to man's life should help the firm (company where he works) and society, too. Only then can a civilisation survive. Thus, using goals of man for the firm will help man serve self through the firm and society. Profit will not be the only goal in such a strategy.

Preventing recession will need self confidence. How to develop it?

Recession is not a natural calamity. It is man-made. Problems like recession, disorder and crime result from man's actions. How to transform these actions? How to improve quality of life for both man and society? *What can convince man to reject undesirable action?*

Transformation of man can do so. It creates balance in man and society. This transformation, in ancient Indian tradition, was made possible by its education ideas.

This book merges the best of ancient Indian wisdom and spirituality with the best in management thought. It searches for a learning that can help 'manage' a firm and man's life. Ancient Indian tradition uses *Moksha* or liberation, as a goal of life, to inspire man to follow morality. Morality gives man self confidence to overcome odds. For, deceit always fears getting exposed while Truth is self confident. Hence, Truth, as part of a strategy for life, gives self confidence. Work, too, based on Truth and morality, gives self confidence.

In modern theory of human psychology, Maslow refers to Self Actualisation as the highest order need of man. This need motivates him to become the best person he possibly can, in service of both himself and others.

To inspire man, a commonality between ancient and modern thought is sought. *Moksha* is one among four *Purusharthas* or goals of life. Management concepts 'fit' into these goals – with ethics as their basis. This creates a common framework of practice by man – in daily life as well as at work. This helps man, firm, society and nation.

Faith in God, in all spiritual traditions, promotes faith in good – and goodness. Goodness is a global currency. Every USA Dollar currency note carries a legend: 'In God we trust'.

6

Education must bring out the goodness in a student. Such goodness conquers greed and selfishness to benefit society. Only then excellence of action can occur.

The authors of the book 'In Search of Excellence' (R.H. Waterman Jr. and T. Peters) created a 7S model used by consultancy firm McKinsey. The core of this model is 'Shared Values' which guides business (firms) to achieve the best. This search of excellence brings out innate goodness in man at work. All religions inculcate values, which give confidence.

Religions promote values of Truth and Righteous Conduct. Jesus highlights the principle of Selfless Love, and, the meaning of Islam is Peace. When these values: Truth, Righteous Conduct, Love and Peace become the core of 'Shared Values' of man, firm and society, this model of management transforms all – man, business (firms) and society.

This 'Ideal' in education (how knowledge will lead to practice of Jesus' Love) creates self confidence in man to overcome all problems. It creates balance within man and firm, within nations and with nature – simultaneously. It deals with 'Management of man's life' in a manner that creates balance in society.

Once management study successfully demonstrates application of 'Ideal', other disciplines, too, can integrate the best of academic theory with service to society. This leads to Best Management Practices – for managing life, firm and society.

How can we prevent recession?

Recession is curable by imbibing the medicine of human values which help man control greed. Since ancient times, all spiritual traditions have been instrumental in building man's character by inculcating eternal values. Truth and Righteous Conduct lead to Peace, Non Violence. This leads to Selfless Love.

When these values are missing in man's actions, greed guides behaviour. Then social disorder, chaos, recession can occur. Education can use ancient Indian wisdom to help man take responsibility of actions by teaching values to save society. These values of ancient Indian tradition are integrated with 'Shared Values' of current management theory, here, to suggest a way of preventing recession. Similar studies in all traditions, too, should conclude that man's actions should not hurt society. This approach will impact current ideas that business has about maximising profit.

Some common sense questions are asked and answered here – even before the book starts. In this manner the author, who had predicted the global economic recession*, seeks to learn and share a way of preventing it. Restoring balance in man and society enables it. This is achieved when men pursue the goal of *Moksha* or liberation. A commonality of Maslow's Self actualisation need and man's 'Search of Excellence' integrates practice of management with ancient Indian thought.

Using the best of all traditions and faiths, through education, brings out the best in Man

Society suffers due to collective impact of choices of all. Education trains the mind towards choices that benefit society. Religion enabled man to lead a moral life. Parents reaffirm moral ideas, through example, at home. This benefits man, society, nation and the world. Thus, education, religion, parents give a Strategy for living Life. This helps unify body, mind and intellect of man. It develops Integrity or wholesome approach to living life. This integrity is called morality. Ancient Indians refer to it as *Dharma.* Ancient Indian wisdom believed that practice of morality can help the world attain greater levels of prosperity which will be sustainable, too. This would ensure happiness for all. All religions share the same goal and, thus, establish the same truth for society.

The idea of both religion and education is to concentrate on transformation of man so that he follows a Strategy of Life that creates balance, gives happiness and enables prosperity. Then not only man but society, too, is in balance.

A recession occurred in 2008 even though some educated managers were in decision making roles. Were these managers convinced about the importance of morality in creating prosperity? Or, did greed guide their decisions? Either way, creating prosperity through

*__*__ Published in Business Times, Singapore: October 4, 2007 – about seven **trading** days before the **first down tick** in USA stock markets. It predicted end of 'Goldilocks' growth and that USA housing market will take the world into the house of a Bear Market.*

8

selfish means hurt society. What could be lacking in their strategy? Did their strategy at work conflict with a Strategy of Life that family, society, teachers and religions inculcate? If so, why did managers lack self confidence to follow morality, ethics, truth, compassion?

How to integrate strategy at work place or strategy of firm with strategy of life? How to convince students that management strategy without Truth, Morality, Compassion (Strategy of Life) harms all? If morality deteriorates, religions, society and the student, too, will suffer! Thus, can academic theory merge with ancient wisdom? If achieved, students will know that a common strategy based on Truth and Morality is needed – at work and in Life.

What is the need for this book?

Management study develops problem solving skills. These skills enable man to accept responsibility for problems. So, solving problems like recession can happen through management study. But it must involve and use the best of all disciplines to achieve this task.

Managements always try to improve quality by seeking a zero defect state. This can be achieved by constantly improving each small fault. Thus, management seeks its own faults first before finding others. It accepts responsibility for problems. An automobile manufacturer will replace even a million vehicles if the life of one passenger is at risk. It does not pass the buck. How to use this approach when millions suffered due to recession? Let us try a self critical audit:
• Can society ignore the fact that unethical use of derivatives led to the recession? Despite educated people, social problems increased…
• If use of tools and techniques harms society, some thinkers may feel that without integrating them with ethics, these are not of use.
• Should schools show disinterest in what happens to society… especially when application of education is not preventing social problems? Recession shows interconnectedness between firms, customers and society. So, all may suffer if such problems are ignored.

The question that troubles thinkers is: 'Why ethics taught is not implemented – despite separate courses on ethics? Cases, even though they integrate ethical questions in real situations, fail to help'.

Therefore:

- Should some ideas about education be revisited? Many believe that current management theory has led to great advancements. So, how to retain the best of current thought with a way that prevents recession and other social problems? This book addresses this task.

If above is the case, then what initial ideas can we start with?

- Practice of ethics is sometimes left to religion. Academic models can try to integrate ethics with strategy of firm and life. Life without ethics is like swimming without water. So, academic theories must apply to life, first. Then student will be incapable of harming society.
- Also, education must apply to life for retaining relevance. So, its use must help society and lead to prosperity – not recession and social conflict.
- Business, customers and society suffer during a recession. Students must 'experience' this interconnectedness before acting in society.

So, where should we look – to seek a change for the better?

- There is a need to strongly integrate education with practice or life.
- The practice of education should help man, society and business.
- The presence of recession, social strife and conflict (both within man and society) shows a need to take action.
- Education integrates the best of every discipline and prepares man for social action. By building Character of man, it prevents problems.
- How can it meet this challenge of recession and social conflict?

This book seeks to answer these questions.

It concludes that:

- Strategy is needed not only for corporate firms – but for man's life.
- This strategy should add value to man's life and to society.
- Only then can it add value to the firm or corporate entity.
- This strategy, based on Truth and morality shows man's character.
- Strategy of firm must emanate from 'ideals' of this strategy of life.

How does it address this task?

Before a new automobile technology is accepted, it must run tests over long time durations and many test conditions. Similarly, new thought in management should have stood the test of time. If it has led to prosperity and balance in society in the past, it can be trusted to do the same again. This book chooses to incorporate ideas of ancient Indian tradition into current academic theory. This should promote balance within man, in the firm and in society's processes.

Strategy must teach that society benefits only when man overarches selfishness and greed to discover enlightened self interest.

(*Purushartha* converts *Swartha* to *Parartha* to *Parmartha* – equivalent words of ancient Indian tradition to describe how to achieve this objective)

This truth was realised by the ancient Indian civilisation. It incorporated this belief in education. In today's world this implies:
• The purpose of all subjects – management, study of religion, law, sociology, psychology, philosophy etc is to prepare man for life.
• Life is understood as living in society – for no man can be an island.
• The above understanding is most relevant for management.
• For, even those who do not study management 'manage' their life.
• Thus, concepts of management should be same – whether for business or life. Else, there will be conflict within man which will lead to conflict in society. Strategy of life and firm must be similar.
• Management or 'Man' 'age' 'meant' includes all that is 'Meant' for 'Man' in this 'Age'. Its study encompasses awareness of many subjects. The practical application of all subjects in life should help man contribute to society. This enables him to 'manage' his life. Then, society, firm, cluster, industry, nation get 'managed'.
• The purpose of education is to make man overarch selfishness and greed. The focus is to make him realise enlightened self interest.
• Without adherence to Truth and morality, man cheats himself and society.

Therefore, only character of man can lead to development of society. Ancient Indian education, thus, focussed on character of man – building it with *Purusharthas*. This transformed *Swartha* (self interest) to *Parartha* to *Parmartha* i.e. to the highest interest of society.

With the above understanding, balance in society prevents recession and other social problems. Therefore, tools and techniques in all subjects need to be taught to enable balance in man and in society.

Management study can break inter disciplinary barriers. A common focus of use of knowledge can lead to a Renaissance and prosperity.

Education based on Truth, morality and social concern removes myopic self interest. Ancient Indian tradition's ways show how this was done earlier:
• This book brings together ideas that ensure value based management study. For, without values, despite management study, crisis occurs. The use of derivatives, means used to sell them and also used to sell housing in USA are examples.
• Means lead to ends... wrong means should not lead to end of society! Academic theory should demonstrate this to convince all.
• The book uses diagrams to show this integration of two diverse streams of knowledge. It diagrammatically depicts balance in man, firm and society. This is achieved by merging the best of management theory and ancient Indian value system. It can, thus, demonstrate to a student that **without ethics it is not practical to use tools and techniques, for it harms society.**
• European Renaissance began when academicians taught thousands of years' old knowledge. They integrated it with current thought. This, first, led to a creative explosion in art and craft followed by a period of inventions and discoveries. It also created multi dimensional talents in man – Leonardo da Vinci being one example!
• Management study should include all streams of learning – for management is an inclusive discipline. It freely uses concepts from all subjects to teach man how to 'manage' his life. Management of the firm should be a natural byproduct.

Ancient Indian civilisation was prosperous for thousands of years using these ideas. Its concepts of management and how they merged with ethics are integrated in popular education for a Renaissance – to lead to prosperity.

• It integrated ethics with way man lives life using the concept of Divinty. This idea was used by many other civilisations, too, giving it different names. Ancient Indians used the idea in great detail to convince man to practice ethics. Their academic approach to Divintiy is integrated here.

• This book is a first step. Similar studies in all subjects and traditions will prove the point: What is taught in the classroom should apply to life and contribute to society. The idea of Divinity helps achieve this.

How did ancient Indians use idea of Divinity to uplift humanity?

Ancient Indians used the idea of Divinity to add values to life. Then, economic value was added. This led to balance within man and in society and prevented social problems.

Thus God represented Goodness. Education was designed to bring out latent goodness in man. Goodness should help others. This was the purpose of its texts and spiritual practices.

Ancient Indian Wisdom's use of Divinity

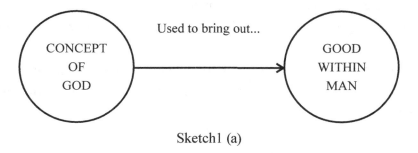

Sketch1 (a)

This idea applied to how man managed life. God was not just an idea of goodness alone. He also represented Excellence. When man observes nature or creation closely, a comparison of his size with the size and scale of nature can occur. Then, he can be filled with an awe of creation. The ancient *Rig Vedic* texts of Indian tradition show such awe. They also wonder if God exists at all. This questioning led them to realise the idea of excellence in the way survival of species occured. Excellence was understood as God. The supreme Godhead was not excellence in one dimension – but in all dimensions, simultaneously. Inspired by such excellence, man's actions can seek to attain it. The desire to maintain 'balance', like nature's cycles and seasons, leads to management of life and society. Sketch 1(b) shows this diagrammatically.

Ancient Wisdom applied to Modern Management Thought

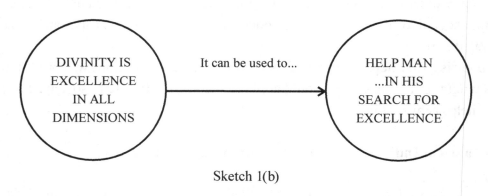

Sketch 1(b)

The role of Education is to bring out goodness in man by inspiring him. The purpose of such inspiration is transformation. This inspiration is about two things: Goodness and Excellence. Goodness does not let man hurt others. Excellence makes him do his best. This excellence should not be limited to just one act or a small series of acts. The idea of education is to help man unfold the excellence in all dimensions hidden within. During the period of European Renaissance this was unfolded and it led to prosperity. Leonardo Da Vinci the painter, sculptor, architect, musician, mathematician, engineer, inventor, anatomist, geologist, cartographer, botanist, and writer is an example of multiple talents.

When man seeks excellence with an idea of goodness, he achieves balance within himself. Social problems occur when man is not in balance. Then, society, too, suffers as his actions can harm others.

Thus, education inspires man and transforms him. It helps unravel the goodness and excellence within. This process leads to balance within man. Balance in society, then, is the result. Sketch 1(c) shows this.

Role of Education in Ancient Indian Tradition

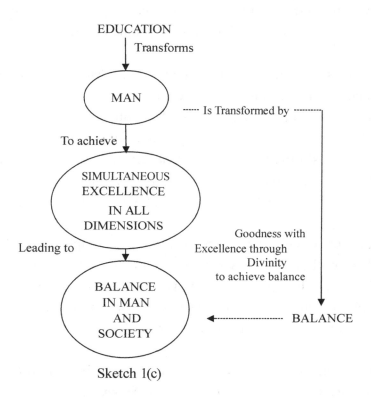

EDUCATION

Transforms

MAN

------ Is Transformed by ----------

To achieve

SIMULTANEOUS EXCELLENCE IN ALL DIMENSIONS

Leading to

Goodness with Excellence through Divinity to achieve balance

BALANCE IN MAN AND SOCIETY

BALANCE

Sketch 1(c)

Reform of society begins with man –
Reform of man begins with education

This book is about role and impact of education in society. Education should help create balance within man. This will prevent problems when he serves society. If man is not in balance, can society be in balance? Obviously not! Education gives balance. So, one question remains unanswered: **What is Education**? An answer, in ancient Indian style:

Education begins when **man searches for Truth** – asking questions like: 'Is the Earth Round or Flat? It ends with **'realising' Truth**. An example of Truth is: If man is just a human body then why preserving it after death does not add value? If he is not just the body, what is he? His mind is invisible, yet it creates visible value for him self and society. This Truth, man has to '**Realise**'. The 'Introduction' explores Nature of Truth and answers the question: what is the highest learning leading to 'realisation' – promoting excellence within man and in society? It shows ancient path for achieving excellence. Illustration 2, then, gives the book's roadmap for study of Man and Management. Following Truth and Morality is the **Best Management Practice**. Hence, India's education system developed it. Truth transforms fear that is inherently ingrained in deceit, to give self confidence.

But, how does an understanding of Truth impact Man or education?
The 'Background' discusses it. It explores the ancient Indian concept of Truth and discusses 'Truth about Man' as well as 'Truth about the Universe' (or the world). It explores implications of these on education. Its case studies of reform of robber Angulimala by Buddha or transformation of thief Ratnakara to Sage Valmiki hold hope for all. Finally, integrating education with life occurs when man is in balance within himself. Then, society, too, will be in balance when man speaks, knows and *experiences* Truth.

Balance occurs when man masters the mind. Then, implications of Truth(s) on education are realised and each student acts upon them – in life. What will be the impact on Management theory? How do 'best practices' emerge? The answer is found here. Like George Bernard Shaw's plays, here too, the Synopsis, identification of Shared Values, Introduction and Background is as large as the new understanding of Management study elaborated later.

Reform of man, society leads to 'balance' – within man and in society
Balance occurs with use of ethics, concern for society and excellence. This helps manage both: business and life.
This excellence unfolds when man has mastery over his mind – then:
- There is no duplicity in behaviour of man.
- Man learns to speak the Truth and search for it.
- He follows morality and does not cheat himself.
- He can contribute to family, his firm (where he works) and to society.
Otherwise, he is not in balance. If he cheats himself, he will cheat his firm and the firm will cheats others: finally, society suffers.

When strategy of life is based on truth, strategy of firm will benefit society. For, man's actions mould a firm (man's work place) and the impact it has on society.
When strategy of firm is driven by morality and Truth – cluster, industry and society will be in balance.
When society is in balance, each nation will experience unity.

Removal of greed will lead to balance with nature and halt environmental degradation, too.

In human history, which society achieved balance in this way?

The ancient Indian tradition transformed human capital – by imparting human values through education. **How?** Its practices are explored here – to create balance within man and society. Can these be integrated with education – and life?

Ancient Indian thought is integrated with Management Theory, here. It helps discover what this balance will diagrammatically look like. Some work of Harvard Business School's Prof. Michael Porter has been used for this integration. This is because his body of work stretches from strategy of firm to competitive advantage of nations...

Ancient Indian tradition's approach to education

The ancient Indian tradition does not just rely on mass transmission of information for education. Instead, it seeks to inculcate values and culture in man, first. It recognises each individual as unique. However, values are common and find expression through action in society. If man lives alone he will work in a selfish way. Society gives an opportunity to develop human qualities of sharing, caring, sacrifice of petty selfishness etc. – by control and direction of senses. Education helps apply human qualities in life. This helps discover man's true nature.

Education also attempts to transform each student through discipline. Its purpose is to make students live by ideals (of Truth, honesty, selflessness etc.) in daily life. This achieves control over the mind and balance within man.

(Though, why speaking the Truth or indulging in righteous conduct is considered a spiritual practice, not a part of education, today – is a question best left unanswered...)

Balance results from an understanding of Truth. Disciplined spiritual practices enable man to see it. Such discipline can change man's vision. It prepares him for liberation and society for balance.

Grasping subtle truths is never easy – as they are not visible – just like the human mind. Ancient Indian Seers took years to teach them through rigorous personal discipline and difficult practices. Realising Truth (and its nature) is the goal of education. Realising Truth about man's life achieves this goal. Understanding Truth about Man and about the world is the path of education. This helps man achieve balance within him. Education helps man realise the Truth of life. If man is in balance, society, too, will be in balance. The ancient Indian civilisation survived as students lived by these Truth(s) in life.

This book is an information booklet if it is not understood as a transformation tool...

Let us explore how...

Interrelationship of Education and Truth with life of man

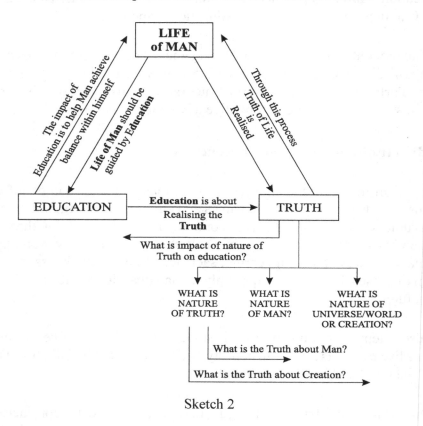

Sketch 2

Scientists have sent satellites to space. How did they achieve it? Hard work develops their capability. Then, power – that is already within them – is manifested. Ideas come, skill develops and perseverance leads to achievement. Man, finally, achieves his goal. The ancient Indian tradition gives a direction of Truth and Morality to this power. The student works hard on these – first. This disciplines the mind and, later, helps control it. Then, he undertakes hard work in a chosen field. This manifests power within man – once again. It leads to Best Management Practices for managing both – life as well as a firm. Then, balance among all – man, society and nature results.

Let us see how...

What is role of Education for balance in society – Ancient Indian way?

Society is in balance when man transforms into a 'gentleman'* – with high moral character. The control over mind (detailed in Chapter 1 and 7), commitment to Truth and Selfless Love add value to society. Human Values help man overcome selfishness. They shape character, giving balance to man – leading to balance in society. Both, spiritual and secular education added value in ancient India: training man for life as well as specific trades.

Balance through education – 1

```
┌────────────────────────────────────┐
│ MAN  BECOMES  'PRODUCTIVE'  IN       │
│ SOCIETY – 'BALANCE IN SOCIETY'       │
└────────────────────────────────────┘
                 ↑
```

SECULAR Education - that gives skills according to individual choice for specific trades or professions.

```
┌────────────────────────────────────┐
│          MAN + VALUES                │
│        (BUILDS CHARACTER)            │
└────────────────────────────────────┘
                 ↑
```

SPIRITUAL Education – Common concepts across all religions – that help transform man's perception about 'How to live life as a Gentleman'

```
        ┌──────────────────┐
        │       MAN         │
        └──────────────────┘
```

* Old English proverb: "Education begins a <u>gentleman</u>, conversation completes him!"

Sketch 3

Why do problems exist in Society today?

Character Building, the foundation of Education, is not the prime focus

Man has progressed and made life comfortable through inventions etc. Yet, many social problems exist. Competition is healthy – until it focuses on winning at any cost. If: 'only those who won have excelled' – then means are no longer important. Only the end is. Man forgets "It does not matter if you win or lose – it's how you play the game!" The compulsion to win makes man forget 'what is a gentleman?' Then, society suffers. Schools take pride in shaping character of students. If society is so harmed, schools need to rethink.

Cause of problems in society

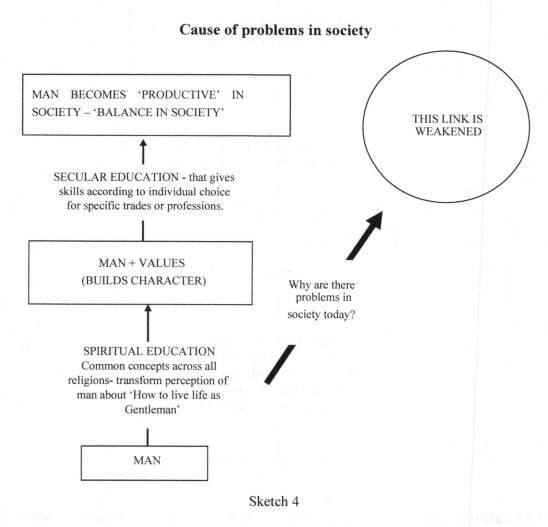

Sketch 4

What creates balance in society?

When Gentlemen with high moral character add value to society

Balance within man emerges through personal transformation and discipline of mind in each individual. Then, enlightened self interest replaces selfishness.

Balance through education: 2

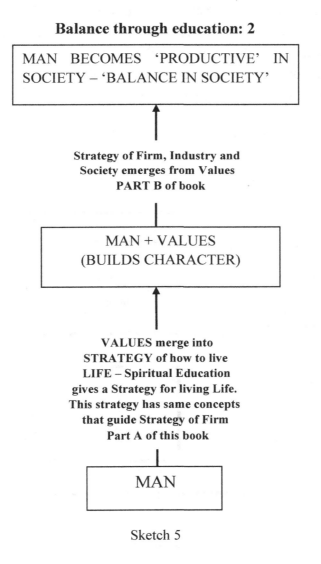

Sketch 5

Civilisations that survive entrust the task of character building to education. Which ideas on 'how to live life' enable survival of society? Can we incorporate them in our education (and Management Education), today – so students can live by them in daily life? If secular education remains value neutral, its misuse will always be possible.

21

Which ideas made ancient Indian civilisation last?
Applying its basic idea to Education and Management Education
Ancient Indian educators seek to train students as 'gentlemen' who adhere to values and have high moral character. They **translate eternal human values** (of Truth, Righteous Conduct, Non Violence, Peace and Selfless Love) **into action by** following the **goals of life** – called *Purusharthas*. This book identifies the *Purusharthas* of modern management: thus integrating management theory with ancient Indian tradition's Strategy of Life. This understanding is Meant for Man in this Age. It revives ancient ideas by removing selfishness: thus promoting 'best practices' for managing both the firm as well as each individual's life.

Application of ancient Indian wisdom to life and management education

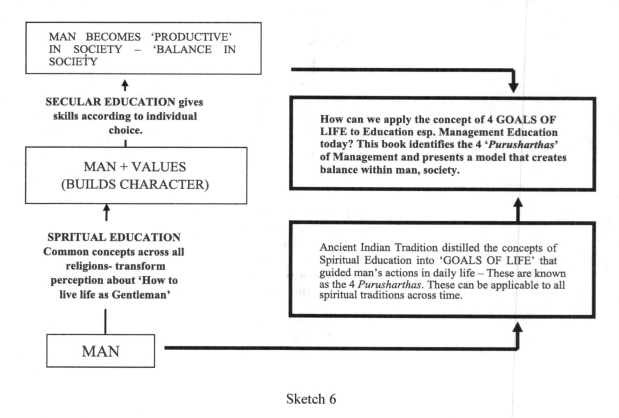

Sketch 6

Integrating ancient Indian tradition with education, including management education
How to practice three Indian philosophies in daily life

Education (both secular and spiritual) develops **Best Management Practices** for life. For these to be used at work, man should realise the Truth that his ability to think cannot emerge from matter. Yet, his body is matter – and he can think! So – 'what is man' if he is not the body? The Truth is that man is body, mind and Soul. Truth that body experiences through sense organs (called Duality or *Dwaitha*) can be called *Nijam*. As many objects are subject to a constant flux, this truth keeps changing leading to false perception (*Maya*). We can not conclude that this truth is permanent. Character helps man to control and direct the mind and the senses. Then, balance in man results. This creates balance in society. Spiritual education firmly ingrains man's linkage with society (this is *Vishisht Adwaitha* or qualified nondualism). Then, Truth that emerges from this conviction is *Satyam*. This creates balance within man (and society – as his actions are incapable of hurting others).

But, life's goal is to realise Truth as *Ritam* – Socrates calls it Soul. (This is *Adwaitha* – when unity of creation is experienced: as 'One' Soul). Education leads man towards this goal. Only spiritual and secular education, together, can fulfill this goal – of education and life.

It is fruitful to live in duality (*Dwaitha*) with a feeling of Qualified nondualism (*Vishisht Adwaitha*) to reach the goal of Non dualism (*Adwaitha*). This path implies following *Bhava Adwaitha* (feel non dualism) **not** *Karma Adwaitha* (i.e. always act within limits of Dualism). Thus, there should be non duality in thought but actions should be according to the demands of duality. This means: treat all with equal respect and Love. However, fulfilment of duties must respect differences existing in the physical world. To give a practical example: the practitioner must have equal love for King and farmer – but give a King the respect his position demands. This explains the ancient Indian adage: 'Hands in society, head in forest'.

Sketch 8 shows the Circle of Education to achieve this goal – through Part A and Part B of this book. Part A gives spiritual education while Part B transforms man's actions through character. When character guides action (management of life of man, firm, cluster, industry, nation and family of nations) – balance for man and society results. When four *Purusharthas* are followed as **two** 'pairs' – living in Duality becomes fruitful. Then, profit Optimisation replaces profit maximisation in capitalism, economic theories and management strategies.

Circle of Education through Part A and Part B of book

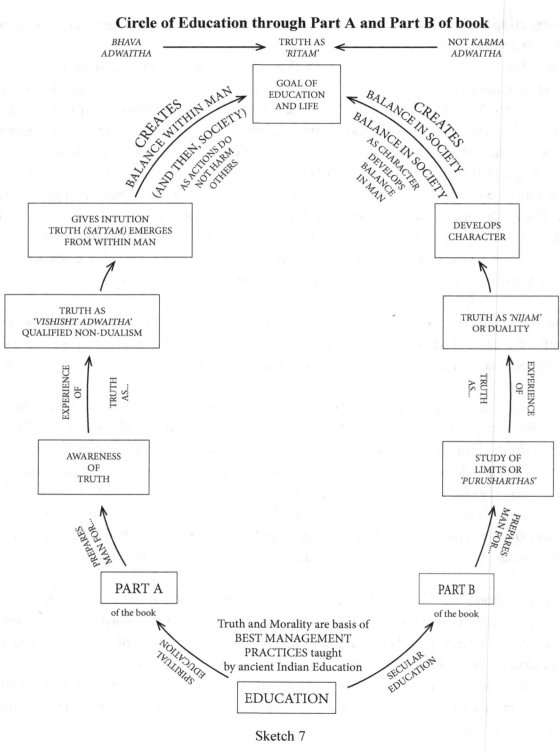

Sketch 7

Test the Truth of book's hypothesis: Apply it to education and life, today!

Best Practices of Ancient Indian Tradition: 4C Approach of Management

This book does not impose ancient Indian ideas of life on strategy of firm. It does the opposite. It starts with Porter's definition of strategy and applies it to ancient Indian idea of how to live life – thus wording it in modern management language.

Michael Porter of Harvard Business School has given three ingredients of Strategy: 1) Simple Consistency, 2) Reinforcement and 3) Optimisation effort. This ancient tradition states that man's life should rotate on the axis of morality, sticking to path of Truth. This occurs when he speaks and acts according to what he thinks. If there is duplicity in behaviour then man, firm, and society suffer. This tradition refers to it as: 'Unity of Thought, Word and Deed' (*Trikarana Shuddhi*). It builds character and brings out the best in man. This is an expression of Porter's simple consistency – at work in life of man! When man's soft, sweet words reinforce thoughts – and deeds reinforce words – Porter's Reinforcement ingredient is in action – in a 'Strategy of how to live life'!

Strategy of Life is the basis of strategy of firm in ancient Indian tradition. Porter's definition of strategy, thus, fits into 'Strategy of Life' of this tradition. Then, Simple Consistency exists among shared values in strategy of firm and life (as firm's strategy emerges from life's Strategy). This removes possibility of conflict between man and management – and between man and society. Optimum balance results – for all – society, cluster, industry, firm and man – simultaneously! This Optimisation effort is Porter's third ingredient! It prevents social conflict, chaos, disorder and recession. It overarches profit maximisation compulsion in economics, strategy and marketing. Similarly, Optimisation (not maximisation) in use of nature's resources gives balance with nature. These 'limits' are set by the conscience of man.

Ancient India's ability to strengthen value creation and improve value delivery made it a great civilisation. Its economic prosperity made it the target of many foreign invasions. What was the source of prosperity for thousands of years (barring last few hundred years)? Its greatest wealth was its academic tradition – which is restated here – in a language understood today.

In fact, this book can be applied to both education and life by making a simple beginning: "Speak the Truth, follow morality". Ancient India's education tradition incorporates this Ideal as the **Best Practice of Management.** It is applied to man's life as well as at work. This disciplines the mind and leads to a clear vision – enabling man to 'C' strategy as part of a 4 C Approach to Management. This book uses ideas of Maslow, Porter's definition of Strategy and Competitive Advantage of Nations, Mc Kinsey's 7S Model and Kotler. It integrates them with ideas of ancient Indian tradition of 'how to live life'. This integration of education with life shows how same can be done for all topics in management – and education!

The ancient Indian tradition manages the mind and life through four goals or *Purusharthas* – referred to as the 4C Approach here. Current management scholars' ideas, too, can fit in this classification. Thus, ancient Indian tradition fits into modern management theory of strategy. Secondly, modern management concepts fit into the four fold classification of 'Strategy of Life' of ancient Indian tradition. The integration of these seemingly diverse streams of learning is simplified by diagrams of this book. They make the merger of these two traditions valuable for society – by application in life and corporate world!

If students wish to check its power, they need to transform – into a good human beings. Then, they will be useful to society. This commitment can be practiced – if divided into smaller goals. Deviation from truthful and moral behaviour needs daily review and rectification. A diary must record progress – daily, without fail. A vision of how man's actions can harm society is needed. If selfishness is forgotten, the significance of ideas here will emerge from within. With character and this vision Strategy, Quality and Marketing can be applied. This helps society achieve balance. Then firm, industry, cluster and man will be in balance – simultaneously. And, education will achieve its goal.

Ancient India's productivity created value and delivered it for thousands of years in this manner – contributing significantly to global GDP. Its best practices are called: 'The 4C Approach of Management'. This approach is useful for man and society as it prevents recession and other social problems. Their chapter wise study here is shown in Sketch 8:

Merger of Modern Management and Ancient Indian Goals of Life:
Chapter wise flow

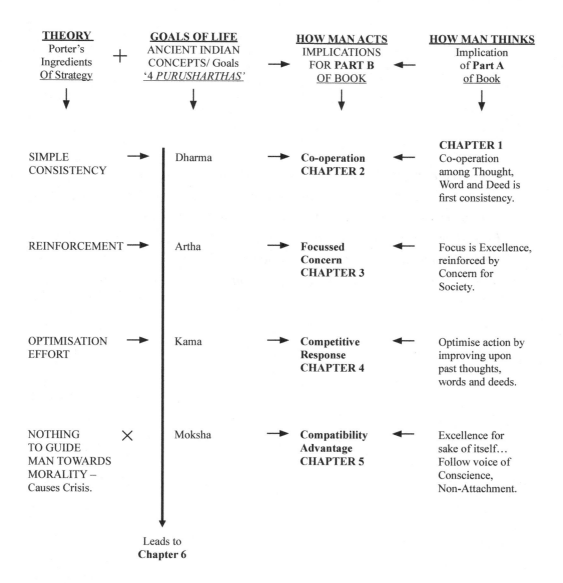

THEORY Porter's Ingredients Of Strategy	GOALS OF LIFE ANCIENT INDIAN CONCEPTS/ Goals '4 PURUSHARTHAS'	HOW MAN ACTS IMPLICATIONS FOR **PART B** OF BOOK	HOW MAN THINKS Implication of **Part A** of Book
SIMPLE CONSISTENCY	Dharma	**Co-operation** **CHAPTER 2**	**CHAPTER 1** Co-operation among Thought, Word and Deed is first consistency.
REINFORCEMENT	Artha	**Focussed** **Concern** **CHAPTER 3**	Focus is Excellence, reinforced by Concern for Society.
OPTIMISATION EFFORT	Kama	**Competitive** **Response** **CHAPTER 4**	Optimise action by improving upon past thoughts, words and deeds.
NOTHING TO GUIDE MAN TOWARDS MORALITY – Causes Crisis.	Moksha	**Compatibility** **Advantage** **CHAPTER 5**	Excellence for sake of itself… Follow voice of Conscience, Non-Attachment.

Leads to
Chapter 6

The journey of four Goals of Life is embarked upon to experience the Unity of Creation (Chapter 6), following dictum 'Help Ever, Hurt Never'. This leads to the 'experience' that helping or hurting others is like helping or hurting our own self. The Simple Consistency of Unity of Thought, Word and Deed is reinforced by a focus on excellence with a concern for society and it is optimised by improving on past work of man. Finally, Self Actualisation is realised when man seeks excellence for its own sake and not because he is attached to rewards. Then, he follows the voice of his conscience.

Sketch 8

The Introduction of new people is sealed with a handshake.
The Introduction of new ideas may have many shaking their heads
– in agreement, disagreement or to show their insouciance.
Honest criticism is the best source of growth of society – from
time immemorial. For, it shows a sincerity of quest. All new ideas
request not for praise but for this quest and a sincerity about it.

INTRODUCTION

A sincerity about achieving excellence leads to self actualization. Though it is the larger goal, other goals help achieve it – both in life and at work.

DESIRE FOR SELF ACTUALISATION CREATES AWARENESS OF EXCELLENCE 'WITHIN' MAN – IN ANCIENT INDIAN TRADITION

Way of achieving goal is Strategy. Way of achieving goals of life is Strategy of life. Self Actualisation (*Moksha*) is the goal of life. Awareness about it was created in ancient India with questions that help discipline the mind. The answers became basis of action in life.

What is Man? Awareness about this reveals man's capability of 'Excellence' in all dimensions.

Man

In this age, what should he manage? He must manage the mind, restrain greed.

Man+Age

How? Self Actualisation or *Moksha* desire is awakened through Awareness. This makes man realise that expressing Excellence 'within' him is purpose of action – in all work including for firm and society. *Kama*, desire, leading to greed, is restrained by such purpose. This benefits man, society and prevents recession.

Man+Age+Me(a)nt

A Management perspective **meant** for man, firm and society – merging ideas of ancient Indian tradition with writing of modern management thinkers. The techniques for man to study and train himself – for inculcating the desire of self actualisation 'within' – leading to excellence in action are elaborated upon here. Such a study of management is meant for man in this age.

MANAGEMENT – A STUDY THAT RESTRAINS GREED IN MAN, PREVENTS RECESSION

Sometimes, old ideas can help when success also fails. If some men could not prevent the recession, maybe some old ideas can – if used in a novel way.

IDEAS THAT PREVENT RECESSION

(i) (a) **Four Shared values that unite religions, society, mankind**

   (b) **Four Goals of Life implement four shared values – How do they add life to each Chapter?**

   Abstract – Two versions – Ancient wisdom and modern management points of view

(ii) **Introduction: Part A: Understanding Education and management education**

   Part B: Understanding this Study

(iii) **Background – Four Questions that lead to wisdom in Ancient Indian Education**

A concern:

"I'm sure a crash like 1929 will happen again. The only thing is that one doesn't know when. All it takes for another collapse is for the memories of the last insanity to dull."
John Kenneth Galbraith.

An effort:

A friend once asked **Michelangelo,** the Italian sculptor, "Why are you working so hard chiseling this piece of rock?" He replied: "I wish to bring out of this lifeless stone the living Divinity that is embedded in it". A sculptor tries to bring the latent image of Divine out of a stone.

Can a stone hearted man, then, not chisel out latent goodness within? God is goodness and excellence in all dimensions, simultaneously. Desire for goodness and excellence, the ancient Indian tradition states, leads to discovering Divinity within man.

Education chisels by purifying the heart and mind, teaching the moral path. This brings out the latent Divinity in man.

Exhibits 1,2,3,4 – what do they exhibit?

When a word is used to describe an action, it becomes a verb.
If the merger of ancient ideas in modern management is acted upon,
the behaviour of men will change – to prevent recession.
The meaning of exhibit (as a verb) is to manifest a quality or type
of behavior. Man's innate quality is to seek excellence. Ancient
wisdom helps man exhibit this quality.

PREPARING FOR MERGER OF:
ANCIENT WISDOM WITH MANAGEMENT IDEAS

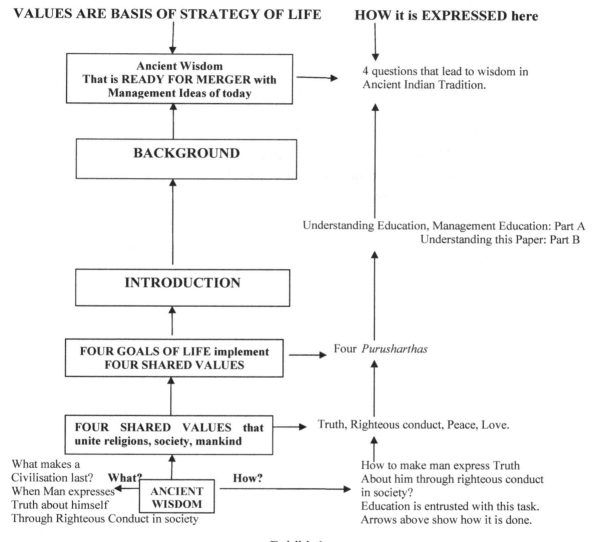

Exhibit 1

There is an old saying: "Joy shared is joy doubled – sorrow shared is sorrow halved". The value of values increases manifold when they are shared – by all. The sorrow of recession is reduced – when values are shared to cure it...

FOUR SHARED VALUES unite religions, society and mankind

Fig 0.30 (in Background section) shows how these shared values form the basis of the 4C Approach of the book; Chapter 2 uses them as 'Life forces' of man

Recession is understood as implying loss of money. Money and wealth are used interchangeably today. The idea of money itself has changed over time along with its form. Gold, silver, precious stones, grains or even stock in trade – anything which had value, could be traded, was a store of value, a medium of exchange and a measure of value for society was earlier considered as money.

For those who believe firmly in cycles of time or business, these are the cause of recession. If such analysis is taken further, Time and its cycles are the stealer of wealth causing recession. For others, man's actions cause it.

What is the wealth that cannot be stolen by Time also? If this wealth is identified, recession can be prevented – by man's actions.

In the ancient Indian tradition, this wealth was created by ideas. Such ideas formulated human behaviour. This wealth of wisdom could not be stolen by any thief, including Time.

To make sure that such wealth is created and preserved in society, they entrusted the task of imparting it to education. Youth were trained and values ingrained in them. There is an old saying "Build a strong foundation in the early days of youth. Life will shatter and shock you with its storms of stress and strain. But on a strong foundation you can build and build again".

The ability to preserve wealth even when money is lost and create money, once again through it, was the wisdom of ancient Indian civilisation. Its education imparted this wisdom to its students.

What was the core of this education? It convinced the student that the link between man and society is eternal. Education prepares man for action in society. So, society helps man achieve purpose of life. If transformation of man leads only to individual prosperity – will this be sustainable if society loses something? Education seeks answers to this question in ancient Indian tradition.

If excellence within man emerges through education – the right question is: What is excellence used for? Education added value to man's life in a manner that he could add value to society. It led to best management practices – for living life. When educated men were in responsible positions and society faced a crisis (whether financial, social, political or moral) they identified two possibilities. Either education is not applied – or it needs to be reengineered to meet challenges.

Both alternatives led to soul searching. Some questions that help this search are given here: What was missing in the technique that it could not transform man or could not apply to society – and, if applied, why did it fail? In this manner education transformed itself to meet current challenges whenever a crisis faced society. When Best management practices for life that emerge through such soul searching are applied in the firm, it shows the relevance of education. Soul searching unravels awareness of excellence within man. Its results convince him that his actions should be within limits that do not harm others. Therefore, education must inculcate – (a) An Awareness of the potential of excellence (that lies within man) and (b) Limits to his actions in society. Then he can fulfill his self interest in a manner that enlightens, does not harm others and adds value to society.

When politicians serve the people they rule, when business serves customers first, petty self interest later, when teachers of morality practice what they teach – then, disorder, chaos, crime and falsehood will not find place in society. This was the conclusion of this tradition.

What is missing in man that allows these social problems? The answer is given in the Synopsis and lies in one word: Character. So, ancient Indian education sought to build character. How? It taught how to **forget individual differences and move with everyone with a spirit of harmony and equality. This spirit of unity adds beauty to all group activities**. This is called moral character and does not allow anybody, whether a sportsman or businessman, to cheat. How is character building incorporated in academic theory that man practices in life? When man learns to live within 'Limits' of norms, character develops.

Almost all academic institutions, today, promote group assignments and group learning to promote character building – preparing man for social action.

In schools, physical, mental and emotional development occurs through sports, academics and extracurricular (like dramatics etc) activity. A sport promotes physical development creating an enabling environment for individual excellence in a manner the team excels. Orchestra participation, dramatics etc. enable emotional fulfilment. The gestalt of a performance benefits from individual excellence of each performer. Man learns discipline of humility, stays within norms of a group and enjoys the benefit of excellence. Everybody contributes their best for a larger cause. Discipline and limits help build character.

Thus, this appreciation: 'The whole is greater than the sum of parts' develops in each student.

A sportsman learns: '**It is not important whether you win or lose – it is how you play the game**'. This statement sums up philosophy of education and life, together.

The presence of doping in sports and statements like: 'without performance enhancing drugs no sportsman can reach the top' imply that practice is different from what is taught and learnt (or theory). The story of the 'game of life' is no different. If it matters little how you play life's game – the only relevant question is: did you win? Then recession, chaos, conflict can occur. Character development leads to balance within man. This leads to balance in society as individual's and society's goals merge. When individual's and society's goals diverge, there is imbalance in society. Then, education and life get divorced; imbalance within man is the consequence.

How to create an academic thought which prevents such a divorce between education and living life? This happens when goals of education and life merge with goals of firm. How to create academic learning around goals of life so it does not repeatedly need review with change in time and circumstance? Then, it will be Meant for Man in this Age. It should study Management in the corporate world (or the firm), in society and nation. It should also study management of life for each individual to nurture 'best management practices'. These practices flow from life to man's contribution to the firm.

The next question is: How to judge if society is in balance? For, balance makes man overarch greed, preventing recession. Society achieves balance through education. The study of various philosophies shows that balance in society is a result of the practice of **four cardinal principles**. These principles are common across religions, cultures and are valid for mankind. They build Character of man, control mind: replacing greed by enlightened self interest. When inculcated in behaviour, they impart that wealth that cannot be stolen. They bind a society together and ensure that a civilisation survives…even if money is lost. These are the **four shared values**:

1. Truth (called *Satya* in ancient Indian tradition). It is the foundation of all philosophies and traditions – the world over. Man must discover the truth about himself, truth about the world and seek Truth in action. Search for Truth involves discrimination – which is the basis of man's distinction from the animal world. This search for Truth thus gives meaning to his life.

2. Righteous conduct (called *Dharma* in ancient Indian tradition). It is the central teaching of all religions emerging in Indian sub-continent i.e. Buddhism, Hinduism, Jainism and Sikhism. It is also a guiding principle for any collection of beings to survive in the long run. No wonder, it finds primacy in human thought and resounds in all religions and uplifting philosophies. It disciplines the human mind and makes the body follow it.

3. Peace (called *Shanti* in ancient Indian tradition). It is the meaning of word Islam and among its central teachings. Visibly, society is in balance when there is Peace. An individual, too, in balance is peaceful.

4. Love (called *Prema* in ancient Indian tradition). It is the central teaching of Jesus "Whoever does not love does not know God, because God is love" (John 1, as quoted in many sources, including the easily verifiable Wikipedia). Balance results in a family when there is love. Similarly, if society is a large family then Love is basis of balance. The principle of 'Love thy neighbor as thyself' declares that Love should not be petty or selfish (I, me, mine). When benefit of others is seen as clearly as we see our own benefit – then expression of love emerges as selfless service to society. This Selfless view makes man incapable of harming others or society. If practiced, this teaching completes education. Therefore, it is the central teaching of all religions.

All religions and uplifting philosophies, since the coming of mankind, have stated the same four cardinal principles for education. These promote discrimination within him. He, then, realises his distinction in the world. It seems that they are different shores of the same ocean of knowledge designed to help man reach the goal of life.

These cardinal principles evidence that man needs society to reach the goal of life. By harming others or society he is only harming himself. Education teaches Man to rotate on the axis of Truth and Morality (through Righteous Conduct) and act with love to create peace and harmony. It makes man satisfy his needs without infringing on others rights. Following Truth and morality, man is at peace within himself. This creates peace in society. Non violence is, then, practiced. Man, then, gets the experience of Selfless Love.

How does this reflect in social action? What goals of life, which imbibed in education, help man to 'man-age' his life and work, together?

A study of a civilisation that has survived can guide academics to create balance within man and society. For such research, ancient Indian tradition provides rich material. It clearly lists ideas that lead to Awareness (described in (a) above) and practices that comprise Study of Limits (described in (b) above). There are also ideas of Management whose documentation allows a merger of ideas of Man and Management or Man Management. Their study helps putting this book into practice.

*The value of achieving a goal is lost – if it is achieved
without adhering to values. For, that makes success a failure.
The 2008 economic recession is an example...*

FOUR GOALS OF LIFE implement four Shared Values – how do they add life to each Chapter?

Illustration 2 (in the Introduction that follows) shows the integration of study of man and management through the Chapters of the book. Fig 0.27 shows goals as car wheels.

The study of man and world by ancient Indians gave Awareness (which is total understanding of a subject). This Awareness inspired action in society. Awareness results from the application of the four shared values in daily life. This application, in ancient Indian tradition, is implemented through the four *Purusharthas* or goals of life. Thus, following the *Purusharthas* is like implementing the four shared values identified earlier.

The *Purusharthas* give life to this book's Chapters.
Actions of man, in ancient Indian tradition, were guided by education to follow Goals of life. Speaking the Truth – *Satya* – (in a manner that does not hurt others) and following Morality (with Unity of thought, word and deed) helps achieve them. This is **Chapter 1** of the book – and life! It leads to 'best management practices' in life. These are carried from life to firms – by all.

The Synopsis starts with linking education to the search for Truth. How does the search for Truth lead to righteous conduct – the first *Purushartha* or Chapter 2 of the book? Righteousness (*Dharma*) is a feeling (*Bhava*) that should be generated within man. Faith in Truth leads to this feeling of Righteousness. Therefore *Dharma* is called embodiment of Divinity or Excellence within man – by ancient Indians. When all uphold righteousness there is *Shanti* or Peace. Then, actions of man are an expression of Selfless Love (*Prema*) for society. Thus, education starts with search of and faith in Truth. This leads to the first *Purushartha* of *Dharma*. When there is faith in Truth there is *Dharma* – which is treated as Divinity or Excellence. Truth, by implication is also Excellence, so is faith. So, *Satya* leads to *Dharma* – which leads to the four shared values emerging within man and in society. For, *Dharma* is the guide to economic activity *Artha*. The practice of *Dharma* leads to actions for righteous purpose and not out of false attachment or *Moha*. The ending or *kshaya* of *Moha* is the fourth *Purushartha* of *Moksha* which guides the *Purushartha* of desire or *Kama*. Where there is *Satya* there is *Dharma*. Where there is *Dharma* there is

Peace or *Shanti*. Where there is *Shanti* there is Love or *Prema*. Thus, from shared value of Truth other shared values emerge and the four *Purusharthas*, too.

Four goals of life – the purpose of management education

A common theory of Management and life prevents possible divorce between them. Goals of individual and society must merge. This creates balance within man and society. The ancient Indian civilisation survived due to such balance. The 4C Approach incorporates balance by detailing the four *Purusharthas* of Management which discipline the mind and direct action. It gives reasons for choice of these ideas as the relevant *Purusharthas*, today. Here is a summary:

Education prepares man for action in society (to make Awareness productive). So, he must understand the importance of Co-operation (1st C) which is the basis of society. This is **Chapter 2** of book – as well as of life!

Co-operation makes man contribute his excellence to the team. He also benefits from the excellence of team. This gestalt reflects that a 'whole is greater than the sum of parts'. In this manner, man follows his *Dharma* or duty or righteous conduct. Just as *Dharma* supports society, co-operation is the support for society to be productive. Of course, such co-operation must be on the axis of Truth and Morality.

In ancient Indian tradition, *Purushasuktam*, from *Vedas*, points out man is a limb of society, society of nation, nation of nature – which is a limb of Divinity. Nature is part of God, society is part of nature and man is a part of society. Therefore, inter-relationship exists between all: man, society, nation, nature and God. Inter-dependence is the basis of co-operation with others and nature.

The next step includes the stages of value creation and value delivery (**Chapter 3 and Chapter 4** respectively) in society. Value creation emerges with a focus on need. This focus, if purely selfish, will disturb balance. A concern must direct focus towards the larger goal. Thus focussed Concern is the second *Purushartha* of Management.

Through value delivery, a firm gives its Competitive response to fulfill its desires (*Purushartha* of *Kama*). This competitive response delivers value without hurting overall interests of society and nation. Thus, the fourth *Purushartha* (or *Moksha*) guides competitive response.

The fourth *Purushartha* (**Chapter 5** of the book – and life) contains the training given to every sportsman: 'It does not matter whether you win or lose – it's how you play the game'. This excellence coupled with a non– attachment to results is critical. Concentration on seeking excellence should guide competitive response of man and firm. Man and firm's value addition becomes compatible with needs of society, nation and family of nations. All benefit from the fourth 'C' of Compatibility Advantage.

When compatibility need guides behaviour, understanding of competition changes. A competitor is only a benchmark in early stages. Finally, expression of Individuality of firm and its manager has only one competitor – past work of man or firm. Need for self improvement and serving Individuality of customer in firm's individual way adds value – to man, the firm and society. Firms seek benchmarks in their own past performance and keep finding unique ways of delivering value.

The book's idea is not to give a new theory. It only seeks to classify knowledge (that has worked for thousands of years) in the present context – to create balance within man and society. To merge this study of strategy for man and firm, it relies on:
• **Michael Porter** (faculty, Harvard Business School) then applies it to McGraths writing on Transient Advantage published in June 2013.
• **Maslow** (psychologist who taught at Columbia University, USA)
• **McKinsey**'s 7S Model: Prepared by Waterman and Peter – authors of book 'In search of Excellence' for management consultancy firm McKinsey.

The ideas that ensured survival of a civilisation use words of current management theory here. Various charts and diagrams display balance in man, firm, society and among nations –resulting from their application. (This book has 101 diagrams, figures, illustrations, exhibits and sketches – sketches in Synopsis, illustrations in Introduction, figures in Background, exhibits before sections and chapters and diagrams in the main book to enable easy search). Most ideas work if man disciplines the mind. Academic study should imply study of techniques of disciplining mind. Theory must, thus, show the way to practice. Presence of corruption, unethical and immoral behaviour in society reveals an inability to control mind.

When purpose of education is forgotten, it leads to recession

The important question for society is: What does the human mind seek from education? Is In-come the focus of learning or Out-come of actions important? Is purpose of education to get a job or is it to contribute to society? How many view a job as a means of contributing to society? What declares distinction of man? Education must train Intellect of man for declaration of distinction.

Does education only guide the intellect? If so, every educational institution is doing a commendable job. The intellect, unfortunately, is a double edged weapon. Its misuse is easy. Education must try to remove wickedness in man's heart. Then, there will be no misuse of intellect. Education guides intellect (through use of discrimination) to transform heart of man. Education makes man productive. However, this productivity should add value to society. Corruption, unethical behaviour, social unrest and crime – especially by degree holders hurt the educators. 'Educated' people control levers of power in society. Qualifications guarantee better jobs and positions of power. All decision makers during the global financial crisis, too, were 'educated'. Why did society suffer still? Knowledge is imparted to create balance. How does its misuse disturb it through recession?

When firms maximise profit not optimise, they can overuse resources. A single minded pursuit of self interest harms customers and society. Without study of limits, man and firms maximise use of resources – guided by selfishness. Thus they harm environment, society and – themselves. For, the circle of selfishness that starts with harming others completes itself, one day. When greed for unrealistic bonus makes managers sell harmful derivatives to customers, a financial crisis results. When man forgets interests of the customer or society, balance is lost. Then, skill of the manager (like a sharp knife) becomes a murderer's knife instead of a surgeon's. It kills the balance. Both, life and the market, need this balance. If performance driven culture leads to disservice towards others, society loses the purpose of education. Then, a recession occurs.

When recession hits, demand falls. Demand for a product falls due to decline in quality or over-production. If production increases without value addition, demand will fall one day. If price charged is too high, demand falls. Of course, spurt in sales and profit due to economies of scale can come. However, value addition should be the inner driver (or focussed concern). Demand for product due to such value addition should lead to scale economies. The right price and quantity gives value and prevents recession. Demand may also fall due to lack of quality. Quality is an attitude: it originates from the attitude of the manager. Education focuses on developing inner qualities of a man. Then, good quality processes emerge, enabling single minded devotion to quality. All scientific advancements and strength of society depend on quality – of an individual. Without individual character, knowledge is meaningless. Quality implies performing duties as an act of service to society. It is not to trick management or customer.

Thus, high customer satisfaction, low complaints or absence of product recall are signs of Quality. But, the first signs of quality must emerge 'within' man, through education. An aware manager knows that compromise in quality finally leads to wastage and higher costs. Tricks to earn bonuses harm all. When good of society overarches such concerns, no trickery increases short term profit. Then, focus is on quality of raw materials and proper use of skill of workers, contractors (and others in value addition process). This ensures overall quality. Such positive attitude, not selfishness, is meaning of quality. Thus, Total Quality Management should be focus as well as concern of managers. Positive Attitude leads to personal development and development of the firm and society. When quality is basis of firm's competitive response, it creates balance within man and society. It leads to, as well as benefits from, compatibility advantage. This results from behaviour that is compatible with others and with nature.

When everything is in balance, society and firm are in balance. The manager will get value by adding value in a selfless way. This is how *Upanishadic* law (another ancient Indian text) of seed and tree works – within man, in firm and in society. The seed contains within itself the full tree. If one seed is taken, can the fullness of tree reduce? This is explained in **Chapter 6** of the book.

When man works in such a selfless manner, he adds value to himself, society and nature – much like the selfless tree. The highest wish of a tree fulfills itself as the seed. The highest wish of a seed fulfills when it becomes a tree. Similarly, the highest wish of man and society are fulfilled simultaneously by education. If we give full education (seed), what will remain? The tree, representing wisdom, remains full and ocean of knowledge does not become shallow – despite everybody benefitting from it.

The focus of education is to raise the quality of life

Standard of living for a few is not the focus. Education expresses itself when man willingly decides not to exploit nature and others. The use of natural resources in a limited and balanced manner is a result of control of desires by man. When there is no control over desires, environmental degradation results. Similarly, an inability to control desires leads to exploitation of others and finally an economic recession. Education teaches man how to control desires following Truth and morality. It directs them to a path that achieves a higher purpose for man and society.

The four *Purusharthas* are the path for achieving this. Thus they too constitute the Best Management Practices for man and the body of society. They can be compared to man's body. *Dharma* or Morality is like the feet. Everything stands on the basis of *Dharma*. *Moksha* or desire for Self Actualisation is like the head. It guides actions. *Artha* or business pursuit is like the stomach. *Kama* or desire (unrestrained, it leads to greed) has its seed in the heart of man.

What happens when *Dharma* and *Moksha* are not incorporated in education? Without feet and exercise can the body digest well? If the head does not guide the heart, man can eat without restraint. Then, slowly, the body deteriorates in health. Even though, initially, it seems to be fun and enjoyment. Therefore, the head must guide the seat of desire i.e. the heart of man. Marketing targets the seat of desire. The head gives discrimination to guide desires of man. Education transforms the heart of man. It directs desires towards noble goals. *Dharma* is the basis for the body to stand. Without it the body will not be in balance. This holds equally true for the body of man and society.

Hence, the four *Purusharthas* are best practices interconnected with the way man lives life. They help control the mind; implement education in man's life. They help man and society actualise the four shared values that bind mankind. They take the car of man forward so that society travels to its destination. For this, the air pressure of the four wheels of man's car has to be balanced by education (Chapters 1 reveals Truth from 'within' while driving, Chapter 2 to 5 fill in the correct air pressure) – both create balance in journey.

ABSTRACT

Do Ancient Wisdom and modern theory converge?

This Abstract shows how...

Transformation of Man through Education –
Ancient Indian tradition and Maslow's Theory used in Management

This Study treats them like two sides of same coin

Everybody will agree that man can do self analysis, self motivation and self improvement. Then, it does not matter whether we study ancient Indian tradition or modern management theory. The results will be similar. All man needs is a commitment to personal transformation – along the path of Truth and righteous conduct. The technique of achieving transformation varies across traditions. However the result serves education's goal. It prepares man to serve society. Such a broad approach allows this book to integrate modern management theory and ancient Indian tradition.

The Abstract presents two points of view. The first is man committing himself to rising in Maslow's hierarchy of needs. The second viewpoint is *Bhagavad Gita's* (ancient Indian traditions important text). Both ways of seeing ('C'ing) lead to similar directions for man to act in society. They use different words but convey the same idea. Their practical application – to the life of man – is same. They are like two sides of the same coin:

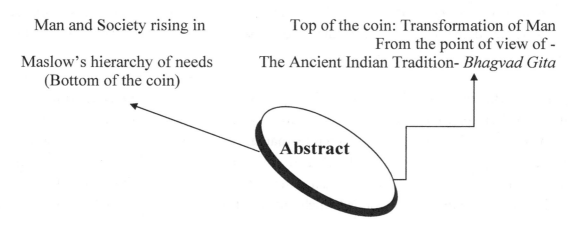

Man and Society rising in

Maslow's hierarchy of needs
(Bottom of the coin)

Top of the coin: Transformation of Man
From the point of view of -
The Ancient Indian Tradition- *Bhagvad Gita*

Abstract

One side of the coin– Man and Society rising in Maslow's needs hierarchy

Maslow, an eminent psychologist, has given a hierarchy of human needs while proposing a theory of human motivation. The ancient Indian tradition gives a path of directing these motives to reach the highest human endeavour, as researched by Maslow. The role of education, in this tradition, is to help man reach the highest human need – in Maslow's hierarchy – in the shortest possible time. Its enabling practices would be **Best Management Practices**!

From his study of exemplary people, Maslow found a pattern of upward movement of human motivation from the physiological needs of food, clothing and shelter to higher order needs. After fulfilling physical needs, humans sought safety, morality, family, health etc. Then, the next order of need was for togetherness of family and friendship etc. Some fulfilment, here, led to higher order need of respect from others – or the need for esteem.

As soon as the satisfaction of immediate physical needs occurs, the social nature of the needs starts emerging. This recognises that man lives with others in society. To enjoy the satisfaction he seeks from others, he must learn to give the same satisfaction to them, first. Only then he can receive the same from them. Therefore, the first lesson is co-operation. It also helps man if he treats others as he would like to be treated by them.

While co-operation is the 1st C of the 4C Approach, treating others as man treats oneself leads to highest state of balance within man and society. Chapter 6 shows how – and helps man see the underlying unity of creation. The 1st C helps value creation by creating a common focus. A Concern for others (2nd C) leads to value delivery or competitive response (3rd C). Their compatible nature with the needs of society and nature (4th C) is the end of journey.

In Maslow's hierarchy, man's journey begins with co-operating, within him and with others. This helps him realise the highest need – which is Self Actualisation. This is defined as "What a man can be, he must be". Therefore, man must realise his potential – of achieving excellence in all dimensions – fully. Realising this potential is called *Moksha* (*Moha–ksheya* – the end of delusion of attachment) in the ancient Indian tradition. It makes man Realise excellence in all dimensions (which this tradition calls *Atma* or Soul). It manifests the power that is dormant within him. This fulfills purpose of education and life. Their merger occurs in the state of Self Actualisation.

The ancient Indian tradition uses different terms for man's transition from a focus on satisfaction of physical needs to higher order need of self actualisation. This has implications for man and his actions in society. How should man fulfill his physical needs? What does the ancient Indian tradition say? Simply put, this tradition believes that nature has enough for everybody's need, but not for their greed. So, while man has a right of Self Preservation, fulfilling his needs should not harm others or society. Education sensitises man about this – encouraging him to sacrifice ignorance and that selfishness that harms society. Therefore, education transforms the heart and prepares him for such Self Sacrifice.

How to make man travel this journey from Self Preservation to Self Realisation? The ancient Indian tradition, unlike popular education, did not believe in passing on information to the student. It believes in revealing such information only after transformation of the heart. This tradition addresses this aspect through developing an understanding of four basic ideas:

a) What is Man? (b) What is Truth? (c) What is the nature of Creation? (d) How does integrating 'purpose of Education and Life' take place?

Understanding above ideas leads to an Awareness or total understanding about himself. Filled with Awareness about himself, man performs his role within Limits without harming others and society. This is the 4C Approach of Management.

Part A of the book creates Awareness or total understanding of excellence that exists within man.

Part B of the book is a Study of Limits for man. He is free to act so long as his actions are not harming others.

A common theory of living life and Management emerges when there are common principles for managing life and managing a firm. Then, managing society is easy – as man's balance leads to society's balance. Following common principles of Truth and morality, man uses the four fold path of *Purusharthas*. The practices used for following Truth and Morality that guide him along the four fold path are the **Best Management Practices** of this tradition. They apply to life and from there they flow to man's contribution at work.

Other side of same coin: Using grammar of the ancient Indian tradition

Bhagavad Gita, delivered during *Mahabharata* battle, explains the ancient Indian idea of education. *Mahabharata* is a battle between good and evil. 'Good' and 'bad' exist **within man** and **within society**. This battle is going on: (a) within man – tackled by Part A of the book (b) in the outside world he 'sees' (Cs) – tackled by part B of the book. Winning the battle within man leads to winning outside.

The ancient Indian tradition: Lord Krishna is the teacher and Arjuna the student. The text is educating us. (For those who do not believe in God, Lord Krishna symbolises the voice of conscience. This emanates from what Socrates calls Soul. In this tradition the Soul is perfection in all dimensions or God. Man has to Realise such perfection at the end of education. As man is the Soul and the Soul is God, therefore, Self Realisation – or the realising the full potential of excellence – is the goal of both: education and life)

What does Lord Krishna teach Arjuna? He teaches the Highest Truth. However, first he 'transforms' Arjuna to prepare him for action. Therefore, the first step of education is transformation of the student. How is transformation done? Krishna compels Arjuna to pick up his bow. This bow is *Buddhi* or intelligence. On this, Arjuna has to put the arrow of discrimination. (Please see background Chapter Fig 0.2 and (d) (i) to (iv) which lists the four ideas that give the background of education and help create discrimination). The head of the arrow consists of two questions: 'What is Man' and 'What is Truth' and the answer (The Truth about Man) meets at one point that pierces the target. The body of the arrow is the third question – 'Understanding the nature of Creation'. The fourth question is the feathers at the back of the arrow. It gives balance to the flight of the arrow. (Please see Background (d) (iv) – 'Integration of the common purpose of Education and Life'). When answers to questions are correct, the arrow will reach its target – the 'heart' of man – which is the target of transformation.

Transforming heart of man, education makes selfishness disappear enabling experience of Selfless Love. Now, he is able to Realise full potential of excellence within himself. Education makes him fit to act in society using arrow of 4 *Purusharthas*. Transforming society happens itself, then. The 4C's are Co-operation (Dharma), Focussed Concern (Artha), Competitive Response (Kama) and Compatibility Advantage (Moksha). Their correct pairing is essential: *Dharma* must guide *Artha* and *Moksha* must guide *Kama*. Crisis occurs if desire fulfilment guides *Artha*. When selflessness is the guide to action, man wins the battle of life.

Therefore, transforming oneself is first step before transformation of society is attempted. Krishna lists spiritual practices done by Arjuna, qualifying a student. Similarly, students, today, become qualified for transformation by the process of character building. Education builds character of student. Academic theories are means to this end. Such practices are foundation of education in ancient Indian tradition. They prepare man for transiting from living in Duality to a non-dualistic experience through stage of *Vishisht Adwaita*.

How to make living in Duality fruitful? Understanding *Vedas* makes man ready to follow his *Dharma* or righteous conduct. He, then, Co-operates with others (1st C) for fulfilling the highest goals of man and society. A focussed Concern (2nd C) guides him to add value to the customer, society and himself. This value addition leads to value delivery through his Competitive response (or 3rdC). When conduct rising above selfishness and attachment to fruit of action guides the 3rdC, Compatibility advantage (4th C) emerges. Man and society achieve balance.

The last C or fourth *Purushartha, Moksha,* is the key to this transformation of man as it implies overcoming the 'delusion of false evaluation'. When desires are fulfilled without attachment to the fruits of action (*Karma Phal Tyaga* or *Nishkama Karma*) this happens. This is the central teaching of *Bhagavad Gita*.

The merger of ancient Indian tradition with modern management ideas:
Harvard's Professor Porter has given 3 ingredients of Strategy. This book applies them to Life of man, to help remove the 'delusion' that Arjuna suffered in *Mahabharat*. A common theory of Management and Life, thus, creates a common basis of understanding of management, life and 'management of life'. This removes cause of conflict – both – within man and society. **The book is in two parts: The first** shows how Values merge into Strategy. **The second** shows how Strategy is effective when it emerges from Values. Thus, modern management thought co-operates with spirituality (*Bhagavad Gita*), here, to fulfill goals of man and society.

Ancient Wisdom may need no introduction. For grandparents,
parents, teachers or even our religions have given it to us.
How it applies to many modern ideas may need an introduction.

INTRODUCTION

Part A: Understanding Education and Management Education – common context of ancient wisdom and modern ideas

Education is about realising the Truth:
Civilisations endure through education. **Education** is about **realising** the **Truth**. Understanding nature of Truth should transform the way man sees the world. A different perception of Truth marks distinction of man from the animal world.

Adding ancient wisdom to modern ideas: Our schools design syllabus for each subject and explain properties of physical matter, treating them as Truth. This is useful but is it the only understanding of Truth? Philosophy of a subject can explain it. Physical matter is visible to animal world also. A view of Truth leads to impulses and actions. So, how does man view the world differently from animal world? What understanding of a subject will make man's actions – and society – different?

Importance of the invisible in life: The philosophy of education in every discipline deals with Truth. It tries to inculcate a view of Truth that is not easily visible. Self interest is visible and motivates both humans and animals. So, what is invisible? Physicists, when they add up the visible matter can not add up their equations to account for movement of galaxies and stars. They deduce that there must be some invisible matter to explain rotation of objects and existence of gravitational forces. Force of gravity and even the smallest atom are invisible. The power of a small atom was misdirected towards a bomb! Truth reveals gravity of life. The mind that understands it, too, is invisible. If visible world, that breeds selfishness, limits Truth – can society survive? Therefore, man looks beyond self interest – to realise enlightened self interest. This is higher Truth. It is invisible. Education reveals it.

Myopic self interest is visible: The presence of social strife and crisis is evidence that man lacks a view about a Truth higher than visible myopic self interest. Truth that creates balance, within man and society, is not necessarily visible as physical matter. Yet, it is basis of man and society – so, man should gravitate to it.

Invisible Truth: What is Truth about Man's body? Everything is a mass of atoms always in a state of motion. Scientists and ancient wisdom agree that there is nothing like matter. Table, chair, nose, face, eyes mouth are all in active motion. Their atoms keep moving. Body cells die and soon what man calls 'mine' is dead. How soon new body cells come and replace old ones surprises all. So everything is not what it used to be. It is always changing. Indians call this is *Maya* or illusion. The world, according to them, is an illusion. So, they search for Truth in a world where man's body also changes. The greying of hair, falling of teeth, wrinkles and slowing of human response with age evidence it. Scientists take it as a natural phenomenon. There is an eternal question: What is Truth behind natural phenomenon? Ancient wisdom has taken search for Truth in this direction.

Swami Vivekananda is credited with a conversation with his secular teacher. Ancient Indians believe that world emerges from Truth. As Truth is God, world emerges from God – such is their belief. Vivekananda's teacher once asked: "You say that world emerges from God. There is evil in the world. So does evil, too, emerge from God?" Vivekananda asked counter questions: "Do you agree that there is darkness and cold? But, do we teach it in Physics? We teach heat and light. Absence of heat is cold and absence of light is darkness. In same way absence of God or Good is evil." So, this Paper believes that cultivating goodness removes evil, at once. Darkness disappears when sun comes out. If educated are not committed to goodness, society suffers. If society suffers, man, too, suffers.

Balance is also an Invisible Truth: If society is in balance, education has transformed man so individual good merges with higher good of society. Converging of individual good with higher good leads to balance within man and balance in society. This is an invisible phenomenon. Yet, all stages of life need this convergence – from childhood to adult life. It is evident at school, college, within a family or in society. Sports requires team effort, orchestra creates melody through it, unity of family leads to peace and balance at home.

How does Invisible Truth work in society? In each group, if individual goal merges with larger goal, balance is achieved. If an individual is not serving goals of the group, balance is lost. Neither individual nor group will, then, be in balance. History gives examples of how great empires have fallen. Lack of unity is the most important cause. Empires fall due to lack of unity in ruling family, between the ruler and those managing far off provinces, lack of unity in armed forces or lack of unity in society because of policies of a king. After an empire or civilisation collapses, it is irrelevant to find fault. However, we learn from mistakes.

Invisible Truth emerges from an 'Awareness' 'within' man: The responsibility of the future rests with man, society and education. Man has a body limited by laws of physical matter. The study of these laws is useful for his role – in society. However, man's distinction from the animal world is his Awareness which transcends his body. The capacity to think does not emerge from matter – man's physical body is matter. What leads man to set up United Nations when world war occurs? What leads to environment protection agencies? What leads him to ensure justice through courts at the local, national and international levels? Man's nature seeks Truth and justice. He is aware that some actions can harm all – even though his own nation may win a war, today. Many philosophers believe that the world emerges from Truth. They delve into the subject of Awareness. If what they discover is true, what nature of Truth is experienced by Awareness – using the mind? It is obvious that mind is beyond a human body. So, to understand matter we need something that is not visible – the human mind. What impact does knowledge, emerging from such awareness, have on man's actions?

Man and Truth: Man has a physical body that is visible in a mirror. What is not visible is his mind, yet can anybody deny that it exists? Therefore, man himself is the biggest proof that what is not visible can also be Truth. According to Socrates and ancient Indian Seers, man is really Soul or *Atma*. This is highest Truth about man which is neither gross nor subtle but eternal. It cannot be seen; it cannot be grasped but is an experience full of bliss.

Visible Truth, Higher Truth and Highest Truth: Truth, when it is a description of gross facts is called *Nijam* (this *Nijam* or level of truth seeks to describe the ever changing nature of things that are in a constant flux – permanent conclusions about impermanent things is difficult as a veil of *Maya* or delusion is said to cover this truth – so a search of truth should look beyond so as not to be deluded by such a veil) in ancient Indian tradition. It is a description of what is experienced by man's sense organs. The purpose of education is to help man get the subtle experience of Truth as *Satyam*. This is not found in textbooks but it emerges from within man after years of discipline and practice of Truth and righteous conduct. It guides man on how to act in a way that creates balance within him and society. The highest Truth of man cannot be easily grasped. It is discovery of 'Self' which is known as *Atma Vidya* and realisation of *Atma* or Soul –which is Truth. Even Upanishads, sometimes, use *Ritam* and *Satyam* interchangeably. The difference is that *Satyam* is Truth beyond Time while *Ritam* is beyond Time and Space. Education, thus, makes man realise the Truth. Awareness about it should lead to the highest learning.

What is the highest learning resulting in Highest Truth? This question needs a background before an answer is understood. The objectives of a student today are: to earn well, to find a good job, to enjoy a powerful position, freedom, authority, control, increasing remuneration levels and promotion of self in organisation and society. If these result from recognition of their service to society, it is agreeable. If these are to be achieved by hook or crook – it defeats purpose of education.

It is sometimes difficult to understand spiritual education through the lens of secular education. It needs a different background. To appreciate this Paper, it may be important to understand this background. The next chapter titled Background gives education the context of Management and Society. It explores background of education while seeking answers to three questions:
(a) Which civilisation or culture can give a context for study of Management today?
(b) What is the role and significance of man as part of nature?
(c) What ideas have been central to the survival of man through the ages?
The Indian spiritual tradition has been chosen here for developing a framework for integrating education (including management education) with life. The reasons are given in the Background. The nature of Truth, the Truth about man and Truth about the world/universe, are all elaborated upon there. The impact of study of these Truth(s) on education is also detailed in the Background.

The highest learning has to deal with the topic of Soul or *Atma* – which is beyond the mind of man. An experience of the Soul gives the realisation of the potential of excellence in all dimensions that is inherent in man. Which path for man can help transcend his mind – while being in the physical body? The ancient Indian tradition has a path of four goals of life. A journey on this path is capable of taking man beyond the mind, slowly – overtime. The terminology of this tradition has to be, thus, incorporated in the curriculum of management to enable a realisation of man's potential for excellence in all dimensions.

In the current study, terminology and concepts of this tradition have been integrated with management curriculum that today's decision makers were exposed to. Of course, other studies using other spiritual traditions may also be done. But, as we have seen that this tradition is inclusive – hopefully, results will be same.

This Paper, for brevity, assumes a familiarity with basic **ideas** of this tradition. These ideas include its understanding of Truth, *Atma* or Soul, Theory of *Karma*, *Moksha* or Self Realisation and goals of life or *Purusharthas*. Some exposure to its basic **texts** *Puranas, Vedas, Bhagavad Gita, Brahma Sutras, Upanishads* and its **philosophy**– of *Dwaita*, *Vishisht Adwaita & Adwaita* (dualism, true-false nature of the world & non– dualism) will be useful. However, a patient wait by those unfamiliar will show a use of concepts for common sense conclusions. Simple words are used to interpret essence of message from Source of study.

What is Spiritual Knowledge? Many feel that above knowledge is spiritual in nature, thus outside academic scope. The dictionary defines 'spirit' as that which gives life to vital organs. Similarly, spirit behind an act gives meaning and direction to action. This spirit is not found in textbooks but within man himself. Why should speaking Truth or acting on its dictates be considered a spiritual practice? It is a normal practice, but it deals with the spirit of man's intentions and observations. Hence, it becomes spiritual, too – as it gives meaning and direction to man's actions in society. This meaning and direction discriminates him from other species.

Spiritual Knowledge starts within man, enabling discrimination knowledge. Knowledge based on discrimination is useful at all times. It imparts quality to education for it helps differentiate between good and bad. Action is an important ingredient of this knowledge. One of the important criteria for judging knowledge is that it should have prepared students for right action. In fact, it should give them self confidence to face challenges and unforeseen problems which are not in any textbook (developing the 'spirit' in students). Application of knowledge requires helping others in society boldly and skilfully.

Technique of ancient wisdom: Ancient Indian education trains man for difficult situations. How? In difficult situations, using discrimination and spiritual training, right knowledge (that is relevant to that situation) should emerge from within man. Then, their education will be permanent and will have a sound basis – this is referred to by Seers as *Satyam*. Speaking truth and implementing what you speak, consistently, prepares man for higher Truth of

Satyam – emerging naturally from within. This is experience of ancient Indian Seers. **Therefore, before any process of education begins, the student has to practice sticking to the truth always – in thought, word and deed.** Overtime, it will help him experience Truth as *Satyam*. Unlike a medical school, where case studies help students operate on human bodies or cure them, life presents different situations at each turn. Only emergence of *Satyam,* from within man, can help him and society at critical turns. Case studies for life should help realise eternal Truths. Only then man can apply them in all situations.

Beyond textbooks: Role of training the mind

Training the mind leads to harnessing its power productively, its conquest and even its elimination. This leads to experience of Soul or excellence within man. Ancient Indian tradition believes that concentration of mind is more important than collection of facts. So, education should train the mind. General knowledge cannot be acquired from books alone but by experiencing life. This implies education cannot be put into practice by closing our mind to the world – i.e. by being narrow minded. A narrow vision is unable to see any subject from perspective of society. A book can only say that hurting society is like hurting our own selves. Ancient Indian education sought to give the experience of interconnectedness of mankind and of Oneness of human race. This was demonstrated by the teacher. His heart was filled with compassion. So, education must fill the heart with experience of compassion. This leads to balance within man, among men and between man and nature. A truly educated person, then, will never commit a deed that will harm mankind. This attitude of caring, deeply ingrained as a permanent experience, is 'educare'.

The ancient Indian path to achieving Excellence:

What is the correct path for harmonious working of society? This Paper explores the Truth revealed by spiritual masters. The validation of this Truth was their direct experience. Their ethical route started with a two-fold approach (which this Paper duplicates). Firstly, Seers seek to explore that Truth which does not change. This was understood as the Soul or *Atma*. Seeking such a Truth reveals full potential of excellence, within man. This leads to inner freedom (or **Awareness** of inner power – or Divinity within one self). Love for virtue and fear of sin can make this experience of freedom become useful for balance in society. Thus, their second concept of 'Study of Limits' guided man's behaviour towards love for virtue – through education. This creates ethical background necessary for social action. The ideas at set social Limits to actions of man are taught along with nature of Soul or *Atma*. Otherwise, freedom can lead to ego, desire for personal glory and power. This way wealth and power, without selfishness in use, enabled long term balance in society.

Difference in secular and spiritual understanding of Excellence:

Goal of Education and its impact on man and society

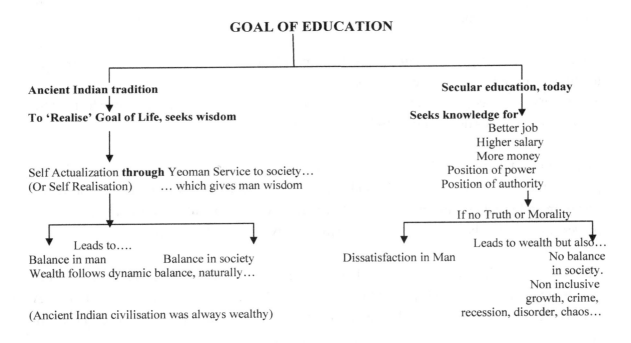

Illustration 1

While secular education concentrates on knowledge, spiritual education seeks wisdom. Wisdom is achieved by realising the goal of life. Maslow would call it Self Actualisation. In the ancient Indian tradition it would imply doing yeoman service to society. This leads to a state of dynamic balance – when men follow the goals of life. Where spiritual education is mixed with secular, prosperity of the highest order is achieved. For, it unlocks the potential of man. Such an approach made ancient Indians wealthy. Wisdom driven society is in balance with nature also. However, when man only seeks the highest goal, the concern for wealth is also overarched. Then, the individual seeks Absolute balance. Socrates, Aristotle, ancient Indian sages sought Absolute balance. Their wisdom inspired society. Following ideas of Truth and morality, ancient Indian tradition gave four goals of life. These helped create dynamic balance for man and society. Dynamic balance can lead to Absolute balance.

Alternatively, when students undertake secular education alone, without following Truth or morality, it leads to fractured society. Without Truth and morality, prosperity will be accompanied by non inclusive growth, disorder, recession, chaos and dissatisfaction in man. Illustration 1 shows this.

Steps for achieving Excellence: The Indian tradition How to ensure that arrogance leading to cruelty, conceit and authoritarianism is removed from mind of man during education? This was the first task for training the mind. If achieved through 'transformation' of habit, then, it is safe to allow students to enter society.

In the ancient Indian tradition, students are convinced that man is endowed with two powers: Individual Freedom **And** Fundamental Law (*Dharma*). **Man is free to enjoy his freedom so long as it does not clash with others – this is a fundamental law.** These two powers are used to help the individual, firm, society through five steps:

The role of morality becomes clear when man feels that all must have the same freedom that he enjoys. With a feeling of One-ness with others, humility emerges, naturally. A comparison of size of man with ocean and sky, too, can generate this feeling. Freedom without humility leads to arrogance, which leads to cruelty, authoritarianism etc. So, the first step, among five, is Humility. These five steps are:

1. Humility: It leads to listening and opening the mind and heart – to others concerns and point of view – leading to social concern and a larger view of men and matters. Market Research, which is essential for product design, is an example of the firm humbly understanding the customers concerns. Arrogance by rulers and judges while listening to complaints of the common man will reflect in their judgement. Humility will create balance. It is, thus, the most useful quality for man in society.

2. Individuality: It is man's treasure. When facts are humbly absorbed, they react with man's voice of Conscience within. The response reflects Individuality. Different firms may design their product differently after research on same customers. Kings and judges may give similar judgements – but in a different way. Though all men live in a conscious state, inner voice or conscience that guides on right and wrong reflects man's Individuality. Its multiple expressions add value.

3. Nationality: The ancient Indian tradition is about expansion and not contraction of the mind (for petty gains). The Love that one feels for one self is expanded to the family and the firm. Then, it is expanded to customers and society and also the nation. This leads to a feeling of Nationality. Porter has discussed the development of National Competitive advantage but from a different perspective. In this tradition, the working together of humility and Individuality should be directed towards Nationality. The voice of Conscience directs man to enlarging the heart to fulfil larger and larger goals identified with the larger interests of the Nation State. The attainment of Knowledge mixed with discrimination which takes care of national interest, prepares man for the next step.

4. Divinity: The above three steps lead to emergence of Divinity or excellence within man. This excellence or perfection is not in a limited area or for a limited task. It should be expressed in all that one does. It is the expansion of Love for work to include all. As it has evolved keeping the best interests of suppliers, customers and environment in mind, many shades of excellence can result. This Gestalt of culture, refinement of thinking and management lead to excellence, perfection or divinity. It blossoms fully after step 5, below:

5. Unity: Striving for excellence leads to an overwhelming feeling of Unity starting from customer. This stems from a realisation that hurting anybody is like hurting yourself. This is the essence of Unity – making man incapable of hurting others or society. This feeling of Unity should extend to all men and nations. Then, it leads to balance between nations and with nature. This is Wisdom that is beyond knowledge and is the final goal of education. It leads to progress and better or unique product and service development – in tune with real needs of society. The ancient Indian civilisation, known as the 'Golden bird' for thousands of years, shows the Truth of this claim. This is the purpose of seeking its management Ideal for study here.

Part B: Understanding this Study

Impact of Truth on this study: This Paper shows how a broader understanding of Truth has a serious impact on decisions of man and, therefore, his actions in society. The Awareness of man's distinction from rest of creation is useful for man to act within the limits imposed on him. Limits exist in society, in firm where he works, in his family and within his physical body. Therefore, this Paper has two sections – one dealing with Awareness followed by the second section dealing with Study of Limits. A proper understanding of both can lead to change in actions of man and ensure balance in society.

Man – focus of Truth and this Study: As outlined above, any study of subject of Management should start with Man. When man transforms, this will impact his family. Each family has an impact on society. Society impacts nation. And nation is part of world. The journey to transform all thus begins with one step: man. If man does not act responsibly first link of chain will be weak. How can society get 'man-aged'? Then, any exercise of management is futile. Therefore, **Management of Self** or Man Management is beginning of education for life. This makes the task of **Management of Society** easier. The Theory of **Management of the Firm** finds relevance only between the two ideas outlined above.

Transformation of man is real education: Change in action of man occurs not just through spread of information but, more importantly, through transformation. Courses in Sciences and Mathematics inform students about important and useful formulae and facts. Is this enough? How do schools transform – not just inform students? Without transformation, man's actions will lead to imbalance, social strife and conflict. The global debt crisis and financial crisis occurred despite 'educated' men (with many derivatives formulae and financial facts) taking decisions.

Purpose of Education: Education should produce good individuals. Most schools state their objective: 'to make a man out of him' or 'make him a gentleman'. So, we refer to educated persons as gentlemen, here. Can a good individual harm society? If society is harmed, have schools transformed students and made them aware that they are good individuals, first? Transformation of man occurs only when man realises what he is (a gentleman!).

Therefore, is curriculum that educated future decision makers fully equipped to give such education? Or, are students not able to absorb it? Where can we draw inspiration from?

Learning from the book of life is always better than learning from a textbook. The book of life, unlike textbooks, does not give solutions but choices – either action chosen will help others or harm them. Society experiences impact of wrong choices over time. The book of life gives experience of Truth to each individual. However, sometimes, it is too late to reverse the clock as experience comes much after an action is taken. The purpose of education, elders and parents is to share their revealed experience – to prepare students for life.

How to integrate Truth about Life with education? If sensitivity about Truth of man (in case experience cannot be given) is non-existent in graduating students – are degrees useful? This is major challenge facing education – not only today, but always in history – whether in oriental or western world. How to integrate book of life with a textbook? If this becomes possible, it would, then, be true study of both Man and Management. This is the objective of this study or Paper.

In many ancient traditions, great teachers taught from the book of life. It was like an examination they gave – for their students to experience and learn from. Their life was an open book; it was their message and teaching. Their personal lifestyle and choices set an example not only for their students but for society at large. Life gives us experience of Truth. Ancient teachers learnt Truth about Life and lived it. Observing them students absorbed it. Examples of how Awareness of Truth is implemented in daily life led to its absorption in society. Teachers taught by example the ideas that led to Awareness of Truth – this enabled management of transformation of man.

Understanding this Study: (earlier ideas presented in format of an academic Paper)

It is important, before pursuing the current study, to understand:
• Why this study?

(This includes an understanding of: Need for study and finding answer to the question: who should take responsibility for crisis in Society?)
• Objective of Study
• Methodology
• Primary and challenging tasks
• Choice of Sources of knowledge which will guide the Study
• Conclusions and some concepts that give context for understanding them

Why this study? (Re stating earlier idea – as if it is an academic Paper)

The first question that occurs to a reader is: 'Why this study?' Another question, which encompasses the reason for this study, is also tackled here: 'Who should take responsibility for crisis in society?'

Need for this study:
Is there a need for this study just because society is facing many a crisis? In fact, presence of crisis is not a reason of seeking an Ideal in education. Irrespective of presence or absence of any crisis, both man and society need an Ideal for reference – more so in education.

The reason for seeking an Ideal is the Ideal itself. It does not need a cause to justify its study. A dipstick test does show that society is not in balance today. The debt crisis faced by nations is not a random event caused by a single unpremeditated act of one individual. Similarly, scams in the corporate sector may not be innocent instances of an individual's stray act. The abuse of earth's resources, leading to degradation of environment, also, has not been result of an exception. When auditors who are the check and balance of corporate sector, participate in wrong practices, it is time to go back to basics. These examples reflect the failure of accountability and governance as they impact balance in society and harmony with nature.

Who should take responsibility for crisis?

What could be cause of crisis facing man and society today? Management education does not search for alibis. Is it possible that what was taught is not implemented? If so: Why? Also, education may not have addressed some issues adequately, or, use of current framework of education in real life is incomplete. Either way, society suffers. Management practice is about taking responsibility and seeking the best path out of any crisis. The presence of imbalance in society and with nature is, thus, a management issue.

What could be a long term cure? **The best solution comes from education.** This Paper gives some inputs for management education. It seeks inspiration from ideas that made civilisations survive to develop a way to tackle problems.

Objective of current study: (Re-stating earlier idea – as if it is an academic Paper)

Education and Life are interlinked. Education prepares man for life. It makes life productive, harmonious and balanced. This is more so with Management Education which deals with managing – a single organisation, any organisation or social structure or even society itself. In fact, education should be such that by managing one's life well, society should become automatically well managed. Therefore, education should benefit the student while producing harmony and balance in society.

Which education removes conflict within man, between individuals and also between man and society – producing harmony and balance for all? If this is found, it can be the course study of Management. This would be the Ideal framework for contemplation and research leading to a theoretical framework for study and action. The Ideal is excellence in all spheres – when man gives the best possible for himself and society. Maslow refers to it as Self Actualisation. Management education should help put it in action for individuals, in society. Therefore, seeking excellence within should lead to excellence in all processes in society. This Paper, thus, seeks Excellence in education, first.

Therefore, ideas that have been important for man, since birth of civilisation are studied – as we try to develop a model of Management that seeks to identify:

(a) **Which management ideas can lead to sustainable, balanced growth of man and society?**

And

(b) **What practices, disciplines/ goals of life can integrate practice and study of management education with life?**

Above questions are answered here. This enables merger of goal of human endeavour with management education. The answers are within context of 'purpose of human endeavour' in Indian spiritual tradition. Expansion of ancient ideas for management practice is undertaken in the language of modern academic ideas of management. Modern management thought is, then, studied using ancient ideas of India's spiritual tradition. This completes the merger of both – spiritual and modern – for practice of management and life.

In the Indian tradition, the goal of life is Self Realisation and purpose of business is to do yeoman service to society. **Illustration 1 and Diagram 1.1 of Chapter 1 show the difference between present focus of education and ancient Indian tradition.**

The achievement of purpose of business, with these ideas, leads to achieving goal of life. In this analysis, where does the concept of Divinity fit? This Paper equates Divinity and 'experience' of Unity of Creation with Self Realisation – which expresses the idea of excellence in every sphere. Self realisation is the result of pursuit of excellence by performing duty to best of ability without attachment to results. Pursuit of excellence begins with the search for excellence within oneself (in the first expression of man: thought, word, deed). This adds value to both man and society – creating harmony and balance in society. Education is not merely transferring of information but should lead to transformation of attitudes. Distributing information about tools and techniques in a classroom is not education. Therefore, **the objectives of this study are**:

i) Firstly, **to show how ideas of strategy and marketing integrate with transformation of a student – enabling a search for excellence within.**
ii) It shows an approach that can be expanded to include all other topics of management (apart from strategy), in a similar fashion. The focus of current study is to integrate transformation with course material of senior managers when they went to management schools in '80's and '90's. If decision makers were transformed, the task of transforming society would be simpler and recession avoided. Not all concepts can be covered in one Study/ Paper/ book. Therefore, the Paper shows this integration through application on few main ideas.

iii) The macro objective of the study is to demonstrate how education in each stream can be integrated with goals of life.

Integrating education with life is a concern for every stream of knowledge – from sciences to arts to medicine. This paper is only a demonstration of one way of integrating the concepts of ethics in an academic discipline. Ethics changes the way of 'C'ing the world – which is the 4C Approach of Management. Integrating ethics with study of strategy shows how strategy for living life and strategy of firm come together. Thus adding meaning to life, man and society. The idea is to catalyse similar thinking in each academic discipline.

The background which follows Introduction here is the source from where the task of 'integration of education with life' can begin for any discipline. This Background prepares man (to 'C' the world in a way and experience it in a manner) that does not permit him to harm it through the practice of tools and techniques imparted by education.

How can this approach be implemented in real life scenario? This issue is discussed in Chapter 7 of this Paper under the title Tests of 'Truth' of Study – in Spirituality, Science, Finance, World. It gives detail of how this approach is being implemented for three decades. It also shares how these ideas can be practiced in real life.

The purpose is to **integrate** ancient ideas (practiced for thousands of years and, now, implemented in a deemed university for three decades) with what is taught to graduating students today. The need for a way of learning that integrates the two systems of education is addressed by this Paper.

The purpose of study is also to **demonstrate** that current concepts fit in with ancient Indian tradition. Only, a need for adaptation of focus exists. This change of focus is best seen in the section that deals with Marketing (referred to, here, as Competitive Response). The two approaches view everything differently here – even identifying the competitor! The difference in understanding of ideas of Strategy is shown in Chapter 4. The strategy of firm and man's Strategy of living Life are interlinked. They have an impact on society. Therefore, such a study is useful. It shows that most ideas of management easily assimilate ethics of ancient Indian tradition – only the nature of understanding changes.

The application in life of ancient Indian education's goal fulfils purpose of study.

Methodology: (Re-stating earlier ideas – as they would appear in academic Paper)

Indian business tradition is a sub set of its culture which has emerged from its ancient education system. This study focuses on:
- Understanding the primary goal of education.
- Then, the understanding expands to include management education.
- Finally, current management theories incorporate ancient India's management tradition. The merger of ancient practices with modern management concepts is attempted.
- The central idea running throughout the Paper is to ensure that life and education should no longer be detached from each other. Therefore, it seeks to integrate education with life... This has been done by integrating goals of education with goals of life.

This is the methodology used in this Paper.

Primary and challenging tasks: (Re-stating of earlier idea – as in an academic Paper)

The primary task of this Paper is to understand the Ideal for practice of Management in daily life. To make study of management relevant to daily life, goal of its study needs to be integrated with goals of life.

The challenging task has been to bring together different approaches – of secular and spiritual, popular, western and orient – in a common framework. The current management education system has different understanding of goals than ancient Indian one. The respectability of an Institute of higher education, today, is directly linked to the kind of placements its students get. The students from these institutions, when they join the corporate world, indulge in practices that led to financial crisis and other problems listed earlier. The approach of Indian education was different. It taught to become useful for man for living Life – not just to give help in earning a Living. While current management education has a lot of logic and skill development in its study, the ancient Indian education system focuses on moral character first. It instills detachment, loving service, fraternity, humility, sincerity, fortitude and fearlessness. The purpose of education, in Indian system is to change man himself. The end of its education or transformation achieved is described by one quality in the student: character.

Choice of sources:

To enable a study of two streams of thinking, a primary source from each stream – modern management thought and ancient Indian concepts – is chosen. Sometimes, a different source uses different terms to explain the same idea. Having a single source avoids such confusion, leading to easy understanding. The author and reader, thus, have a better appreciation of their main ideas.

For choosing a source from current management thinkers, importance was given to nature of work. It should be expansive and cover a wide range of issues researched in depth. Therefore, source should have done original research, not just at level of firm but also expanded it to industry/ industries and also to the nation. The expanding application of management ideas across contexts will be useful for our Study. For, ancient Indians, too, view everything in the context of expansion – as the universe expresses expansion. A common style of analysis and similarity of terms used will make ideas easy to understand.

Keeping this in mind, the work of Michael Porter till '90s is relied on. It forms the backbone for unifying two streams of thought (ancient Indian and modern management). Of course for Marketing, Philip Kotler's and earlier textbooks in Management (studied by today's senior managers) have been used. Multiple sources, here, do not lose advantage of synergy in Porter work (from the strategy of the firm to the competitive advantage of nations). The range and coverage of his work helps unification with the Ideal (as elaborated in the ancient Indian idea). This work is then applied to McGraths idea of Transient Advantage published in 2013. This hopes to give academic shape to sage Parmahansa Yogananda's last words (expressed before taking *Mahasamadhi* during His last speech). He gave hope for a united world combining the best qualities of efficient America and spiritual India.

For choosing a source in the ancient Indian thinking, the criterion was simple. There are innumerable sources, but for ease of understanding of context, one primary source was chosen. The belief *"ekam sath vipra bahuda vadanti"* or the Truth is One but expressed differently by different people – is put in practice, here. When it comes to the highest Truth, the teachings of all Masters merge – this is the path of ancient Indian tradition. As 'Paths can be many but destination is One', we trust the reader (in case he can't identify with the path) will meet us at the final destination.

Across cultures, civilisations and traditions, the works of all Masters are useful. We need to study, first, the principle of "Unity of Thought, Word and Deed" and the principle that the "Purpose of business is to do yeoman service to society". All Masters have shown "busy"ness in exhibiting unity of thought, word and deed. They have also done yeoman service to society by elaborating on the nature of Truth and making others experience it.

For our study, however, we have used the private and public discourses as well as writings of Sri Sathya Sai Baba. He has written and spoken extensively on all sacred ancient Indian texts and also spoken on ancient Indian view of Management to MBA students of His University. Therefore, there is ease of academic research and possibility of direct verification of Truth from Source. The link between education and its practice in life is, therefore, easy to research, study and share. His interpretation of ancient Indian texts has always highlighted unity in core teachings of all religions. This should make results of our research valuable to all irrespective of their individual faith (or lack of it!). Such an interpretation is in the true spirit of ancient Indian education and learning. He has also done yeoman service to society by forming and running institutions that give:
(a) Free education (from primary schooling to PhD)
(b) Free drinking water and
(c) Free healthcare on a scale that not been seen in recorded history

While (a) sets an example of management and execution of education and related services, (b) and (c) demonstrate the use of education to do 'yeoman service to society'. Offering such services requires management abilities showing application of His writings on ancient Indian texts. His idea of 'unity of thought, word and deed' is, thus, demonstrated by Him.

The Source has given discourses on Management in '80s and '90s – when today's senior managers were students. Using Porter's work of this time gives research material for merger of ideas. The projects of the Source give validity to His teachings.

His project of providing free drinking water, for example, entailed laying 2000kms of pipeline, building sumps, balancing reservoirs and overhead reservoirs apart from pre cast cisterns in the drought prone region of Rayalseema, Andhra Pradesh. This was followed by similar schemes in Medak and Mehboobnagar districts in AP, India in 179 and 141 villages respectively. Two million poor in 1000 villages were provided free drinking water. Further, a 63km stretch of canal was developed to give drinking water to Chennai – irrigating 300,000 hectares of agricultural land on the way. Apart from this, two General hospitals and two world class Super Speciality Hospitals give free treatment. These hospitals have performed – till 2012 – some 700,000 cardiac and neuro diagnostic tests. They have also undertaken over 35,000 cardiac surgeries, 40,000 eye surgeries, a million lab and blood tests and treated millions more – all free. Apart from this, a primary school in Puttaparthi and Colleges in Bangalore, Anathapur and Puttaparthi are part of a Deemed University giving free education. From primary school to PhD, children of poorest and even powerful in society study together – free of charge. Just like Medicare is free – for all.

In this manner He has put into practice teachings of ancient Indian texts He has written about. Such an effort requires organisation capacity and management. Not only of finances but also of dedicated individuals who need to be mobilised. They should deliver service continuously sharing His ideal of Service with Love. These services continue to be provided to poorest of poor even after He has left His temporal body. This shows the transformation within those who impart free service on a continuing basis till date.

The Truth or validity of Paper is shown by how His ideas have been put into practice for 3 decades. This topic will see elaboration separately at the end of Paper under the title: 'Tests of "Truth" of Study in Spirituality, Science, Finance, World'. The educational institutions started by Him prepare man for service to society. This service is reflected in free Medicare and free drinking water projects implemented by His Trust. It is not surprising that some of His students involve themselves in service activities of His Trust.

These, and other such service organisations, are case studies of management. They work with no selfish motive – through **co-operation** of those giving their services free of charge or at nominal charge. The organisations, further, give services freely to society. There is a **focussed concern** for the basic needs (educare, health and drinking water) of the rural population (or users). A desire to excel continuously (**competition with one self to improve** further) leads to a **compatibility** with needs of society (in areas of educare, health and drinking water). The wealthiest of societies may not give these services on such a large scale as delivered by one individual with Love. Love is totally experiential – only those who have been touched by it feel it. This paper is for academic wisdom seeking only. Hopefully, it will familiarise us with possibilities of human action and awaken desire to cultivate it. When such change occurs within, it benefits individual as well as mankind.

After choosing the Source, to avoid repetition, all unacknowledged quotations henceforth should be understood as being from this Source only.

Roadmap: Integrating study of Man and Management – Illustration 2

Ancient Indian tradition and current management theory integrate with achieving balance – within man and society. The road map of this paper shows how:
Developing excellence (within man, firm, society and nation), as discussed above involves the five steps for achieving Excellence (in the ancient Indian tradition):
a) Humility b) Individuality c) Nationality d) Divinity d) Unity

With the above understanding of Man and Management, this study begins in a two – fold format – chosen both for Introduction and this Paper, too. This is similar to man's need to have Awareness within limits of fundamental law as described in Part A. So, Part B sets Limits of this Paper within the Awareness outlined in Part A. The Background gives reasons for choosing the Indian tradition. Some aspects of Conclusions of the Paper, too, are given here.

Illustration 2 expresses these steps through various chapters of the book. Each chapter, then, gets expressed as a *Purushartha*, which is, then, integrated in the 4C Approach of management. Chapter 1 depicts Part A of the Paper and Chapters 2 to 5 Part B. Chapter 6 and 7 integrate and validate the study.

Integrating Study of Man and Management through Chapters 1 to 7

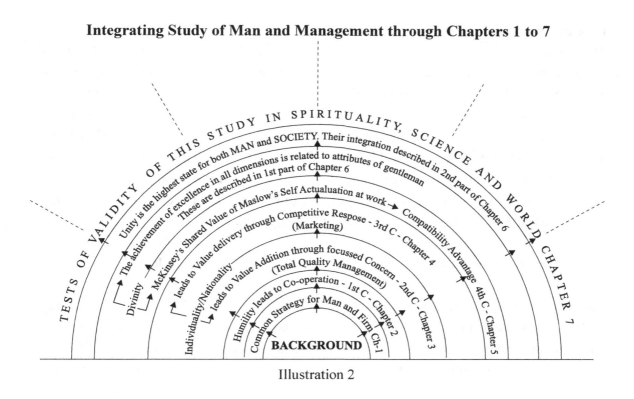

Illustration 2

The 2 fold format of the Paper: Reason (restating earlier idea for academic Paper)

In keeping with the dual nature of things (that Awareness works within limits of a human body) the Paper has been broken up into two sections. This follows the ancient Indian spiritual practice of living in *Bhava Adwaitha* not in *Karma Adwaitha* i.e. live in the Awareness of experiencing the underlying Unity in Diversity (*Bhava Adwaitha*). Yet actions should be in limits (*Karma Adwaitha*). These limits are determined by duties/ obligations (at that moment, as required of man, as per his role in family and society). Therefore, Part A and Part B of this Paper are separated showing this aspect of education:

Part A: The Awareness

This section deals with man's potential for excellence and his capacity to realise this potential within himself. It gives the theoretical basis of ancient Indian thought and creates understanding that integrates with concepts of management in later chapters.

Part B: The study of Limits

This section views firm as an interconnected part of body of society. Just as all parts of a human body are interconnected, the same is case with both firm and society. In case any part of the human body gets hurt, the body directs resources from all over to cure it. Also, what the eyes see and ears hear is used by the brain to direct other body parts to act. Though each body part works within its limits, yet, together, with co-operation, they fulfill all tasks. This helps achieve natural balance of the human body. This balance results only if all parts are in balance. To achieve purpose of life, ancient Indian tradition limits man to four *Purusharthas* or goals. To achieve purpose of business in/of society, can we identify the equivalent *Purusharthas* for our study of Management?

What does the Paper identify – how, why and what does it conclude?

This Paper attempts a framework of management as fulfilling goals of life by identifying:
A) What these goals of life translate into (in language of management theory today).
B) Which management concepts fulfill which particular goal or *Purushartha* of life
C) In above, as smaller truths lead to bigger truths, if something new emerges, it is recorded here.

This way of seeing ('C'ing) things is the 4C Approach to Management or Man Management (as man is the focus and starting point of study). The Paper's focus expands from co-operation within man to co-operation between men – and between man and society. The 4C's are:

Dharma which is Selfless Love in action – creates natural trust among men which results in heart to heart communication and Co-operation. Parts of a body, of man and society, follow *Dharma*. The 1st C is, therefore, Co-operation whose role has been highlighted adequately both in strategy of firm and competitive advantage of nations by Porter.

Artha or business conduct requires a 'concern' for customer and society with a 'focus' on their needs to add value to them. Focussed Concern is, therefore chosen as the 2nd C.

Kama or desire fulfilment is 3rd C of Competitive Response which fulfills firm's desires.

Moksha or '*Moha-ksheya*' (removing illusion of false attachment) emerges from Shared Value (McKinsey 7S model) of Self Actualisation (Maslow's need hierarchy). It gives balance when shared among all men in society. This makes output of the firm 'compatible' with needs of society. The 4th C is, therefore, Compatibility Advantage. Sensitivity about environment makes society benefit from compatibility of man and nature.

The **expression of 4 'goals', *Purusharthas'* or 4C's** within man as well and through the firm, cluster and home nation **must show lack of selfishness. This makes way for expression of Selfless Love.** Their inter relationships are expressed through diagrams.

Education transforms selfish love to selfless love. Following *Dharma* and desire for *Moksha* prevents petty gains at the cost of society in the business of life. *Artha* without *Dharma* and *Kama* without *Moksha* create imbalance. Students of Indian tradition use four *Purusharthas* or 4C Approach in the business of life. For, it moves man from a desire of maximisation of selfish gain to making an Optimisation effort. Man, thus, rejects mindless profit maximisation and prefers profit optimisation. This is the route to equilibrium or balance in society. It removes darkness from mind of man and from society. This can be discovered following the spirit of teachings of sages and indulging in righteous conduct which reflects Truth, Beauty and Goodness. Integrating study of Indian culture with management education can influence qualities imbibed in students. The philosophy of Vedas and Upanishads co-operates with management thought to fulfill the *Dharma* of Management – using inspiration of India's ancient Seers to fulfill aspirations of society.

Management education, thus, emerges like a wave from the ocean of knowledge and merges back in it again. The flow of Chapters is designed to replicate the flow of Life. Ancient Indian tradition identifies the flow of life with the flow of four '*Purusharthas.*' The Ocean of Knowledge can be understood in many ways. *Satyam, Jnanam, Anantham Brahman* is one way. Its expression through Chapters of book is depicted below.

How does worldly action emerge from this and how does this worldly action lead back to the Highest Wisdom? Illustration 3 depicts it. It removes selfishness by giving experience of Unity of Creation through percept and practice. It prepares man to only 'Help Ever, Hurt Never'. This creates balance within man, within society and with nature, simultaneously. When man realises the Truth about Himself, goodness or God within man or excellence in multiple dimensions expresses itself. Then, beauty of action emerges as non – attachment. **Chapter 1 (signifying Awareness) emerges from the Background and Chapter 6 merges back in the same ocean of knowledge. Similarly, the similarity of Synopsis with the Summary validates that they are from the same ocean of knowledge.**

Wave of Management Education
emerges from Ocean of Knowledge and merges back in it again – Synopsis to Summary, Chapter 1 to Chapter 6

Step 1:
Wave of Management Education emerges, fills man with 'Awareness' - created by 'Background' as Part A of the Book (Chapter 1).

Step 2:
It is put into action by man through Four 'Purusharthas' (Chapters 2 to 5)

Step 3:
This prepares man for merging back in the Ocean of Knowledge by realizing the Unity of Creation (Chapter 6 of the book)

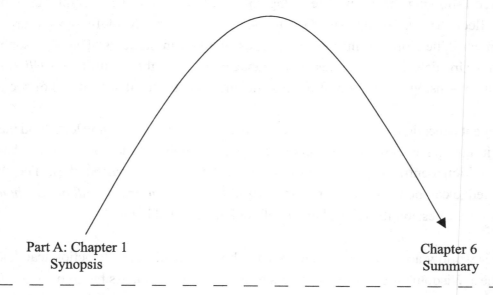

Part A: Chapter 1
Synopsis

Chapter 6
Summary

Ocean of Knowledge: (Background of Book)

Satyam, Jnanam, Anantam Brahman

Satyam (True/Truth), *Jnanam* (Wisdom), *Anantam* (Infinite) *Brahman* (Supreme Consciousness/Self)
True Wisdom lies in understanding that all we see is Infinite manifestation of
Brahman (Self) only:
So 'Help Ever, Hurt Never'
For helping another is same as helping your Self,
Hurting another is same as hurting your Self.

Illustration 3

BACKGROUND

FOUR QUESTIONS that lead to wisdom in Ancient Indian Education

Everything gets its meaning from a context or background. The same act done in different contexts may mean opposite things – just as use of a knife by a surgeon and a murderer. The murderer harms with use of knife while a surgeon cures. The context of use of knife gives meaning to an act. Education (and management education) should be in context of man and society. But, what does context mean?

Context has been defined by Oxford online dictionaries as: "The circumstances that form the setting of an event, statement or idea, and in terms of which it can be fully understood…" Man's education should be understood in context of society. If actions that harm society come from educated men, then education becomes like a murderer's knife.

Importance of Context: Convergence of contexts of Education, Management & Society

Society works in a context of social structures. These operate to generate balance and harmony. To understand background of education and management (in and of societies), we need to study a society that has been a survivor and see reasons that led its settlements to become a civilisation. Tracing reasons of survival could lead us to concepts useful for education and management education when applied in today's context.

Management is not just about managing business but, at individual level, about managing life. The understanding of management should be common whether one manages a business or one's own life. In this process society also gets managed. This convergence of man's goals with society's aspirations should logically lead to harmony, balance and survival of society and civilisation. Education should learn the process from such a civilisation, adapt it and promote this convergence in today's context. However, it must, first, itself learn how this convergence can be achieved or has been achieved in the past. To learn from history, it is important to study a society that merges the concept of individual welfare and Optimisation (Management Prof. Porter's ingredient of Strategy) of individual's efforts with societal welfare to achieve goals of society.

Which ancient society has had such a broad understanding of the inextricable link of welfare of society rooted in highest aspiration of man? Has this society outlasted others with this concept ingrained in its education as well as way of life? Can the way of thinking of this society that ensured harmony and balance be incorporated in current thinking of how to manage life, business and society?

Such a universal understanding of management of life, business and society usually evolves from four things. These are: the way man understands himself, his role in society, background of society and an answer to the question: what ensures its survival? These ideas influence education which Reinforces them (Reinforcement – Porter's ingredient of Strategy). For education, searching for Truth about man and society is the underlying idea. Its understanding is the basis and starting point.

Four basic questions that give background of this Paper/ Study:

All men and societies may have similar beginnings, yet some outlast others. The nature of processing that happens within man (through education) makes a society or civilisation different. To refresh present approach to education, it is important to learn from concepts/ ideas of such civilisations that can add value to education today. Therefore, the first question is:

(a) Which civilisation can give a context for study of Management today?
As part of our search, we conclude that ancient Indian civilisation can upgrade our approach to education. The reasons are elaborated later.
However, it is important to understand some basic concepts first. The most important are:
(b) What is the role and significance of man as part of nature? – History of man
(c) What concepts are central for man's survival?
(d) Which ideas create background of education?
After answering the above questions the process of education starts – which prepares man for living in society.

(a) Which ancient society can give a context for study of Management today?

A civilisation that outlasts others should reveal management tools for learning and practice. By using this criterion, the ancient Indian civilisation is not only ancient but has survived the vicissitudes of time and circumstance. It has a clear concept of an Ideal way of living life. A study of its approach, goals and fundamental concepts can be the basis of a unified approach to management of life, society and business.

The purpose of study will be fulfilled by exploring training of mind and use of human intelligence in this tradition. This will be incorporated for man in this Age for education or management education.

Why study Indian tradition?

A study of achievements of ancient Indians has been done by many authors, but it is good to choose one. The Shankracharya Sri Chandrashekarendra Saraswati, who died in 1994, is a recent authentic source whose views can summarise work of many scholars.

He states that matters of this world were never ignored in a concern for the 'other world' by ancient Indian seekers. In fact, he confirms that ancient Indian knowledge and texts are a storehouse of science and all other disciplines. For sake of brevity, we will only highlight mathematics as an indication of sophistication.

He gives examples of various ancient texts as source of modern mathematics. For example, he states: "The *siddhanta-skandha* deals with arithmetic, trigonometry, geometry and algebra.... The higher mathematics developed by the west in later centuries is found in ancient *Jyotisa*". Arithmetic, he contends, was called "*vyakta-ganita*" in Sanskrit and included addition, subtraction, multiplication and division. "*Avyakta-ganita*" is algebra. "*Jya*" means the earth and "*miti*" is method of measurement. "*Jyamiti*" evolved with need to measure sacrificial place: "geometry" is derived from this word. The "geo" in geography is from "*jya*". There is a mathematical exercise called "*samikarana*" which is same as "equation". He also mentions branches of mathematics like *"rekhaganita"*, *"kuttaka"*, *"angapaka"*, etc.

He feels that while ancient Europeans may have opposed science and burned scientists as heretics, ancient Indian tradition has been inclusive by nature, always. He also questions the European claim that they were the first to discover that earth is like a ball and not flat like a plate. He answers the doubt by asking a simple question: 'what word do Indians use for "geography"?' He, then, gives the answer: *"Bhugola sastra"*, (text of earth being a sphere) – and not – *"bhu-sastra"* (text about the earth). Ancient Indians, he thus concludes, have known from early times that the earth is a *"gola"*, a sphere. These texts spoke of heliocentric system long before western astronomers or scientists. He has pointed out that very first stanza in *Surya Siddhanta*, (a very ancient treatise) refers to the force of attraction of earth – Gravity. In Shankara's commentary on Upanishads, he adds, there is a reference to earth's force of attraction. The force which pulls down an object thrown up is *apaana* and earth has *'apaana shakti'*. Prasnopanishad (3.B), according to him, states – "The deity of earth inspires the human body with *apaana*". He further states "there are many such truths embedded in our *sastras.*"

In fact, the Shankaracharya has checked calculations of scientists who, seeing the diminishing heat of the sun, arrive at a time when it will no longer be able to sustain human life. He has, then, compared it with the *'avanta pralaya'* or intermediate deluge given in ancient Indian texts. He states that the calculations match perfectly. He proves the superiority of ancient Indian knowledge and mentions there is an equation in the *'Apastamba sulba sutras'* which could not be proved until recently. Modern mathematicians, he states, had thought it to be faulty as they could not solve it. Now, they accept it.

History proves Indians were convinced that the earth revolves around the Sun and the moon revolves around earth. Earth's gravitational force was known – so was modern decimal system and use of zero. (This was called Arabic numeral system given to Europeans but it was known as *'Hind se'* meaning 'from India' since it originated in India). Aryabhatt from India has recorded the rule of finding area of Triangle before 500 AD. He can be credited with knowledge of Trigonometry (which is a derivation of the words *'Trikon mitri'* or understanding or being friends with triangles).

There are many illustrations of excellence achieved by ancient Indian civilisation in worldly and spiritual matters. They were known for establishing a link between them – the understanding of zero and infinity is one such example. Shankracharya Saraswati also states that Bhaskaracarya established the subtle truth that any quantity divided by zero is infinity ("*ananta*"). His mathematical treatises conclude with a benedictory verse in which he relates zero to the Ultimate Reality. "When the divisor goes on decreasing the quotient keeps increasing, does it not? If you divide16 by 8 the quotient is 2; if the same quantity is divided by 4 the result is 4. Divided by 2, the quotient is 8. Divided by zero? The quotient will be infinity. Whatever the number divided, the result will be infinity if the divisor is 0." Bhaskaracarya says: "I pay obeisance to the *ParamAtman* that is Infinity". Infinity is manifestation of Divinity – or excellence in all dimensions – which is purpose of spiritual pursuit or goal of education and life. To understand manifestation of divinity as infinity popular folklore in India sings: "*Hari ananta, Hari katha ananta….*" i.e. Divinity or Excellence cannot be limited by dimensions. Expressions of glory of excellence or Divinity are without limits – or infinite. Human potential gives 'experience' as infinite and purpose of spiritual pursuit is to take it towards such 'experience'. Humility of being zero leads to it.

The excellence achieved in sciences and arts by ancient Indians was synchronous with their spiritual pursuits and not restricted to mathematics, physics, chemistry or astronomy. In fact, inspiration for such higher knowledge came from their power of single-minded concentration which spiritual pursuits enabled.

The formal system of medicine of ancient Indians, for example, is recorded since 2nd century AD and may date earlier. Their skill in metallurgy and scientific study of metals is evident in an iron pillar that dates to 415 AD. The universities giving secular and spiritual knowledge, temple architecture, paintings, sculptures and literary arts of Gupta period from 320 AD to 540 AD, among other such historical evidences, reflect this excellence.

Nalanda and Taxila universities in India had students from different parts of the world. The spiritual discussions were not restricted to a single faith. They gave an understanding of philosophy and purpose of human life. The Jains and Buddhists came to these universities. They did not have faith in *Vedas*, yet the system of education was relevant to their daily life and was of use to society. The 14th Dalai Lama says that Tibetan Buddhism draws a true lineage from Nalanda in India. This pristine breadth of vision and its inherent quality of inclusiveness enables it to be of use across all cultures.

What is this tradition and what made it so inclusive? Even non-believers could find meaning by studying it – even if they rejected its texts or scriptures! Its society practiced and protected a large number of customs, traditions, languages and religions and fiercely protected the Individuality of each. What has made this appreciation of apparent diversity possible? For a society that preserves its spiritual traditions, the answer, too, lies in its spiritual roots! The faith of ancient Indians revered and accepted all faiths. They believed that if factionalism entered their heart, it would bring disgrace to them and their forefathers – who taught the essence of unity in diversity. So, they never disturbed the faith of others.

To answer the question 'Why study Indian tradition?' let's ask another question: 'what is the essence of ancient Indian tradition?' This answer can be given in 5 points:
1. The tradition sincerely believes no one should ever try to bind another by a fixed attitude or interpretation of way of life. Also, man's sincere application of higher knowledge does not need approval of a single individual or group – so long as it does not harm anyone. Using any force in matters of spirit is a crime. Hence, all religions prosper here.

2. The eternal universal *Dharma* or righteous conduct is taught in *Vedas*, which were revealed along with creation. They have no beginning or end. Enquiry into spirit with faith finds fulfilment in them. For all problems involving differences in spiritual attitudes and aspirations, convincing solutions can be found here. They are endless – just as creation is. All that is elevating and beneficial, all that is holy and sacred to believers in Indian thought, is available and has been available at all times, from and through *Vedas*.

For those who do not have faith in God, Indian spiritual seekers ask a simple question; "Do you have faith in yourself?" This faith is enough to begin with. Strengthening this faith is the main task. This can be easily achieved through attaining excellence by righteous conduct, truthful behaviour and purity of intention in pursuit of all activities. The only precaution is eliminating the ego. The experience man attains, after ego elimination, will be same as attained by following righteous conduct etc along with a belief in God or universal power. The Indian spiritual tradition concludes that 'you are God, yourself' in the later texts of Upanishads leading to *Atma Vidya* or Knowledge of the Self. The capacity to experience excellence or Divinity within and absorb Truth is different, hence this tradition moves from higher to highest Truth in stages. However, the desire for excellence is hallmark of a seeker in this tradition.

3. The *Vedas* state that there exists One transcendent eternal Power, everything has originated from It and will merge in It again. Diverse beliefs about this power (formless or with form – and which form?) find Vedic declarations supporting each point of view. This proves that the nature and characteristics of this Power is an irrelevant question. The later texts and *Atma Vidya* (Knowledge of Self) point out that the world is the reflection of mind. When the mind dissolves into Excellence or Divinity, it can become one with this Power. However, merging with excellence and achieving power of creation is attainable only by a very few people.

4. From childhood a belief is ingrained that no qualification like wealth or disqualification like poverty exists for spiritual discovery. This idea ingrains a broad feeling among spiritual aspirants and helps create humility and ability to see all as onself.

5. This tradition believes that Creation or this Universe has no beginning or end. According to the laws of evolution, it will recede from gross into subtle stage and after being there for some time it will again recede into causal stage from where it emerged. From the One into which it merges, it will gradually manifest itself as many through subtle and gross stages of expression. The later texts and *'Atma Vidya'* make man aware that he is not gross or subtle body but causal body or *Atma*. The journey from gross to subtle to causal body is the journey of education or *Atma Vidya*. The universe, in the highest stage of realisation or most purified state of consciousness, is nothing but a reflection of that within man and can dissolve within him.

The ancient Indians did not expound the above 5 principles to confront any dogma or theory and score victory over it. Their goal was not empty faith but was evident through experience of two things: (a) *Sthithi* (or the stage of experience reached) and (b) *Siddhi* (or the wisdom won). The experience of both was self evident to a practitioner. The attainment of fullness of experience is the merging of mind selflessly in excellence or Divinity (which is Love for work expanded in all dimensions). Even after thousands of years practitioners vouch for the experience that this technique of education imparts to them. Their experience is individual and is not easily described in words.

However, an answer to "Why ancient Indian tradition should be studied for Management of man and society?" is not just because of the aforementioned points but also by other considerations. These are:

i) The most important guideline for action in this tradition.

ii) Other determinants like: its highest prayer, its similarity with other religious faiths or philosophies, being source of other traditions and ability to generate economic prosperity and scientific excellence. These realise the purpose of life of man and give an ability to generate inner and outer excellence, simultaneously.

– The first determinant is its guideline for action. How is action judged in society? What gives basis for guiding choices of action? The ancient Indian tradition has goals of life and defines the first goal of life or *Purushartha* as *Dharma* or Righteous Conduct. One dimension of *Dharma* is that its application makes the whole world prosperous. Therefore, the understanding of life and balance of society also encompasses economic activity and seeks to promote prosperity of world. Such an inclusive tradition is both spiritual and worldly and can, therefore, promote balance within man, among men, among nations and the world. It can thus be worthy of study for living life by practicing business and its management.

– The highest prayer denotes highest objective of man. If this objective is selfish, it may be inappropriate for functioning of society (and also for balance within it). If its highest objective is all inclusive, it can be applied to other societies across time. Only those who pray for happiness and welfare of everybody and everything in all circumstances can support an inclusive society. For such a society establishes the essential linkage between prosperity of self and prosperity of all others! Prayer comes from the heart and when such a tradition incorporates such emotions and feelings in the hearts of men through prayer, it becomes a tradition and culture worth emulating. Thus:

– The ancient Indian tradition becomes a preferred choice as it always prays for "*Loka Samasthaa Sukhino Bhavantu*" or "*Samastha loka Sukhino Bhavantu*" or "May all the worlds be happy and prosperous". This prayer and its feeling is ingrained in education process as stepping stone to Self Realisation or achieving the highest goal of life for man. The close interdependence between achieving man's highest goal and society's welfare achieves harmony and balance – enabling it to last for thousands of years. This harmony and balance is achieved within man first, through education. Thereafter, harmony and balance between men, between man and society and between man and nature emerge as natural corollaries.

– The similarity of teachings of Socrates and Greek philosophers with ancient Indian concept – of man not being just the body but also the mind and the Soul is well known in philosophy. In fact, even before Christianity, the dominant philosophy of Hellenistic period recognised four elements (out of five propounded by ancient Indians) as basic cause of Universe. Many similar concepts about evolution, devolution and primacy of Divinity are also found. The concept of Love propounded by Jesus is the backbone of ancient Indian wisdom and was also given by Socrates, Plato and Greek philosophers. It, again, resounds in the words of Rumi in another period of time and at other places in the world. Therefore, ancient Indian tradition absorbs highest tradition of philosophy of ancient and medieval world. The task of this Paper is to study how these concepts apply to education today.

– The 13th century Muslim mystic Rumi brought together not only central Asia and India for seven centuries but also the world. He has been one of the most popular poets of United States. United Nations announced 2007 as the Year of Rumi while Pope John XXX111 wrote "In the name of the Catholic world, I bow with respect before the memory of Rumi". What were his ideas that have moved the world for centuries? These ideas are ingrained in ancient Indian wisdom and are universal concepts across cultures, religions and time. Some of these ideas are: Man unconscious of his Divinity (or excellence and expansion of Love) is akin to animal. His desire of union with the beloved (excellence) is achievement of Divinity within man. He believed that separateness from this Divinity at the beginning of time (re-interpretation of Fall of Adam) led to evolution of everything in universe. To follow this inner urge and move back to union with this excellence or Divinity is purpose of human endeavour. He advocates tolerance, goodness, positive reasoning and awareness through Love. While Rumi taught this passionately through music and poetry, Indian tradition has elaborated philosophy behind concepts making it easier for academic study.

– Baruch Spinoza, the rationalist who died in 1677 examined 3 things: structure of world, nature of God and life of man. The infinity and wholeness of world or its Perfection was characterised as the substance of world by Spinoza. God, in his explanation, was the World for He is all pervading, everlasting and complete. Every object in the world is like a momentary idea or attitude of God. Each one of us is a definite part of Him – a cell in His body – but our limited intelligence makes us understand only a limited part of Truth. The world is like a symphony in which each one of us is but a note. God, then, is universe and everything in it is part of body of God. This philosophical doctrine is called Pantheism (Greek word Pan means whole or everything and Theos means God) which is an ancient Indian concept. Its implications for action, too, are the same as Indian thought: happiness of each one of us depends upon well-being of whole body of mankind. Therefore, love others as one loves oneself. Desire only that what you would desire for all others for all are equally important parts of God. Love, declares Spinoza, transforms our life into eternal ecstasy. The Soul, he contends, is not destroyed as it is a part of God. His concepts are part of ancient Indian *Sanatana Dharma* and detail reasons behind the prayer "may all worlds be happy".

Thus ancient Indian wisdom shares concepts with all religions, ancient European, medieval Muslim and medieval rationalist thought. In fact, its idea of Nationality includes all who sincerely implement this wisdom in daily life (irrespective of outward differences in expressing the same). The desire of excellence and single minded pursuit of it (following path of Truth and righteousness with purity of intention) makes all such aspirants share a common nationality irrespective of outward differences. This is the Indian approach that reflects broadmindedness. Such an inclusive nature makes this tradition a suitable candidate while choosing a single tradition for academic study.

• Professor Max Mueller (who received his PhD for a study of Spinoza's Ethics) worked under Franz Bopp who undertook the first systematic study of Indo-European languages. From history of language to history of religion was his next journey. Many references exist for his work. For ease of reader's verification, the Wikipedia's correct summary about this period is restated: "…In particular the Vedic culture of India was thought to have been the ancestor of European Classical cultures, and scholars sought to compare the genetically related European and Asian languages in order to reconstruct the earliest form of the root – language. The Vedic language, Sanskrit, was thought to be the oldest of the IE (Indo European) languages." Max Mueller studied *Vedas* in detail and commented: "Into whatever unknown realms of experience their causative and positive inquiry led them, the Indian seekers ventured boldly therein. They never hesitated to discard, for the sake of success in this adventure, whatever they felt as an encumbrance. They were not affected by fear of how others might judge them". He felt Indian spiritual aspirants sincerely walked on the right path and the path of Truth. So, he asks others to join in this adventure and discovery.

• Wikipedia's accurately gives Max Mueller's views. They are restated for easy verification by the reader: "For Mueller, the culture of the Vedic peoples represented a form of nature worship…. He saw the gods of the Rig-Veda as active forces of nature, only partly personified as imagined supernatural persons. From this claim Müller derived his theory that mythology is 'a disease of language'. By this he meant that myth transforms concepts into beings and stories. In Mueller's view 'gods' began as words constructed in order to express abstract ideas, but were transformed into imagined personalities. Thus the Indo-European father – god appears under various names: Zeus, Jupiter, Dyaus Pita. For Mueller all these names can be traced to the word Dyaus, which he understands to imply shining or radiance. This leads to the terms *deva*, deus, theos as generic terms for a god, and to the names Zeus and Jupiter (derived from deus-pater). In this way a metaphor becomes personified and ossified." With European scholars making such a strong case for understanding this tradition, the choice of ancient Indian tradition for purpose of our study becomes simpler.

• A study of economic history of the world shows that, but for the last 500 years, India has contributed very significantly to global economic activity. It is also recorded in history that India was attacked by Turks, Frenchmen, and the British etc. If India did not have riches accumulated through productivity and value addition, why would it have evoked such repeated interest amongst the conquerors? Such wealth and prosperity must have resulted from its working ethos and culture – which must have been nurtured by a good education tradition. When the world always seeks its skills (through trade) or wealth (through conquest), it becomes relevant to ask: what led to productivity over many a thousand year? What was its education that enabled such skill development? Is this a sign of excellence? What are dimensions of such excellence we can incorporate in our education?

• The ancient Indian spiritual tradition is commented upon in the Encyclopaedia Britannica under 'Ethics' where it states: "In the oldest of the Indian writings, the Vedas, ethics is an integral aspect of philosophical and religious speculation about the nature of reality. These writings date from about 1500 BCE. They have been described as the oldest philosophical literature in the world, and what they say about how people ought to live may therefore be the first philosophical ethics......".

It also agrees with Mueller's views when it states: "The Vedas are, in a sense, hymns, but the gods to which they refer are not persons but manifestations of ultimate truth and reality." Further, it states; "In the Vedic philosophy, the basic principle of the universe, the ultimate reality on which the cosmos exists, is the principle of *Ritam*, which is the word from which the Western notion of right is derived. There is thus a belief in a right moral order somehow built into the universe itself. Hence, truth and right are linked; to penetrate through illusion and understand the ultimate truth of human existence is to understand what is right. To be an enlightened person is to know what is real and to live rightly, for these are not two separate things but one and the same."

The Encyclopaedia also states: "The ethics that is thus traced to the very essence of the universe is not without detailed practical applications. These applications were based on four ideals, or proper goals, of life: prosperity, the satisfaction of desires, moral duty, and spiritual perfection – i.e., liberation from a finite existence….. Because the eternal moral law is part of the universe, to do what is praiseworthy is to act in harmony with the universe, and accordingly such action will receive its proper reward…."

• In all religious and social traditions, including Indian, the focus shifted overtime from the inner to the outer. However, the clarity of concepts in the Indian tradition about: **man's understanding of himself**, understanding the **nature of Truth** as well as **understanding creation** – all were **integrated into education** with a focus on **the way life is to be lived**. Understanding the **common purpose of education and life** was the backbone of its education system. This created a **unity of purpose within man and society** thus preventing a fractured society.

However, the 'formal' approach slowly began to obliterate the spiritual. The original way became obscure for common man as rituals became more important than spirit behind actions. The divisions of society undertaken for harnessing potential of men, as per their skills and inner urges, became dogmatic creeds for exploitation. The role of women began to be misinterpreted for serving selfish ends. The leaders of thought lost confidence in their own innate excellence and tried to safeguard petty interests instead.

Such actions created a culture of mental weakness in society which impacted morality and understanding of Truth. This has led to attempts by reformers to revive purity of ancient path. Overtime they also began to be understood as cults, sects or religions. However, original message said in different words by different reformers, continues to be relevant for mankind today, just as it was thousands of years ago. Its understanding of life is as relevant to education today, as it was thousands of years ago when it founded a civilisation.

The understanding of Management and its application within a nation emerges from the culture of society which, again, emerges from its tradition of education. Different nations have different cultural traditions depending on conditions and nature of evolution of society. As Management deals with people, its practice should have relevance to conditions in society. Thus, for practice of management to be effective, it has to be in consonance with culture of society. The application of management techniques may thus be different in different cultures, nations and traditions. Or, the same concept may be implemented in different cultures through different routes keeping sensitivities of culture and tradition in mind. The attitude of hiring and firing employees, for example, may be different historically among firms managed by Japanese and Americans. However, concepts of Indian culture that emerge from its ancient wisdom are so broad minded that they have universal applicability – and can be applied in all cultures and traditions.

Secular education enables man to fly millions of miles in outer space. Which education thinks of going half an inch in the inner realm to discover what lies *within* man? Can such exertion and energy spent on education be called meaningful? In which tradition, today, is knowledge and scientific temper practiced along with sense and mind control with character development?

Thus, it is relevant to study this tradition and revive its universal applicability. This Paper merges concepts of management with highest Truth of this tradition and education.

Lessons from history: A case study of European Renaissance

In 15th and 16th century Europe, scholars made new translations of work of ancient writers to discover that those who lived a thousand years earlier understood the world better in many ways.

The interest in ancient learning of humanist scholars led to great discoveries in both art and learning. Historians record this period of time as The European Renaissance. History states that Erasmus, the scholar of Europe, saw no contradiction between Christianity and ancient cultures – and referred to Socrates as 'Saint Socrates'. He also believed in practicing and learning humility which is an important principle of ancient Indian tradition ("It is vain to gather virtues without humility…"). Cardinal Ximenes set up a university with a very humanistic curriculum. The search for indigenous culture combined with an appreciation of the commonality of cultures, religions and ways of seeking excellence (Divinity) paved the way for using education for more secular purposes.

The tradition of ancient learning is: 'seek and you shall find'. Those who seek secular purposes will achieve them. Those who seek the highest education, too, will find it. The growing fusion of ideas as well as art and science, in the view of historians, anticipated the scientific revolution that was to come two centuries later in Europe. Even during the Renaissance there was a rebirth of learning where scholars studied many subjects. Leonardo da Vinci was one example of a 'Renaissance man'. Apart from being a painter, he was a military expert, engineer and inventor who also studied the human body very closely. He has written fables on importance of humility. Such excellence in many dimensions simultaneously does not lead to defocusing but is the result of a deeper focus resulting from a higher level of education.

Can a Renaissance in management education be achieved by appreciating and integrating ancient Indian spiritual truths in the practice of management? To enable this, the Paper seeks to add a focus of ancient Indian education system to current management thought. This allows an integration of 'study' of management education with practice of life. A renaissance will fulfill the objective of this study.

(b) What is the role and significance of man (as part of nature): Context of human life?

For nature or creation to exist and not collapse, it must be in a state of balance. Man is, thus, a part of the balance of creation. Two questions emerge when this point of view is accepted: What is man's role in maintaining this balance? How does this balance (or what Buddha refers to as middle path – not too much, not too little) emerge within man, naturally? What should be the purpose of human endeavour that enables man to achieve his natural state? The process of education can begin after understanding this.

If everything is in balance in a natural state then man too should be in balance in his natural state. As his actions help maintain the balance in Nature, it is important to determine what are man's natural actions. To answer such a question, man must first understand himself as well as his context. We know that man operates in the context of society. Is there an inner context which prompts him on how to operate in society?

To answer the above, two questions naturally emerge:
(a) What is the difference between man and the rest of creation? For, if he acts according to this natural distinction, balance of and with nature will be maintained.
(b) Who is a man really?

The natural difference between man and rest of creation gives a background or context for man's actions. To put it clearly, if we say "I am a man" it does not give the full picture but if we say "I am a man NOT an animal" it gives the full picture. Why? This is because the latter statement gives both the context and differentiation of man. Man will fulfill his role and attain balance, in and with nature, only if he operates in a manner that maintains this differentiation. Society, too, gets its differentiation from herds in animal world by highlighting this distinction.

The above understanding by man of his context and role should help maintain balance within man, between men and with nature. The next question is: who is man and what is his nature? Both popular and ancient Indian thought study man in the context of society. For understanding man, Socrates gave the term Soul which Indians called *Atma*. Indians believe that man achieves balance by following Truth and Morality. Why study this balance? For, if society is already in balance, why proceed further?

Balance with nature needs balance within Society: Is society in balance today?

Balance in society is reflected in social behaviour. How can we, at any point of time, check if society is in balance? Ancient Indians checked proper functioning of society through observing political behaviour, social conduct, economic activity and spiritual pursuit. Society's current activities reflect a lack of balance in each of above spheres. Political behaviour is marked by corruption. Social conduct sees disorder, chaos, crime and falsehood. Economic activity shows unethical behaviour while spiritual pursuit without applying control over human mind is useless. Fig 0.1 illustrates this here:

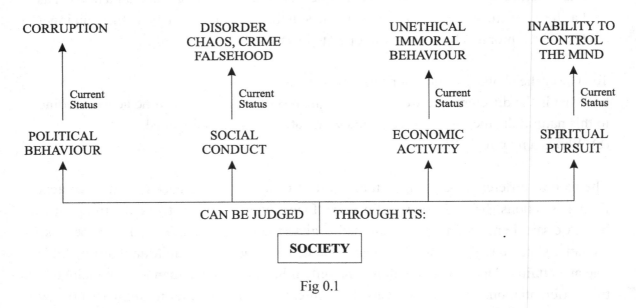

Fig 0.1

Background of society: Popular lessons and Indian lessons from history

Historians believe that man was a nomad first. He travelled in search of food in groups (where men co-operated to meet common objectives) before settling down, learning how to grow food and rear animals. Farming also needed co-operation with nature (understanding seasons and using them for cropping patterns etc) and took less time than hunting and gathering food daily.

Better use of land led to surpluses which led to trade and exchange. Settlements grew into towns and cities where thousands lived. Even more co-operation was needed for doing different tasks which support others. This led to advancements in farming, crafts and trade. There was also classification in society according to skill, trade or job being done – all point out to great deal of co-operation in society. There were inequalities yet there was balance in society. When cities did not co-operate with each other due to rivalry, jealousy, low level instincts or unfair practices being followed by any one or both, war resulted.

All survivor civilisations showed high degree of co-operation within cities. Also a feeling of belonging leads to a willingness to sacrifice petty self interest for a larger cause of welfare of all. Selflessness in serving others – in country or family – was the hallmark of social bonding. It was also an expression of natural affection that humans' interactions with others show. The decline of empires is usually linked to weakening of this feeling in society for ruling classes. The lack of co-operation between the centre and its territories results in weak governments ready for breaking up or being conquered. The history of mankind is, therefore, closely linked with the trait of co-operation, selflessness and sacrifice.

The ancient Indians explored even beyond such an understanding of the origin of society. They sought to comprehend the evolution of the universe. They focussed on learning from nature to understand the nature of world. Their search was 'how to seek satisfaction through human endeavour?' Their understanding of the phenomenon of universe, nature, and world brings into focus two concepts:
• The ever changing nature of things (*Prakriti*) across time. The ancient Indian sages or seers arrived at a realisation that nothing will remain the same (*Jagat*, or the world means that which comes and goes). They, then, found it most meaningful to identify what should remain constant within man in an ever-changing world. This is useful for both – individual progress of man as well as betterment of society. Accordingly, they postulated that the goals of human endeavour (*Purusharthas*) never change. These are guides of human action, in every age, time or human condition. While the world keeps revolving and creation keeps evolving, the goals of human endeavour remain constant. These should always remain the focus of man, teachers and society – in shifting sands of time, circumstance and events.
• The concept of Absoluteness cannot be found in an ever changing world. Hence the absolute Truth, also, is found within man and should not be searched for in society by a person whose locus of control is outside. An inner vision is necessary for experiencing

absolute Truth. The history of *yugas* (time cycles) shows that there never has been a time when there has been absolute perfection in outside world or society. Hence focus of this tradition is on inner world of man. For this, the process of education seeks to create an inner vision within each individual. Even in the perfect kingdom of Lord Rama there was a washerman who made society unhappy. Thus, it is unwise to seek absolute things in the world. This is because the nature of the world is to evolve continuously.

Hence absolute contentment/balance (in financial facet or otherwise a search for a continuous all perfect state) is possible only within man. Not outside him. Equilibrium in society does not imply perfection achieved in all aspects of society as a steady state. The changing nature of things, in worldly matters, does not allow perfection in all aspects permanently. Excellence is achieved within man. In a particular time and circumstance man's actions seek perfection in the outside world. Therefore, the search for excellence, in worldly matters, is a continuous ever evolving process, keeping pace with the changing nature of things. The world is in Dynamic balance. Absolute balance in man makes him see society similarly.

The ever changing nature of things in creation (*Prakriti*) is the context in which man survives in nature. There is another starting point of education here. To appreciate Indian tradition, we can begin with its understanding of movement of time and man's role therein. There is a natural equilibrium, according to ancient Indians, in the repetitive process of creation and destruction. This is a continuous cycle and there never was (or will be) a time when this did not (or will not) happen.

The balance of time and creation is maintained by a process of change. As time progresses from one age (*Yuga*) to another, nature of life in each age changes. Despite this, man has to remain focussed on goals of life irrespective of age or circumstance. These remain the same and the final destination of these goals is also constant – Love for God or Excellence. Though essence of adoration of God remains the same, this highest goal was executed in different ways in different ages (depending upon circumstances, availability of time with man and nature of society). This realisation of uniqueness of every situation and demand for a different response according to circumstance is the key to understanding ancient Indian approach. The acceptance of plurality of paths does not in any way deviate from the need to follow the same set of goals of life irrespective of time, circumstance or reason.

The four ages or *Yugas (Krita, Treta. Dwapara and the present day Kali)* follow each other. In the first age the human population is very small compared to natural resources. There is little need for exertion of man so he devotes full time to meditation on God. People are generally noble and driven by high goals. In the next age, as population increases, there is a need to use skill to harvest resources of nature. Social structure and kingdoms result and traces of egoism and selfishness enter. Man can no longer meditate for long spells due to greater responsibilities and worships God through *Yagya* or sacrifice. The text of this time (the *Treta Yuga*) is *Ramayan* where evil is outside and has to be conquered in society.

In the next age, the population increases furhter, causing greater preoccupation with activities that leave no time for meditation and little time for *Yagya*. Prayer or *archana,* which takes less time, is the mode of adoration of God to achieve excellence in human endeavour. The *Mahabharat* is the common text referred to for this period. Here (in the *Dwapara yuga*) the evil has entered within the family as depicted in the fight for kingdom among cousins. In the present or *Kali* age, it is said, there will be no time left for anything but worldly pursuits and evil will enter man himself – man will have dual nature of being both man and devil – depending on how he uses his intellect and mind. Understood differently, different Yugas have different degrees of difficulty for attaining the goal. The evolution of human intelligence is increasing with progress of *Yugas,* making faculty of intelligence highest in current age. The increasing level of human intelligence, across *Yugas*, unfortunately, can be misused by man.

Some academicians may not find much significance in such an understanding of movement of time. Even if it is treated as a story, it has a moral – like parables used by Jesus. For Indians, who respect ancient wisdom, this understanding of *Yugas* highlights critical importance of correct education and training of human mind – especially in today's context (of *Kali* Age)! It also implies that given the nature of advancement of intelligence in each age, it is possible to attain the goal of education (Self Realisation) in the easiest possible manner today! The only constraint is to figure out correct path and incorporate it in education system.

(c) Which concepts have been central for survival of man through the ages?:

Popular thought and Indian thought

While biology determines how man survives physically, philosophy determines his intellectual growth. Man and animals differ because the former depend on food for survival while man depends on ideas for progress. Thus, philosophy has been useful for understanding background of academic thought in many a subject of study.

Even biology accepts that cell is the basis of all human beings and is, thus, proof of the unity of creation. When the question 'What is Life' emerges, all 3 concepts of Biology (gene theory, 'cell is the fundamental unit of all life' and theory of 'evolution by natural selection') come together. The special way cells reproduce gives the conditions by which natural selection takes place which makes living organisms evolve. The organisation of chemistry within the cell provides explanation for life's phenomenon. Just as organisation of thoughts within man makes some civilisations survive.

A new idea in biology is 'the nature of biological self organisation' on which living cells and organisms process information and acquire specific forms. Philosophical concepts direct thoughts within man and allow a 'self organisation' within man and society making both of them process information in a particular way which gives both man and society a specific form. When thoughts of man are noble and for higher good of all and also in consonance with words and deeds, society can survive longer and man can evolve higher. The world is a family as it shares the 'cell' as a common unit of life. However, organisation of chemistry of thoughts through the gene of education helps some civilisations evolve differently – just as men get differentiated from animals even though both have cells as basis of life. This Paper seeks to identify survivor 'gene of education' for study and practice.

The unity of all creation, as symbolized by the cell, can be understood through *Vishisht Advaita* and *Advaita* philosophy of ancient Indians. While there is no equivalent to *Advaita* Vedanta in the world, yet some western studies come near to other ancient Indian concepts – even though stated in somewhat different contexts. Indians always believe that the world is *Vasudeva Kutumbakam* i.e. one family and true education suffuses them with this feeling.

A Western school of thought believes that all Homo sapiens originated from the same set of species and, therefore, belong to one family. Neil Grant in Oxford's History of the World says: "Humans today do not look alike. But we are all related. Everyone in the world today is probably descended from one small group of people...". The current differences in appearance, body measurement, language and customs happened over time according to local climate and other conditions that developed over time in places where they settled. He also states that "The scientific name of modern man is Homo sapiens (wise man)." Therefore, those who are wise are human beings.

Thus, in popular thought also, two concepts emerge:
(i) There can be a basis to treat the world as one family and
(ii) The basic nature of human being is wisdom seeking.
These conclusions raise the questions:
(i) What bonds a family together? (ii) How to realise Wisdom – the hallmark of man?

A family is strengthened by bonds of love and selflessness. Strengthening these two qualities should naturally lead to wisdom as both concepts are interdependent.
Thus there are two common ideas in spiritual education of Indian tradition and among thinkers who influence popular education. These are: (i) Selfless Love and (ii) wisdom seeking nature of man (which differentiates him from other forms of life).

The idea of Love has also been interpreted by Plato and Rumi among others. In the Indian spiritual tradition (which is the earliest known spiritual tradition in the world) selfless Love is the basis of spiritual progress. For, Selfless Love is the basis of natural co-operation and trust among all, beginning with the immediate family.

This Love is understood as Platonic Love by western society. Socrates relates ideas of Prophetess Diotima, presenting "Love as a means of ascent to contemplation of the divine". Aristotle merged teachings of Plato with ancient Indian Seers by teaching that Truth, Selflessness and Beauty are very important. Indian Seers refer to them as *Satyam* (Truth), *Sivam* (auspiciousness that comes through Selflessness) and *Sundaram* (Beauty – which is basis of Love – will be beautiful only when there is no attachment). Selfless Love for Truth is, thus, the common dictum of many western thinkers and all ancient Indian thinkers.

When men act, guided by wisdom, they co-operate with each other based on Truth and Morality – approaching the concept of society being like a family. Therefore, ancient Indian spiritual tradition: "pray for the well being of all men at all places", 'Love All' or treat 'humanity as one family' can find parallels in Western thought. These parallels are not new. They date back to time before Christ when value and belief systems seem to be similar to the ancient Indian thinking.

The oldest civilisations also had a strong concept of Divinity and gave a central place to it in their lives. How do we interpret this common source of strength of ancient civilisations?

Even before Christianity came to the Western world, a philosopher, Zeno of Citium, propounded the dominant philosophy of the Hellenistic period. He believed that the Universe is God where all parts belong to the whole. He talks of evolution through elements of fire, air, water and earth (as propounded in ancient Indian thought). There is a stark similarity of views regarding formation and destruction of universe. He believed, like ancient Indians, in Goodness and Peace. This Peace is gained by living in harmony (within man – through practice of virtue – and with nature). Zeno recognised **Good as the only goal to strive for**. Happiness is the good flow of life which can be achieved through right reason coinciding with universal reason (logos) which governs everything.

Thus some key ideas have had an impact on man. They have led to development of civilisations that outlast. These ideas should be the sources that can create background of education today: Meant for Man in this Age.

(d) Which ideas have created the background of Education?

Education is the result of philosophy – as ideas signify progress of man. Which ideas have been responsible for giving a background to Education, since time immemorial?

Background of Education emerges from 4 main ideas:
i)   **Understanding Nature of Man – Implications for Education**
ii) **Understanding Nature of Creation – Implications for Education**
iii) **Understanding Nature of Truth – Implications for Education**
iv) **Understanding common purpose of Education and Life: Integration of both**

i) Understanding Nature of Man

"Who is a Man?"

The difference between man and animals is simple. One depends on food for survival while man depends on ideas for progress. Of all possible ideas, the most significant is: What is man's idea about himself? This leads to the first question: 'How does Man understand himself?' This understanding gives impetus for action as well as a focus to education. Man has something which the animal world is not gifted with: discrimination. Using this ability he chooses between right and wrong course of action. He differentiates between good and bad. This is his superiority over the rest of creation. By sharpening this ability continuously, he can achieve purpose of life. Man's sense organs help him recognise and interact with the world. But is he limited to them and by them? Or can he overarch them in understanding the world and himself? If he has to overarch them what helps him do it?

In Indian tradition following universal principles helps man discriminate between right and wrong, good and evil etc. These are: Truth, **Righteous Conduct, Peace and Selfless Love**. When man follows these principles (of Spirituality – common in all religions) he develops discrimination. With discrimination, he can reshape his behaviour and make the best emerge from within – for himself and society. Thus, he can rise in Maslow's need hierarchy. Both Maslow and ancient Indians do not view man as a static entity but as a dynamic being. All concepts of ancient Indian tradition make man evolve into a better human being. This is also the purpose and task of its education system.

Therefore, ancient Indian education begins with inculcating a habit of speaking the Truth. It should be sweet, soft and stated in a manner not to disturb balance. Following righteous conduct is the other side of the coin. *Satyam Vada, Dharmam Chara* (Speak the Truth, follow righteous conduct) is a four word summary of its education. Peace and Selfless Love keep emerging through practice of above two – for, education is a process not an event.

Understanding basis of Man

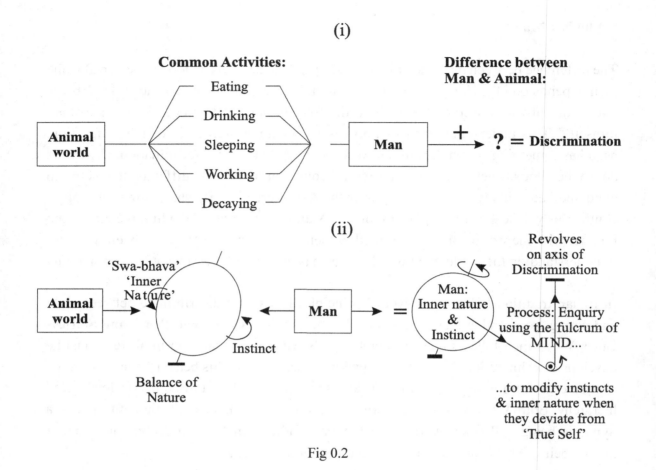

Fig 0.2

Through inference and observation ancient wisdom concludes that Nature or Creation is in natural balance based on its *swabhava* or inner nature. For example: the natural instinct of some animals is to eat vegetation and others to prey on other animals. Though man has an inner nature and instinct, there is difference between him and other objects in Nature. The attraction to sense objects is due to instinct – which comes from the body and does not need training. For example, no training is needed for infant to seek milk from the mother. However, to walk and talk the infant needs training. Even for use of sense pleasures, proper training is needed. A wild and untrained search for such pleasures produces anger, malice, hatred, envy and conceit. Man can use process of enquiry and through discrimination modify his inner nature and instinct in a significant manner. The mind of man has the power to choose any path. Thoughts direct actions and if action is harmful, its impact will be felt by others. To control actions, man has to direct his thoughts in the right direction – in line with his True Self. In this manner man can use his intellect through a process of enquiry using the mind as a fulcrum. This is shown in Fig 0.2 Man revolves on the axis of discrimination which helps him modify his instincts and inner nature whenever they deviate from the 'True Self'.

Man: Indian Concept

Human activity, today, gives a lot of importance to the body and use of techniques by the mind. It does not devote much time for ways to direct or control the mind. The ancient Indian tradition views man as not just the body but also mind and Soul or *Atma*. The triad of body, mind and Soul/ *Atma* form a continuum from destructible to indestructible. While the body is destructible, the Soul or *Atma* is indestructible.

In this tradition all knowledge that relates to the outside world is useful only if Self Knowledge is realised. Therefore, experience of excellence and goodness within man is the first step. It leads the search for knowledge and wisdom. Without such an inner experience, use of human mind will remain uncontrolled. Without goodness, it deviates to undesirable paths.

The original sin in ancient Indian tradition is to consider man to be just the body. Such an assumption leads man towards animal instincts. Education and social action, sometimes, may find it meaningless to discuss study, teach or learn about objects and subjects not directly visible to human senses. These intuitive, inspired or inferred subjects find acceptance with difficulty. Many seekers have sacrificed their life to have intuitive, inferred or inspired thoughts like: 'earth is round not flat'! However, there are no examples in ancient Indian tradition of treating people (with opposing viewpoints) with violence. Figure 0.3 below shows the difference between the two approaches:

Understanding Nature of Man

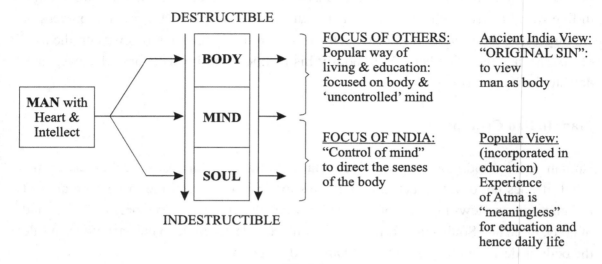

Fig 0.3

Indian spiritual thought views man as a complex of gross body, subtle body and *Jivi* (Individual or Soul/*Atma*). As man is part of creation, the two are closely interlinked. We will study in 'Nature of Creation' (next section) that Individual Soul/*Atma* does not have its origin in either *Akasa* (Ether) or *Prana* (Primal Energy). It is not material in nature. It is eternal, without change. The gross body is a result of combination of *Akasa* and *Prana (Ether* and *Primal Energy)*. Therefore, it dissolves itself into its components. The subtle body, too, dissolves but only after a long, long time. The Soul/ *Atma* or *Jivi* is not brought together, so it does not fall apart. It has no birth, no moment of origin. It is *Nithya* (eternal, unchanging, everlasting). The same Soul/*Atma* that is beyond birth and death pervades the Universe. It is the essential Unity behind apparent diversity.

Based on this understanding ancient Indian education trains man to perform his role in society. With detachment, yet equal love for all. The influence of opposing assumptions is based on man's experience of the objective world. This leads to an underlying assumption that man think, feels and experiences that "I am the body". The ancient Indian education guides man to experience his real nature or feel: "I am the *Atma, Jivi* or Soul. As Soul pervades the universe, hurting others is the same as hurting One Self.

Understanding Nature of Man

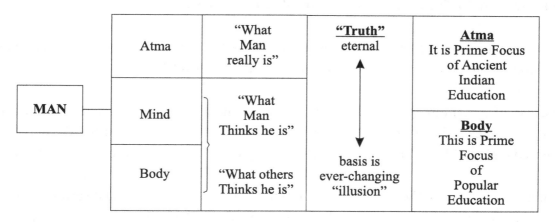

Fig 0.4

These two views are totally opposite and give rise to opposing conclusions. The difference in view has serious implications on attitude of living life and education. Some scholars describe death as "the act of giving up Life". However, life is *Jiva* in ancient Indian thought. Indian wisdom understands death as giving up only the body. The other school of thought understands man as a bundle of matter – subject to laws of physics and chemistry. Ancient Indians give the experience of unity of creation, enabling man to experience himself as Soul.

Discrimination is basis of Indian Education which cures social problems

Discrimination, through Education, seeks to change activities of man within society. This happens through goals of life given to man. Use of discrimination in ancient Indian society was tested by some indicators. These are: morality in commerce, humanity in application of science, principles used in politics and emphasis of character building in education.

How is Discrimination acquired in this tradition? Living in society teaches discrimination. How to sustain economically by helping society is discrimination in action. Education prepares man, through *Dharma*, for society by developing discrimination.

Thus, Discrimination can be acquired through:
a) Education. b) The process of honourably earning wealth.

Education ensures discrimination is not just useful for the individual (individual discrimination) but also applies at societal and universal level.

The use of discrimination in business is closely linked to practice of Truth, Righteous Conduct, Peace and Selfless Love in life. Education enables this. The study of Management is based on two things. These are: enquiry into nature of man and use of Discrimination.

Management study is, therefore, 'Meant for man in this Age!' Acquiring discrimination is the best way to study management. For, discrimination is applying *Dharma* or righteous conduct, in life. Education is one way of acquiring discrimination. Ancient Indians believe it is not the only way. Serving society through business is the second way. Thus business or management is practical application of education in life. Following four *Purusharthas* enables it. Ethical business teaches man discrimination. Just as education does! Fig 0.5 shows this idea graphically. **Chapter 6 will explain this diagram's implications fully.**

How to acquire Discrimination
Indian view (Study of 'Man Age Meant')

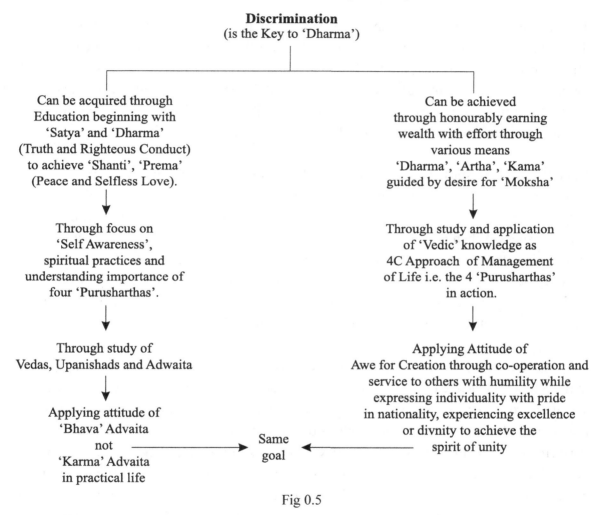

Fig 0.5

The use of discrimination results in righteous conduct or *Dharma*. Therefore, the route to acquiring discrimination is meant for man in this age (and every age). Discrimination can be acquired through the highest education and through honourably earning wealth – through use of 4 *Purusharthas* as goals of life. The fourth goal of *Moksha* is the common meeting point of education and goals of life. This is shown in Figure 0.5. The first three goals prepare man for experience of the highest wisdom – which is also the purpose of education. That education or 3C Approach that does not prepare for 4th C cannot promote balance within man, among men, in society and among nations. Instead of the highest peace, there will be social strife and other problems illustrated in Fig 0.1 earlier.

The difference between animal and man is that animal reacts as if it is only the body. Man thinks he is more than a body. Man realises that it is impossible to prove that capacity to think grows out of physical matter. So, man's body is not responsible for his capacity of thought. What enables thought – that makes man different from animals? The capacity to ask this question is distinction of man from animal. This starts discrimination within man. Animals succumb to craving of sensual attraction. Human effort overcomes such craving.

Once this process starts within man (called *Dama* in Indian tradition) the veil over man's inner eye starts is slowly removed. This unveils Truth. Practice of Truth with philosophical enquiry and discipline of six-fold *Sadhana* (spiritual practice) leads to purification of consciousness. When consciousness becomes like a clean mirror, it reflects Truth within man. This is the experience of ancient Indian Seers. For attaining highest Truth, cleansing of consciousness is the best path. It is easy for those with a pure heart. Purity of intention purifies heart of man. The search of ultimate reality begins and ends with purity of thought. Thought is directed by discrimination and proper education.

A focussed concern for achieving Self Awareness makes higher knowledge emerge – within man. When knowledge of *Adwaita* or non-dual knowledge is imparted, it does not lead to social disorder. For, its application in daily life is also taught. An attitude of *Bhava Advaita* not *Karma Advaita* is central to application of non-dual Knowledge. This makes man perform actions with a feeling that all have same divinity within. However, actions must be guided by limitations of physical bodies. Therefore, status in the world of a king is to be respected. The status of the farmer is also to be acknowledged. The outward difference in behaviour exists despite awareness of same inherent divinity. Fulfilling duties in this manner detaches man from fruit of action. This makes actions 'selfless' and not selfish. The goal of education and correct use of discrimination is, then, attained. The implication of difference between *Karma Advaita* (non Duality expressed in action) and *Bhava Advaita* (non Duality expressed through thought only) is explained in 'Implications for Education', later.

The route map given in fig 0.5 above, then, becomes an easy path. It makes difficult concepts of education easy to understand. The path of action, too, through *Purusharthas* of *Dharma*, *Artha* and *Kama* leads to honourable earning of wealth. For, earning wealth by honourable means is practical application of Vedic Knowledge. The attitude of awe of creation applies in life by service to society – which is part of creation. Humility and co-operation allow a cleansed consciousness to express Individuality with pride in nationality. The experience of resultant excellence is guided automatically by a spirit of unity with all.

Why Indian civilisation survived

When man views himself as only the body, he seeks worldly pleasures. His value system is one of self aggrandisement. This does not promote welfare of society. Therefore, a civilisation built on sand of shifting nature of worldly pleasure can last only for some time. All countries that follow ancient Indian approach can survive for thousands of years. Refreshing signs of creative life come from an approach looking beyond self centeredness as a sole goal of life.

Implications for Education

The conclusions emerging from 'What is man?' view of ancient Indians are integrated here. These are:

• Man is not just this body but still has to act within limitations of the body. He is *Atma* – a concept beyond physical senses – yet within the realm of his experience.

• Man is capable of using intellect to direct his mind to differentiate himself from animal world. The use of intellect, through education, leads to balance.

• Man has the capability of achieving excellence latent within.

• This excellence can manifest itself only through whole hearted pursuit. The transformation of heart is a goal for pursuit of excellence.

• Man is, therefore, not just the body but also intellect, mind and heart. Discovering their correct role while discovering who man really is (i.e the *Atma*) – is the goal of education that fulfils purpose of life.

• Man, to achieve goal of education, must live in awareness that he is *Atma* while performing tasks through the physical body.

• The nature of *Atma* is without limits while the body is nothing but a Study of Limits.

• Therefore, intellect and mind of man have to be directed. Only a whole hearted pursuit of excellence within him will reveal the Soul principle or *Atma*.

• This has to be achieved while performing daily tasks. Limits set by role that man is allotted fulfils his search within. Fulfilling his role, following path of Truth and morality, unravels mystery of *Atma*. Then, man undertakes tasks without desire for their results. Figs 0.6 to Fig 0.9 show process of achieving balance which is basis of ancient Indian education.

Keeping the above in mind, Part A of this Paper i.e. Chapter 1 (along with Background) deal exclusively with this Awareness. Part B of the Paper deals with expressing this Awareness by a Study of Limits (Chapter 2, 3, 4 and 5). Chapter 6 deals with the Highest Truth. Truth of conclusions is validated in Chapter 7. In this manner this Paper integrates secular education with spiritual learning as shown in Fig 0.6

What is man?
Integrating Ancient Indian View with this paper

PART A	PART B
(of this Paper & its Background)	(of this Paper & its Background)
'AWARENESS'	'STUDY OF LIMITS'
(of excellence or divinity of 'Atma' or 'Self')	(of the human body and environment in which it operates)

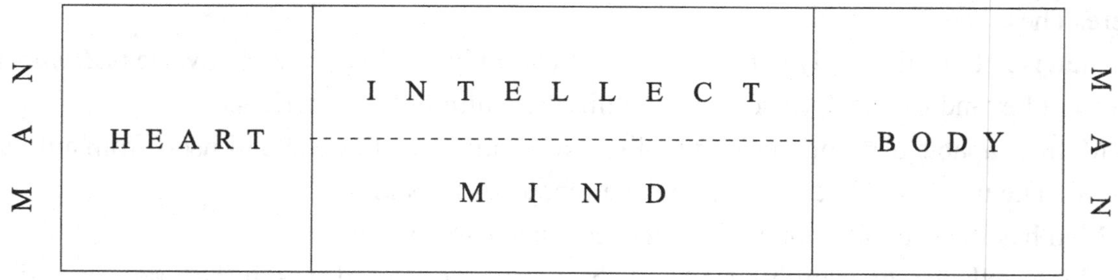

M A N	HEART	INTELLECT / MIND	BODY	M A N

Fig 0.6

The attitude for Education and Life – Indian view The belief that man is the body leads to hedonistic ideals. Such attitude can lead to over exploitation of natural resources, global warming, wars, violence, social unrest etc. It gets reflected in business too. Insensitivity to others divorces education and life and leads to a fractured society as depicted in Fig 0.7.

Education and Life must be inter related

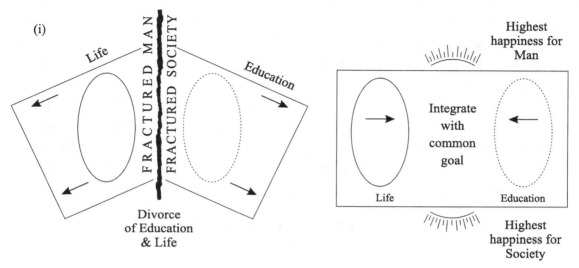

(i)

Fig 0.7

Vidya Vahini
'Flow' of Knowledge in sync with 'Flow' of Creation

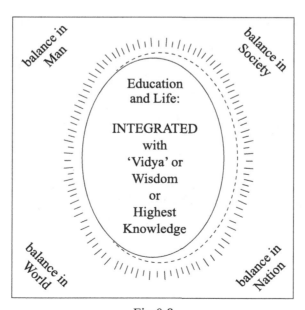

Fig 0.8

The ancient Indian tradition views Unity in diversity of creation – i.e. to view all as one self. The logic is simple: If a person is happy that he has one body, should he not feel doubly happy that he has two? In this way, the knowledge that he has increasing number of bodies leads to manifold increase in happiness. When the whole world is known as one body and world-consciousness becomes part of awareness of man, he achieves bliss or *Ananda*. This is shown in Fig 0.8. Here, such a focus leads to expansion of thoughts of man – which unlocks the Selfless love in his heart – as shown in Fig 0.9. Current techniques do not recognise need for unlocking of heart. Limited ego-centric prisons in mind of man are created. A multi-consciousness that is the basis of education in this tradition is forgotten. Ancient Indians used education to guide the intellect to discriminate. Then it decided direction in which key of mind has to be turned.

Education & Man Interaction
Nature of Popular & Indian Technique

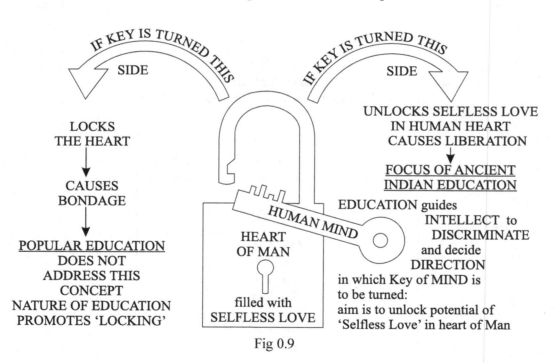

Fig 0.9

ii) Understanding Nature of Creation – Implications for Education

There exists a different understanding of origin of universe among ancient Indians and others. However, there is similarity in the understanding that elements are the basis of universe. The same is found in Greek, Buddhist and Japanese thought. Classical five elements pre date Socrates and persist through Middle Ages and Renaissance influencing European culture. Thus, a common understanding of elements of nature has always existed.

What is the need for man to understand the nature of creation? What does modern science state? What implication does it have for education? How will this understanding be applied to education and daily life of man?

The Purpose: The ancient Indian tradition uses education to prepare man for living life. Understanding nature of creation develops the correct attitude to view it. This attitude guides thoughts and action of man. When thoughts and action seek noble goals, there is balance within man and harmony in society. Then, purpose of education and life are achieved.

Basis of Universe: Indian view A popular system of education uses matter as the basis of the universe. It studies matter through various disciplines. It guides man how to use and apply this education for daily living. The ancient Indian tradition viewed Primal Energy as basis of the Universe.

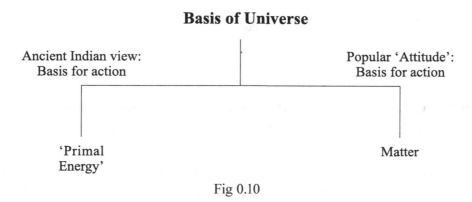

Basis of Universe

Fig 0.10

Constant Transformation: Indian view The ancient Indians view transformation of energy to matter to be a continuous, never ending process. This includes transformation of matter back into energy also. The conversion of energy into matter can be understood as atomisation while action of matter being converted back into energy can be termed de-atomisation.

Indian view of Creation

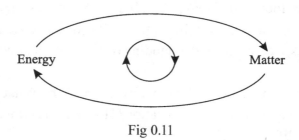

Fig 0.11

Creation: Continuous Transformation Process

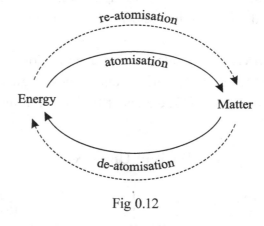

Fig 0.12

Ever Expanding Process The continuous process of atomization of energy into matter, its de-atomisation and re-atomisation into matter is an ever expanding process.

LBNL – The Lawrence Berkeley National Laboratory of USA – works with Department of Energy, United States Government. It lists its breakthroughs on its website. One of these breakthroughs listed was understanding nature of the universe. This was undertaken as part of the Supernova cosmology project. They concluded that universe is three quarter dark **energy** which causes it to **expand at an accelerating rate.** Lab detectors on NASA satellites helped arrive at this truth. This was revealed long ago by an ancient civilisation.

Of course, implication of this discovery for application in daily life has yet to be announced by LBNL. Ancient Indians discovered the Truth to apply it to the life of man.

Creation: Ever Expanding Process

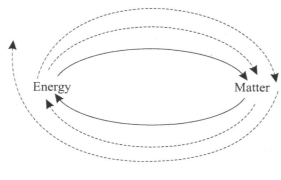

Fig 0.13

The LBNL study, however, does recognise two critical things: a) The primacy of energy in the creation process and (b) the implication of ever expanding nature of the universe. If energy is the cause of creation then why is education so obsessed with studying matter alone? Also, universe is ever expanding and nature is constantly changing. Then, can education achieve its purpose if it chases the ever changing? Should it not try to grasp that which is not prone to change? Can it use that understanding to react to what is ever-changing? This is the difference in approach between present and ancient Indian education system. If LBNL can agree with two main points of Indian tradition, it may be worthwhile to understand what else it states about creation. For, that may also be true – even if not studied or confirmed by USA's top laboratory – as yet.

Primal Energy: How it acts The 'Primal Energy' consisting, among other things, of various types of rays (physical light rays, magnetism, electricity, X-rays, *Dharmic* rays, laser rays etc) materialise into colour, form, name etc converting energy into matter. The five elements ether, air, fire, water, earth are interacting with each other in innumerable permutations and combinations to form matter. Figs 0.14 to 0.17 detail this process.

Creation is not just an event but a continuous process The objective world is caused by Primal energy and Ether *(i.e. Prakriti* is caused by *Prana and Akasa)*. The objective world that man experiences is known as *Prakriti*. It is eternal, but with a difference. It undergoes perpetual change. It is never the same and persists forever.

How does Creation take place*?
View from 'Primal Energy' side of coin

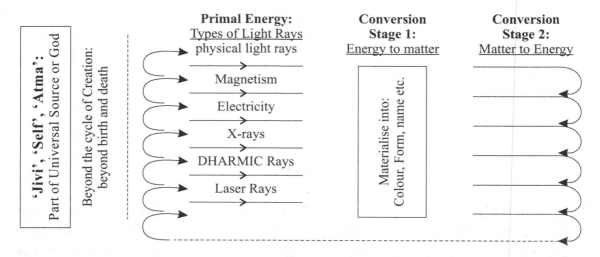

*Creation is not just an 'event' but also a continuous 'process' or flow.

Fig 0.14

Its impact on education is discussed in the next section

The basis of objective world is Primal Energy or *Prana* (the Life Force). This is also eternal just as ether (space or *akasa*) is. *Prakriti* or manifested world is the result of *prana* (Primal Energy/Life Force) and *akasa* (space/ether). They act together and interact – and are like two sides of the same coin.

The manifestation of this continuous, never ending process is creation. This process of creation occurs, viewed from Primal Energy side of coin, not only through light rays but also with x-rays, laser rays, electricity, magnetism and, above all, rays of morality. Creation, as per ancient Indian Seers is the expression of Selfless Love in action. The sun, moon, earth, seasons, oceans etc are a Study of Limits for they follow their *Dharma* or morality. Their motion is within Limits/ *Dharma* or morality. The energy level of these subtle, moral/ *Dharmic* rays sustains creation. From the ether side of coin, same concept is explained

116

in Fig 0.15 and 0.16. Here the five elements emerge from imbalance of the three *gunas/* attributes (*Sathwa, Rajas, Tamas*). The subtle attributes are recognised by man's subtle senses. Even the gross form needs subtle senses for recognition. Therefore, the difficult task of recognising the subtle Primal energy is left to education.

How does Creation take place*?
view from 'Ether' side of coin

	Physical Attributes	Subtle Attributes	Subtle senses of man to recognise these	Subtlest
expresses itself as 3 Gunas				

Primal Energy → [Sathwa] [Rajas] [Tamas]

Prakriti: Mirror of Divinity 'eye' thru which God sees himself

imbalance in the 3 produces

Earth — Smell — Nose
Water — — Tongue
Fire — Taste Form — Eye
Wind — — Skin
Sky — Touch Sound — Ear

Mind & Ego arise from same principle

When in Balance it is called 'Prakriti'

'SARGA': PROCESS OF CREATION

Creation is not just an 'event' but also a continuous 'process' or flow.

OR

How does Creation take place*?
view from 'Ether' side of coin

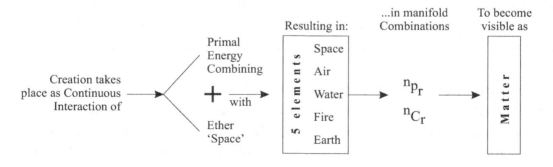

Creation takes place as Continuous Interaction of

Primal Energy Combining + with Ether 'Space'

Resulting in: 5 elements — Space, Air, Water, Fire, Earth

...in manifold Combinations $^{n}P_{r}$ $^{n}C_{r}$

To become visible as — Matter

* Creation is not just an 'event' but also a continuous 'process' or flow

Fig 0.15 and Fig 0.16

Their impact on education is discussed in the next section

Impact of understanding of Creation on Man: Unity in Diversity

What is man's role as a part of creation? Man is part of creation at the gross level. Yet, at the highest level, he is untouched by it. Indian spiritual thought views man as a complex of gross body, subtle body and Jivi (Individual, *Atma*, Soul). The Soul did not have its origin in either *Akasa* (Space, Ether) or *Prana (*Life Force, Primal Energy). It is not material in nature. It is eternal, without change. *Akasa* (Space) and *Prana* (Primal Energy) impact each other. The gross body is the result of combination of Ether/*Akasa* and Primal Energy/*Prana* and so dissolves itself into its components. The subtle body consisting of the mind, too, dissolves but only after a long, long time. The Soul is not brought together, so it does not fall apart. It has no birth, no moment of origin. It is *Nithya* (eternal, unchanging, everlasting). A person can discard as many gross bodies in which he takes temporary residence but the subtle body will outlast the number of times he pares his nails. **The same Soul (*Atma*), is beyond birth and death, pervades the Universe as the essential Unity behind the apparent diversity**. As *Atma* or Soul, creation does not touch man. He remains a witness to it. Only the mind experiences creation and, therefore, till the mind exists creation exists. However, conquest of mind and thought is prescribed through action called *Nishkama Karma*. This is righteous action done for its own sake with no desire of reward.

This understanding of creation tells man that waiting for the world to be perfect is useless. The nature of creation is ever changing. The continuous interaction of Primal energy and Ether will always result in the five elements. These will continue to interact in manifold permutations and combinations to give matter. Therefore, any wait for perfection in the outside world will be endless. Such a wait serves no purpose. Action must be taken by achieving a perfect state within and not searching for the same, outside.

Such action, by implication, begins within man. What is action that occurs within man? The mind and its thoughts are within. The mind of man, according to ancient Indian Seers, is the source of all problems and solutions. The thought of man, if impacted, gives both bondage and liberation. Energy which impacts mind and thought, if harnessed, can change man's world. This is the Awareness that this tradition seeks to inculcate. The Study of Limits that emerges from observing creation is given below:

Creation implies that two or more of five elements are combining in varying proportions. The basic lesson using observation is: Excessive usage harms – just as inhaling too much air, drinking too much water, exposure to too much heat or sound etc. Balance comes through use of natural resources intelligently, in moderation. Use nature with humility and with an idea of loving service to community. This is the culture of ancient Indians. The Middle Way of Buddha (not too much, not too little) has a similar echo.

Man & Energy levels
Indian view

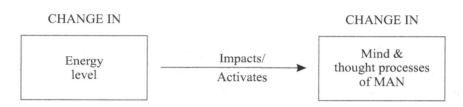

Fig 0.17
Change in Man leads to change in firm, society and nation

Understanding nature of creation helps guide man in achieving purpose of life. This understanding can achieve balance. There is an energy that flows through creation. Does the energy that flows within man differ from the energy in the rest of creation?

There is an energy produced by mind and its thoughts, too. Fig 0.18 shows how to harness and direct this unique energy. This ability differentiates man from rest of creation. It can be achieved by making man's energy level flow to be synchronous with flow of creation. The nature of creation is expansion. If man's heart, too, expands – like the flow of creation – the synchronization takes place. Then flow of human life is, then, integrated with the flow of creation. By expanding the heart with Love for all, its purpose can be achieved. The sublime rays of morality, then, energise both man and the world.

Implications for Education

The study of the ever changing aspects of nature, the appearance and disappearance of its working, may be a fine subject of study. The material objects have no value. They depend on man for awareness of qualities which impart value to them. The relative world, thus, depends on relative consciousness of man. This helps understand inherent value of things.

The Indian tradition believes that knowledge of principles governing objective nature can best provide man with food and clothing. It does provide ways and means of gaining them. However, such knowledge does not prevent exploitation of weak by strong. Material objects get their value by how man understands them. Similarly, man will realise his own value only by his understanding of Self. The understanding of value of man by man himself imparts values and value to human life. This is the goal of education and purpose of understanding creation. It reveals man's desired role therein.

The viewing of world as a true false entity generates ability to experience its apparent diversity as an illusion. This stops the urge of exploitation within man. This is the gift of ancient Indian education through visualisation of process of creation.

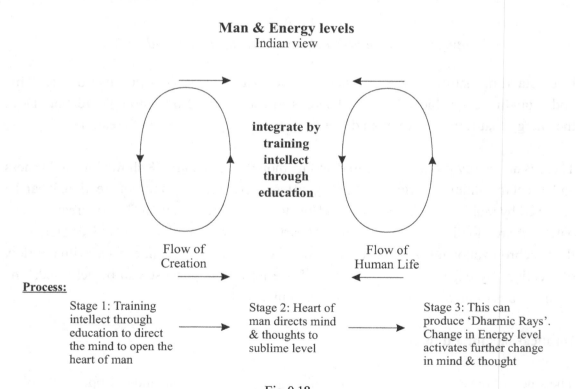

Man & Energy levels
Indian view

integrate by training intellect through education

Flow of Creation

Flow of Human Life

Process:

Stage 1: Training intellect through education to direct the mind to open the heart of man → Stage 2: Heart of man directs mind & thoughts to sublime level → Stage 3: This can produce 'Dharmic Rays'. Change in Energy level activates further change in mind & thought

Fig 0.18

Transforming Man transforms society: Implications on Education are explained next

Using understanding of creation for transformation of man

What is creation? Creation can be thought of as projection. When the mind is trained, the thoughts it projects change. Hence, this book is about training the mind to project the right thought. Before it does that, it must have attitude of equanimity and acceptance towards the world and universe. It should not have feelings of hatred towards anything. As Jesus says – 'Hate the Sin, not the Sinner'. What understanding develops this attitude of equanimity towards creation? The ancient Indian tradition provides it: The human cell and the cosmos, ancient Indians believe, are sustained by the same reality, called *Brahman*. When this reality is visualised as the infinite cosmos it is called *Paramatma*. When it is thought of as the core of an individual being – the '*Para*' prefix is dropped and it is called *Atma*. All three (*Brahman* – whose study is Brahma Vidya, *Paramatma, Atma*) are one entity – but appear as different due to delusion or *Maya*. The Supreme Power uses the Three *Gunas* i.e. *Satwa* (serenity), *Rajas* (activity), *Tamas* (inertia) to express itself differently. The *Gunas* urge a person towards Knowing, Desiring or Working. When *Maya* impels Brahman to project itself leveraging *Satwa Guna* it appears as God. Thus the holy see God everywhere and in everything. This *Brahman*, ancient Indians state, projects itself as living beings leveraging *Rajo Guna*. It becomes Nature (*Prakriti*) when it leverages *Tamo Guna*. *Brahman* is, thus, the basis of all three: God, living beings and Nature. *Maya* is the mirror in which *Brahman* is reflected. Education polishes the mirror so that the image of Brahman is clearly seen everywhere and in everything – enabling the *Tat Twam Asi* realisation (Chapter 6). Thus:

a) Popular education gives primacy to elements (not Primal Energy) in understanding creation. It understands creation through elements present in nature. Further, it seeks to understand their diversity through various sciences. The ancient Indian tradition gives importance to Primal Energy and treats it as basis of the Universe. This is the fundamental difference between these two approaches.

b) Man seeks perfection and excellence by nature. Where can he find it? As primal energy continuously interacts with ether, ever changing nature of things makes waiting for perfection futile. Creation is ever expanding too. Any study concentrating on elements alone would need continuous up gradation. Therefore, an understanding that does not change is needed. For, it would give a better understanding of nature of things. It would also give a firm basis for action to man. It is best to assume that creation is perfect, now only man needs to perfect himself. Therefore, the basis of action for man is search for excellence. This perfection or excellence cannot be achieved in the outside world.

c) So, excellence or perfection is to be achieved within man. How can this be achieved? It can be achieved by synchronizing the flow of life with creation. Education is a tool for executing this task. This understanding of creation helps transformation of man.

d) Study of elements in creation trains the intellect to give skills for maintaining the physical body of man and society. However, training of intellect for study of inner self imparts skills that uplift both man and society. This inner science needs different tools than physical science. It uses tools of sense control, mind cleansing, concentration and inner silence. These tools result in controlling mind and directing it. They increase capacity of intellect for higher knowledge which, now, directs the mind. Such use of mind differentiates man from rest of creation. It comes through man's transformation – through education.

e) Unlocking the difference between man and rest of creation requires the key of discrimination. Ancient Indian education sharpens and uses this key. It unlocks heart of man and sows in it the seed of human values. These seeds sprout by use of human mind distinguishing man from rest of creation. Understanding Nature of Creation enables this.

Education, as depicted in Figure 0.18 earlier, trains the intellect to direct mind and thoughts to a sublime level. It opens the heart of man to experience Selfless Love that lies within. This Selfless Love finds expression through human values.

A study of musical instruments shows that when a person hits, strikes, strums or plucks them, they are set into vibration at their natural frequency. Education seeks to do the same to man. The natural frequency of man is experience of bliss – a stage he experiences only in deep sleep. Education stretches the string (man) to the desired length and tightness and plucks at it. This forces the attached sound box (human body) into vibrating at the same frequency. The music of human behaviour created is conducive to functioning of society.

The experience of creation is cognized by the mind. So, one view is that man is part of creation. However, the opposite is also true – that creation is in the mind of man. So, at the spiritual level, creation is like the sound box attached to mind of man.

Excellence is Divinity. For, it is simply Love for work – which expanded infinitely to include everything – becomes Divinity. This divinity of education tightens the string of man's mind. It does so by training the intellect to open the heart of man. Now, the heart recognises creation and finally plucks man's thoughts selflessly to make the sound box resonate with natural vibration of 'bliss'.

This is depicted in the visualisation of the ancient Indian Goddess of Learning. In her left hand she holds the musical instrument with strings and Her right hand is free to adjust the length, tighten the string and play. If the sound box is creation, then creation is in left hand of Divinity. The right hand is free to work on man through highest education. This produces a melody of bliss within man. It can be heard through the sound box of creation. Within society it emerges from the sound box of the physical body of man. When man realises his innate divinity or excellence within himself, his own right hand is free to play the melody of life. This melody brings harmony in society and within him. His left hand supports creation by looking after needs of society while fulfilling his own obligations.

iii) Understanding Nature of Truth – Implications for Education

The search for Truth is man's eternal search differentiating him from other forms of life. In many ancient traditions, great teachers taught from the book of life. Their personal lifestyle and choices set an example not only for their students but for society at large.

Life gives us the experience of 'Truth'. Ancient teachers learnt the Truth about Life and taught it. There can be different approaches to searching for the Truth. One approach can be to find out truth about matter. The ancient Indian tradition concentrated on finding about Truth of Spirit. Excellence in the former does not lead to excellence in latter. However, Shankracharya Saraswati has detailed how excellence in the latter was accompanied by excellence in the former in ancient India.

Understanding truth about material things was not a prime focus of ancient Indians. Instead, experience of Truth integrated purpose of education with the purpose of life.

Understanding Nature of Truth
Implications for Education

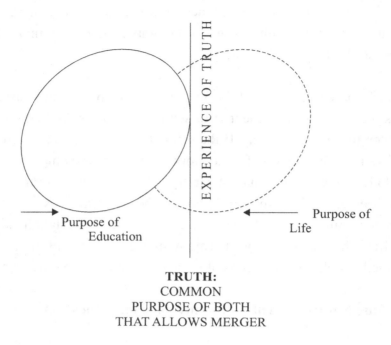

EXPERIENCE OF TRUTH

Purpose of
Education

Purpose of
Life

TRUTH:
COMMON
PURPOSE OF BOTH
THAT ALLOWS MERGER

Fig 0.19

Fig 0.19 shows that experience of Truth was purpose of education and life, both. The awareness of the 'Universal Immanent Impersonal' is Truth and goal of education. They discovered that no satisfactory solution could be found through study of matter alone. Therefore, pursuing qualities of external nature was not thought to be goal of education. Understanding qualities of man himself was desired objective. For, then, man could transform his inner nature to attain balance, joy and highest peace for himself and society.

The truth about man can be experienced or realised by observing behaviour of man. When man's desires are fulfilled, new ones arise and this is never ending. Can fulfilment of desires give peace and contentment to man? If this was the case kings and conquerors like Alexander the Great would die content. Yet, Alexander the Great asked that his open palms be displayed to the world after he dies. This was to show that he carried nothing back with him. The acquisition of wealth, power and land man dreams for – left the emperor of emperors with a feeling of emptyness. This lack of contentment he wanted to share with all.

The ancient Indians had learnt about this long ago – through experience. The pleasures are, they concluded, temporary while contentment is permanent. Indian education concluded that putting the cart (body) before the horse (mind) will only give the cart strength while the horse grows wild or starves.

The observation that man does not achieve contentment by fulfilling desires leads to important inferences. He realises that pleasures are transitory and do not give permanent happiness. This begins the search for contentment. Feeding the mind with thoughts not related to worldly pleasures begins a fulfilling journey.

How to Discover Truth?
Indian View

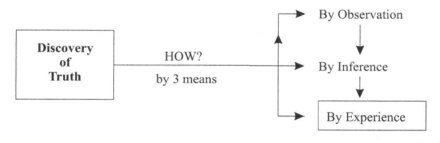

Fig 0.20

Experience shows that when man concentrates on inherent excellence within himself, he achieves contentment and lasting bliss. This experience reveals that harmony at home and in society comes only by experiencing one-ness of all. Virtues alone can endow love and sympathy, peace and joy for one and all. This is the process of discovery of Truth about man and his interactions in society.

Discovery of Truth
Ancient Indian Way

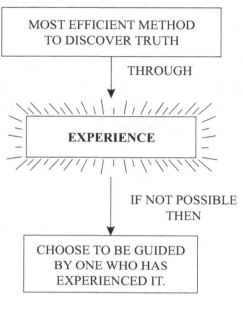

Fig 0.21

The ancient Indians believed that the experience of Truth is beyond the scope of words and is, therefore, difficult to teach through books. It is to be experienced as part of life. Thus students stayed with the teacher to observe him closely. The Truth may be stated here but will not be absorbed till it is experienced. It can only be taught by one who has experienced it. For, it will be integrated into his life. The life of a Master becomes his message and students learn from it. This was ancient way of learning and is shown in Fig 0.21.

Ancient Indian Way

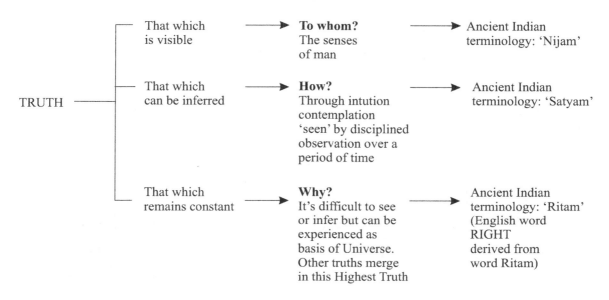

Fig 0.22

The questions regarding search of Truth are answered in Fig 0.22. Truth that is visible to senses of man is called *Nijam*. It is not regarded as the full Truth (it is also called *Maya* – or the illusion of truth – just as a dry stump of a tree in darkeness can be feared to be a bizarre human being or a ghost due to a faulty perception based on the feeling in the mind – this is caused by darkness and this misperception reflects the 'darkness' of the mind that education seeks to throw light on). The world we see is called half Truth only. This leads to a search for Truth that can only be inferred. This inferring requires contemplation and disciplined observation. *Nijam* is perceived immediately. Contemplation or disciplined observation develops over a period of time by man. Then, *Satyam* emerges – within. However, why is this also not complete Truth? The complete Truth is difficult to see or infer – it can only be experienced as basis of universe. All other Truths merge in it. Ancient Indians refer to Highest Truth as *Ritam*. It is said that the English word 'right' is derived from *Ritam*. Such an explanation of truth immediately evokes a question: What is Highest Truth – or 'One Truth' in which all others merge?

This question is answered by Fig 0.23

What is the Highest or 'One' Truth?
Ancient Indian Wisdom

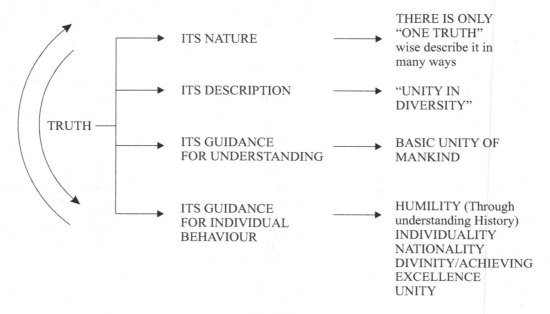

Fig 0.23

Implications for Education

The ever changing nature of creation and its working may be a fine subject of study. The material objects have no intrinsic value but depend on man's awareness of their qualities. This imparts value to all objects. The relative world, thus, depends on man's relative understanding to fix inherent value of anything. The Indian tradition believes that knowledge of principles of nature only provide man with material comforts. However, such Knowledge does not prevent exploitation of weak by strong. Material objects get value by man's understanding of them. Similarly man realises his own value by enhancing his understanding of himself.

The understanding of value of man by man himself is the goal. Many faiths, sages and religions seek this 'One' Truth. If words could describe this Truth, they are: see the unity in diversity. This is the best description of experience of Truth.

To understand Truth, man has to first be convinced about basic unity of mankind. Once Truth has been experienced, behaviour of man is steeped in humility. For, he sees everybody as one self. However, this experience heightens his expression of Individuality. The expression of Individuality is directed towards Nationality. Here, all who share the same experience belong to one nation. Such broad mindedness comes from Divinity.

What is Truth?

Nature of Truth	Finite **'Nijam'** Finite That you can experience with senses of physical body	◄---- **'Satyam'** ----► experienced by controlling senses experience through intution contemplation & disciplined observation	◄---- **'Ritam'** ----► Infinite: Eternal Truth can only be realised through EXPERIENCE	INFINITE
Nature of Eduction Needed	SECULAR Education	SPIRITUAL + SECULAR EDUCATION	Self-Realisation through guidance by one who has Experienced it	
Tools used for Education	BRAIN + physical senses	Control over senses through Brain to transform heart	Heart. Filling with Selfless Love (beyond comprehension of brain, physical senses and imagination)	
End Product of Education	Education based on 'Material' aspect gives tools & techniques for getting worldly pleasures only. Selfishness increases.	'Character' of student is end product of education	Realisation of perfection/excellence within One-self expressed as selfless Love for all results in 'balance'	

Fig 0.24

Fig 0.24 shows that moving from *Nijam* to *Satyam* to *Ritam* is a continuum – of Truth. It moves from finite to infinite. The experience of Truth rises above senses of a finite physical body (*Nijam* – based on everchanging principle – hiding the true nature of man). It then experiences what comes from controlling these senses. Finally, consciousness – within man – reflects Truth as an experience beyond words. *Nijam* is explained with help of secular education. Experience of *Satyam* needs discipline, control over senses, contemplation and use of resultant intuition. The experience of Infinite Truth, *Ritam,* is only by a purified consciousness. *Satyam* and *Ritam* require cleansing of impurities of thought, word and deed. *Ritam* reveals Truth like a perfectly reflecting mirror. The best person to guide towards this experience is one who has experienced the Truth.

Different tools are used for different levels of Truth. The human brain and physical senses can understand evident facts and takes these as truth. However, when nature of creation and its ever changing, ever expanding expressions are understood, the transience of facts becomes evident. That is why secular Knowledge based on facts alone is amenable to changing with new discoveries. The ancient Indians concluded that Truth does not emerge by uncontrolled use of senses. Controlling them, through use of intellect can transform the heart of man and reveal the Truth. This results in character building which gives personal satisfaction and builds a strong foundation for a sustainable social order.

The pursuit of material pleasure gives innumerable inventions for acquiring them or worldly wealth. However, lack of emphasis on character makes any pursuit selfish. This can upset social order. Pursuing highest Truth, on the other hand, aims at filling the heart of man with selfless love. It gives contentment and a state of mind beyond comprehension of senses, intelligence and imagination. The realisation of excellence within man is the end product of this search. It is fulfilled when excellence is expressed through actions which elevate and add value to man and society. The achievement of goal of life results in balance within man. It promotes balance among men and in society.

iv) Integrating Education with Life

The integration of education with life by ancient Indians needs to be both understood and emulated. This integration occurs when goal of education fulfills purpose of life. The goal of education is achieved through imparting both secular and spiritual education. This leads to acquiring highest knowledge and wisdom – referred to as *Vidya Vahini*. This signifies that knowledge is a flow and not static. However, the flow is guarded and directed by **same principles** – irrespective of time or age.

The principles that contain flow of Knowledge in any age, time or circumstance for man are expounded as 4 goals of life. These we refer to as 4C Approach. If flow of Knowledge is understood as a stream, it always flows within the twin banks of Truth and Morality. These contain the flow of both education and life. 4Cs direct it at all times and circumstances. Understanding 4Cs in today's context helps rejuvenate ancient knowledge and make it relevant to current circumstances. The practice of *Dharma* or righteousness is expressed when man co-operates within and with others. This removes falsehood, jealousy and selfishness and achieves tasks for common good. Such co-operation is directed by a focussed Concern for *Artha*. It expresses distinction in a manner that adds value to both man and society. In economic sphere this value addition is expressed through business activity and its management.

The result of co-operation and focussed concern is fulfilment of desire or *Kama*. It is expressed through competitive response of man and groups of men (firms). In this manner it is conducive to promoting balance in society. When man's response is compatible with own nature, society and nation it fulfills purpose of education and life together. This is shown in Fig 0.25.

Integrating Education with Life

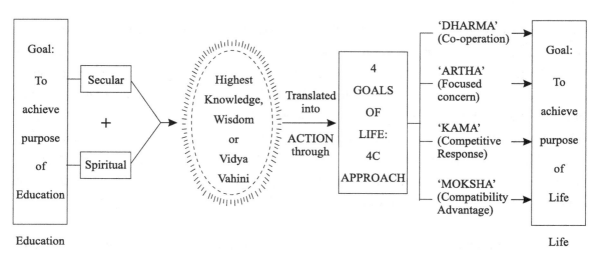

Fig 0.25

Purpose of this Paper: Cure for all social problems *including* Recession

The Paper's Purpose is to **prevent recession** and other social problems. It is to explore nature of education in context of nature of Truth and Indian path of 'how to live life'. This tradition gives guidelines for action. They enable integration with the purpose of education. This, finally, merges in purpose of life. Fig 0.26 summarises the approach followed here.

Ancient Indians believed that secular and spiritual education should be imparted together. Only then purpose of education and life can be achieved simultaneously. The realisation of potential of excellence within man or Self Realisation is purpose of both. The secular education referred to here is not the current method of imparting education. It is the Indian approach to imparting secular education – emerging from moral values.

Education helps unravel nature of Truth. Secular education, ancient Indians believed, only gives knowledge of truth as perceived by sense organs of man i.e. *Nijam* (sense organs, if directed by an uncontrolled mind, can not see this impermanence). Spiritual education which is achieved through control over senses opens mind of man through intuition. This makes *Satyam* emerge from within. Finally, it leads to realisation of highest Truth or *Ritam*. Such understanding of Truth solves **all** social problems, not only recession.

The ancient Indians lived in a world of facts as experienced by the senses. These senses 'feel' a separateness from creation known as Duality or *Dwaita* – which emerges from experiencing the truth only as *Nijam*. The higher Truth *Satyam* is experienced through education in the *Vishisht Adwaita* philosophy tradition. This states that creation is One but that One/Brahman or Unity expresses itself through multiplicity. The experience of 'One-ness of creation' is achieved only through spiritual education. The full realisation of excellence within comes through experience of *Adwaita*. This is the non-dual nature of creation. It is known as *Atma* Vidya or knowledge of Self. This enables man to perceive excellence both within and without in a manner that removes distinction in them.

What is the guideline for action for following secular and spiritual education of ancient Indians? Secular education teaches man how to live in society. Spiritual education teaches man to keep elevated thoughts – i.e. keeps his head in the forest (where Seers lived). Man's actions in society must be guided by a non – attachment to fruit of action, always.

Man's potential is realised and purpose of education fulfilled when the only desire of man is for excellence in all dimensions. This unravels divinity latent in him and solves social problems. The above may sound theoretically romantic. The ancient Indian tradition shows how it works for man in society. Man has to fulfil obligations in society based on righteousness while having equal Love for all. This occurs by executing duties in selfless manner. Such an approach reveals the 'true inner self 'of man to himself. This is purpose of education whose implementation in daily life leads to achieving purpose or goal of life and goals of society.

Purpose of Paper
Indian Approach

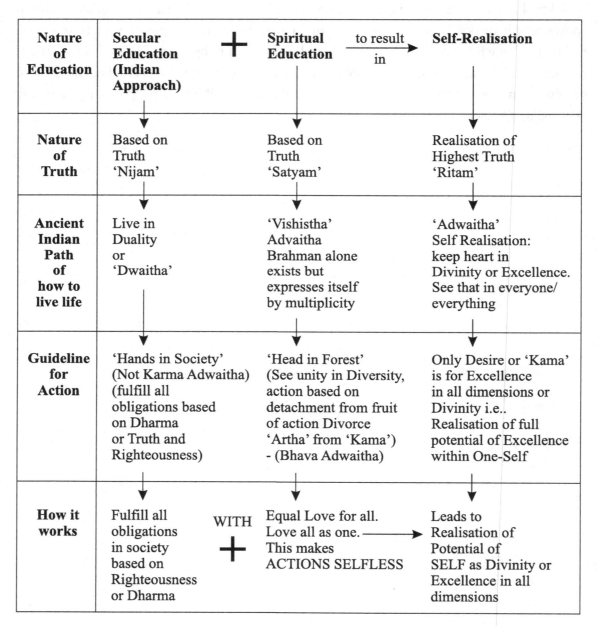

Nature of Education	Secular Education (Indian Approach)	**+**	Spiritual Education	to result in →	Self-Realisation
Nature of Truth	Based on Truth 'Nijam'		Based on Truth 'Satyam'		Realisation of Highest Truth 'Ritam'
Ancient Indian Path of how to live life	Live in Duality or 'Dwaitha'		'Vishistha' Advaitha Brahman alone exists but expresses itself by multiplicity		'Adwaitha' Self Realisation: keep heart in Divinity or Excellence. See that in everyone/everything
Guideline for Action	'Hands in Society' (Not Karma Adwaitha) (fulfill all obligations based on Dharma or Truth and Righteousness)		'Head in Forest' (See unity in Diversity, action based on detachment from fruit of action Divorce 'Artha' from 'Kama') - (Bhava Adwaitha)		Only Desire or 'Kama' is for Excellence in all dimensions or Divinity i.e.. Realisation of full potential of Excellence within One-Self
How it works	Fulfill all obligations in society based on Righteousness or Dharma	WITH **+**	Equal Love for all. Love all as one. → This makes ACTIONS SELFLESS		Leads to Realisation of Potential of SELF as Divinity or Excellence in all dimensions

Fig 0.26

How is purpose of Paper achieved?

Fig 0.27 illustrates process of achieving purpose of life and education in this Paper. It takes the example of life of man being like a moving car. As life is a flow, just like education, to keep the car moving requires co-operation and compatibility. The tyres on which it moves have to co-operate and be compatible.

Fig 0.27 further illustrates that four wheels of the car of life are like four goals of life / *Purusharthas*. When man moves according to goals of life, the journey ends at the destination. This can be achieved by ensuring two things:

a) That correct pairing of tyres of goals of life/ *Purusharthas* takes place:
For car of life of man to reach its desired destination, Righteousness or *Dharma* must be paired with *Artha*. The expression of distinction of man through pursuit of material wealth is *Artha*. Righteousness is the basis of *Artha*. Similarly, *Kama* or desire has to be directed towards *Moksha*. All desires have to be directed towards realising excellence within which leads to *Moksha*. Only such a 'pairing' can create balance within man and in society.

b) The correct 'pressure'/ emphasis has to be maintained or given to each goal of life or tyre. The current situation in the world suggests that there is too much pressure on *Kama* or wish fulfilment. This wish fulfilment is misdirected. Also, there is too little pressure in the tyre of *Dharma* or righteous conduct. This is reflected in the actions of man in society.

The purpose of this paper is achieved by creating awareness of the above two. The path for achieving correct pairing and correct pressure is also shown. This ensures co-operation and compatibility in seeking of material wealth and fulfilment of desires of man in society.

How is purpose of paper achieved

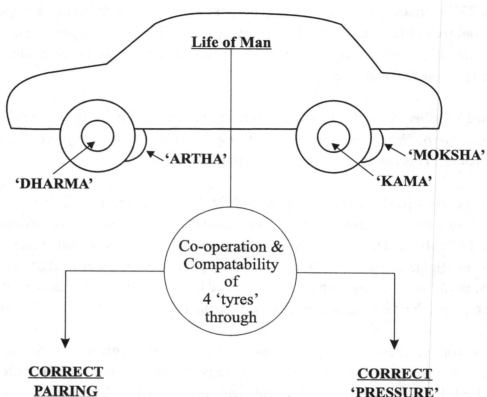

Life of Man

'DHARMA'

←'ARTHA'

'MOKSHA'

←'KAMA'

Co-operation & Compatability of 4 'tyres' through

CORRECT PAIRING
OF 'TYRES'
'DHARMA' must be paired with 'ARTHA'
'KAMA' must be paired with 'MOKSHA'

- DO NOT ALLOW 'KAMA' TO MARRY 'ARTHA'
- DHARMA IS BASIS OF 'ARTHA'
ONLY DESIRABLE THING ('KAMA') IS TO REALISE POTENTIAL OF EXCELLENCE OF 'SELF'

CORRECT 'PRESSURE'
IN
TYRES
All tyres must be with 'just right' pressure. Less pressure in any one will harm the car

- REDUCE PRESSURE OF 'KAMA'
- INCREASE PRESSURE OF 'DHARMA' & 'MOKSHA' IN SOCIETY TODAY

Fig 0.27

The Difference between popular education and ancient Indian education

Fig 0.28 illustrates the difference between the two education systems. It must be clarified here that the 3C Approach of popular education and ancient Indian education are not comparable. In 3C (popular approach) knowledge about the world is given without emphasis on 4thC of *Moksh*a. The 3C's of ancient Indians lead to the 4th C, teaching man to follow the four *Purusharthas* or goals of life. This is not the focus of teaching currently. Individuals, today, do their own spiritual search. The ethical training of following truth and morality is gained from individual teachers, some courses, parents and other influencers. Many follow four goals of life (*Purusharthas*) and achieve excellence within the self. However, system of education does not formally promote such an understanding as prime focus of education. The difference between present system and ancient Indian education system is presented here in three contexts studied above i.e.

- What is man?
- What is Truth
- Understanding the nature of interaction between man and creation.

Education has an impact on Heart of man at one end in Figure 0.28. The consequences of actions of man in society are concluded at the other end.

These are detailed as follows:
- The present education system does not lay emphasis on spiritual knowledge while ancient Indian system seeks to impart both. *Para Vidya* or worldly Knowledge along with *Apara Vidya* or Spiritual Knowledge is taught, together.
- The purpose of *Apara Vidya*/Spiritual Knowledge is to open the heart of man. Worldly *Para Vidya*, pursued singularly – ignoring *Apara Vidya*, leaves man's heart locked.
- *Para Vidya*/ worldly Knowledge, therefore, is unable to transform heart of man. It, thus, remains a collection of theories, inferences, concepts, conjectures and constructions. These theories are material in nature and, therefore, cannot lead to Awareness. Nature of man remains a mystery. *Para Vidya* or Spiritual Knowledge inculcates this Awareness.

The Difference Between
Popular Education &Ancient Indian Education

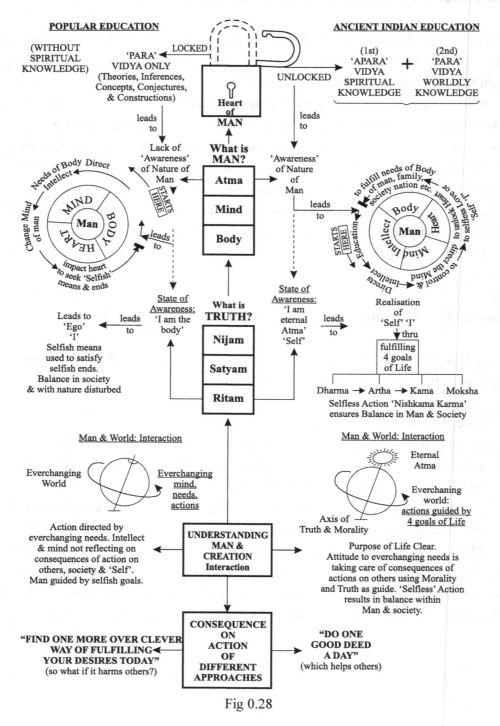

Fig 0.28

• The popular education system makes man emerge with a conviction that he is the body. He, then, starts a circle of interaction both within and with the world. This revolves around the body, mind and heart – as depicted in fig 0.28. He concentrates on needs of his body. Needs direct his intellect and influence his mind to seek material gains. The concentration on material needs leads to selfish responses by fulfilling them. The development of ego 'I' leads man to seek self importance and self aggrandisement. It develops a selfish way of looking at the world. He begins to treat life as a zero sum game. He feels his gain comes at the cost of someone's loss. The material world is ever changing. So, man's actions too chase these ever changing needs. Each action is, then, a zero sum game. Therefore, result of actions on society can be very harmful. This disturbs balance within man, in society and with nature.

• The ancient Indian education system sensitized man to awareness of Soul or *Atma*. This led him away from the delusion of being just the body. When education begins with this background it directs intellect to control the mind. This unlocks potential of the heart for selfless Love. The result of search for meaning in life is discovering real nature of man – i.e. Soul. With such feelings and motivation man now interacts with society. He adds value for others and himself in a selfless way. The way of living life is through four goals of life (*Purusharthas*). This leads to actions performed with excellence without attachment to results. This selfless approach helps man view his role in society in a correct perspective. It leads to a vision of life as a non-zero sum game. Man's interaction with the world through such education revolves on axis of Truth and morality. With purpose of life being clear, the attitude towards ever changing needs is different. Man wishes to take care of consequences of actions on others using Truth and morality as a guide. This attitude produces selfless action promoting balance within man and in society.

• The consequences of action of man in both approaches become clear once attitude, which prompts actions, is understood. In present system of education the attitude can be: "Find one over clever way of fulfilling desires today!" In ancient Indian tradition, goal of education is to transform heart of man. It seeks to inculcate an attitude: "do one good deed today" which helps others. The consequences of actions that emerge from these attitudes result in balance in society or lack of balance. All educators (not only now – but at all times in history) have to choose either of above techniques of education.

What is the major difference between these two approaches of education? The emergence of Selfless Love within man after transformation of the heart is the major difference. How does this emerge within man?

Selfless Love is the major difference between 2 systems of education – how does it emerge within man?

Fig 0.29 details how Selfless Love emerges within man. The understanding of creation, the understanding of man and understanding nature of Truth help in transforming heart of man. What is the natural expression of this transformation in life? What enables Selfless Love to emerge within man?

The eternal Soul of man is in union with highest Truth of creation. This is the basis of universe – as well as ancient Indian tradition. Man experiences world through his sense organs (circle of *Nijam* as depicted in Fig 0.29). After ethics based education, this experience begins to revolve on axis of Truth and Morality. The inner nature of man is *Ananda* or bliss. This is an experience above senses of the body – but experienced within it. This Truth about man is what has to be 'realised'. This becomes simple after reading Chapter 6.

Man absorbs inputs of education through purity of intention, patience and perseverance. The concept that man is not just the body is the foundation of education. This holds true in ancient Indian tradition and also is the belief of thinkers like Aristotle.

The resultant 'Truth, Goodness, Beauty' of Aristotle is known as '*Satyam, Shivam, Sundaram*' in Indian tradition. It represents similar concepts. *Shivam* means auspiciousness in the Indian concept. It reflects auspiciousness that results when myopic selfishness is ignored while seeing the bigger picture.

The expression of Truth should always be in words that do not hurt and upset balance. The dictum '*Satyam bruyaat, priyam bruyaat*' lays down guideline of action while speaking truth. The beauty – that is the inner nature of man – has to be uncovered through this inner cleansing. When the inner beauty is experienced by man he will automatically be able to experience beauty outside him. Such is the understanding of Indian sages and See'rs.

Emergence of Selfless Love in Man
The Process

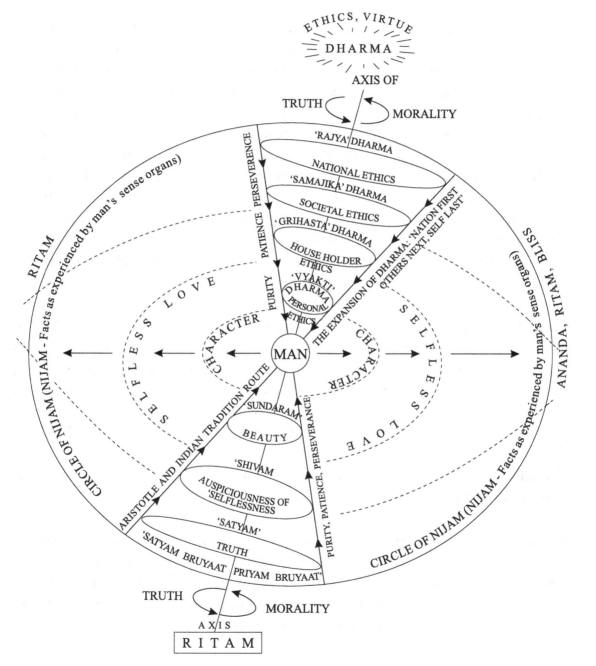

Fig 0.29

The ability to experience beauty within and without prepares man for action in society. The expression of action is through different dimensions of *Dharma*.

Dharma has many dimensions. It starts with *Vyakti Dharma* i.e. individual *Dharma* or personal ethics. This is the focus given to each student. Then, it graduates to *Grihasta Dharma* (householder ethics) when man grows up and gets married. While fulfilling role of householder, *Samajika Dharma* (societal ethic) emerges. *Rajya Dharma* (national ethics) becomes a natural responsibility of man as a social being. The nature of expansion of *Dharma* deals with expansion of the heart of man till he acts with the conviction; 'Nation first, others next, self last'. The expression of such righteous action promotes harmony in society. Harmony in society is a collective expression of individual character resulting from such education. The character of man enables him to pierce through perception of truth as *Nijam* – called *Maya* or the deluding veil that covers the higher Truth. This occurs through emergence of Selfless Love within man. His intuitive nature is then able to perceive *Satyam*. Experience of inner nature is beyond senses organs. However, this experience occurs not by sacrificing his body but by living within it.

The understanding of Selfless Love helps in executing the four goals of life or *Purusharthas*. Alternatively, following the four Cs, develops Character of student – which helps the understanding of Selfless Love to emerge, slowly. This prepares man for action in society and for piercing the circle of facts (*Nijam*) to experience Truth about man's life (or *Ritam*). Here, good feelings are more important than religious beliefs. Mutual regard (*mamatha*), equal mindedness (*samatha*) and forbearance (*Kshamatha*), too, help develop Selfless Love.

Conclusion: Truth is basis of everything – Four Shared Values of society, Four *Purusharthas* for man emerge from it

The purpose of the Paper is to produce harmony or balance within man, between men and finally between nations. How is balance achieved? To achieve it, first, we have to comprehend it! How can we understand the concept of balance? Can it be communicated through words, metaphor or pictures? The ancient Indian tradition gives a good route for easy comprehension of this concept. It uses the concept of God.

The description of God has two dimensions: *"Yaatho Rudrassivaathanoraghora Paapa naasinee"*. The above verse depicts God as having two distinguishable forms – the serene and the terrible. The same God appears serene to the devotee (Please read story of *Prahalad* – an easy source is internet). However, he appears as terrible to (*Hiranyakashipu*) whom the Lord kills. The idea is that Nature has these two concepts of mild and fearful present simultaneously in it. Water is both life-giving as well as cause of death under some circumstances. The same can be said for food. Food gives life but when too much food is partaken, it eats the body through ill health. Hence balance is essential in every aspect of life for the fearful aspect to be eliminated. The mantras and stories, like parables, ingrain such concepts in a simple way in this tradition. Even when God is understood as excellence in all dimensions, this excellence needs to be kept in balance through man's actions. These actions must be within two banks of the river of education – Truth and Morality. Otherwise, Divinity will appear fearful – as it did to *Hiranyakashipu*. For, man's untrue and immoral behaviour causes harm to society by misdirected use of skills emerging from false understanding of success as 'excellence'.

Fig 0.30 gives the basis of emergence of 4C Approach. The 4C approach is multidimensional and covers both the spiritual and worldly aspirations of man. These dimensions depict how concepts of balance of man and balance of society merge in each other. What are the pillars of balance in society? The pillars of *Satya, Dharma, Shanti* and *Prema* (Truth, Morality, Peace and Love) in social behaviour ensure balance in society. Non violence or *Ahimsa* is their natural corollary and follows *Shanti* and *Prema* – or Peace and Love. Balance within man emerges by basing his life on the four goals of life or *Purusharthas*. **All these ideas have Truth as a basis**.

Education starts with Truth. This leads to humility in man on one hand and Morality in society on the other as shown in Fig 0.30. For the individual, Truth is both – gross (*Nijam*) and subtle (*Satyam*). The subtle Truth of 'Unity in Diversity' is realised through education as humility emerges from within man – leading to respect for others. At the gross level man education gives man the experience that 'no two things in nature are the same'. This makes man observe that there is Individuality in everything in creation. Hence, there must be Individuality in man. It convinces him to unearth it through pursuit of Truth.

The humility in man, prompted by education, leads to a willingness to Co-operate with others. Truth and Morality have to be the basis for this. This is *Dharma* (The first *Purushartha* – expressed as Co-operation) or morality with Truth as a basis. This, as Fig 0.30 shows, leads to experience of Individuality of man which is expressed through action. Such action should have a focus on adding value and generating wealth for himself with a Concern for society. This is *Artha* or the second Purushartha – which is expressed through his 'focussed Concern'. Both – *Dharma* and *Artha* – emerge from Awareness with Truth and Morality as basis (Fig 0.30).

The focussed 'Concern' for customer, self, society and natural resources marks the 'distinction' of man from rest of creation. Everything that marks this 'distinction' of man while fulfilling his desires is included in the definition of *Artha*.

Fig 0.30 shows that pursuit of *Satya* or Truth with application of *Dharma* or Morality in society leads to *Shanti* or Peace therein. Also, pursuit of *Dharma* (Morality) and *Artha* (or Wealth generation) leads to his desire fulfilment. This should express distinction of man and society through expression of Selfless Love. Then, a Compatibility Advantage emerges between man's and society's goals. This gives progress and prosperity – which promotes harmony within man and harmony between men.

In the meantime, the process of Peace or *Shanti* in society is expressed through peaceful co-operation of cluster and industry with a focus on national competitive advantage. This leads to *Prema* or Selfless Love. It generates 'Compatibility Advantage' on other side of the Figure. Thus, for man and society the search begins from Truth and ends with Selfless Love. Here, man's self interest merges with higher interests of society and nation. This is the root and origin (as well as the destination) of the 4C Approach of Management. The focus of this approach is on transformation of man. By not imparting information on how to be cleverer than others, it helps all. This difference in focus gives a civilisation the capacity to outlast.

Let us refer to Fig 0.5. Education prepares man to create balance in society. Education begins with *Satya* and *Dharma*. The dictum: *Satyam vada, Dharmam chara* (Speak the Truth, follow morality) guides this process. This helps man discover inner Peace *Shanti* which makes him experience Selfless Love or *Prema* towards all. This is the role of Truth in Society. It also translates the four *Purusharthas* of man into action. *Dharma* makes him see the best in everybody – resulting in humility and, therefore, co-operation. This leads to Peace within man and society which generates mutual respect and Selfless Love.

Similarly, when this Truth was to be put into action by man, he had to follow the four *Purusharthas*. The *Satyam* aspect of Truth makes man follow Righteous Conduct. The *Nijam* aspect of Truth helps man appreciate Individuality of creation, customer and himself. He can express this individuality to serve individuality of others – in his own unique way. This gives shape to *Artha* (to fulfil others needs) and *Kama* (to fulfil his own legitimate desires). This process does not harm others but adds value and balance to man and society. The highest goal of man and mankind is, then, achieved.

The dimensions of 4C Approach merge balance within man with balance within society. This leads to balance within nation (and within family of nations). Chapter 5 on Compatibility Advantage will describe this concept through the Study of Limits. This Figure details how study of Truth (or The Awareness of reality of man) leads to it.

Four Shared Values of society, Four *Purusharthas* of man, 4Cs of firm emerge from Truth

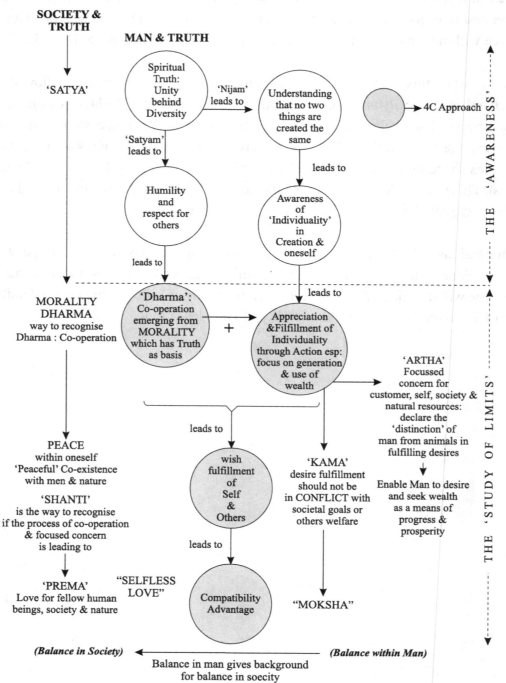

SOCIETY & TRUTH

'SATYA'

MAN & TRUTH

Spiritual Truth: Unity behind Diversity

'Nijam' leads to

Understanding that no two things are created the same

4C Approach

'Satyam' leads to

leads to

Humility and respect for others

Awareness of 'Individuality' in Creation & oneself

leads to

THE 'AWARENESS'

leads to

MORALITY DHARMA
way to recognise Dharma : Co-operation

'Dharma': Co-operation emerging from MORALITY which has Truth as basis

+

Appreciation &Filfillment of Individuality through Action esp: focus on generation & use of wealth

'ARTHA' Focussed concern for customer, self, society & natural resources: declare the 'distinction' of man from animals in fulfilling desires

leads to

PEACE
within oneself 'Peaceful' Co-existence with men & nature

'SHANTI'
is the way to recognise if the process of co-operation & focused concern is leading to

wish fulfillment of Self & Others

'KAMA' desire fulfillment should not be in CONFLICT with societal goals or others welfare

Enable Man to desire and seek wealth as a means of progress & prosperity

THE 'STUDY OF LIMITS'

leads to

'PREMA'
Love for fellow human beings, society & nature

"SELFLESS LOVE"

Compatibility Advantage

"MOKSHA"

(Balance in Society) ← *(Balance within Man)*

Balance in man gives background for balance in soecity

Fig 0.30

146

Some of the dimensions of 4C Approach are:

• The difference between *Bhava Adwaitha* (non Duality in thought) and *Karma Adwaitha* (non Duality in action). This difference needs to be absorbed within man. This is incorporated by the 2 fold approach: The Awareness and Study of Limits.

• The 4 pillars for Balance in Society are expressed through *Satya, Dharma, Shanti, Prema*. They lead to social interactions based on Truth, righteous conduct, promote peace within man as well as society and promote Selfless Love at individual, social and national level. These common sense concepts are not explained further.

• It merges four things: (a) Flow of Life (b) Flow of Education (c) Process of man Realising One Self – explained in Background (d) Concepts of how man should live in the World to Realise Him Self.

These happen simultaneously and concomitantly with each other.

• From an understanding of Truth, righteous action *Dharma* and expression of distinction of man i.e. *Artha* emerge.

• From *Dharma* or righteousness and expression of distinction of man (*Artha*), the desire or *Kama* should emerge (for Selfless Action or *Moksha*). Then, process within man (and in society) emerges as Selfless Love (which is the basis of Compatibility Advantage or *Moksha*). The manifestation of Selfless Love or *Moksha* is universal '*Prema*'. Equal Love towards all or everything – fellow human beings, society and nature – ensures balance in society, nation and family of nations.

The first difference is between *Bhava Adwaitha* (non-Duality in thought) and *Karma Adwaitha* (Non-Duality in action). This difference has to be understood and absorbed within man. Therefore, first dimension is difference between education that comes as part of the Awareness and the Study of Limits. The Figure is, thus, broken into two parts. Each part is based on difference between areas of the Awareness and the Study of Limits. The awareness that man needs for life is awareness of Truth about himself. This Truth is known as *Satya* and is the first pillar of 4C Approach. This includes the spiritual Truth of unity in diversity.

Truth, absorbed as both *Nijam* and *Satyam* (secular and spiritual education), impacts man's actions in society and create balance. Interpreted in a spiritual way, Truth (*Satyam*, leads to respect for others and inculcates humility in man. Interpreted in worldly way, through

147

observation of matter or *Nijam*, it leads to an understanding that no two things are created same. This leads to understanding Individuality of everything in creation and, therefore, of man also. The expression of Individuality in society is through co-operation with others. This is a reflection of *Dharma* or righteous action of man in society.

The understanding of Truth in both i.e. *Nijam* and *Satyam* leads to application of *Dharma* in action (which is Co-operation emerging from morality with Truth as a basis).
The appreciation of Individuality in creation and, therefore, in man comes from understanding Truth through the senses or *Nijam*. A focussed Concern for creating wealth guided by the intuitive perception of unity in diversity through application of *Satyam* leads to *Dharma*. This guides application of focussed concern in generating value for man and society. Such Concern for customer, society, self, and natural resources declares distinction of man from animal world. Then, fulfilling desires, *Kama*, (of society and man) occurs in a harmonious way. The societal goal is achieved by ensuring lack of conflict in goals of man and society (in processes associated with value creation). This enables man and society to fulfill wishes by seeking wealth as a means of progress and prosperity. This lack of conflict reflects in peace within man (and among men) known as *Shanti* in society.

The unfolding of Truth (*Satya*) within man (which emerges from balance within man) creates background for balance within society. This balance is expressed through actions based on *Dharma* leading to *Shanti* (Peace). This is expressed through universal Selfless Love (*Prema*). The process of balance in man leads to balance in society. The Introduction starts and ends with this idea – giving a background to its application by man in society.

The simultaneous and spontaneous occurrence of all above processes – in a repeated manner – leads to a Compatibility Advantage. Man in society benefits from it. It creates balance within nation, among nations as well as between man and nature. Selfless Love once experienced within man is reflected in every action as *Nishkama Karma*. This leads to *Moksha* for man while ensuring Compatibility Advantage for society. Thus, *Moksha* is not something to die for – it is something to be achieved by living for it!

Chapter 1 makes Truth about correct Strategy needed emerge from 'within' man;
Chapters 2 to 5 give Strategy that creates balance through all activities of man.

Part A

Ancient Indian Education seeks the following:
"Yad Vijnaanena Sarvam vijnaatham bhavathi"
"That, which when known, everything becomes known"

EDUCATION MAKES MAN MASTER OF HIS MIND: CREATES BALANCE IN MAN
Mind of man spins a spider web of thoughts. Ancient Indian tradition seeks to purify thoughts. This creates balance within man – when he becomes the master of his mind, not its slave. It also helps develop an attitude that makes Truth about right Strategy to use emerge from 'within' – when man is in the driving seat. Then, correct decisions prevent crash of the car of society in the journey of man's life. Attitude of man is responsible for his thoughts. Hence education should create an attitude that enables balance in man, society. It should transform attitude of selfishness and greed to one of seeking peace and excellence. Attitude emerges from intentions of man which need to be purified. This purity comes from values and represents Truth about man – which can be expressed through righteous conduct in society. Righteous conduct creates balance within man, society.

Part A details how balance in Man can emerge using ancient widom.
Part B describes how balance in society can be achieved using life's goals – righteous conduct being the first among them.

Values exhibit the character of man.

But, how does that prevent recession?

A recession refers to an act of reduction or moving back, not forward.
Then, instead of helping each other they indirectly or directly cause harm
The impact on society of the summation of such individual actions is recession.
Preventing a recession would imply effectively blocking movement backward.
When humans receed from their natural state, they receeed into selfishness.
For, it is in basic human nature to care for others.
Values prevent recession of man into selfishness and society into a recession.

Many current ideas esp. those about competitiveness need to be changed for this.
Present ideas of competitiveness are based on the assumption of comparing
achievements of ones company, industry, society, nation with others. This can lead
to jealousy which signifies the end of consciousness of man about his potential.

In fact the expression of competitiveness, if expressed through selfishness, will be
the core of the problem. It will reflect the inadequacy of education concepts.

Merger of Ancient Wisdom with Management Ideas
VALUES ARE BASIS OF STRATEGY OF LIFE

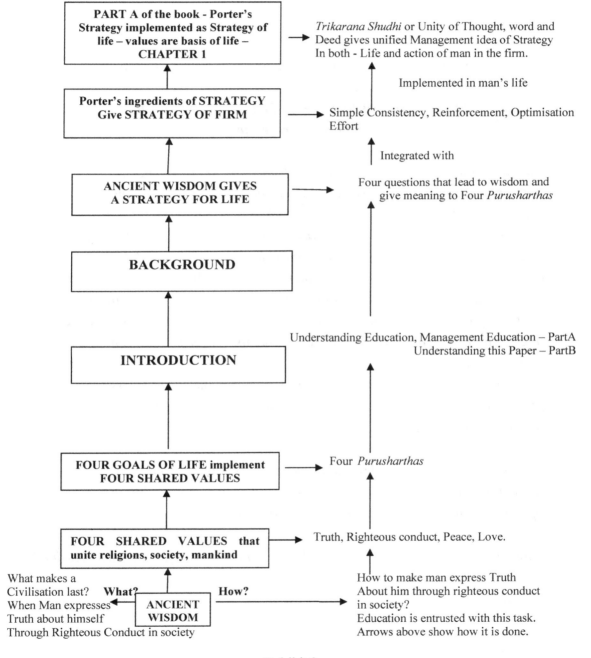

PART A of the book - Porter's Strategy implemented as Strategy of life – values are basis of life – CHAPTER 1

Trikarana Shudhi or Unity of Thought, word and Deed gives unified Management idea of Strategy In both - Life and action of man in the firm.

Implemented in man's life

Porter's ingredients of STRATEGY Give STRATEGY OF FIRM

Simple Consistency, Reinforcement, Optimisation Effort

Integrated with

ANCIENT WISDOM GIVES A STRATEGY FOR LIFE

Four questions that lead to wisdom and give meaning to Four *Purusharthas*

BACKGROUND

INTRODUCTION

Understanding Education, Management Education – PartA Understanding this Paper – PartB

FOUR GOALS OF LIFE implement FOUR SHARED VALUES

Four *Purusharthas*

FOUR SHARED VALUES that unite religions, society, mankind

Truth, Righteous conduct, Peace, Love.

What makes a Civilisation last? **What?** When Man expresses Truth about himself Through Righteous Conduct in society

ANCIENT WISDOM

How?

How to make man express Truth About him through righteous conduct in society? Education is entrusted with this task. Arrows above show how it is done.

Exhibit 2

From values emerges wisdom. From wisdom emerge values.
Values are wisdom in action.
But, how does wisdom change ideas of competitiveness,
and prevent recession?

Comparing with others is the very initial stage of competitiveness.
When man, companies, industries discover their potential of adding
value to society by expressing their individuality – they serve the customer
in their own unique way. Today, all are copying each other in some way
or the other. This experience of ones individuality comes only through
a deeper sensitivity about self, customer and society. When such individuality
is experienced, the only competition is with ones own past work. Society has
yet to fully experience such creativity – which can come only after practice of
ancient Indian wisdom. Today we face problems of over exploitation of
resources and harmful waste material – for many try to do the same thing
using the same resources or they just pump up demand by unnecessary
product obsolescence leading to wastage of resources and material that
harms the environment.

We have only reached the level of thinking of recognising that above
activities cause harm. How can this be stopped needs a very different
approach which can be inculcated by proper education

How to develop that awareness of Self that benefits society, prevents recession?

ANCIENT WISDOM – VALUES ARE BASIS OF STRATEGY OF LIFE
Part A emerges from 'Background'

- The Ancient Indian tradition did not begin education by imparting skills.
- It concentrated, first, on developing an attitude towards work.
- Recognising Individuality of man, three paths of developing attitudes in tune with 'inner nature' of man are given: *Karma, Bhakti, Jnana*.
- It also identified man's 'inner faults' that impede implementing these attitudes. These are: Anger, Desire, Greed, Envy, Attachment, Pride.
- It then showed how using 'inner nature', and attitudes natural to it, helps overcome these inner enemies.
- Its experience of thousands of years helped it classify what path would appeal to an individual's 'inner nature'. This led to transformation of man.
- Man uses his body, heart and intellect. All three, together, create balance. Different people have different skills in using each of them. Some have stronger inner skills of using the intellect, for example. They are naturally inclined to asking questions and searching for meaning.
- The task oriented people were recommended the path of *Karma.* Those with inclination to devotion were recommended the *Bhakti* path. Finally, for the intellectually inclined the *Jnana* path was recommended.
- This led to optimum use of the human body, mind and intellect through various paths which led to attitudes of work. Balance results from using special skills of man. Based on these attitudes it was possible to achieve excellence, harnessing optimally the 'inner nature of man'.
- How do the three paths of *Karma, Bhakti* and *Jnana* help man overcome their inner faults is shown in this tradition.
- When these inner faults are removed, it is a natural Optimisation effort of man's output in society. Transformation, thus, benefits man, society.
- Man's output starts with personal interactions. Ancient Indian tradition teaches him how to interact with others.
- This happens best when man learns how to manage his thoughts. For, training the mind is the first priority. As all faults start from the human mind, true education concentrates on 'how to train the mind'.
- So, how to 'manage' thoughts is important. How can people with different 'inner nature' or inclinations manage their thoughts? This is shown here – using ancient wisdom.
- The objective of the above is to transform the heart of the student, first.
- Until the transformation of the heart takes place, skills imparted are likely to be misused. Skills give a strategy of performing work optimally.
- Values, in ancient Indian tradition, merge into Strategy.
- Awareness that 'Values are the Strategy of Life' makes man ready for acting in society. Then, skills imparted will not be misused.

What is the nature of man, Him Self?

The ancient Indian tradition states that what man thinks as Him,
The One who is filled with excellence, is nothing but the Self.
*Him is there (*Tat*) while Self is you (*Twam*). That* Tat *is* Twam *(Asi).*
Chapter 6 is designed to show the path to this union with excellence
through seeing the unity of creation. Man is capable of 'realising'
this excellence within himself – so the ancient Indian tradition states.

How does this Awareness prevent recession?
When profit is the sole goal of business, it shows a lack of sensitivity
about other things that may be important for society. Rosabeth Kanter has
given many examples of how the work of seekers of excellence has helped
society – even during the Tsunami. If such effort remains isolated to few
individuals or companies, their beauty will be like a individual pearls.
Until a theory binds such pearls together into a string that can be worn
the beauty of their work will not be appreciated. It will be taken as an
individual effort of good human beings – not a way of doing business
that prevents recession in society. The solution for a recession comes
from a change in attitude – that will emerge from a different awareness.
Ancient wisdom gives this understanding – but it requires a training of the
human mind over many years to experience its Truth.

Rita McGrath found that Milliken USA did not shut its textile plants in 1980
like others when the whole industry manufacturing shifted to Asia. They
closed slowly till 2009 to help relocate workers! This firm survived to
become a leader in speciality materials and high IP-speciality chemicals!

The Search for Excellence within "One-Self"

Management

Man in this Age is Meant to

Realise Him-Self

Scribe:

Satya Saurabh Khosla

INTEGRATING MANAGEMENT THEORY
(From strategy of firm to competitive advantage of nations)
WITH GOAL(S) OF LIFE

"All this talk of Awareness is good, but how do I recognise it within?"
This is a relevant question

Buddhism talks of Sunyata (emptiness) as there is no independent Self.
Ancient Indian tradition talks of the gap between two thoughts as wisdom.
"But how will all this make me see things differently?"
This is another valid question.
His Holiness The Dalai Lama often begins a speech by pointing
out that He does not see any difference between Himself and all those
listening to Him. This feeling of One-ness with all is a state where the
ego has been eliminated. It is also a reflection of the ability to always
see the unity of creation (Chapter 6). A feeling of being between
brothers and sisters emerges. Vivekananda's speech at the 1893 World
Parliament of Religions in Chicago started with a thunderous applause
as He began by using the expression:"My dear brothers and sisters..."
as all could experience His ability to 'C'everybody with a feeling
of unity. This shows the first step of Humility, outlined earlier. Emerging
from such humility, Individuality manifests. Awareness is a state of
silencing the mind or becoming a master of the mind.

Chapter 1

Values create Awareness of Excellence 'within' man

Education creates Awareness through inculcating values. School, college and textbooks give building blocks for a strategy of life. Education is a continuous process of multiple life experiences that test this learning of values and application of strategy. Each individual has different (or a different mix of three) ingredients of inner nature of *Karma* (activity), *Bhakti* (devotion to excellence and excellence seeking) and *Jnana* (Wisdom seeking). However, all (except Seers) have to indulge in *Karma*. In the ancient Indian tradition *Karma* transforms to *Bhakti* and *Bhakti* to *Jnana*. This three stage transformation is an experience. It cannot be explained in this or any Chapter. The outline of transformation in three steps is:

1) First, Work becomes Worship. This is when *Karma* is prompted by *Bhakti*. This is known as *'Samsara Bhakti'* or Worldly devotion. It seeks gains in the material form for material satisfaction. The seeking of maximising gains for the firm and the unending desire to maximise efficiency for activities can lead to discoveries, inventions and breakthroughs in the field of endeavour – whether it be in new production processes, R&D or market share. When work is enjoyed for its own sake, the attachment to results wears off. Then, excellence is sought as the search for excellence itself gives a unique self satisfaction – this is worship or *Bhakti*. Initially this devotion leads to worldly gains but when attachment to them, too, wears off then the larger picture emerges slowly in the mind of man – this is the birth of wisdom.

2) When, some wisdom (*Jnana*) is added to *Bhakti* or worship, it transforms the above 'Work is Worship' dictum to *'Vanaprastha Bhakti'*. The experience 'Profit is not the No.1 priority of business', then, emerges. (*Vanaprastha* is the third stage of life or *asrama* of man – the earlier two being *Brahmacharya* which is a period meant for study and *Grihasta* or householder where youth may seek maximising efficiency without use of discrimination). Rosabeth Kanter of Harvard Business School has given examples of many individuals in firms who kept up their research because they were convinced that it is useful for mankind – irrespective of whether it would lead to immediate profit for the firm (P&G's decade long R&D on a water purification product that was finally used during the Tsunami – and other examples). Chapter 4 on Competitive Response mentions how *Vanaprastha* idea is used in the Product Life Cycle to show detachment from selfishness to set an example in society.

157

3) The last stage is when *Bhakti* transforms to *Jnana*. Then, devotion transforms to wisdom. This is '*Sanyasa Bhakti*' which denotes the last stage of life or *asrama*. This is Self Actualisation or *Moksha* itself. The motivation to collect resources of men, material and money to create a permanent and everlasting infrastructure that delivers free services of primary to higher education, free healthcare and free drinking water in a drought prone area are examples. This is the Ideal of transformation of skills and knowledge to wisdom. Of course, wisdom alone is not sufficient; it must be accompanied with detachment. For the benefit of such activities are not for the individual who has created them but for society at large. The life of Seers and teachers of ancient India also set such an example of selflessness.

What can motivate man to seek higher goals while indulging in action or *Karma?* The above transition elucidated by the ancient Indian tradition can be explained using an example of a bus travelling on a dusty unpaved village road. So long as *Karma* is continuous or the bus keeps travelling, dust of *Karmic* implications will not settle till it reaches the road of devotion or *Bhakti* – which is slightly paved. Here, too, it should not stop till it reaches the highway of *Jnana* where no dust rises as bus travels. The desire of stopping is equated to getting attached to the result of actions. If selfish motives of enjoyment of results guide actions, then the consequences of actions will impact man. Seeking the welfare of others makes actions like the flow of a mighty river – whose speed can purify the water as it travels.

This Chapter shows how: (a) **simple consistency through 'unity of thought word and deed'** (b) its **reinforcement through individual and social effort...** (c) ...**creates an Optimisation effort.** This enables translating knowledge into value addition – for man and mankind. Optimisation effort prevents social conflict, chaos, disorder and recession. It translates knowledge into wisdom.

Ancient India's framework led to 'managing thoughts' of man. This was the gateway to education and management of society – it is shared here.

This book can be applied to education and life by making a simple beginning: "Speak the Truth, follow morality" This makes **values merge into strategy**. India's educational institutions incorporated this Ideal as per three 'inner natures of man' – identified by it. This led to morality and clear vision of man – enabling him to 'C' strategy as a **Best Management Practice** using the 4C Approach

Man Age Meant: Creating Awareness of Excellence 'within' man

It is not possible to reform anybody or anything without reforming one's own self

Man has conquered the whole world but he has not conquered himself
Winston Churchill

Education should integrate with life by transforming it. True education should get upgraded, not outdated with change, new inventions or new ways of doing business. When education is designed only for earning a living, it may serve immediate goals of prospective employers. But long term goals of society may not be the focus. Changes in technology, techniques and ways of doing business can make such education irrelevant with passage of time. The timeless quality of education emerges when it fulfils man's goals of life as well as goals of society. Then, it can adapt to new ideas, within its natural framework.

What would such a natural framework look like for management education?

Search for universal idea of management: Even small tasks, to be performed efficiently, require management – of resources and time. Thus management ideas should apply to all tasks (big or small, in business or life). They should apply beyond *businesses* to any purposeful human activity or '*busy*'ness – that wishes to achieve optimum results. Can such a broad understanding integrate study of management with life? Can a commonality of ideas among man's actions in life and in the firm be discovered? Can there be a similarity of concepts in devising a strategy for both? Will these concepts help in executing all activities of man in an optimum manner? Can we execute business with same ideas of management and strategy followed for living life – and *vice versa*?

If these ideas can be identified, then there is just an easy question to ask: "Can we simply impart them as a way of seeing things – in simple manner? If so, how do we show their universal application – whether to business or life?"

Our study should incorporate an ethical framework or a way of analysing that directs human behaviour. All actions of man should be transformed towards achieving excellence. The impact of such transformation should extend *to* business *from* life. Education is a discipline. Training for life and business simultaneously will promote harmony between them and, therefore, among man, society and nature.

Merging ancient wisdom and Porter's idea: Ancient Indian thinking has many concepts of – 'management of Self' – and – 'strategy for living life'. How do they integrate with business and with present management theory and thought? Can answers of all these questions be fitted into a simple model? This task is attempted here.

Michael Porter is a Professor of strategy, competitive strategy, competitiveness of nations at Harvard Business School. He identifies **three ingredients of strategy** for **firms.** These are: **Simple consistency, Reinforcement and Optimisation effort**.

Can these ingredients of strategy apply to strategy of man for living life?

1.1 'Man Age "Meant"': Beginning with Man: – Search for and **adherence to Truth** (by man) **is the first exercise in Porter's 'Simple Consistency'**

How do simple consistency, reinforcement and optimisation effort relate to an individual? Any study of management relates to man, is devised by man and is executed by man to impact him and others. So, he will be a direct beneficiary if best practices of management are ensured. Hence study of man needs to be incorporated in study of management. This establishs a Simple Consistency between man and the purpose he wishes to pursue. Truth about man will then be the basis of management Truths.

Any activity or study has a purpose. This purpose should align with the purpose of the user or target audience. The target audience of management is man himself. So, a Simple Consistency is needed in search for Truth about Man and Management.

With the above objective we begin our search for a self-sustaining framework for man and management. We will conclude that ingredients of strategy for the firm and for man (whether they be customers, workers, suppliers etc) are same. They have the same three ingredients for consistency. This will enable a study of both simultaneously – in a common framework. Therefore, when three ingredients of Strategy (Simple Consistency, Reinforcement and Optimisation effort) relate to goals identified for Man – the likelihood of crisis diminishes. The overlapping nature of study of both Man and Management should reveal itself in study of three ingredients of strategy. More so, when these ingredients are applied to man's efforts – in life and at work. A simple consistency in search for and adherence to Truth guides man to implement them. Both, in life – and at work in the firm!

How does the search for Truth start within society and man? The search for Truth (even of meaning and purpose of life) comes from two sources: Either from an 'inner quest' natural to man or it can come from a sudden crisis.

A crisis is when something coveted, dear and desired is taken away or threatened to be taken away. This is the time when man becomes most alert. In a world where focus of activity is money, a financial crisis generates alertness for preventing future ones. Progress can take place with such an approach. In every crisis, man falls back upon the body of knowledge he has created. However, what happens when one seeks to question the universal applicability (across time) of the body of Knowledge itself? This can lead to a deeper and more meaningful search.

Crisis motivates man to search for Truth: Today management education and practice are at such crossroads. A crisis is the right time to question practices that allowed it to develop. When managers and managements do not have tools to prevent a crisis, a closer look at management education is needed. For, it provides a curriculum for training of managers and influences management practice. The purpose of current management curriculum is to enable the students to earn more. The focus is on teaching tools and techniques. The higher salary levels of the graduating class are directly co-related to the reputation of a business school and demand for admissions. The perception of employers and job seekers is to seek instant gratification – the former in commercial value addition and the latter in higher salaries. Both perceptions allowed a financial bubble to blow bigger. This level of Truth could not prevent a crisis. A higher level of Truth is needed to guide society to prevent a crisis.

What Truth was forgotten – that led to the financial crisis? Employers, educators and practitioners forgot to reaffirm through theory and practice that Management tools (derivatives etc.) are for ethical managers only. Without values any strategy will make society lifeless. The end, therefore, was as inevitable as the need for a new beginning now.

Consistent Truth about man, management and society: The primary task of management education should be to enhance the quality of life of customers, companies and society. It should initiate a process in which managers can add tremendous value(s) to their lives – emanating from a never-ending search of excellence. This should bring out the best in themselves – which is excellence! A Latin word *educare* which means "to bring out what is within" aptly describes it. Society and educationists need to address a question: can 'earning more money' be the sole end of education? Wealth is created through 'creating value'. Discovering and creating 'value' is a process that may not necessarily be measured in terms of money. The role of non-financial value creation and human values is not included in value creation taught to man – for use by business in society.

Values are non-financial, yet add value: A mother, for example, adds tremendous non-financial value to her child's life while bringing out the best 'within her'. As she brings out excellence and values 'within' her, it empowers the child with human values to bring out the best 'within him or her'. A summation of such value addition adds much value to society. It happens at home and both parents enable it. Morality by teachers, in and out of classrooms, reinforces it. This is a non financial value creation process. The child, then, grows up to add value for self and society. A summation of this process across all children prepares a workforce that is empowered for 'bringing out the best within individuals, firms, clusters and nations'. This is *educare* which implements *Vidya Vahini*.

The idea of *educare* is to train for life through imparting human values. It is not just for earning a living (aiming for money alone) – yet it creates prosperity for all. It recognises that fortunes of man and society are closely interlinked – promoting balance in both – leading to prosperity. This prevents a crisis in society. A change in focus is needed. The desired focus will enable individuals, firms, clusters and nations to 'bring out the best within them'. **This will ensure simple consistency between study of management and goals of man and society.**

The purpose of Management Thought

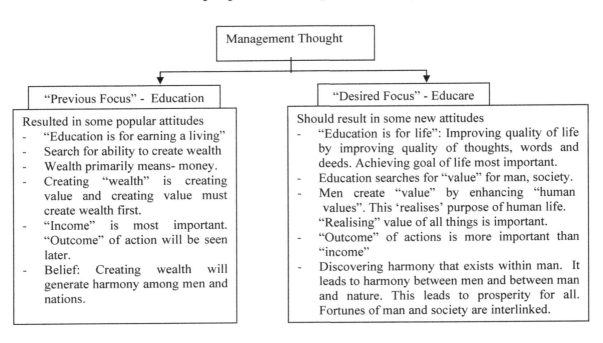

Diagram 1.1a

163

1.2 When Knowledge leads to Practice of Management: Exercise in Porter's "reinforcement"

A simple consistency between 'educare' and its focus on man in society should be followed by reinforcement. This reinforcement is done by man when he implements 'educare' ideas in life. First, man's innate potential for excellence is awakened by 'educare'. Then, men seek excellence – reinforcing values and best practices in the firm, cluster and home nation. **Diagram 1.1b** shows how simple consistency of 'educare' and its reinforcement is followed by optimisation effort – which results in best practices in society. These best practices, thus, emerge from 'within' man as an optimisation effort for him and society. Unity of thought, word and deed is the best practice for managing man's life. It removes duplicity and creates balance. This best practice transforms man's contribution at work and home, too. At work, it leads to best management practices for firm and then of cluster, industry – and finally society. It also promotes balance within man, for family and society – creating balance for all. Thus strategy through simple consistency, reinforcement and optimisation effort adds value to both man and society.

Simple consistency, Reinforcement and Optimisation effort add value to man, society – by creating Best Management Practices

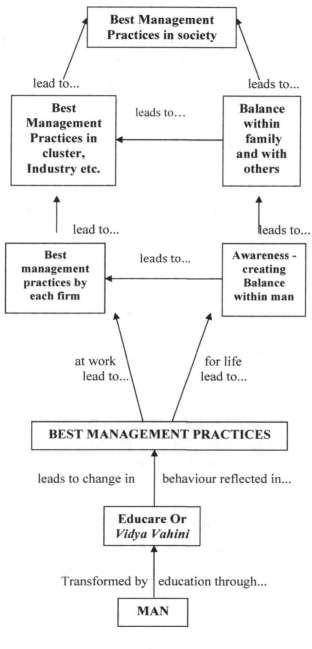

Diagram 1.1b

Best management practices are not an accident. By the time man reaches the firm to add value to society, it may be too late to inculcate values! Hence, ancient Indian tradition incorporated them in education as Educare or *Vidya Vahini*.

Sketches 6 and 7 give the idea how spiritual and secular educations, together, initiate Best Management Practices – for both man and firm. Diagram 1.1b elaborates how this process works. Finally, Diagram 6.0 in Chapter 6 shows how these Best Management Practices lead to balance in society.

What are these Best Management Practices?

Truth and Morality are the first Best Management Practice for man. Chapter 1, here, in Part A explains how they can emerge from within man. This is based on 'experience' and its practice over thousands of years. The ancient Indian tradition, through such practice, designed thought processes that lead to Awareness emerging from 'within' man. These are shared here, in Chapter1.

The meeting point of Part A and Part B is Chapter 2. It uses the Awareness generated within man from Chapter 1. It shows how Best Management Practices emerging from this Awareness are put in action. This needs to be done within man, first. Then, they should be implemented by man is society. What is this Awareness?

a. Study of Man: Awakening Awareness of man's potential for Excellence For Best Management Practices to emerge from within man awareness about himself is required, such Awareness creates balance. This chapter focuses on concepts of Awareness that are common across various traditions. It presents their academic understanding and practice. Finally, the practice of Management has to be done only by Man. Hence, man has to first learn to manage himself. Hence Man Management is the correct beginning and purpose of any study of Management. Management is about controlling and directing through leading. If man is unable to control himself, there is very little he can contribute towards directing others or leading. Thus, ability to lead, control and direct thoughts, first, has to be both imparted and imbibed by each student. The test of ability is shown by nature of control man demonstrates over himself. Then, he can productively direct thoughts and action to achieve higher goals for all. This gives confidence in his leadership and enables others to allow giving him control.

A recap: True education, therefore, works first on man and his nature To identify the nature of man, ancient Indian philosophy has important inputs. It begins the process of search by asking the basic question: 'What is a Man (individual or human being)'? Is he the body, the mind or something else? Is not man beyond the mind also? If so, what lies beyond the human mind? Socrates gave it a name – calling it the Soul.

Using ancient Indian and Greek concepts, we identify three aspects of man: (i) Soul/ *Atma* encapsulated by the (ii) body and (iii) mind. *Atma* is that which makes the eyes see, ears hear etc (as a dead body can't do these). Hence, the conclusion: the body, mind & soul together are man. Aristotle also pointed out that the human body has five sense organs while Immanuel Kant proposed that knowledge of the outside world depends on our modes of perception.

Indian Seers ('C'ers) depend on this mode of perception or way of seeing things to achieve goals of life. They state that the mind can help differentiate a man from an animal by his control of sense organs. How? Being in touch with *Atma,* they state, transcends vagaries of the mind and man then responds to the call of his conscience. Conscience is the keeper of morality within man. Honesty in identifying Truth *Sath* (which is also his true nature or Soul, excellence in all dimensions or God) gives man self confidence. This shapes individual consciousness or *Chith* (mind) to follow dictates of his conscience or *Atma*. Such a merger of Truth with individual consciousness gives man the experience of *Ananda* or bliss. This can only emerge from righteous behaviour. Education, in ancient Indian tradition, concentrated on imparting values that generate righteous behaviour. This was the primary purpose of education. Tools and techniques useful for enabling efficiency in performing tasks were imparted later – otherwise man can efficiently harm society.

Diagram 1.2a depicts that the mind is capable of enquiry and *discrimination*: a quality not shared by animals. Hence body consciousness alone is animal quality existence. The *Atma* is the source of excellence in the body and may be equated to the experience of *Ananda* or Bliss. The body, mind and soul together are called *Sath* [Truth] plus *Chith* [Mind] plus *Ananda* [Bliss]. Constant Integrated Awareness of actualisation of excellence within oneself is Self Actualisation. This awareness is beyond attachment to anything except the Truth. It is, therefore, expressed in action as Selfless love – which is fair, just and beneficial for all – 'self less' as it is not performed with a myopic selfish motive.

Man's actions, directed by Selfless Love for all, reflect this Awareness and actualisation of his potential for excellence. Man manifests his nature through actions which reflect a mix of Soul consciousness, Body consciousness and use of the mind. The use of mind is evidenced through his enquiry or use of discrimination. A higher degree of body consciousness leads man towards behaviour identified by sub-humans. An awareness of *Atmic* (Soul) principle brings out the best 'within' man i.e. a constant integrated awareness of his potential for excellence or what ancient wisdom calls divinity.

Study of Man: Functions of Body, Mind and Soul

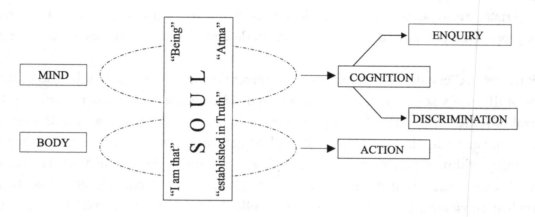

MAN = Body + Mind + Soul
Excellence in all dimensions + individual consciousness="Sath"+"Chith" lead to... "Ananda"

Diagram 1.2.a

For any execution of business or strategy, both **man** and his **mind** are involved. If these are trained to achieve excellence, the purpose of education is achieved. As education gives man an Awareness of his innate excellence, Part A of this study is titled: **The Awareness**

b. From Knowledge to Practice: Unity of Thought, Word and Deed: Porter's 'Reinforcement'. Non – attachment (criteria for *Moksha*) begins with thought.

The mind is capable of thoughts. The body acts to express them through words & deeds.

When thought, word & deed are not in unison; man's actions lack reinforcement. Therefore, they cannot achieve optimum results – both for him and society. Their unity is the first sign of simple consistency. However, nature of mind is to to waver with many thoughts. As all of them may not be beneficial, man must not attach himself to thought – and view it as an observer. Ancient Wisdom gives Awareness to reflect on the never changing. Thoughts are everchanging. When the mind is trained through spiritual practices in this (Chapter 7), then choosing the right thought for action becomes beneficial for man and society. Watching thoughts and ending them with an elevating thought is management.

Optimum activities are directed by selected thought (using *Dharma*), reinforced by words and deeds. For man, this overall strategy of optimisation is implemented using *Dharma* of choosing and creating elevating thoughts. It is helped by a technique of telling the mind "*Neti, Neti*" i.e. 'Not this, Not this'. This helps make man aware that he is not the body or the mind as both are ever changing. Man seeks the never changing which is the Soul and, thus, chooses thoughts which will direct his actions towards such Truth.

The three criteria of Simple Consistency, Reinforcement and Optimisation Effort can only be fulfilled if thought, word & deed of top management, manager & workers are in unison. Diagram 1.2b shows it. If thoughts are neutral to positive, words sound helpful to all but acts damage some, firm's activity cannot achieve balance.

"Unity of Thought, Word and Deed imply
Reinforcement for Optimisation Effort"

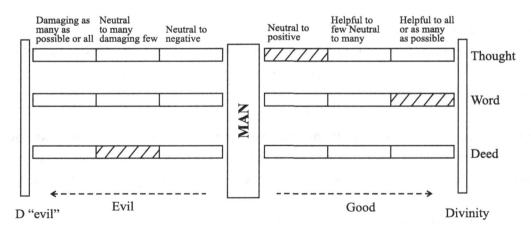

When all 3 are perfectly aligned at extremes human action is most effective
Usually, man may want to help a few, appear to be helpful to all but due to selfishness may harm a few

Diagram 1.2b

c. Three types of knowledge (Self, Work Related, Social Environment Related): Their Simple consistency and Shared value requires Reinforcement and Optimisation effort

The knowledge of Self (actualisation of excellence within man) needs to be directed in the context of the firm and social environment. Then, man's actions can be effective, balanced, efficient and productive. This requires reinforcement and optimisation effort of: – knowledge of Self with knowledge of work and knowledge of social environment. A shared value of simple consistency in thoughts words and deeds is the first step for this. Use of these three types of knowledge helps configure activities (of both man and firm) and the way they relate to each other. This occurs in the following manner:

1. Knowledge of Self: As discussed in 1.2.a & b above, until man can control himself first, he cannot control others effectively. For this man must achieve Unity of Thought, Word & Deed. This leads to the experience of Self. This Self expresses itself in the character of an individual. Ancient widom postulates that individual character requires daily practice of ethics, good company and good behaviour. Individual character should be expanded to give national character. This requires patriotism and spirit of sacrifice (of pettiness), too. These emerge from *Atmic* awareness (understanding of unity of man and nature) – which expands man's heart with concern for others. Immersed in awareness, man emerges as a humble, soft spoken, sensitive human being – incapable of harming others or the system.

2. Knowledge related to Work: This refers to skills that man requires in executing tasks given his role in society, organisation, family etc. These skills are very specific to the given task and need training. Secular education is currently fully equipped in this area. So, no elaboration is needed.

3. Knowledge about Social Environment gives the context for actions of man: Social norms, customs differ across time and place. Knowledge about them is necessary for both communication and actions to ensure proper understanding and generate social harmony.

When three types of Knowledge are used in organisations (firms) and society in context of shared values, balance emerges. The nature of shared values is excellence seeking, if they are based on Truth and Morality. More so, when there is both a simple consistency, and reinforcement in use of skills and communication for executing tasks. An optimisation effort, then, results from knowledge dissemination (or *educare*) and knowledge application. This creates balance 'within' man, in the firm and in society – simultaneously.

Requirements of simply consistent shared values in firms (reinforced with optimisation effort)**, role of top leadership, role of three types of knowledge: their interrelationship**

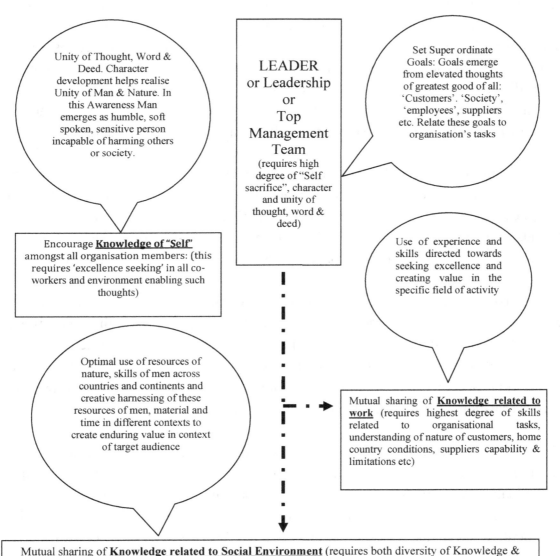

Diagram 1.3a

d. Role of sacrifice and national character (the understanding that enables sacrifice)

To give effective leadership to men, society and nations a spirit of sacrifice is necessary. How did ancient Indians understand sacrifice? Real sacrifice is the sacrifice of ignorance. First, man must understand the cause of bondage in his life. Then, severing this bondage of ignorance about the true nature of Self can be done. Sacrifice is, thus, not of wealth. Education removes ignorance and prepares man to sacrifice that which is essential to maintain social order and perform duties. Also, sacrifice includes all actions done for achieving any of these three goals: (a) leveraging the Universe for pursuit of excellence in all dimensions (Divinity) – called *Yajna* (b) to establish peace and justice in society (understood as charity or *Dana*) and (c) to control and co-ordinate the body for ethical life (called *Tapas*). The glossary gives more details of sacrifice for those interested.

Man's instincts are guided by such sacrifice to become different from an animal's. Then, he works in the spirit of his true nature – of excellence and naturally following ethics. This reinforces behaviour emerging from a simple consistency of what is taught and practiced. It leads to an optimisation effort for both man and society – simultaneously. Here, Selfless Love can help man conquer body consciousness – which is the basis of sacrifice.

Let us take an example to explain this otherwise difficult idea: A mother loves her child and is willing, if needed, to sacrifice the health of her body to further the child's welfare. The feeling of identification (or 'one-ness') with the child enables such a reaction – without any external prompting. Similar feelings, if developed, for the firm, cluster, industry, nation and world reflect an expansion of the heart and sacrifice. Leadership (in any group: firm, cluster or nation – not just family) needs similar traits.

The above understanding of sacrifice is used in the following pages. For giving leadership, apart from individual character, national character is also important. When groups of individuals in a firm show sacrifice and national character, it can achieve excellence and establish leadership. This helps build the cluster, industry and, finally, true National Competitive Advantage. The spirit of unity in a family is based on sacrifice – so, too, for a firm, cluster, society and nation. National character emerges from such a broad feeling for the nation. This phenomenon is studied in more detail in chapters 2 and 5.

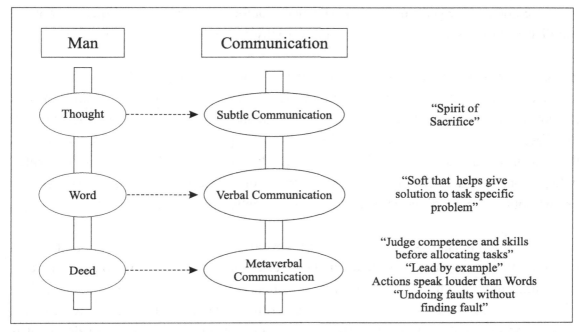

Consistent, reinforced communication: A tool for optimisation effort in firms, society
Diagram 1.3b

e. Role of Communication in Organisations & Society

To work together in a firm, society or nation, communication is needed. There are three types of communication: **a) Subtle (b) Meta verbal (c) Verbal.**

The desired expressions of Thought, Word and Deed – through each mode of communication – are shown in Diagram 1.3b. These, when executed together continuously, lead to consistent, reinforced communication. This is a tool for optimisation effort within a firm. Subtle Communication is powered by shared thoughts for a common goal and is the most powerful. Meta verbal communication uses gestures, indications and signals and demonstrates that a context and understanding is mutually shared. This is a powerful and quick method of communication. Verbal communication is used to build upon the above two. Communication should be consistent both within man and firm, cluster, suppliers, home nation etc. It is reinforced through types of communication above in an optimisation effort. This adds value to man, firm, industry, cluster, home nation and society. The ideal communication is heart to heart communication. When the sense of identification with each other is complete, the heart understands the needs of the other person (customer, co-worker, supplier or family member) subtly or meta verbally and without formality.

Allocate tasks according to skills: The use of communication in firms will only be productive if tasks have been allocated according to a proper understanding of skills of each employee. The understanding of the Self helps man understand his strengths correctly and, therefore, project the correct picture of his skills to employers. Training can only enhance these skills to make them productive. It is a difficult task to create skills that have mismatch with personality traits. When man has learnt only tools and techniques, their indiscriminate use without understanding the context hampers excellence seeking by firms.

Thus, education must make man understand himself, first. For, he who has not understood himself can not manage himself or anybody else. Hence, first, man should be able to communicate within himself to communicate about himself. When proper understanding of skill sets is there tasks can be allocated accordingly. This enables excellence in firms, cluster, industry etc. and enables balance. The area of human resource development is the foundation of creating excellence at workplaces. The ancient Indian tradition enables excellence in life and work by entrusting education with the task of developing human resources. It also gives guidelines how to interact with others and ensure balance at workplaces. Leaders should not only have a spirit of sacrifice but should lead by example. Hence they should have learnt tasks of all departments to enable them to add value and understand the problems correctly. This will enable them to undo fault without finding fault. When this is done in an atmosphere where only soft words are used, then the workforce can achieve excellence. However, correct matching of skills to tasks ensures that the soft words will be productive, sooner or later.

1.3 Ancient Wisdom (Four *Purusharthas* – The path of *Dwaita*/Dualism) **and Management Ideas** (Porter's ingredients of Strategy) **lead to an optimisation effort** through this paper

Man's purpose of life (Self Actualisation or realising the Truth about himself – Self Realisation) is achieved through four goals (called *Purusharthas*) which direct human activities. Can the same technique be extended to apply to the human activity of management? The effort of extending goals of life to management study by identifying them would optimise use of ancient wisdom for modern management – through this study.

A recap: The goals of life, or the four *Purusharthas,* as guided by ancient Indian Seers ('C'ers), are: *Dharma, Artha, Kama* and *Moksha.* These are useful only if viewed in pairs i.e. *Dharma & Artha* come together (where *Artha* is guided by *Dharma).* The second pair is *Kama & Moksha* – where desire fulfilment (*Kama*) is guided by the *Kshaya* or dissolution of *Moha* or illusion (*Moksha*). Their **simple consistency** (shown as a flow from Truth in Fig 0.30) is **reinforced by** their working together and **optimised by** working in pairs. The practice of human effort guided by these 'two' pairs is called *Dwaita.* It is considered fruitful to live in this duality or *Dwaita.* Here, attainment of goal of life helps man achieve his purpose of life and also promotes welfare of society. Then, management thought, if fitted into goals of life, too, should promote welfare of society. Management study, by identifying four *Purusharthas* fits the work of recent thinkers in management within the framework of ancient wisdom. This is attempted here through identification of 4Cs or four 'goals of management'.

The first duty of man in a firm, organisation or society is to understand and fulfil the role assigned to him. This implies that Co-operation, based on Truth and morality, is the first duty of man. This co-operation is between Thought, Word & Deed within man and also between men in organisations. This is like *Dharma.* The human body depicts co-operation among various body parts & sense organs in execution of daily tasks. "On the foundation of mutual respect, understanding, sharing through co-operation the greatest tasks can be fulfilled. The pursuit of desires, wealth and welfare of all is best achieved through co-operation which implies a healthy respect for all". **Hence the first 'C' is Co-operation.**

The attainment of wealth requires a focus on and concern for nature of tasks to be achieved and means of achieving them. **This focussed Concern is, thus, the second 'C'.** It requires a focus on excellence and a concern for society.

The desire to excel implies competing and doing the same things in a better way. The firm's ability of doing better emerges from a focussed concerns shared by all. Executing this focussed concern in a unique individual way is Competitive Response. This is inspired by the actualisation of excellence. **The third 'C' is, therefore, Competitive Response.**

Finally, competitive response should impact society positively. The spirit of excelling should not harm others, natural resources or long term interest of man or mankind. Thus, nature of competitive response has to be compatible with needs of society, man and nature. The advantage offered by such a compatible response is a desired goal of human effort. **The 4th 'C' is, therefore, Compatibility Advantage.** Current management theory, when studied in this format, merges it with ancient wisdom. To demonstrate what is being said above we ask a simple question:

Does this Paper fulfil criteria of ancient wisdom and modern management?

• This Paper's approach illustrates the idea of: (a) co-operation amongst ancient and modern thought (b) with a focussed concern for developing a common understanding that creates value in a better way (c) the purpose is to help man and society realise goals in a sustainable and beneficial way.

• It seeks to show how (a) **simple consistency through 'unity of thought word and deed'** and (b) its **reinforcement through individual and social effort** (c) **create an optimisation effort.** This enables translating knowledge into value addition – for man and society. It also addresses different contexts of worldly and spiritual achievement and finds a commonality. This is possible as they relate to man, his mind and its achievements.

• It fills the gap between spiritual and secular education. Each is incomplete without the other: "Spiritual education should be part and parcel of all types and levels of education. Spiritual and secular educations are like two halves in the seeds of pulses..." The germination that occurs as a sprout (between the two) optimally uses effort of both halves. This can be understood as an optimisation effort by each half.

Thus, management ideas are optimised with ancient wisdom through this paper's effort.

1.4 Study of Man: Ancient Indian Wisdom, Management Ideas & *Adwaita/* non–dualism – knowledge translates into wisdom by conquering six inner enemies

The study of man in ancient Indian tradition begins by identifying six inner enemies which hide his true nature. These are: **greed, anger, desire, false attachment, pride and envy.** They act like a veil of illusion or *Maya* and hamper man's ability to see or 'C' the truth about himself. Just as a beautiful design of a necklace diverts the sight from the material it is made of – so, too, a focus on the diversity of the material world diverts the human mind from the innate unity or excellence that binds it. The six inner enemies rob man from his wealth of peace and joy. Only man's action or *Karma* can translate knowledge about this into wisdom about how to act in society.

Indian spiritual tradition realises the **differences in 'inner nature' of men**. Three paths help conquer inner enemies as per innate nature: *Bhakti* (Devotion), *Jnana* (Wisdom) and *Karma* (Action). Though these paths are different, the goal is same. This is detailed below:

Theory of *Karma*: Theory of *Karma* is a restatement of the dictum of the Bible: 'as you sow, so you reap'. As *Karma* (work) is motion, it can also be explained by Newton's third law: 'every action has an opposite and equal reaction'. It simply states that whatever you do the same will happen to you sooner or later. Hurting others will rebound in a equal and opposite way – it will hurt you in future! If, on the other hand, you help somebody, it shall rebound and you will be helped in a similar manner in the future. This theory is a mirror image of the 'Great Truths' or *Mahavakyas* (that emerged out of contemplation of Spiritual Truths) or *Advaita Vedantic* truths or *Jnana Yoga*. All of these lead man to the understanding of Truth. The awareness of impact of results of actions on man's future makes them conducive to others and society at large. Selfishness that harms others is, then, avoided. When this thinking guides daily activities, it transforms man. He can evolve to higher order of needs using an understanding of righteous conduct.

Theory of *Karma* guides man to watch his thoughts, words & deeds. For, they determine the future that awaits him. Deeds and words will follow thoughts – hence watching thoughts can be very useful. Each individual has a different mix of proportions of innate nature. Depending on the stronger inner urge of man (for *Karma, Bhakti* or *Jnana*) the thoughts maybe managed to lead to better words & deeds. The method is shown in Diagram 1.4.

**Education begins with Realising the Truth through "Managing" –
'thoughts', 'words' and 'deeds'.**

FIRST WATCH...   THE 'MANAGE'

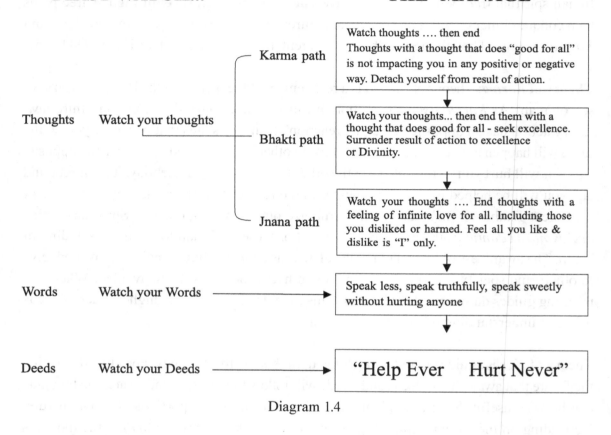

| | | Karma path | Watch thoughts .... then end Thoughts with a thought that does "good for all" is not impacting you in any positive or negative way. Detach yourself from result of action. |

Thoughts   Watch your thoughts

Bhakti path — Watch your thoughts... then end them with a thought that does good for all - seek excellence. Surrender result of action to excellence or Divinity.

Jnana path — Watch your thoughts .... End thoughts with a feeling of infinite love for all. Including those you disliked or harmed. Feel all you like & dislike is "I" only.

Words   Watch your Words → Speak less, speak truthfully, speak sweetly without hurting anyone

Deeds   Watch your Deeds → "Help Ever   Hurt Never"

Diagram 1.4

How to manage thoughts? The Indian text of *Bhagvad Gita* gives the classical route: systematic practice (*abhyasa*), relentless enquiry (*vichara*) and detachment (*vairagya*). It gives a shorter route also. Thoughts (esp. in this age) come rushing as an overwhelming flood mixed with six inner enemies. They are a continuous process. To slow this process the Seers also (out of their practical experience) have recommended *namasmarna* (nonstop mental repetition of any name or form which is associated with perfection). This mental visualisation of excellence slows the mind. Withdrawal of the mind leads to wisdom. So, the thoughtless state between two consecutive thoughts is defined as spiritual wisdom. However, if senses act as if 'I am the body' (selfishness), this name repitition gives ability to achieve wordly not spiritual tasks. Case studies in this tradition of *Ravan, Bhamasura* and

Kamsa illustrate this. There is another way which merges good physical health with mind management. Observing the inhaling and exhaling of breath is a practice recommended in this tradition. This helps slow down the working of the mind – leading to its management and mastery. The last stage, when man is the master of his mind, is known as 'master mind'. So, **firstly, recognise the distance between man and his mind**. Secondly, observe it. Thirdly, indulge in either of above or Chapter 7's practices. The management of mind is the beginning of journey of education. Without this realisation, education will result in a crisis – moral, spiritual, social and personal. This will lead to recession, chaos, crime and disorder.

Theory of *Karma* is a restatement of the *Advaita Vedantic* truth or *Mahavakyas* (Great Realisations) of *Aham Brahmasmi & Tat Twam Asi*. It explains their practical application to one who is seeing the world as Duality.

Theory of *Karma* simply states in non dualistic language – "if you hit yourself, you will get hurt. What you think is another person is only you! So, hitting others will cause pain to you. Therefore, do not hit yourself!" The ancient Indian text of *Upanishads* translates this idea from non dualism for students to understand. Its explanation is as follows: The Soul pervades the universe. It is indivisible and the same for all – signifying the underlying unity behind the apparent diversity. The same Sun gets reflected in many pots. As all is "I" – any thoughts, words & deed that hurt someone is hurting "I" only. This is the realisation after constant dwelling on the Theory of *Karma* – which leads to *Dharma* or righteous conduct. This is the true conduct for man – for it recognises his inner nature.

Therefore, when man cannot comprehend his infinite nature, Theory of *Karma* holds a mirror before him. The mirror expands the feeling of space & reflects back all. Man stops hurting others – for that will hurt him ultimately. The only difference is that a non dualist will feel pain immediately. The dualistic will fear pain in future. Both serve the same purpose. Both guide man towards righteous conduct: to help, not hurt others.

Theory of Karma helps move Realisation slowly from 'Dwaita/ Dualism' to 'Adwaita/ Non-dualism'

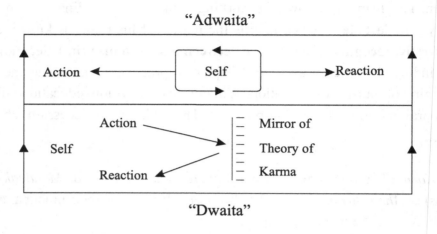

Diagram 1.5

In both *Adwaita* (non– dualism) & *Dwaita* (dualism), Self receives impact of actions on others. Theory of *Karma's* practice leads man to same goal as *Adwaitha*. Thus, progress from *Dwaita* to *Adwaita* philosophy occurs naturally by following *Dharma*. When such a theory guides actions, it leads to righteous conduct by man in society – creating balance.

The Highest stage of Selfless Love is to see all as One Self: i.e. Love everything as oneself. This is the stage of *Aham Brahmasmi*. The final Truth is that 'I am the Soul' – present everywhere. When man sees two – world and me – instead of the unity of Self with world, it is duality. The highest stage is the *Tat Twam Asi* ('I am That' which is Truth) Realisation. Even if this realisation is not accepted, the conduct it leads to creates harmony and balance.

The Theory of *Karma*, thus, is very useful for society and for those who experience the dualistic nature of the world. Its – "Reflection, Reaction, Resound" of 'Thought, Word and Deed'– principle educates man. For, it postulates that what you do to others will happen to you. Then, thoughts that harm others will be reflected back, harsh or angry words will resound and actions that hurt others will lead to reaction on oneself. This realisation guides man to act in a manner that does not hurt others. Then he is in balance. When each man is in balance within, society will be in dynamic balance. The state of Absolute balance is

Aham Brahmasmi. Here, society is experienced as part of man – This is *Moksha* or a state of non – dualism and non – attachment. It emerges from equal Selfless Love for all.

Beyond *Dwaitha* (Duality) and Theory of *Karma*
(Reaction, Reflection, Resound) lies *Adwaitha* (non– dualism)

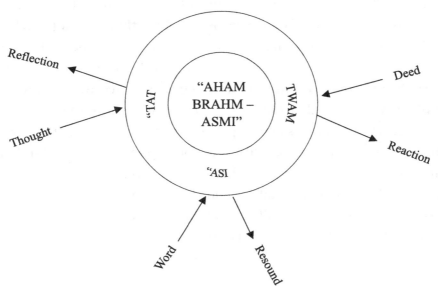

Diagram 1.6

The other path is *Bhakti* – which is of nine types – the highest quality that it generates in Man is of Surrender (Islam, too, means Surrender). When total Surrender (to the visualisation of excellence in all dimensions) takes place there is no room left for anger, greed, envy, pride etc as they, too, are surrendered. Here the ideal of "*Esha vaasyam Idam Sarvam*" makes one see the object of devotion ('Him' in Diagram 1.7 – which demonstrates approach on four inner enemies, interpretation for other two will be similar) "here" "there" and "everywhere" (All). Thus, everybody and everything is finally loved as a picture of the object of devotion. Society can not, then, be harmed as it is now visualised as filled with excellence. Chapter 7 mentions about how a psychotherapist used this to make hijackers free their passenger victims. The devotee is filled with Selfless Love for excellence. The '*Tat Twam Asi*' *Mahavakya*, then, helps in the next step of realisation that 'Thou art That'. This state is no different from experience or *Jnana* – the ability to see all (complete identification with customer also) as projection of Self. In Chapter 6, section **6.11** will show how this vision/ ability to 'C' benefits man and society. **For business of life, any action dedicated to excellence in all dimensions is *Bhakti*.** Thus, Spiritual and Secular education merged as *Bhakti* merges into *Jnana* or Awareness and *Bhakti* gives *Jnana* automatically.

For those living everyday life, the path of *Karma* is the easiest. The essential ingredient of the path is *Karma-Phala-Tyaaga* or renunciation of fruit of action. Therefore, simply put: **All actions are to be guided only by what is the right thing to do (or *Dharma*) with no concern for reward.** When man seeks highest good of customer without attachment to fruit of action, then devotion to work adds value to both man and society. If this is sincerely done then **six inner enemies of man – greed, anger, desire, and attachment naturally fall away**. Finally, all actions are guided by love for truth or love for *Dharma*. This Love manifests from thoughts into output of man as righteous conduct. Love by nature is sacrificing and selfless. Therefore, selfless action becomes *Dharma*. Similarly:

Self Actualisation/Selfless Love for all + Words = Truth (*Satya*)

Self Actualisation/Selfless Love for all + Action = Righteousness (*Dharma*)

Self Actualisation/Selfless Love for all + Thinking = Peace (*Shanti*)

Self Actualisation/Selfless Love for all + Discrimination = Non-Violence (*Ahimsa*)

All spiritual paths lead to same end result
(Transformation of man recognises Individuality, first. 3 paths exist. Education is according to inner nature)

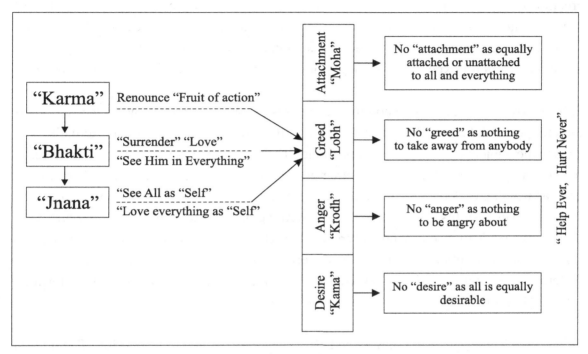

Diagram 1.7

Jnana: It is identified with **realisation of wisdom**. It is elaborated in the *Mahavakya* (eternal truth) – "*Ekoham Bahushyam*" the same "One" being reflected as "many". This means the Sun is One but its reflection in many pots is seen as many. The unity underlying the original and image is understood and realised thorough education – as all are images of the same Sun. This, however, does not change the nature of the Sun. Such an understanding makes man realise the all pervasiveness of Self. Wisdom realisation occurs as all paths merge ultimately. The search in this path remains dry unless it is filled with Love i.e. when the whole creation is loved as oneself, the goal is realised. Therefore, just as one loves oneself, everything is to be loved with the same intensity – then, all greed, anger, desire, attachment, dissolves. For, there is nothing but "I" to desire or get attached to. It is pointless being angry at oneself or greedy to snatch something from oneself.

The core of wisdom (*Jnana*), as stated earlier, is Selfless Love. This implies that love experienced for oneself is same as experienced for others. Without Love there is no *Jnana*, there is no Truth, Peace, *Dharma* (righteous conduct) or *Ahimsa* (non violence). Loving creation with same intensity as one loves oneself is the purpose of work and essence of Man Management. Finally: *Dwaitha*, *Vishisht Adwaita* and *Adwaita* are not distinct but are stages of mental transformation. Their understanding occurs slowly: like fruit ripened by the sun and soil (of experience) through intermediate stages of raw, tender and ripe fruit.

Selfless love emerges from 'Thoughts' expresses as 'Words' and changes 'Deeds'. This is the end point of *Karma, Bhakti* and *Jnana* paths. All of them lead to Self Actualisation. This is the subject of Chapter 6. Thus, though paths may be different, the goal is same. In the end, all paths dissolve into each other and meet at the same destination. When work is done as worship or dedicated to seeking excellence, it leads to 'Awareness' and *Jnana*. This wisdom gives insights or makes Truth as *Satyam* emerge within man. Walking on any of these paths leads to discovering Nature of Man. One of these three paths appeals to man's inner nature. Education recognises the difference in inner nature of men. It recommends different routes for each. However, education 'Actualises' this inner nature, transforming it to Selfless Love.

To sum up: a Manager truly understands Management as knowing Mankind. The highest way of viewing Mankind is with eyes of Selfless Love – which is the core of Shared Values.

1.5 Practice of 'Awareness' needs Total understanding & 'people-related skill'

Only when man understands himself (Soul) can he completely understand others and other disciplines properly. This requires understanding of *Dwaita*, *Adwaita* and his own culture. It requires Awareness about the inner and outer world. Awareness includes understanding the fact that everything, starting from every human body part, operates within Limits.

Awareness implies a total understanding and communication of the same: The intellect and mind, for example, are inter-connected and communicate with every part of the body. This is based on perfect understanding of requirements of each part at all times. This is an example for business. Understanding is through heart to heart communication.

Developing understanding develops people related skills: Man management begins with Awareness of Self, understanding of limits and real communication. This, and selfless love, develops people related skills of managing men. A task orientation is a necessary condition of Selfless Love. Man management, therefore, is not about sitting and contemplating over the nature of the Soul. It requires working within limits including:

• moving around the workplace ('Managing by Walking Around') & understanding every task performed in an organisation fully.

• It requires understanding of conditions of inputs, raw materials and workers as also market conditions.

• It requires understanding of reasons of success of competition & present productivity levels of the firm.

Then, bookish Knowledge is converted to practical Knowledge. This practical Knowledge has to then be channelised by:

• understanding nature of home nation, culture and realities of conditions prevalent. Thus knowledge is converted to skill. This leads to balance. Just as cycling, walking or even speaking requires balance. Similar balance in business leads to progress.

Education in general (and management education in particular) should produce socially responsible citizens. Such education is best imparted within the cultural framework of the student. This enables him to relate to it. Ancient wisdom encompasses many cultures, therefore, a need for understanding and integrating its values in a study that manages life.

Among ancient India's four *Purusharthas, Dharma* refers to the entity that bears and sustains creation. This concept is easily stated but not so easily understood. *Dharma* is the unique quality of every object. Fire burns and gives light, which, when lost, changes the nature of object itself. Sugar, for example, would be like sand without sweetness. These qualities of objects constitute its *Dharma*. What is *Dharma* of Man? Indian culture postulates that Man has two essential qualities: Truth and Morality. These are considered to be the eyes of society through which we can 'C'. Hence, we postulate a 4 C approach to management. The two inner eyes are co-operation and compatibility. The two outer eyes are focussed concern and competitive response. There is a natural understanding and trust between men due to these qualities. This trust makes co-operation a natural quality. A concern for fellow human beings and focus on how to help them, are then, a natural urge.

When natural trust between men occurs at work with customers, management, workers, suppliers etc any task can be accomplished. Then, the next set of questions becomes important:

- "what is the impact on society of products produced"
- "what is the utility of the output"
- "is it useful to society"?

Such concerns make the output of firms compatible with needs of society.

However, a need to excel and express Individuality gives the best results. Healthy competition in serving customers – by each in its own individual way – helps all. The basis, however, must be ethical business values. Competition is expressed in terms of quality, price and durability of product. Quality is not sacrificed in name of competition – as it is the true mark of Individuality of men and firms.

When natural trust between firm and customers is formed, it results in productive long term business equilibrium. This is referred to as dynamic equilibrium earlier. The beginning, however, is when each manager learns how to manage himself and his mind. Only then managing a firm or others will lead to balance. By helping manage the mind, Educare prepares a student for life. This involves sensitising the student with his inner nature. This inner nature is not based on instinct but on a philosophy of life. The word philosophy is itself derived from Roman language. Phils means love, Sophos means Divinity and their combination Philosophy means Divine Love. Divinity is the realisation of perfection within man. This can be achieved through practice of selfless love for all. This natural urge of love of man for his 'own' self is expanded by Educare makes him feel that all are his own. It enables man to experience the excellence within him, and actualise his potential.

Porter's 3 ingredients of Strategy: simple consistency, reinforcement and Optimisation effort, therefore, **relate first to man, then to organisations**. We have seen above how values merge into strategy. **Thus, strategy is effective when it emerges from values.** The **simple consistency** of thoughts, their **reinforcement** with words and deeds are expressed as an **Optimisation effort** in the 4C approach. Selfless Love is the basis of **co-operation** with a **focussed concern** to achieve a **competitive response** with a **compatibility advantage**.

Practice of Awareness: an example from daily life of Truth, Righteous Conduct

Education should transform thoughts and intentions before unity of thought, word and deed. Life gives many opportunities to test the level of transformation and improve upon it.

Unity of thought, word and deed is the 'Strategy of Life' for man in ancient Indian tradition. Man's actions in society are a sub set of his actions in life. To prevent conflict within man and, therefore, in society the idea of Strategy of Life and Strategy at work place must be same. Only then balance, not conflict, will prevail within man and society.

Practical problems faced by man in daily life: an example

Given below is an example of how practice of Awareness seems difficult to many. This example will try to prove how unity of thought, word and deed is not possible in daily life. Thus, some may like to conclude that the 'Ideal' should be reserved for textbooks. However, later, a correct understanding of texts is given to show one way of practicing Awareness in the same situation. Of course, using individuality, each person may find a different way of achieving the same objective – depending on his inner nature and level of practice. The idea is to demonstrate that it is possible to transform and elevate thoughts to practice Awareness. Also, the idea is to demonstrate that the purpose of education is not just to prevent recession, crime, social conflict etc. It is to bring out the best 'within' man in service of himself and others (self actualisation).

What training of mind enables this? What ideas naturally transform behaviour of man enabling balance and true culture or refinement? Tranformation does not apply to each idea, separately – but is a gestalt. *Dharma* (righteous conduct) enables rules of conduct to transform thoughts.

When we practically live in society, many people would experience that it is difficult to have unity of thought and word. Deeds will come later. Let us take the example of a person who loves his sleep and has an unexpected visitor in the morning when he is still sleepy. Even though he feels irritated he greets the visitor with 'I am happy to see you'. Is this not a demonstration of lack of unity of thought and word? Many such instances abound in our daily routine. If such social courtesies are not followed there is bound to be lack of harmony in society. Is this formal approach not making our life artificial and demonstrating lack of harmony? Can we not conclude that to remain a civilised and well mannered society we have to encourage indulging in lack of unity of thought, word and deed? For, if all start stating truth as they see it this will lead to relationships at home, work and in society falling apart faster than we can imagine...

Ancient Indian way:

A backgound to the explanation first: A commitment to inner transformation is necessary for practice of Awareness. Thoughts give us our imagination; they also give us our ideals and expand upon the yearning in our aspirations. These leave an indelible impression on the mind and find expression as little deeds. When these deeds are repeated they become habits. These habits shape man's intelligence and mould his outlook to life. The achievements of scientists, inventors etc. demonstrate the high level of skill in their limited sphere of activity. They are mere expressions of their greatness. However, without personal character, these are meaningless for they can be misused to harm society (use of the atom bomb, for example). Society values goodness of a human being more than greatness. Therefore, education concentrates on giving an imprint about the attributes of a flawless character in the impressionable human mind during early years. The qualities that constitute flawless character are Love, forbearance, patience, steadfastness and charity. Character is like the fragrance of the flower (of high level of skills in a particular field) that blooms. The fragrance of character gives value and worth to human life.

What is the training of ancient Indian tradition? One of the concluding paragraphs (before this sub section) in Chapter 1 states: "The beginning, however, is when each manager learns how to manage himself and his mind. Only then managing a firm or others will lead to balance. By helping manage the mind, Educare prepares a student for life. This involves sensitising the student with his inner nature. This inner nature is not based on instinct but on a philosophy of life..."

Two ideas emerge from the above quotation. The first is that a manager has to learn how to manage his mind. The second is that education should transform the inner nature of man so that it is not based on instinct (as in animal instinct) but on a philosophy of life. These ideas belong to the area of practice, not theory. So, two questions should arise 'within' man after such a feeling of irritation. First, man should explore and search for an answer to the question **'why did this feeling of anger or irritation arise**?' Next, he should be ready to make an attempt so that it should not arise the next time – or intensity of the feeling should diminish overtime. The search for practices that enable this is education.

(a) Managing the mind

The practice of managing the mind in daily life is assisted by spiritual practices given in Chapter 7. It is also enabled by an understanding of *Dharma* or righteous conduct and other ideas of this tradition. The first practice is Self Observation. So, to transform his reactions man has to observe himself. Only if he has the intention to change is it worthwhile to read further. Such transformation is easiest in the formative years of childhood – therefore, children were sent to a hermitage to live with a *Guru*. The teachers taught by demonstration. How to practice without such a teacher? When the feeling of irritation or anger arises, putting it in words gives man the ownership of the feeling. This adds fuel to the fire. If, however, the feeling is observed and man distances himself from the thought without giving it words, the mind will slowly get diverted. In case of anger, this tradition advises that drinking a glass of water and walking up and down help divert the mind. Managing the mind by a reminder that 'I am a human, not a dog' helps control anger. So, managing the mind is the second practice necessary for man.

(b) The philosophy that transforms the inner nature of man: This philosophy cannot be summarised in a set of points. Its gestalt is greater than any words or expressions. Its great teachers prefer silence lest impurity of words create more problems than they solve. Words are by their nature limited and cannot capture selflessness which, by its nature, is infinite and an expression of divine. Words can be misinterpreted by limited understanding of the audience. This, according to some, is the problem with interpretation of spiritual texts, too. So, man relies on *Dharma* for a solution. To help us understand some possible solutions for avoiding negative human reactions, some guidelines of *Dharma* are shared below:

1. *Satyam bruyaat, priyam bruyaat* (Speak the truth, speak it sweetly – the complete *sloka* strongly urges – do not speak that truth that is not sweet). Help Ever Hurt Never is the first dictum of this tradition. This should be implemented in the speech of man, first.

2. Speak only if it improves upon silence by its contribution to others or society's welfare. The limits to speech are tested by its utility to society. Unnecessary gossip, slander and criticism that will hurt others are avoided. Constructive criticism is given with *Yukti* – which is a way of adapting that is pleasant and helps in managing things. This comes from 'within' man when he 'sees good, is good and does good' only.

3. Valedictory teaching of the Upanishads: '... *Matri devo bhava, pitri devo bhava, Acharya devo bhava, Atithi devo bhava...* (Treat Mother, father, preceptor and guest as God). This *sloka* or verse helps man visualise *Dharma* or righteous duty or faultless deeds. These words urge man to perform such good deeds always.

4. It is difficult to give all teachings in one place. The life of the *Guru* demonstrated the gestalt of the application of teachings in daily behaviour. This is the reason why society revered them – for they moulded the future. In seeking excellence 'within' themselves they contributed the maximum possible to society – by securing its future. Thus, they demonstrated the convergence of the highest good of man and society.

5. The primary reason for not speaking the truth in a way that can anger others is that doing so is indulging in violence through speech. From the four shared values the fifth emerges naturally – non-violence. Hence, the importance of sweet words.

Practical tips of ancient Indian tradition: How to purify intention

The four *Purusharthas* are both the goals of human behavior and the limits for man. Their repeated practice leads to purity of intention overtime. The practice of restraining behavior to righteous conduct helps purify thoughts and intentions of man overtime. Without such restraint immediate action for gratification or rewards tempts man towards the wrong path. The stimulus of such a reward will lead to further responses which are not righteous. Then, prosperity – not based on righteousness – will show its side effects. Peace, happiness and joy will not emerge in man or society. Porter, too, talks of decay as the last stage of development of society. This stage is avoided by righteous restraint in daily behaviour.

The capacity to overcome temptation of the easier path (which may give immediate rewards) is increased with repetitive behavior. This results in purity of intention, overtime. The mind (which is referred to as a mad monkey – jumping from one branch of thought to another all the time) is by its nature ever in motion. If the mind is calmed to a standstill through spiritual practices, man becomes the master of the mind. In ancient tradition, the *Guru*, initially, gave all types of physical tasks to students to help purify their mind. It is through action that he judged the purity of their mind and intention. Only after they passed the test was initiation into the Supreme Knowledge (Chapter 1) imparted. How can a simple beginning be made, today, in the direction of purifying the mind? Two initial steps are shared:

• Watch your thoughts as if they are passing clouds. Do not get involved in them. Detachment should start from thoughts esp. those that discrimination guides us are not as per *Dharma*. Do not take ownership of them by putting them in words. Watch them go away and they will not leave a mark on the sky of the mind. The clear sky of purity of mind will remain. Do not follow the mind (which is a mad monkey).

• Manage the thoughts using Discrimination. This implies being Aware of a power that is above thoughts which guides man. This is the use of intellect or discrimination. It results from education. Then, man is not a helpless victim of his thoughts – but begins the process of having mastery over the mind.

It is important to remember that this process is a continuous one. Ancient Indian wisdom gives many case studies of *Ravana* etc. who after many spiritual practices confronted excellence in all dimensions (or Divinity). This was the test of purity of intention. The boon asked for was 'to become great'. This was made possible – but ultimately it led to decline – for, goodness is greater than being great. That is why Jesus, Buddha and Vivekananda or Shankracharya are remembered and followed more than Alexander the Great (who is confined to history books – and does not find a place in the heart of millions). Thus, life gives repeated tests to test the purity of intention of man. In this tradition, difficulties are welcomed as tests of the absorption of ideals. When difficulties are overcome, without compromise on the ideal, it increases man's capacity to contribute to the welfare of society. Such thought leaders show the way for thousands of years – even though some give up their life taking upon themselves the ills of society.

So, what can man's reaction be to the problem described? Some alternatives:
If irritation is strong at being disturbed by a visitor, it is best not to use the expression 'I am happy to see you' when receiving him. It is better to just say 'Welcome, Welcome, Welcome!' This expression is following the *Dharma* of treating the guest as God. Of course, it is good to visualise the guest as God. If there is success in such a visualisation, overtime, then truthfully the expression 'I am so happy to see you' can be used. Thus

choice of words is important for speaking the truth. The mind, if in control, can be directed towards happiness on receiving the visitor. Now, for the next natural question: 'Does this imply that God has come to see me – so I cannot refuse what He asks for?' This is where discrimination guides us using 'study of limits'. The Upanishads state that the same Sun is reflected in a thousand vessels. This does not mean that jumping into these vessels will make you catch the Sun. The reflection of Divinity is to be seen in each individual – even when he is harming you. However, actions of man are to be 'limited' by the physical reality and *Dharma* that is applicable according to his position and circumstance. Also, man should be guided by *Bhava Adwaitha* NOT *Karma Adwaitha*. Of course, it is impossible to oblige all who approach you. Ancient wisdom, therefore, guides 'speak obligingly, even if you cannot oblige'. In this manner man's actions should create harmony and balance within him and in society.

Righteous conduct helps Truth emerge from 'within' man, transforms heart

The above example shows that ancient wisdom focuses primarily on inner transformation of man. Its conception of *Dharma* (Righteous Conduct) and practices are designed to create simultaneous harmony in man and society. *Dharma* (Righteous Conduct) uplifts and refines thoughts of man for benefit of all. Ancient Indian education uses it to make the best 'within' man come out – in service of self and society (self actualisation). This best 'within' man is the Truth about his inner nature. This Truth 'inside' enables him to see Truth in the outside world, beneficial for him self and society. Thus, education makes Truth emerge from 'within', by transforming man's heart and thought, word and deed, leading to balance.

Chapter 1 makes Truth about correct Strategy emerge from 'within' man;
Chapters 2 to 5 give Strategy that creates balance through all activities of man.

PART B

Values add value to a firm's output by using goals of life

EDUCATION MAKES MAN'S ACTIONS CREATE BALANCE IN SOCIETY

Step 1. Knowing this everything else can be known:
Man is capable of excellence in all dimensions – simultaneously. Part A and spiritual practices of Chapter 7 give an 'experience' of values 'within' man. Selfless Love, not selfishness, then, is the motive for action.

Step 2. Applying ideas and values to daily life and work:
With the above 'experience' man follows values through four goals of life and learns skills of a trade or profession. Excellence, in this skill or its management, is sought with detachment from fruit of action.

Step 3. Truth should emerge from 'within' man if helping society by applying skills is undertaken – with detachment from result of action:

How to ensure that *Satyam,* Truth, guides actions of man? After doing detached analysis with application of skill to the best of ability, Truth should arise from 'within'. As each situation is unique, this Truth applies values and guides man towards right action. An example of this is given at the end of this book – as a published prediction of the global economic recession in October, 2007. The Truth of the then bull market emerged in a different way in this prediction.

In praise of the Purusharthas:

Man has a body, a mind and the Soul.

Then there is the heart.

Breath gives life or Prana *to the body.*
Management of breath can help cool the mind, even direct it.
But, until the heart has a pure thought, what will be the result?

Thoughts are the breath of the Soul principle. They can bring it to life.
Thoughts get managed effortlessly when human effort is guided by excellence.
This is the reason for designing the four Purusharthas.
They can make techniques like observing the breath unnecessary.

When work is indulged in endlessly with a desire for excellence in the heart
it elevates thoughts – till the pleasure of working is more satisfying than results.
This is ensured when righteous conduct and detachment restrict desire and work.

When the focus shifts from results to seeking excellence
work transforms into worship.

Such worship transforms the heart slowly and leads to wisdom.
Karma *transforms to* Bhakti *and* Bhakti *to* Jnana

Wisdom emerges only when the heart is transformed fully.

STRATEGY OF FIRM EMERGES FROM VALUES

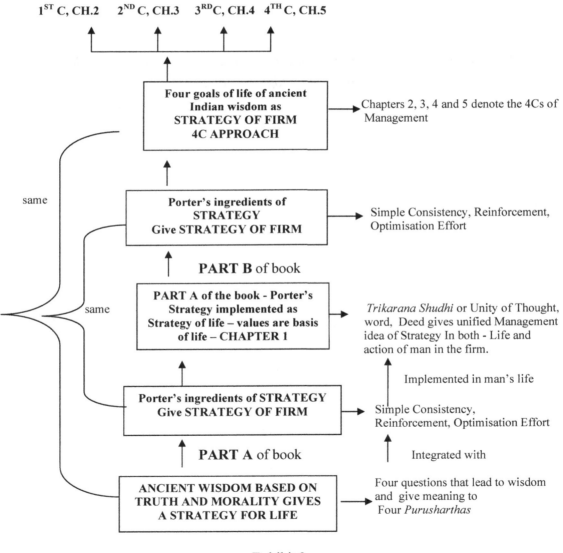

1ST C, CH.2   2ND C, CH.3   3RDC, CH.4   4TH C, CH.5

Four goals of life of ancient Indian wisdom as STRATEGY OF FIRM 4C APPROACH

Chapters 2, 3, 4 and 5 denote the 4Cs of Management

same

Porter's ingredients of STRATEGY Give STRATEGY OF FIRM

Simple Consistency, Reinforcement, Optimisation Effort

PART B of book

PART A of the book - Porter's Strategy implemented as Strategy of life – values are basis of life – CHAPTER 1

same

Trikarana Shudhi or Unity of Thought, word, Deed gives unified Management idea of Strategy In both - Life and action of man in the firm.

Implemented in man's life

Porter's ingredients of STRATEGY Give STRATEGY OF FIRM

Simple Consistency, Reinforcement, Optimisation Effort

PART A of book

Integrated with

ANCIENT WISDOM BASED ON TRUTH AND MORALITY GIVES A STRATEGY FOR LIFE

Four questions that lead to wisdom and give meaning to Four *Purusharthas*

Exhibit 3

Part A and Part B are like two sides of the same coin: they create balance only if they come together, as a pair.

PART B

Management Ideas – Strategy of firm emerges from values Ethics set 'Limits' through Goals of Life (4C Approach to Management)

• Management education trains man for performing a role in society. This role should be within Limits of ethics in both firm and society. These limits are set by conscience of man. Awakening this conscience is the task of Awareness, dealt in Part A earlier. Practices that awaken consciousness are the Best Management Practices. Speaking the Truth and following Morality are the first of these best practices. They translate into goals of life.

• Ancient Indian Tradition defines four *Purusharthas* as goals of human behaviour. These shape values of man in society. They restrain man's choices through practice of morality. They, thus, define the Study of Limits for man.

• Part B of this Paper deals with their interpretation or application. This is within the context of ideas of present management thought and practice.

• The essence of Michael Porter's idea is used here. His ideas on Competitive Advantage of Nations deal with the world which is subject to change – i.e. knowing truth as *Nijam*. As the nature of this truth is to change – hence some aspects of these theories may not remain true across time. If the *Satyam* or the bigger Truth hidden in them is identified and used – the education resulting from this can be a permanent asset – across time – for mankind.

• The interplay of ancient Indian ideas with academic concepts of management, today, is rechristened here as: The 4C's of Management.

• The Awareness of Part A co-operates with action in Part B. Best Practice in Management, then, emerges. The sum of these promotes balance within man and in society. This balance can prevent recession and other social problems.

The Awareness man has about his potential for excellence and its realisation is dealt in Chapter 1. Attaining this excellence within enables man to contribute it to society. It is also important for him to develop an understanding of Limits. Both are interrelated and form the basis of the other. Awareness implies excellence by knowing every small thing properly. More importantly, 'Total understanding' is Awareness where the whole is greater than the sum of parts (Gestalt). The study of Management begins with a study of man. For, one who has not understood himself is incapable of understanding anything else. Controlling, directing or managing the same comes later. This is the basic hypothesis here.

What is 'Study of Limits'?

A study of nature of mind and Soul is needed along with an understanding of the body. The physical body personifies a study of Limits. A human body demonstrates importance of co-operation. Similarly, observing its functions should generate an Awareness of Limits. The body's ability to tolerate heat, cold, to eat, drink or sleep all operate within a 'limit' – just a horse needs reins and a car brakes. Every part of the body, too, operates within limits. A body is endangered when limits are crossed. Similarly, the body of management practice is also endangered when limits are crossed. As the human body works within limits – like a Limited Company, so should men working within a firm. Ethics and social norms set limits outside, conscience sets them inside.

The succeeding chapters explore how Awareness of potential and understanding of Limits help man, firms and society attain balance. The ancient Indian "C"rs or Seers 'limited' the goals of life to four *Purusharthas*. As practice of management fulfils goals of life, its study is aligned with their study. This enables experience of synergy that exists between life and practice of management. The four *Purusharthas* or goals (four ways of 'C'ing) are identified as:
Co-operation (though *Dharma* is much more than co-operation, it is the first step for man in society). Even factors of production must co-operate to enable a business to be active.
Focussed 'Concern' for others will lead to prosperity with morality – this includes material prosperity. The use of morality for material prosperity makes a civilisation last.
Competitive Response, ('first deserve then desire'. Fulfilling this dictum makes one compete only with oneself). This ensures continuous improvement and excellence.
Compatibility Advantage (Duty detached from desire leads to a compatible response).

The above understanding starts the study of 'goals of life' (*Dharma, Artha, Kama, Moksha)* for management practice.

The Study of Limits is not restricted to understanding four goals. More important is their interdependence and pairing for balance. For example, *Artha* which includes business or management is limited or controlled by *Dharma* or righteousness and *Kama* or desire fulfilment should be directed to *Moksha* or *moha – kshaya* i.e. vanquishing attachment.

To conduct business, a lot of information is needed. This is available in books also. **However, from all such information a transformation must result**. The purpose of studying current management ideas with four *Purusharthas* is to transform the way man analyses information. This should transform the heart of man and conduct of firms, clusters, industry etc. Long term valued addition comes through a Competitive response devised through heart to heart co-operation within the firm. Similarly a focussed concern for the customer gives value in new ways for current or emerging needs. A focussed concern for the environment and society occurs simultaneously. It generates compatibility between output of firm and long term needs of society. Compatibility between man and nature occurs, then.

Chapter 2

The 4*C* Approach to Management
(Management ideas – Strategy of firm emerges from Values)

Co-operation: The recognition of interdependence
First 'C' of Strategy: (First way to 'See' Strategy: through the eyes of Truth, Morality)

Man performs duties or *Dharma* using his physical body. What enables it to perform *Dharma*? Does the body of society, too, depend on the same factor? Man's body performs tasks only if all parts co-operate. Society, too, will collapse without co-operation. If one limb of man or society is incapacitated, ability to achieve excellence diminishes. Interdependence enables excellence.

• Man's body co-operates with his inner nature, too. This inner nature is seeking Truth and acting according to Morality. A similar co-operation is needed in society.

• Co-operation between thought, word and deed makes man rise up Maslow's hierarchy of needs. Man becomes more moral and ethical.

• Co-operation begins within body of man. Similarly when all of society co-operates using Truth and morality, harmony and balance is achieved to ensure prosperity.

• Co-operation within the body has many dimensions. When thoughts co-operate with words and actions, optimum output is achieved. Similarly, for the body of society – actions and intentions of all should have the same guides – truth, morality.

• Thus, co-operation helps firm, industry and nation – all integral parts of the body of society. It is, thus, the first ingredient of growth.

• The national diamond (as identified by Michael Porter) depends upon co-operation. Examples from his research prove this. What is true at the national level also applies to development of cluster and industry. It is also true at level of the firm.

• Classical economics, too, states that four factors of production (land, labour, capital, organisation) must co-operate – enabling business to add value.

• Co-operation, thus, is the basis of both planning and executing strategy of a firm. Similarly, it is critical for strategy of man and his life.

• The theory of co-operation applies to strategy of life of man as well as to strategy of firm, cluster and nation. It will promote balance among them.

• Co-operation is the first recognition of interdependence. Just as all body parts are interdependent, all men, too, are interdependent. Spiritual texts ingrain this attitude in man, first. This attitude helps man and society. Ancient Indian spiritual and secular education, thus, begins here.

Co-operation:

Will balance be achieved if opposites are kept apart?

Day and night, as opposites, create balance when they come one after the other.
Two sides of a coin are opposites, yet together they create balance and add value.

Co-operation, even by opposites, is a natural law.

1ST C

Co– operation

implements Porter's first ingredient of Strategy i.e....

'Simple Consistency'

... put in action within man, the firm, with firm's suppliers, cluster, industry, society, nation and family of nations.

When actions of all are in harmony with each other through co-operation the first 'C' of Simple Consistency helps build 'balance' within man and in society.

How does ancient Indian tradition describe co-operation?

Sometimes, what theory can not teach – a story can. The family of ancient Indian idea of Divinity demonstrates it. Lord Shiva demonstrates how balance in a family (of people, societies, nations) can be created. His vehicle is a bull which is scared of the vehicle of His wife, a lion. The vehicle of his son is scared of the snakes that He wears and the peacock vehicle of His other son, too, has this aversion to snakes. Yet they, together, represent a family – as all stay within limits. When co-operation is within a study of limits there is balance – when all work towards excellence, together.

The significant idea behind a story is more relevant than fighting over whether it is or was ever a reality – at some point of time in distant history.

Co-operation: The first 'C' of Management
(The First way to 'See' Management: through eyes of Truth and Morality)

THE FIRST GOAL OF FIRM ALIGNED WITH GOAL OF MAN'S LIFE

C hapter 1 prepares men, therefore managers, workers and organisations to achieve tasks together. Unity between (or co-operation between) Thought, Word & Deed ensures this.

Co-operation is best exemplified also by the body of man in which all parts co-operate fully. Society, too, when it works like one body, can achieve higher goals. Learning from this aspect of his own physical body, man needs to develop the study of Management. Management thought, therefore, needs to start with the first *Purushartha* or goal of co-operation. "What the eye perceives is transmitted to the brain and arms, feet and other limbs act on the cues. A hurt on any part of the body sets an internal co-operation for healing... The body co-operates to absorb that which is useful and reject that is rendered waste. Such perfect co-ordination and harmony enables the experience of life". Similar co-operation between men, firms and society is the purpose and proper study of management.

Co-operation is required for Land, Labour, Capital and Organisation to come together. For man cooperation involves discipline, awareness of others qualities and subjugation of ego (or a false feeling of self importance and superiority over others). It entails use of communication that expresses requirements of co-operation. Such a process lays the foundation for progress of men, firms, society and nations.

When leadership of firms shows spirit of sacrifice (refer 1.2d for understanding of context in which word Sacrifice is used throughout the Paper), individual and national character, a different dimension of growth can open. Working together with even competitors apart from suppliers and other firms in the industry can lead firms and their nations to very advantageous situations. Michael Porters study of 'Competitive Advantage of Nations' has many such examples.

2 Co-operation helps firm, industry and nation

The firm, Porter has shown, is likely to have its fortunes interlinked with the cluster, industry and home nation. Global market shares can depend on competitive strategies built on strength of a home nation's competitive advantage. The skill of understanding customers and their Individuality is critical for this. This competitive advantage is, usually, the result of cooperation and communication.

2.1 Co-operation: The first ingredient for growth

Porter has studied the competitive advantage of nations. His work, at that time, sought to give an agenda to firms and nations that wish to achieve competitive success. The study discovered that firms cannot fight shy of cooperating to build their competitive strategy and nations' competitive advantage. Governments, according to him, do not have a critical role. The dynamics of competition and cooperation has to be nurtured by domestic firms. This is fuelled by their quest for both excellence and competitive strategy. In fact, Porter conclusively observes that greater the degree of competition, the more conducive the environment for cooperation to generate innovative results. Thus, competition is not a threat but a catalyst for co-operation.

Co-operation is essential to augment the firm's capabilities. The consumer needs are not static. They are empowered by dynamism of expanding knowledge, with changing technology impacting the socialisation process. The firm has a national context; an internal structure and the option of building channels of communication. These channels are backed by easy international flow of certain information and offerings. The firm has to adequately meet the challenge of change imposed by influences on consumer. For this it has to recognise the imperative of cooperation.

Often innovation (that reshapes products and creates new products) is the result of cooperation. Information plays a large role in innovation. Innovation is in both methods and technology. Innovation in methods involves new production methods, new ways of marketing, identification of new customers etc. Organisational inertia is the biggest barrier to possibilities of innovation. For sustaining advantages, the firm has to continually move (just like nature of creation or *Prakriti*). The ability of firm to innovate has much to do with information sources available and consulted by it. Information that will be useful is not always sought, or easily available – or needs to be interpreted in new ways. Sometimes it results from sheer investments in R&D and Market Research. Seeking information that helps the firm respond to influences working on customer implies cooperation. Thus, co-operation is an important challenge for communication also.

2.2 The national diamond implies co-operation and communication

Porter identifies four determinants of competitive advantage within a nation (or a national context). These form the "diamond". The favourable factors (and therefore strategic choices before the firm) in producing a product are largely determined by forces working along the "diamond". The four determinants are:

a) Factor conditions **b)** Demand conditions **c)** Related & supporting industries **d)** Firm structure and nature of competition within an industry.

Porter states "The mutually reinforcing activities of the diamond all conceal important channels of communication that add value, give competitive advantage and therefore marketing strength. All these channels, therefore, contribute to both firm as well as marketing strategy".

Michael Porters Determinants of National Competitive Advantage

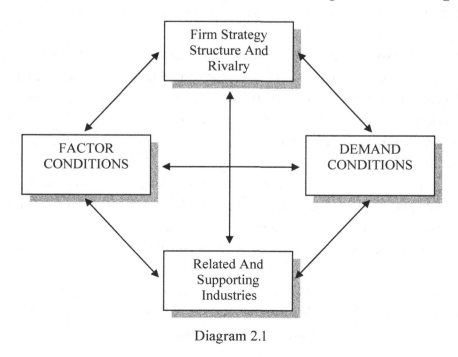

Diagram 2.1

Further, he elaborates "Underlying the operation of the national diamond and the phenomenon of clustering is the exchange and flow of information about needs, techniques and technology among buyers, suppliers and related industries..."

Finally, he concludes that "Advantages throughout the diamond are necessary for sustaining competitive success in Knowledge intensive industries. Advantage in every determinant is not a prerequisite but the **interplay** of advantage in many determinants yields self reinforcing benefits that are hard to nullify and replicate." ***This interplay is the result of cooperation.***

2.3 Role of co-operation in firm's management strategy

The 'diamond' highlights the role of factor conditions, related and supporting industries and demand conditions. Among factor conditions, the advanced factors are critical in Porter's analysis. For, they include modern digital data communication, educated personnel & university research institutes. The advanced factors are, according to Porter, the most significant factors to achieve higher order competitive advantage (like differentiated products and proprietary production technology). They have to be built by human resources and capital factors and may be difficult to procure in the global market.

Porter gives many past examples. Even though **some are not relevant today – the idea is**. Today's case studies can be understood using the same idea. **The book seeks to identify ideas that remain constant even as examples using the ideas change**. New firms and industries follow the same idea while old ones stop using it due to different reasons and circumstances. Denmark's success in enzymes for example was based on interactive communication & cooperation with its base of scientific knowledge in fermentation. Its success in furniture used to depend on its interaction and cooperation with the university that trained designers. The USA's stock of human skills & scientific experience in both computer hardware & software interacted and cooperated to yield advantage. This helped not only these industries but also related ones like medical electronics & financial services.

The advanced & specialised factors reflect the firm's capacity to absorb information, process it and add value. This value is expressed through its products, process & designs. Therefore they reflect the cooperation, communication and innovation abilities of a firm.

Sometimes, the home base advantage itself is translated through a communication strategy to create an international competitive position. Porter illustrated the success of Swiss herbal candy 'Ricolas' in the international market. He showed how a marketing campaign was built around the home base advantage.

Competitive advantage comes not only through using current factors but also through factor creation. It is firms (and not the governments according to Porter's findings, at that time) in most cases that indulge in factor creation. This leads to factor advantage in industries. The Italians indulged in factor creation through cooperation by transfers of knowledge within extended families. For, strong family inter linkages existed between operating firms in most industries. **In the long run, firms taking responsibility survive**. In the ancient Indian tradition society reforms when man takes responsibility for his actions. When firms, too, do the same the 4C Approach helps cluster, industry and nation.

Cooperation or working with buyers, suppliers and channels helps them upgrade & extend their own competitive advantage. Open communication with suppliers can give early access to new equipment, supplies and ideas. These can create competitive advantage. The Japanese case illustrated how working closely with suppliers with free information flow led to superb service and rapid changes. The role of related industries in spurring innovation has been widely acknowledged and recorded. It is cooperation that builds channels of communication which lead to sharing technology, channels and buyers.

Similarly Porter states demand conditions are important for firm's success. Understanding buyer needs requires access to buyers and seeking their cooperation. Building open communication between them and firm's top technical and managerial personnel helps the firm. This interaction should help create an intuitive grasp of buyer circumstances. Again, firms that 'cooperate' – more so with demanding buyers – are more likely to succeed. For, it is sophisticated and demanding buyers who push a firm to innovate. However, working with them *alone* may not be wise – as it ignores the real needs of market. It is close interaction with customer and grasp of his needs that can result in a desirable output.

Ries & Trout call it as "Bottom-up" marketing. This can be the basis of a winning strategy. However, an inability to understand changing market, customers and their need makes many leaders struggle to remain profitable. Global changes, after Porter's work, show it.

2.4 Role of communication in building cooperation (academic theory of '80, '90s)

Firms with strong internal and external communication channels recognise the importance of cooperation. This should be within the firm and with outside sources. They build channels of information with them and are likely to succeed. The features of successful communication strategy would be the same as its competitive strategy. This not only ensures consistency & reinforcement but also optimises firm's cooperation and communication efforts. Porter three generic strategies can be fulfilled if three fits occur in activities of a firm. These fits are simple consistency, reinforcement & Optimisation effort.

Cooperation is a state of mind, which, by its very nature, does not exclude anybody from its ambit. Not even the competitor. However, cooperation with the competitor needs the use of discrimination and can be useful. It should also be based on ethics – not lead to oligopoly.

(i) Cooperation with the competitor can help firm, industry and nation
Some things are best achieved by cooperation among competitors. There are many examples of such an approach. Under certain conditions it is necessary to follow this approach. These are elaborated below:

a) Communicate when factor conditions don't exist: When firms in countries are severely handicapped by lack of a factor, cooperation helps. For, the survival of all competitors may be at stake. Such pressure is often a good breeding ground of innovation. Some of the best inventions in the world have been fuelled by absence of factor conditions. The development of Italian steel Mini mills technology was an example. It developed out of lack of many conditions faced by steel mills situated far away from ports. This led to co-operation to overcome odds.

b) Communicate when international competitive positions are possible for industry: It is in common interest of industry members to develop some factors when all other enabling factors exist. Such factor creation needs communication channels and cooperation. The Japanese industry had successfully produced value added products through cooperation. This had demonstrated their National Character also.

c) Communication within industry and with customers when there is a need to increase generic demand. There are many instances when local competitors have joined together to prepare communication programs that seek to raise consumer interest in a product. The impact of such communication benefitted all brands.

Even joint consumer research by the industry members can be undertaken. The American Coffee Market had seen such an activity by producers. In India generic advertising of milk etc was undertaken to have an impact on level and nature of demand.

(ii) Cooperation has many other dimensions too. These are:

a) Communicate within the cluster: The cluster is one of the most important phenomenons that make a competitive advantage possible. Realising the value of communication and cooperation within a geographical cluster can add value. It has made international competitive advantage a reality for many.

b) Communicate with Industry Association: The industry association has played a decisive role in developing competitive advantage of many industries. Porter gives many past examples. In Italy industry associations helped apparel, shoe, ceramic tile and furniture industries. They played a key role in improving communications and logistical facilities. In USA industry association in electronics worked with schools and universities.

c) Communicate with factors, related & supporting industries and customers: German chemical firms, in the past, had relationships with major German Universities. They sponsored institutes devoted to chemical research & upgrading industry. The firm participated in apprenticeship programs. It involved local technical schools and maintained close contacts with university departments. This enabled factor creation and up gradation. To be close to customers' two world ranking Insulin producers from Denmark owned two hospitals. These specialised in treating patients and conducting research in diabetes.

d) Invest in information, market research, in-company training infrastructure, R&D etc.: A firm's investments in information, market research (MR), in-company training infrastructure, R&D are vital determinants of long term competitive advantage. They lead to capacity to excel within man and firm – and skill development to enable it. This is referred to as *Dakshata* and *Shikshata,* i.e. capacity and training, in ancient Indian tradition, later. All these, combined with cooperation with industry association, determine ability of a firm to achieve competitive advantage.

e) Manage dynamics of competition and cooperation: When interchange of ideas and needs among buyers, suppliers and related industries occur – along with active rivalry – conditions for competitive advantage are most fertile. Porter's research shows this. As many information flows are not one way, a firm has to be prepared for an outflow of information, too. The discrimination ability to manage the inflow and outflow can be an important skill to develop. Development of technology is usually expensive and industry may need to collaborate for it. *Dakshata* refers to capacity of technology also. Developing capacity of technology to serve, too, may need co-operation – not only within the firm but also with suppliers, within cluster and in industry. Firms should focus on development of special processes which save cost, improve quality or ensure better delivery of value added. These express a firm's Individuality through its competitive response.

2.5 Interrelationship among determinants and their influence on stage of National Competitive Development: Theory of '90s

The firm is dependent on determinants of national competitive advantage for its competitive strategy. These determinants are, again, interdependent. They have interrelationships supported by strong under currents of communication and cooperation. The role of cooperation builds the competitive response of a firm. It also enables achieving a competitive advantage for the cluster, industry and home nation. This non-zero sum result of cooperation comes from exploring inter-relationships and building upon them. Such inter-relationships are strong among the determinants of national competitive advantage. This is depicted here:

Interplay among Porters Determinants

INTERPLAY AND RELATIONSHIP AMONG DETERMINANTS				
Variable	**Factor conditions**	**Firm, Strategy, Strategy & Rivalry**	**Demand conditions**	**Relating & supporting industries**
Factor conditions		- A cluster of domestic rivals stimulate factor creation. - Perceived national challenges can also stimulate factor creation	Home demand influences priorities for factor creating investments.	They create or stimulate the creation of transferable factors.
Demand conditions	Sophisticated factor creating mechanisms attract foreign students and participation by foreign firms pulls through the nations products	- Intensive rivalry makes home demand larger & more sophisticated - A group of rivals builds a national image & recognition as an important competitor.		The image of world class related or supporting industries spills over to create demand for the industry. Internationally successful industries producing complimentary products pull through foreign demand for the industry's product.
Relating & supporting industries	Specialised factor pools are transferable to related and supporting industries	A group of domestic rivals encourages the formation of more specialized suppliers as well as related industries	Large or growing home demand stimulates the growth and deepening of supplier industries.	
Firm, Strategy, Strategy & Rivalry	Factors abundance or specialized factor creating mechanisms spawn new entrants		World-class users enter supplying industries. Early product penetration feeds entry.	New entrants emerge from related and supporting industries.

(Adapted from: Michael Porter: 'The Competitive Advantage of Nations")

Diagram: 2.2

The relative importance of each determinant and its nature impacts the stage of national competitive development of home nation. Firms depend on cooperation and communication flows with the determinants for their competitive success.

Similarly, the determinants depend on their interrelationships – i.e. the cooperation and communication flows (among other things) among them – for their development.

Finally, the home nation's stage of national competitive development is determined by such a development of determinants. Cooperation, thus, helps the firm, industry and nation. It is an imperative for competitive success of firm, cluster and industry too.

The development of national competitive advantage depends on cooperation and development of determinants. Porter showed that cooperation enables firms and nations achieve competitive success and higher stage of competitive development. Co-operation even overcomes lack of conditions that are necessary for achieving a desired state of national competitive development. These determinants differ in various stages of national competitive development as shown below:

The 'determinants' in the 4 stages of National Competitive Development

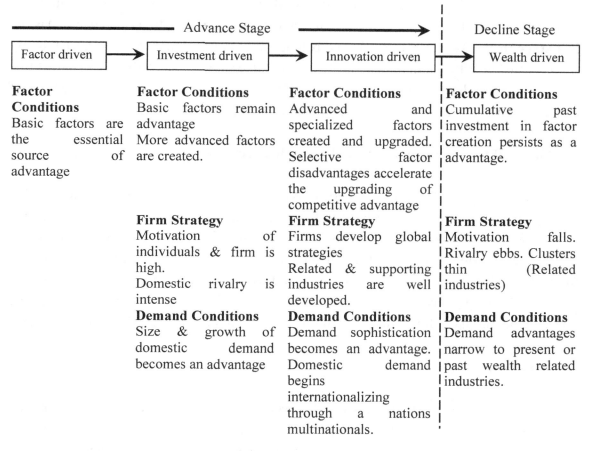

(Elaborated from Michael Porter – The Competitive Advantage of Nations)

Diagram 2.3

To avoid Decline Stage, the 4C approach is necessary. The 4C Approach is not based on textbook ideas. Its practice is based on man achieving control over his mind. When the goal of life is to earn money only there is a lack in motivation to go further, if the goal is achieved. When excellence becomes an end in itself, for both for man and society, decline in motivation is difficult. For, lack of motivation goes against the nature of excellence. With increased affluence, determination and commitment to work can decline. Excellence, however, generates Self-satisfaction. This leads to a regulated and disciplined life and expenditure pattern. Service to others helps in increasing happiness in a life guided by balance. There is no decline when helping others through Selfless Love is the goal of life. Therefore, there is less room for complacency when men & organisations follow four goals or 4C's within the framework of Man Management. **A dynamic balance** (not decline) **is the last stage in the 4C Approach.** Such a balance does not decline but is self perpetuating till its basis (the effort of man to control his mind) does not change. Selfishness harms this balance and a leads to a decline of society. Till the time Selfless Love remains the basis of actions, such a decline does not confront either man or society.

2.6 Limits of Co-operation: Oligopoly, unfair practices

Co-operation is a tool for transformation of business – not for its stagnation. Practices that restrict entry for newcomers unfairly restrict customer choices too. In such a case they extract premium from customers. This, too, is a result of co-operation through oligopoly etc. Sooner or later, it will result in a decline of excellence, innovation and 'closeness to the customer'. Up gradation of knowledge and skills in the industry will suffer if this happens. These practices violate the axis of Truth and Morality. The 4C Approach, like its participating individuals, revolves on this axis – and does not involve selfish practices.

2.7 To sum up

Co-operation between Thought, Word & Deed is the beginning of successful human endeavour. The human body, too, with perfect co-operation executes daily tasks. This spirit of co-operation is the foundation for organisations that seek to achieve laudable objectives. This promotes excellence. Success is the hand maiden of excellence.

1. Co-operation requires discipline, appreciation of others qualities and subjugation of ego. When guided by leadership that has individual and national character with spirit of sacrifice (refer 1.2d) firms can prosper. They can propel themselves, their industry and home nation into an advantageous situation by creating 'national competitive advantage'.

2. Co-operation guides the firm on investment by earmarking sectors with national competitive advantage. It also reveals sectors where advantage does not exist. Finally, it enables a firm to build upon this advantage in these sectors. This helps optimum investment in the use of resources for man, nation and society.

3. The organisational attitude towards cooperation delivers competitive success and is critical. Dynamism within a firm is necessary to upgrade value added offerings to customers. Firms must find ways to keep track of cultural and other influences on customers. They should also translate opportunities into possibilities of satisfying them. This requires an emphasis on both cooperation and communication.

4. In the ultimate analysis, communication helps build cooperation. The firm's strategy cannot achieve competitive success unless it utilises all dimensions of co-operation. Nations, too, achieve higher stages of national competitive development spurred on by such communication and co-operation within the nation and outside it.

Finally, co-operation helps in development of man, firm, clusters, society and nations. How? For example, when a product is produced, all spares too, should be produced in that nation. These give will give easy access to customer. Such a motivation develops the cluster and industry too. This will lead to efficiency, meet present customer demand and enables future development. It also enables economies of scale.

Such an approach leads to better understanding of customer needs and, hence, better products. This leads to comprehensive view of the customer, his requirements and also of products that can fulfil them.

5. Co-operation as *Dharma*: A recap

Co-operation is among the first dimensions of *Dharma*. It is the natural outcome of practice of *Dharma* which creates natural trust among men. If this dimension is practiced sincerely and experienced fully, others follow themselves. **Dharma is not just duty.** The concept of Duty does not have reason in it. *Dharma* encompasses **both duty and reason**. Secular education in India has always revolved around search, discovery and reason. This is both in the "inner" and "outer" sphere. In fact *Dharma* includes all activities that help others. All good works and activities inspired by selfless love to benefit mankind are *Dharma*. The Indian Seers state that "*Dharma* is the basis of everything. There is no virtue greater than *Dharma*". It also operates at many levels. Though it has many dimensions, we will study four types of *Dharmas* here – in the context of man and society:

Vyakti Dharma – Individual Dharma or personal ethics
Grihastha Dharma – Household Ethics
Samajika Dharma – Societal Ethics
Rajya Dharma – National Ethics

While *Dharma* applies for the individual and family, there is also *Dharma* towards society, *Dharma* towards one's country etc. Therefore, when determining a competitive response all four levels of *Dharma* have to be followed by the individual, firm, cluster etc.

The submission of individual ego sharpens Individuality and enlarges the vision of *Dharma*. It increases productivity of man, organisations and society. As man progresses through the stages or *Ashrams* of life, these dimensions of *Dharma* unfold – one by one.

Man, society and world exist in the context of nature. What can we learn from nature? *Dharma* is seen in action in nature according to ancient Indians. For example, the Sun follows *Dharma*. With the co-operation of water, wind etc rain occurs and many cycles of nature are successfully completed. The 'goal' of serving all is achieved in this manner. The movement of Sun is a Study of Limits. By performing its *Dharma* or functioning within Limits, it achieves the 'goal'. It serves everybody selflessly in a detached manner. In this manner it also ensures balance. The Awareness of its power does not interfere with its actions – which remain a Study of Limits. A multi dimensional understanding of *Dharma* is the hallmark of this tradition. Such an understanding generates prosperity for all, operates within limits, encompasses both duty and reason etc. These facets merge as understanding of man reaches a higher 'consciousness'. This two-fold understanding leads to harnessing of potential to serve all selflessly. It is, then, applied for man in this Age – for whom this Paper is Meant!

Business enjoys the benefits of cooperation by four factors of production: Land, Labour, Capital and Organisation. Man, too, is enjoying the benefits of co-operation always. In nature, it begins with chemistry when, say, hydrogen and oxygen co-operate through sharing electrons to give water. Co-operation is the beginning of the journey. Within man it begins with co-operation of thought, word and deed. Among men, co-operation results in effective functioning of families, corporations, society and nations. Co-operation is, thus, the first among goals to be achieved by man, firm, cluster, industry, nation etc.

2ND C

Total Quality of

Concern

...for nation, society, customer, industry, cluster, suppliers and employees is expressed through Porter's ingredient of Strategy:

'Reinforcement'

through a

Focus

on adding value by expressing Individuality with creativity. This makes man and firm move from need of Self Preservation to seeking Self Satisfaction...This focus leads to reinforcing actions taken by man within himself, in the firm, cluster, industry, society and nation.

'Focussed Concern', thus, reinforces the simple consistency of actions that co-operation ensures.

What is focussed concern?

*A focus on the customer with a concern for society is focused concern.
The fixing of the gaze on the customer and how to satisfy his requirement
is the first step. This can be through market research, quality control,
production technique innovation to meet desired cost etc. This is the first
stage. The next stage is when the task can be visualized within the mind –
even when it is not at work – or when the task is directly in view. The final
stage is when the task is internalised within the heart. This enables heart
to heart communication with the customer, supplier, work force etc. to achieve
the objective. These three stages are the three stages defined as leading from
concentration to contemplation to meditation – in the ancient Indian tradition.*

Chapter 3

THE SECOND *C* OF MANAGEMENT: FOCUSSED *CONCERN*

Four Eternal values of Truth, Righteous Conduct, Peace and Love lead to a fifth value: Non Violence. These five, in ancient Indian tradition, may be considered to be the life forces of man and society. They express the 'true' nature of man – that which declares his distinction from other species – in creating value. Of course, for his physical body, too, there are five life breaths (*Panch Pranas*). It is, therefore, not surprising that business (expressing man's distinction from others through use of his physical body) should also have five life breaths.

The use of these life breaths is given a 'focus' by man to express his 'concern' for society. Thus, man creates value for himself and society. A concern for excellence focuses on achieving balance. This creates value – through insights – for self and others. Insights come through meditation also – when senses co-operate (through self control) to silence the mind. Man, too, expresses himself in society through cooperation which directs his 'focus' with a 'concern'. Value creation includes a meditative process – for both man and the firm – to express their individuality through Total Quality Management (TQM) in a unique way.
• Co-operation should be directed towards creating a 'focus' on improving both: Total Quality of life and output (of man and firm). Its Management is undertaken with a 'concern' for customer, industry, cluster, society and nation. This 'focussed concern' shapes strategy which depends on five 'life forces of business'. Given the dynamic nature of man's needs, constant re-engineering of business processes is required.
• Ancient Indians achieved Maslow's Self Actualisation after crossing three stages: Self Preservation, Self Sacrifice and Self Satisfaction... Man's first focus is Self Preservation. It is same for the firm. However, concern for others teaches Self Sacrifice – finally leading to Self Satisfaction. Customer's needs are best fulfilled by a firm that works not for Self Preservation but for Self Satisfaction. Then, it seeks excellence for its own satisfaction.
• Man and firm should share the same goal of quality – of life and output. Balance is, then, created for all – man, firm, industry, cluster, society and nation. Sacrificing selfishness develops clusters to give Satisfaction. When man seeks Self Actualisation, the firm, industry, cluster and nation create balance in society. The roadmap for this is shared here.
• Man has two roles in society. First as a customer and then through the firm – where he adds value. The study of man as a customer, and the firm's total quality management, together, put a 'focussed concern' for quality into action. This is achieved by focusing on and having concern for the quality of his thought, word and deed. This is *Artha* – that which adds meaning or quality to business and the business of life.

How is focussed concern like meditation?

"There are three stages of Sadhana *(spiritual practice). They are concentration, contemplation and meditation. Concentration entails fixing your gaze on one form. Contemplation occurs when you are able to perceive the form within you, even in its absence. Meditation means, when, as a result of this exercise, this form is permanently imprinted in your heart. You should not confine your spiritual practices only to concentration and contemplation. While this is true that these are the first steps in your spiritual practices, you must progress further; you must transform concentration to contemplation and then contemplation into meditation."*

Spirituality is the business of life. Meditation is a day long activity and can be practiced at work and during rest. Meditation gives the experience of the last stage of self satisfaction – leads to the goal of business and life.

The second 'C' of Management: Focussed 'C'oncern

THE SECOND GOAL OF FIRM ALIGNED
WITH GOAL OF MAN'S LIFE

C o-operation is basis of the body of man, society and also Management practice as well as education.

What should direct Co-operation – enabling fulfilment of greater goals by man and society?

A 'focussed concern' leads to setting of goals to be accomplished. It gives meaning to human action and delineates steps for achieving the goal. It helps efficiency, promotes excellence and adds quality to life. However, Self Satisfaction comes only by achieving Total Quality.

Man should promote both – quality of life and quality of output of firm. The firm should promote quality of life of customer, cluster and industry. The clusters and industry should promote quality of life of society. Society should promote quality of life in nation and family of nations. Then, total quality will give a dynamic balance between man, society and nature.

The focus and concern is on quality. What makes quality 'total'? Total Quality implies that it has permeated all processes of man, firm and society. It has to give life to them, just as breath gives life to man. This is the importance of study of Total Quality Management. It gives meaning and direction to study of co-operation within man and firm, cluster and industry. How does this focus on, and concern for, quality give meaning to the concerns expressed above?

3.1 Focussed Concern shapes Strategy which depends upon "5 life breaths of business"

Focussed concern contains within itself pressures of both cooperation and competition. It is like brain bank of a firm. It not only processes received information but perceives information, too. This translates itself through value added processes, techniques, products etc. The Discrimination ability is a key variable here.

The same information may be available to more than one firm. Yet, the response to the same information can be different. Therefore, the task of sifting relevant information from the irrelevant is important.

Viewing all relevant information in a different way (that satisfies customer requirements uniquely as it expresses individuality of man and processes within a firm) is the next task.

Both – cooperation and competition – and managing their dynamics within firm and in the outside world needs discrimination. A firm needs clarity about what to share with competitors, cluster and industry. Also, how to share information is a skill. This is the role of discrimination. It harnesses intelligence and goodness for unique value addition by all.

Finally, a firm has to optimise and reinforce activities in a consistent way. Discrimination plays a role (though a different one) here. Diagram 3.1 illustrates this.

The Indian tradition (refer Source of study) states that five "Life breaths of business" exist. For merging this tradition with current theory, a 'focus' on what it states is needed. This should be merged with a 'concern' for its primary concern. This is executed here by recognising the five life breaths of business. These are:

1. Attitude based costing
2. Business Process Re-engineering
3. Creative Market
4. International Marketing
5. Total Quality Management

3.1.1 Attitude based costing

Using discrimination, a business has to first determine the purchase attitude of customers towards a product. Only then any business should manufacture it. With what attitude do customers perceive value is the first question? Do they consider it as a luxury, necessity or have some other attitude – like is it a useful product etc? If it is perceived as useful – what attitude gives it value in the eyes of a customer? The next question is: how do firms perceive input cost? Similar questions can be asked about quality etc. The importance of 'Attitude' in quality management leading to value creation is shown in Diagram 3.7. The firm has to decide the attitude with which it does business. This is an evolutionary process. After its Self Preservation instinct is fulfilled, it seeks excellence by sacrificing a myopic vision. Finally, it seeks excellence as a goal in itself – without selfishness. This gives Self Satisfaction and adds true value to individuals, firm and society.

The attitude is a state of mind, feeling or disposition. With which attitude does a firm approach the subject of costing? How can firms fructify inculcating the same attitude in the industry or cluster? For example, there can be an attitude towards 'quality first' or an attitude towards 'profits only'. Total cost, itself – for example – can be defined in different ways. Monden (1989) has given the example of total cost of quality in Japanese automobile manufacturing. The necessary steps in total cost management are listed. These are: (i) Plan a product that meets customers demand for quality (ii) Determine a target cost under which the customer's demand for quality is attainable using a blueprint based on value engineering (iii) Determine which processes achieve the target cost in production performance. The firm's attitude influences the way it understands costing. Its attitude towards the customer, commitment to long term customer satisfaction and quality – all of them have an influence on costing. Also, importance a firm gives to market share, attitude to short-term v/s long-term profit, among other things, influences firm's approach to cost.

The firm's attitude towards waste that causes pollution is also relevant. Especially when waste disposal has low monetary disposal cost – but impacts the environment. What is the attitude of firm towards cost in this case? Does it account for the cost to society? Does it prefer processes which have low waste to higher waste? How does it try to impact attitude of cluster, industry, customers etc? With what attitude does it see the cost of changing attitude of others? Costing depends on an understanding of 'relevant costs'. This depends on the attitude towards 'what is relevant' as well as towards business, customer, quality, national resources, supplier conditions, employee satisfaction, innovation etc.

The Indian tradition also states that man has to rise three stages before self actualisation... Depending on the stage the attitude towards one's needs and society is determined. These stages are: from self preservation to self sacrifice (Refer 1.2d for context of usage) to self satisfaction. This simplifies the concept of man rising up Maslow's hierarchy of needs.

First, man is guided by self preservation and physiological needs. Once they have been fulfilled, then he is ready for self sacrifice to protect his family, society and nation. He is also willing to sacrifice something to get prestige and recognition. Self Satisfaction, however, comes only through pursuit of Self Actualisation! Attitude depends on the stage.

How does this transition – which applies to man – also apply to a firm? An answer to this question can enable a common theory and strategy for business and life!

The firm's first response to outside environment may be based on an instinct of Self Preservation. This determines the differentiation it creates. However, to share its 'attitude' of excellence with cluster and industry – to create home nation advantage – it will have to indulge in Self Sacrifice. Such Self Sacrifice is essential for co-operating with suppliers, competitors etc and within the firm. It is also essential for TQM (Total Quality Management – where old processes, ideas, ways of working and co-operating etc have to be sacrificed). Thus, one stage leads to another – as man and firm seek excellence.

A transition from self preservation to self sacrifice results in customer satisfaction. The process is optimised by home nation advantage. This emerges from development of industry and the cluster. Co-operation requires sacrifice of ego and 'I know it all' attitude. Such sacrifice makes firms reject old processes and ideas, develops clusters, industry etc. It helps an industry plan and execute its research, together.

However, customer satisfaction is best created by those who experience Self Satisfaction. This emerges from a commitment to excellence as well as an effort to achieve it. Removal of ego ('I know more') helps selflessness emerge. This helps man and firm become one with the customer. This creates balance, too. For, selflessness optimises use of resources by society. All – suppliers, resources, supporting industries – are optimised with customer requirements when the Attitude developed by education makes man achieve excellence.

Discrimination enables each of these three stages to reach excellence. It also helps man and firm to move from one stage to a higher one.

3.1.2 Business Process Re-engineering

The business processes have to be engineered around a study of customer's wants. This allows them to deliver maximum value most efficiently. It requires a study of how engineering of human wants and their re-engineering takes place. A proper study of the customer is, thus, required.

In Diagram 3.2 below we will see how the customer is an evolving being. This evolving nature of customer gets translated into the engineering and re-engineering of processes. These exist within every firm to help match customer needs through skills, processes etc. Also, the relationship with customers is a lifelong association. After sale of a product, interaction with customer must continue. Ignoring this aspect could make business itself irrelevant some day. That would require business process re-engineering to set it right.

A proactive approach emphasises a continuous business process re-engineering. A reactive approach, on the other hand, helps revival of sick units. Business process engineering recognises the ever changing nature of creation. It translates changing nature of things including customer requirements into a firm's commitment to deliver value. Discarding or sacrificing non value adding activities prevents firms from becoming sick.

3.1.3 Creative Market

The above approach to business meets the important criteria of a Creative Market. Here, every product that the customer desires is available at the correct price point. Close interaction of firms with customers with a long term commitment to the customer changes a firm's perception. The correct price points for various needs can then be understood and delivered. This implies that firms not only remain close to customers but recognise the Individuality and creativity of customer too.

The creative response of firm to a customer's Individuality and creativity lays the foundation of a Creative Market. A continuous interaction between the customer and a firm is the basis of a creative market. The Individuality and creativity of customer inspires product design and development. Diagrams 3.2, 3.3 & 3.4 show the creative market in action. The customer's Individuality and creativity is reflected in current needs (which can be satisfied in creative new ways) and also in emerging needs.

3.1.4 International Marketing

Business has to be carried on in tune with nature, traditions & culture of each nation. This becomes even more important when business is carried out on an international basis. The idea of exporting culture through mass media to suit current products of firms is not acceptable. For, it ignores the inner nature and uniqueness of customers as well as home nation culture and needs. The divorce of customers and their culture while consuming products – influenced by mass media cues – disturbs long run harmony in society.

International marketing should recognise internal and external environment for both, the customer and nation. Marketing needs to recognise different attitudes towards goods and services at different places. Sensitivity to local culture, traditions, climate or historical factors begins the journey to absorbing each of them in the product design.

International marketing, therefore, requires:
• An appreciation of differences in social, cultural perspectives of customers and their impact on human interactions.
• An understanding of difference in attitudes across nations. Also, differences in understanding and ways of communication should be appreciated.
• An observation of differences in ways of satisfying needs and wants.
• A judgment of difference due to local demand conditions and their impact on socialisation process.
• Factoring in impact of exchange rate fluctuations on demand and supply.

3.1.5 Total Quality Management

Engineering tries to create without a fault. Re-engineering is a study of where faults lie. TQM is a focussed concern for delivering faultless product/service, in a zero defect culture. Its proper study can encompass all approaches. Its sole objective is to give faultless value delivery to customers. Given its importance, it is discussed separately in 3.5 below.

The 5 Life breaths of business entail a 'gestalt' of Self Preservation, Self Sacrifice and Self Satisfaction. This will be visible in interactions of firm, cluster, industry and home nation.

The roadmap ahead: Man seeks Self Actualisation and firm creates balance in society Before proceeding further, it is important to have a review of the roadmap to fulfill our objective. This roadmap is that – man should promote quality of life and quality of output of firm. The firm should promote quality of life of customer, cluster and Industry. The clusters and industry should promote quality of life of society. Society should promote quality of life in nation and family of nations. Then, there will be a dynamic balance between man, society and nature.

How can this happen? A beginning by man and firm can be made – as outlined below:
• The life breath of business of life starts with five life forces. These are Truth, Righteous Conduct, Peace, Love and Non-Violence. They are based on unity of thought, word and deed.
• This life breath is infused by man at his workplace in the firm, too – using the life forces.
• Rotating on the axis of Truth and Morality, man seeks to create value.
• This value creation is according to Capacity, Training and skills (*Dakshata, Shikshata*). These relate to men, materials and finance.
• Then, men and firms, with humility, co-operate putting their capacity and training to best possible use to serve society. This creates value and firms deliver it.
• The attitude of man and firm is very important for conducting a business.
• This attitude leads firms to determine costing – which is a necessary step for delivering value.
• Value creation is a result of co-operation with customer. It is based on a focussed concern for his needs. This directs inflow of information for a firms' competitive response.
• The process of value addition analyses needs in a better way and seeks to serve them in new and better ways. This is achieved by discarding non valued added activities.

- This process uses a focus on quality with a concern for total quality – in all processes within man and firm.
- This Total Quality Management concept is, like life, not an event but a process. It is an ever-lasting one!
- Such a continuous process has to re-engineer business to suit ever changing influences on the customer. For, they impact his Individuality and creativity, too.
- Man and firm understand the Creative Market with a Total Awareness.
- This maturity leads man to co-operate within and in the firm to rise up Maslow's hierarchy of needs – towards Self Actualisation.
- This is moving from Self Preservation to Self Sacrifice to Self Satisfaction.
- Self Satisfaction leads to the goal to be Actualised. Diagram 3.1 depicts it.

This movement of man and firm makes the cluster, industry; society and nation share the same goals. When all move from Self Preservation to Self Sacrifice and reach Self Satisfaction, society is in dynamic balance. Then, what is happening at the firm's level (as outlined above) will occur at higher levels, too. As men seek Self Actualisation, the firm, industry, cluster and nation create dynamic balance in society. However, for all to share this perspective, education has to fulfill its responsibility.

Focussed 'Concern' with Five Life breaths of business

The Dynamic Mixture of
Self-preservation, Self-sacrifice & Self-satisfaction
forms the
FOUNDATION OF RE-ENGINEERING

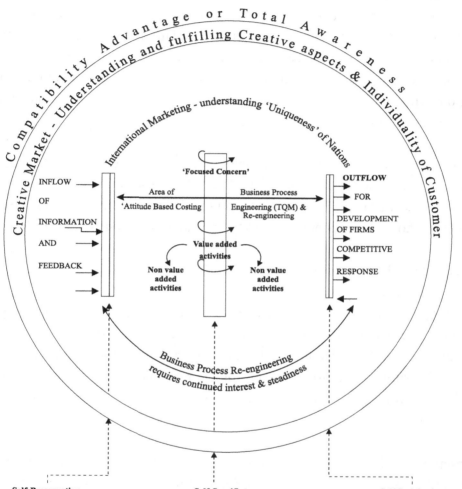

Self-Preservation
Discrimination Filter 1:
The processing of inflow of
information is guided by
Self-Preservation to help
identify & differentiate firms
value offering. Dominant Attitude:
SELF PRESERVATION identify
customer needs & relevant attitude
for costing, choosing raw materials
& product development.

Self-Sacrifice
Discrimination Filter 2:
Identify how optimum value addition takes place.
Discard non-value addition activities
continually. Involves focussed concern for value
addition thru TQM, development of
Cluster & Re-engineering.
Sacrifice current Practices for new,
self interest for development of Cluster,
industry, nation and fulfilling customer needs.
Dominant Attitute :
SELF SACRIFICE. Identify &
add to strength of cluster/industry and
use their strengths too through co-operation.

Self Satisfaction:
Discrimination Filter 3:
How the firm can use this
information to create/ modify
present activities (Role of
discrimination in competitive
response development)
so that they do not harm
environment users & non-users.
This disregard for greed
emerges from Attitude of
Self Satisfaction only.

Diagram 3.1

3.2 Focussed Concern drives firms

Firms need to be driven by a focussed concern. This concern is impacted by three influences on the customer as discussed below. How they impact a firm's activities is important. A focussed concern leads to a search – for information on technologies, skills, processes and, in the initial stage only, competitor behaviour. This concern translates into product and process improvements and also other value added activities. Firms with a focussed concern for excellence enjoy a dynamic work environment. Here, cooperation and subtle competition (with one's own benchmarks) propel innovation in products, processes, ideas and ways to market products etc.

Thus, focussed concern is the engine of growth for firms. Sharper focus and deeper concern create greater likelihood for value addition. Porter, McKinsey and many other contributors have identified how a firm can build and execute this focussed concern. The execution of these concepts, however, depends on a study of Man as a customer. This is done next.

3.3 The study of Man as a customer

The best study of mankind is man. Therefore, study of customers, too, should begin with a study of man. The shaping of strategy needs a dynamic view of the customer. The customer and his wants can not be understood to be static. Marketing is, therefore, is not an exercise of using predetermined cues to ensure customers response. Instead, it is an exercise that recognises the evolving nature of the customer. It seeks to understand the influences working on him.

To understand the primary influences on a customer, those influencers that are internal and external to him need to be identified. The internal influencer on man is an 'inner drive'. For simplicity it is shown as expressed in two ways. First, it is expressed by seeking better value. The second expression of man is his Individuality & creativity. Both expressions are affected by the position of man in Maslow's need hierarchy. For, man becomes a customer in the framework of society. This framework is impacted by him and impacts him, too.

Therefore, study of man is the basis of study of customer.

Customers at lower level of need hierarchy may express their Individuality and creativity in a different way while seeking better value. The inner influencers of man are part the customers private Self. This is shown in Diagram. 3.2.

Creative Market: The 'influencers' and the customer – their inter-play

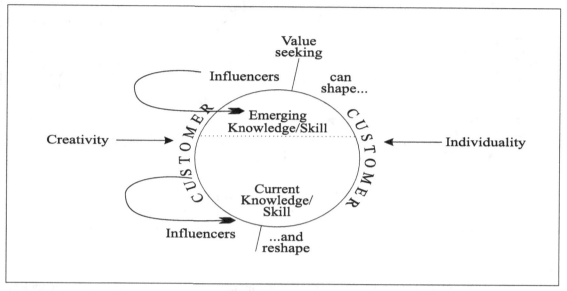

Diagram 3.2

Communication is a thread that ties up customers private self with 'outside influencers'. It also has a role in linking outside influencers with each other. Three 'outside influencers' can be identified. They are:

- Growth of Knowledge and information.
- Technology and its ability to deliver products.
- The socialisation process.

Creative Market: The shaping and reshaping of customer wants

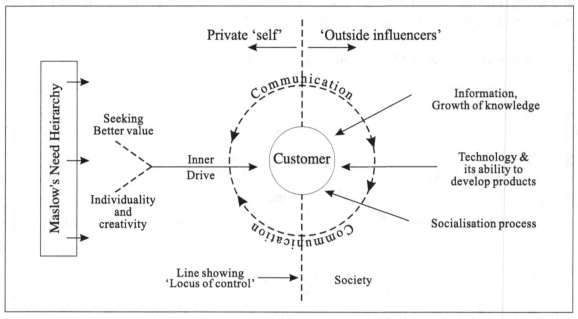

Diagram 3.3

The growth of Knowledge and availability of information has an impact on the process of technology development. This creates not only present products but also new products through a firm's effort. Technology can influence the way customers fulfill their needs. A new way of need fulfilment has social implications. Often, these may be hidden influences.

Diagram 3.3 shows these influencers at work on the customer. They shape and reshape human wants. They tend to shape emerging wants and re-shape current wants. This process is a dynamic and on-going one. The locus of control of man, influenced by education, is shown as the dotted line. If locus of control is 'outside', the socialisation process is less determined by inner drive. If locus of control is within, the inner drive can be purified by education to make man seek higher goals in Maslow's heirarchy and is less influenced by outside influences that are contrary to good social behavior. This line shifts accordingly.

Seeking better value is an inner desire of all customers. However, it is the Individuality of customers which enables segmentation. All customers do not seek greater value in exactly the same way. They have Individuality of needs. Creativity is another important variable.

232

It imparts dynamism to customer wants. This aspect is the basis of study of marketing management. Customers possess an ability to relate to ever-increasing knowledge and information in new and different ways. This creates a need for better or different products to satisfy current wants. It also creates a search of new ways of satisfying current wants.

This creative process shapes new wants. For, the customer is exposed to greater information, knowledge and technology in his socialisation process. Of course, some customers and firms may prefer status quo in varying degrees. Such firms may be less exposed to the growing information and knowledge. Or, they may not be able to develop access to it. Organisational inertia can cause a lack of adequate response to this socialisation process. Similarly, some customers may not be inclined to assimilate a new learning curve that consumption of new product requires. Others may not feel the need for doing so. Their response to the influencers may be slower or non-existent.

The influencer's impact on customers results in emergence of the primary influences for customer wants. These primary influences can be satisfied through present, new & alternate products'. This, too, is shown in the Diagram.

A view of the 'Creative Market' through the emergence of primary influences on' customer needs and wants is shown in Diagram 3.4

Creative Market: Emergence of three primary influences on customer

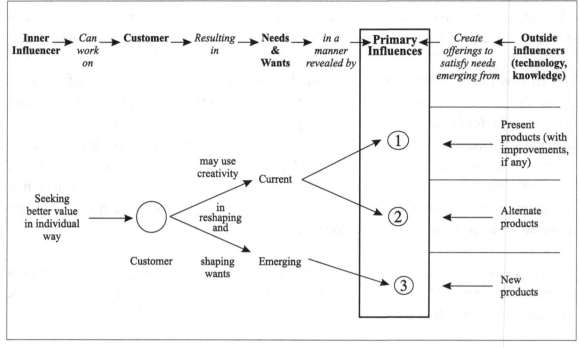

Diagram 3.4

We have seen above that the value seeking customer has three primary influences working on him.

a) <u>Seeking better value delivery for current wants through current products</u> i.e. the desire to satisfy present needs and wants through present products in a better way.

b) <u>Seeking better value delivery of current wants through alternate products</u> i.e. alternate ways of satisfying present needs and wants.

c) <u>Seeking better value delivery of new wants through new products</u>: Here products have to be designed for fulfilling new and emerging needs &wants.

The value seeking customer's needs are not static. He re-shapes his current wants. These can be satisfied with present products. Or, they can be satisfied with modified present products. These could be satisfied through alternate products, too. But, they should satisfy the same want in a different way. Emerging or new wants, being different from current ones, are unlikely to be satisfied with present products or even their alternates.

The nature of these three primary influences gives a new dimension to a firm's dynamism resulting in a 'Creative Market'. Firms ignoring the continuing nature of these influences will lose loyalty of customers whose needs keep evolving. For, their wants are always based on new information and knowledge. To keep their loyalty the firm has to concentrate on these and develop & adapt its products to suit them. This may require different strategic choices.

To offer better value through present products, firms may rely on modification strategies. The modification could be in product features, attributes or in production processes enabling more efficiency or lower cost. The quality of a product could be improved and newer models designed to suit individual needs. The styling of the product, too, could be improved to improve its functional use. Even repositioning could be done to highlight features giving additional value but not perceived in that manner earlier. New or alternate distribution channels may be opened to make it more convenient for customers to access the product.

Technology, fuelled by growth of knowledge, could create alternate ways of satisfying current wants. Such threats could be faced more by firms in knowledge based industries. Development of new software could make many old processes redundant. The use of computers could change delivery of banking services. Internet has opened many new possibilities. In the area of impact of technology Kodak, for example was impacted by the invention of the film less camera and the bearing this had on its film roll business.

The firm also needs to develop new products to meet emerging wants of customers. The customer has many alternatives of firms and countries offering products. However, a firm has to develop core strengths to build systems and structure to innovate. This process should form a part of the firm's strategy. Innovation, often, results from working closely with customers. It also comes from cooperation within the firms' departments. A concerned focus for delivering better value must guide each action in the firm. A firm's own R&D as well as new people joining the firm can help in this. Innovation could also emerge from cooperating with related or supporting industries. For those who still seek benchmarks outside many strategies exist. A firm can keep track of competitors who have inducted new people. A study of the competitor and its new processes could give a firm many ideas. Links with scientific community, laboratories, universities and other research institutions also helps a firm. All firms must prepare for the challenge of change. It is thrown up by new and emerging wants of customers. This challenge unfolds Individuality.

The firm and customers view the changing nature of time differently. Customers view the future based on three primary influences working on them. Firms have to understand these primary influences but prepare for their future using their core strengths. These core strengths have to be supplemented, re-shaped or shaped anew. However, they must keep the three primary influences on customers in mind.

Firms, not addressing these three tasks continuously i.e. business process engineering, TQM, re-engineering etc, are unlikely to deliver value. They may see declining profitability levels overtime. Self Preservation should be only a motivator for excellence. It should lead to higher levels of creativity in a firm thereby expressing Individuality in a unique way that fulfills customer requirements. When firms express creativity, their past performance is the best benchmark to improve – not competitor activity. Rising creativity levels remove fear of Self Preservation. They motivate man and firm to seek higher goals.

While customers can choose products offered by firms all over world, a firm has to produce them in a national context. When firms set up production facilities overseas they operate in a new national context. Firms should plan to achieve competitive advantage through present or future products in a national context. If the national context changes, the product, its production and the way it delivers value must be changed. Firm's internal and external communication, then, must use Focussed Concern and Total Quality Management discussed in section 3.5 below.

Dimensions of Focussed 'Concern'

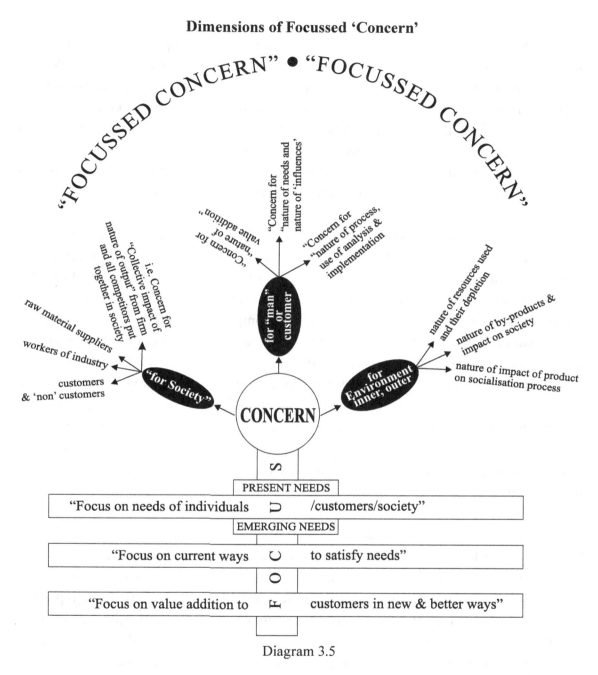

Diagram 3.5

3.4 Communication of focussed Concern adds value (as in Current Theory)

Having a focussed concern is not sufficient. The firm needs to communicate it. Only then can it add value for customers. This may include its suppliers, related industries, scientific organisations, universities and within firm. It also needs to set up channels with outside world or national context. The channels include its sales force, distributors, and employees. They participate in Cost Reduction Strategy, which is a generic strategy beneficial in all stages of a products life cycle. They also help improve firm's production, products and services. Toyota's claim is recorded in books – its employees submitted two million ideas annually. That is about 35 suggestions per employee! Over 85% of them are implemented. Hence internal communication of focussed concern of firm is important. Similarly, external communication with people or groups contributes in the area of concern.

Textbook ways for internal communication to add value and competitive advantage:
a) Communication makes McKinsey 7S model seek excellence: The McKinsey model outlines that firms needs to concentrate on 'hardware' of strategy and structure. They also should develop a 'software' i.e. appropriate systems, skills, staff and shared values. The productive way of organising business activity encompasses these seven variables. It also needs what Peters & Waterman say are "the present and hoped for corporate strengths or skills". Communication theory, as presented here, helps identify and build upon them. The gap between 'hoped for' strengths & fulfilment by present skills becomes a firm's focus. Concern for filling the gap is used to build a response. Innovative firms are those that respond continually to a change in environment. This usually comes from being 'close to the customer' and knowledge of evolving nature of his needs. These firms have strong external and internal communication channels. These help a firm change, adjust, transform and innovate.

Co-operation through communication and sourcing information nurtures innovation. Problems make top heads within a firm communicate with a focussed concern. Their answers are implemented using autonomy given by the firm. This 'bias for action' leads to a culture of 'autonomy and entrepreneurship'. It helps build 'productivity through people', making them 'hands-on and value driven'. Easy communication flows give the firm a 'simple structure and form' with 'simultaneous properties of centralisation and decentralisation'. The resultant higher productivity enables a 'lean staff'. The communication process helps these firms to discover their core strength. This enables them to keep building around it 'avoiding wild jumps in unknown areas'. This leads to a higher success rate. The firm's 7S model seeks excellence in this way.

b) Internal communication to build focus on activities: Ultimately, all difference between firms in cost or price results from activities. These create, produce, sell and deliver their products or services. These activities could be related to delivery of value to customers, assembling final products or training employees. Activities contribute to cost, value delivery & value creation. Activities performed more efficiently than competitors give the firm a cost advantage. The ability to create, sustain and communicate a credible product differentiation based on higher value delivery allows a firm to compete. This differentiation is created within the firm first – before it is communicated to customers. Again, differentiation arises from choice of activities. It also comes from how they are performed together or combined. Activities, then, are basic units of competitive advantage which is the basis of competitive strategy. To generate a competitive response, the firm, therefore, must concentrate on the activities it performs. It must try to see what it can do to them (business process engineering, TQM – these are discussed above). Overall advantage results from not just doing a few activities better but is a result of the entire 'Gestalt' of activities. They must be performed together – in a better or different way.

The firm's value chain is a systematic way of examining all activities of a firm. It disaggregates them into strategically relevant ones. This brings out behaviour of costs and potential sources of differentiation.

c) Communicate Benchmarks, review core processes

The firm's attitude is to examine its cost and performance in each value creating activity. Then, it should look for ways to improve it. The firm can use estimates of competitor's costs and performance as 'Benchmarks' in the initial stage. This can help comparing its own costs & performance (one dimension of Attitude based costing – focus on competitor). These benchmarks can help the firm in assessing which activities can be performed better or at lower cost. This helps a firm achieve competitive advantage. Firm's Individuality is the next step in the ladder of achieving self satisfaction.

The firm should concentrate on improving and managing its core processes better. A firm's competitive strength depends on them. These include new product realisation process. All activities enabling high quality new product development within budgets are covered here. The inventory management process is important. Managing inventory of raw material and finished goods with low overstock costs gives competitiveness. Order-to-remittance process is critical. It covers activities from receiving orders to shipping goods and receiving payments on time. Similarly, the customer service process is the very heart of a business. It makes it easy for customers to contact the firm and receive solutions to problems quickly. A focussed concern on these core processes could help deliver better value for customers or lower its cost. They express Individuality of the firm even when its product looks similar.

d) Better cross-functional communication leads to Operational Effectiveness.

A firm's success does not depend on efficiency alone but on Operational Effectiveness. This includes efficiency – and expresses a firms Individuality. Operational Effectiveness refers to a number of practices that allow a firm to better utilise its inputs. For example, a firm can reduce defects or develop better products faster (through TQM). Often, operational effectiveness depends on cross functional communication. Kotler stresses that new product development is most effective when there is teamwork. This should be among R&D, engineering, manufacturing, purchasing, marketing and finance. Similarly reducing defects in products depends on purchase of components, R&D, study of production processes, SQC. A strong commitment created by in-company communication is needed for all the above.

Cross functional teams and re-engineering of work flows add value in high performance firms. Some companies have a customer operations group. This links sales, shipping, installation, service and billing so that these activities flow smoothly into one another. The application of these concepts is shown in Diagram 3.1 above.

e) Internal Communication System for Competitor Analysis and Tracking

Self Preservation guides firms to track competitors. Diagram 3.1 would include this activity in 'Inflow of Information'. A Competitor Response Profile can be maintained. Even this requires discrimination to decide which competitors should be examined. The four diagnostic components of competitive analysis fall in two categories:

(i) What drives the competitor? – This includes competitor's future goals and assumptions (held about itself and the industry). (ii) What the competitors can do – This includes current strategy (how is competitor competing today) and capabilities (both strengths & weaknesses). The response profile should seek to answer the following questions: • Is the competitor satisfied with his current position? • What likely moves or strategy shifts will the competitor make? • Where is the competitor vulnerable? •What will provoke the greatest and most effective retaliation by the competitor?

In addition, gathering competitive information should be a carefully designed, cost effective process. Sometimes cross-disciplinary teams are used to enable all departments not only to sense, serve and satisfy the customer but also to track competition. The system identifies sources of information, collects data, analyses & evaluates it. Only after validation it is sent to relevant decision makers.

Some competitive tracking tools given in textbooks are:
• Watch small companies in industry and related industries • Follow patent applications track job changes and other activities of industry experts • Be aware of licensing agreements – they give information about where, how and when a company can sell a product. Monitor formation of business contracts and alliances • Find out about new business practices that save cost for competitors • Follow changes in pricing • Follow changes in social environment and customer taste. These alter the business environment.

3.5 TQM: Putting 'Focussed' Concern into organisational action

Total Quality Management focuses 'concern' for quality in all activities towards adding 'Value'. This helps the firm serve customers and society. Deming's 'Quality wheel' below can be expanded from a focus on man in our approach. It can, then, include all aspects of firm's activity and contribution to society.

TQM Quality Wheel

Diagram 3.6

TQM from man to firm

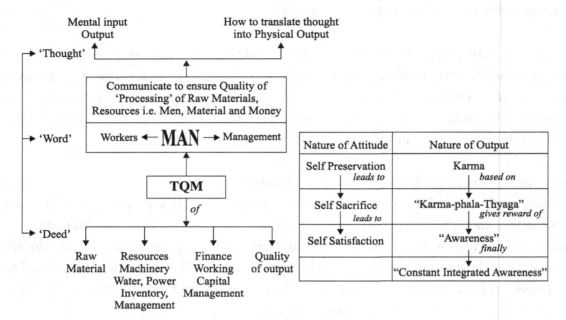

Mental input Output

How to translate thought into Physical Output

→ 'Thought'

Communicate to ensure Quality of 'Processing' of Raw Materials, Resources i.e. Men, Material and Money

→ 'Word'   Workers ← **MAN** → Management

TQM

of

→ 'Deed'

Raw Material

Resources Machinery Water, Power Inventory, Management

Finance Working Capital Management

Quality of output

Nature of Attitude	Nature of Output
Self Preservation *leads to*	Karma *based on*
Self Sacrifice *leads to*	"Karma-phala-Thyaga" *gives reward of*
Self Satisfaction	"Awareness" *finally*
	"Constant Integrated Awareness"

Diagram 3.7

THE TQM WHEEL with Shared Value

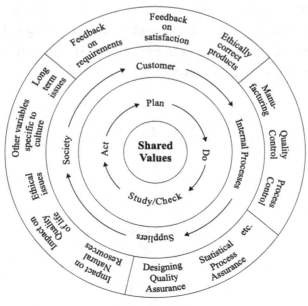

Diagram 3.8

Quality is an attitude. It should permeate thought, word and deed of all in the value creation process. The core of firm's focus should be shared values or human values. These ensure that firm's output does not harm customers or society in the long run. Total Quality Management is not just about checking final output. It operates in a national context to meet international requirements through a three stage process. These stages are quality control of raw material, quality control of workers (to ensure production quality) and final quality. It is, therefore, a process of control from raw material to finished products. As a final product depends on quality of raw material, so a firm needs to check that, first – just as raw material of thoughts become plans. Then, they are communicated through words, and finally result in actions or deeds. So, it is necessary to control quality of thoughts in a firm, first. Quality control of workers implies a recheck of this – if they fully understand requirements of quality by management of a firm. First, quality has to be checked properly during manufacturing or service delivery. Only that can prevent short cuts which are like manipulation. Then, final quality needs to be rechecked. This is like "*Trikaarana Shudhhi*" or Purity and Unity of thought word and deed. If all are in harmony and have unity, quality can be delivered. Then *Karma*, or work or nature of output, is perfect. Hence intention of firm for quality should be communicated in words to workers and should reflect in deeds.

TQM is a wide concept. When applied to thought, word and deed of a firm, it is useful for workers and management. It also applies to processing of resources other than raw material. It is useful for all – men, materials and money. It covers not only mental input and output but physical output as well. TQM, of course, extends to raw material. It also covers other resources like machinery, water, power, inventory management, financial management, working capital management and quality of final output. This is depicted in Diagram 3.7. TQM covers interaction of a firm with customers, suppliers and society. However, it must be around the core of shared values. This is depicted in Diagram 3.8.

To sum up: Focussed Concern permeates all five life breaths of business. It helps understand Individuality and creativity of customers in a Creative Market. It expresses itself through Total Quality Management in a firms output. It enables man to rise above an attitude of Self Preservation by working for seeking excellence only (*'Karma Phala Tyaga'* is the ancient Indian terminology for this). Sacrifice of myopic self interest makes him realise enlightened self interest. This gives self satisfaction or Awareness of his true self. If ways to satisfy current and emerging needs of current and new customers emerge from Awareness, a dynamic balance results. It adds value to customer, society and environment. Processing the inflow of information generates **value addition** through values. Engineering and re-engineering processes with attitude based costing reflect its attitude towards customers, society and environment.

Within man, a focussed concern emerges from an attitude towards life in a changing world. This attitude is a concern for discovering the Self – through service to others. Thus, customers, family, firm, suppliers, cluster, nation etc are served. The focus is on adding value which is guided by creativity in man. This is the creative market place of thoughts and desires. It utilises man's Individuality in the most productive manner. The thoughts and desires emerging from the heart require a focus. A higher level of Maslow's need hierarchy of man is awakened. A concern for excellence is generated within man. This leads to selfless, not selfish action. The process of change in the world requires continuous re-engineering. It discards non value added activities. Man's act of living life is guided by a commitment to total quality – in thought, word and deed. This, then, guides a focus on quality in a firm with a concern for customer and society. Both, man and firm, share a focus on excellence with a concern for society during **value creation** discussed in this chapter. Balance within man and society, then, emerges simultaneously – in **value delivery** of a firm. Value delivery is discussed in next chapter of competitive response.

Chapter 4

COMPETITIVE RESPONSE: THE THIRD *C* OF MANAGEMENT

Excellence emerges 'within' man, restrains greed and prevents recession

• Education transforms man to seek excellence not just success. He, then, joins the firm as a manager to deliver value. Then his Awareness of 'life forces of business' and its national context becomes useful.

• In ancient Indian tradition the Competitive Response depends on Capacity, Training and Protection – of men, materials and finance. Education imparts these to man. Man enhances capacity of firm, protects it and trains others. Then, focus on value creation in Chapter 3 shifts to value delivery, here.

• The manager delivers strategy. The confluence of study of man and firm is the role of manager. His inner qualities, broad understanding, national character are important for the firm and society.

• In this tradition, 'five life forces of business' in tune with 'nature of nation' determine strategy of a firm. The integration of Porter's strategy and Kotler's marketing ideas with this tradition's concepts is shown.

• The concepts of Porter, Kotler and theory of '90s follow a 3C Approach. They do not integrate with 4th C of man's urge for Self Actualisation or *Moksha*. This goal is directly linked to the nature of a competitive response that overcomes greed to prevent a recession.

• Theory of Strategy and marketing, till '90s, is integrated with ancient Indian study of man management for integration with man rising up Maslow's need hierarchy and the 4thC.

• Achieving the highest goal impacts man's actions – in firm and society. He, then, seeks Wisdom. The confluence of three stages of wisdom with Maslow's idea gives an understanding that man can apply in daily life. This understanding is explained here.

• Chapter 1 gives three types of Knowledge. These are: Knowledge of Self, Knowledge relating to work and that Knowledge which sensitises man about impact of his actions on society. Awareness of Self is useless – unless it benefits society. The three stages of Wisdom sensitise man and change perceptions or ability to 'C' things.

• The 4C Approach trains man differently. Man seeks to understand himself and purpose of his life. This changes determinants of demand too. With change in inner influencers, understanding of excellence also changes. This impacts the economic concept of society. Then, the different impact of 3C and 4C strategies becomes clear.

• Indian tradition changes man's view about competition and competitor. Competitor is only a benchmark when lower order needs are important. In later stage, self preservation fear is overarched. Man's Creativity and Individuality remove the fear of survival. His past work, then, is his only competitor. This is true for both: man and firm. Thus, excellence in value delivery within man merges with the five stage process of this tradition.

Desire or *Kama* (3rd *Purushartha*) or greed emerges from duality. What approach makes it fruitful to live in duality while restraining greed? The answer is presented in this Chapter.

Diagram 4.0: Explanatory Note

In the Ancient Indian Tradition the study of competitive response emerges from an understanding of similarity of trinity of five forces that guide both man and the firm. While man is at the heart of the firm, the quality of selfless Love differentiates man from animal world. This distinguishing feature represents the best 'within' man. It is achieved by using the mind – guided by education and the physical body – guided by four goals of life or *Purusharthas*. Mind is balanced by Awareness of Atma, Body by *Doshas*, actions by goals.

Trinity of Five: The 1st Five create balance

Balance in a firms'activities emerges from five things (two plus three): i.e. mind of a manager filled with Awareness of the unity of mankind (*Atma*). These interact with the firms resources: Capacity, Training and Protection (capacity of skills, equipment etc, Training to create the level of skills that generate the desired level of excellence and developing an ability to protect the physical and mental resources of the firm). This is similar to *Ayurvedic* balance of *Vata, Pita* and *Kaph doshas* – which create a healthy body guided by a healthy mind (filled with uplifting thoughts of Unity described in Chapter 6).

Trinity of Five: The 2nd Five are the life forces

The five life forces of a firm are: Production, Connection, Production, Direction, and Collection. The five life forces of man emerge from the five elements: earth, water, fire, air space. Five elements combine to give various dimensions of life forces to man. Some details of these life forces are: Space – (Emotions, Prejudices, Apprehensions, shyness etc.), Air – (Movements and Reflexes – Respiration, Walking etc.), Fire – (Hunger, Thirst, Sleep, Fear etc.), Water – (Blood, mucus, saliva etc.) Earth – (Skin, Muscles, veins, bones, nails etc.). Similar to the body, five life forces of firms power its response. The proportions and management of these forces create balance through use of mind of man or manager.

Trinity of Five: The 3rd Five are Five Life Breaths

Breath gives life to the physical body of man. It consists of five vital airs that enable productivity. These are: *Prana, Apaana, Udana, Samana, Vyana.* They keep the body in balance and perform important tasks (please check Glossary). Similarly for the firm – the five life forces are: Attitude based costing, Business Process Re engineering, Creative Market, International marketing and Total Quality Management.

Only after achieving balance within man and in a firm (by planning Capacity, enhancing and upgrading it with Training and ensuring Protection of its resources) can balance of Five Life Forces and Five Life breaths make firm contribute to cluster, industry and nation.

Body of Man, Firm contributes to Nation using Trinity of Five:

Life Forces, Life Breaths, 'Balanced' by Mind filled with *Atma* Awareness guiding three things

[*Vata, Pita, Kaph* (for man) and Capacity, Training and Protection (for firm)]

Body gets Life from Elements: They form Five Life Forces of Man– Using Five Life Breaths

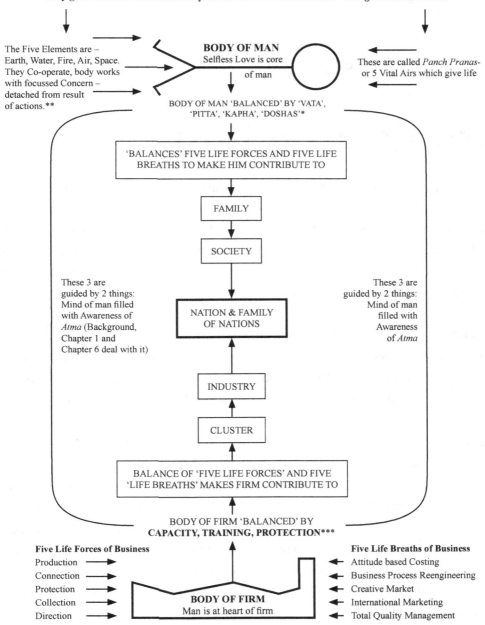

The Five Elements are –
Earth, Water, Fire, Air, Space.
They Co-operate, body works
with focussed Concern –
detached from result
of actions.**

BODY OF MAN
Selfless Love is core
of man

These are called *Panch Pranas*-
or 5 Vital Airs which give life

BODY OF MAN 'BALANCED' BY 'VATA',
'PITTA', 'KAPHA', 'DOSHAS'*

'BALANCES' FIVE LIFE FORCES AND FIVE LIFE
BREATHS TO MAKE HIM CONTRIBUTE TO

FAMILY

SOCIETY

These 3 are
guided by 2 things:
Mind of man filled
with Awareness of
Atma (Background,
Chapter 1 and
Chapter 6 deal with it)

NATION & FAMILY
OF NATIONS

These 3 are
guided by 2 things:
Mind of man
filled with
Awareness
of *Atma*

INDUSTRY

CLUSTER

BALANCE OF 'FIVE LIFE FORCES' AND FIVE
'LIFE BREATHS' MAKES FIRM CONTRIBUTE TO

BODY OF FIRM 'BALANCED' BY
CAPACITY, TRAINING, PROTECTION***

Five Life Forces of Business

Production ⟶
Connection ⟶
Protection ⟶
Collection ⟶
Direction ⟶

BODY OF FIRM
Man is at heart of firm

Five Life Breaths of Business

◄ Attitude based Costing
◄ Business Process Reengineering
◄ Creative Market
◄ International Marketing
◄ Total Quality Management

* Using Mind (thru Education), Body (Thru *Purusharthas)*, Nature (Thru Herbs, *Kriyas* etc). ** Space – (Emotions, Prejudices,
Apprehensions, shyness etc.), Air – (Movements and Reflexes – Respiration, Walking etc.), Fire – (Hunger, Thirst, Sleep, Fear etc.),
Water – (Blood, mucus, saliva etc.) Earth – (Skin, Muscles, veins, bones, nails etc.). *** * … of Men, Material, Money.

Diagram 4.0

3ᴿᴰC

Competitive Strategy is an

Optimisation Effort

…that follows Porter's ingredients of Simple consistency and Reinforcement.

The word Optimum implies right/ perfect amount of anything. It is a dynamic configuration of individuals, activities in a firm and society – and the way they relate to each other. Such multidimensional concepts (v/s single focus) lead to greater Awareness and excellence-seeking in more dimensions – if not all.

Earlier chapters have witnessed this Optimisation effort in action. Part A of the book lists 'Three **Types** of Knowledge' and demonstrates how 'Consistency' in use of Shared values requires 'Reinforcement' and 'Optimisation effort'. This chapter details how three **Stages** of knowledge (and, then, wisdom seeking) transform the 3C Approach to a 4C Approach.

Part B of the book is a Study of Limits. Human Values give limits to human behaviour, demand creation as well as how demand is satisfied. Maximisation implies no limit being placed. Optimisation requires perfection to maintain balance. This 'Optimisation effort' requires Cooperation and Focussed concern. Optimisation effort, emerging from Values, is the 'inner influencer' for the customer and firm. It seeks value in life, influences Value Creation and Value Delivery. This inspires man, the firm, cluster, industry and society – and leads to balance. Man should care for society in the same manner as he cares for himself. Then, Optimisation effort gives true dimension of Corporate Social Responsibility. Balance with nature emerges from Optimum use of resources.

Therefore, Competitive Strategy, too, should be an Optimisation effort...

Competitive strategy is not a
Profit Maximisation compulsion!

A desire for profit maximisation is the basic assumption of capitalism. This was taught in economic theory in 1980's. This leads to a 3C approach in competitive strategy. Profit maximisation, then, was a 'single focus' approach.

Let us take the example of a car. If a car runs on a 'single focus' program of maximum speed only, likelihood of a crash is high. If it Optimises speed, it can satisfy various criteria depending on specific needs at any given time. It can, then, choose a speed to ensure maximum fuel efficiency. Or, it can choose a speed that gives maximum passenger comfort if a track becomes bumpy etc.
Profit maximisation is a simply understood, one dimensional concept.

Optimisation Effort requires a different understanding and different 'software' for programming. It incorporates multiple objectives – and their varying nature – across time. The attempt to comprehend this software from concepts of Indian tradition is made here. Of course, this tradition states that education should, in a new situation, make Truth or *Satyam* emerge from 'within' man. This Truth is the Ideal strategy required at that time. The concepts which prepare 'software' for Truth to emerge are discussed in this chapter.

What optimum strategy makes balance emerge 'within' man, firm, society, nation, family of nations and with nature? An overloaded car can never win a race. Man, too, should not be overloaded with desires. Moderation through 'study of limits' is the key. Greed clouds the ability to 'C' the optimal. Sometimes, a car may choose not to win a race if risk of crash becomes too high due to unforeseen reasons. It should not harm others (crash) and yet achieve optimum results. "It does not matter if you win or lose – it's how you play the game!" The desire to win by harming others is not optimal.

The Truth about this has to emerge from 'within' man. This Truth has to be optimum for firm, cluster, industry and society – in all situations. Man and firm (where he works) have to express their individuality. Their output should satisfy the individuality of a customer in a unique way. All should be guided by a search for the optimum. This chapter seeks to mould the perception of competition itself – which enables this to happen within man and in society.

*Diagram 4.0 shows that **mind of man controls health of body of man and firm**.*

The mind of man has to overcome six inner enemies of which envy is the deadliest. If response to competition emerges from envy, greed etc., it shall harm the system. The recognition of the excellence that others achieve should not subtract from the experience of excellence that ones own efforts create. This can happen only by experiencing ones'own individuality and individuality of customers. Then, the response of man and the firm will add value in a unique way to each other and society.

Rosabeth Kanter's idea of 21ˢᵗ century business is based on these three things also:
   – "The strong potential synergy between financial performance and attention to community and social needs." This is the gist of this Chapter and book.
 – "The unique competitive advantage from embracing the values and expectations of a new generation of professionals." This Chapter and book use ancient values.
   – "The growth opportunities that result from stressing values and supressing executive egos when seeking partners and integrating acquisitions." The role of humility and Co-operation has already been discussed earlier.
All the above ideas emanate from values – which emerge from transforming the mind
Can a theoretical framework be created for management – using values?

The 4C Approach: A theoretical framework using values
The most sustainable ideas for 21ˢᵗ century growth will come from the wisdom enshrined in ancient values like truth and morality.
All Theory (of '90s or today's) needs sustainable values – to prevent recession.

Competitive Response: The Third 'C' of Management

THE THIRD GOAL OF FIRM ALIGNED WITH GOAL OF MAN'S LIFE
Excellence emerges 'within' man, restrains greed and prevents recession

4.1 The Indian ethos

In Indian philosophy, *Kama* or desire fulfilment must be in tune with *Dharma* and *Artha*. In our language it means that third 'C' should be in tune with cooperation and focussed Concern. The three are mutually dependant and interrelated. The dynamics of their inter relationship can be put into action only by a steady mind. A steady mind faces both profit and loss bravely. This is achieved by developing balance or equanimity. It is a state of equilibrium achieved by learning how to convert knowledge to skill. The mind develops an ability to take loss – yet not harm society. Pollution, low quality or arousing baser instincts of customer etc prevent losses. Ignoring this, man and firm seek a balance among all: workers, market, transport, production, raw materials, conserving electric power, water etc. This is idea of business based on balance – creating balance in society.

'Desire fulfilment', *Kama* or 3rd C, then, is not just about profit maximization but also a study from the social or national welfare point of view. It judges impact of products on society. Appealing to base instincts of customer for sake of profit alone may create 'money' for a firm. However, it cannot create value for society. **Ancient Indian Seers state that if *Dharma* and *Artha* are honoured, *Kama* is automatically balanced.** If focussed Concern for customer and society is guided by *Dharma* competitive response will add value to all. Customers, managers, employees and society will benefit. Cooperation of thought word and deed of members of firm and society is the starting point. Truth and morality is the path. This is vision of 'C'ers and cultural ethos of India. This is the disposition, character or fundamental value shared in Indian culture as a guide to living.

4.2 Strategy needs 'scientific enquiry'

The ancient Indian tradition states that strategy needs scientific enquiry: for man and firm. Many firms believe that competitive response requires improving upon what others plan and execute. Even such a strategy, in a competitive situation, needs enquiry. This enquiry should include everything. Needs of customers, capacity of firm, national perspective – all need a scientific enquiry. With internationalisation of business, study of cultures of each nation is important. Cross-cultural perspective gives a proper understanding of national perspective of individual nations. It gives an idea of competitive advantage, factor and demand conditions etc. This 'scientific enquiry' takes three forms:

"Capacity (*Dakshata*), Training (*Shikshata*), Protection (*Rakshata*)"

Before indulging in any activity, a study of 'capacity' of firm to fulfill desired ends is necessary. If capacity doesn't exist among men, it has to be created through training or *Shikshata*. Capacity includes role and scope of the manager and his responsibility (to his *Dharma*, firm, cluster, industry, society and nation). Similarly an understanding of strategy of life of man is based on a realization that the mind is the 'manager'. Capable managers in firms ensure excellence by their inputs and capability to provide all facilities. The mind does so for man. However, these facilities become productive only when Training enables their optimum use. Protection comes naturally from balance. *Dharma* protects man. For firms, ensuring proper circulation of capital, for example, 'protects' business – among other things. Chanakya has expounded this principle. For safety and protection of human body, blood has to be circulated. Similarly, capital, too, needs to be circulated. Protection also implies security of human and non-human resources. The Source of study has, thus, defined the understanding of strategy.

4.3 Who delivers Strategy is critical: 'Role of Manager'

Competitive Response depends on two things. Firstly, how strategy is formulated and secondly, who delivers it. In the ancient Indian tradition, strategy is not a set of words written on a piece of paper. It is a dynamic concept that has to be lived by the firm. If the firm has to implement a strategy, the leader or manager is important. As the manager delivers strategy, transformation of his thought process was addressed, first. Three quotations from Source of Study define some dimensions of this transformation here. They give insights into 'what a Manager should be'. They deal with: (a) his inner qualities (b) broad nature of understanding and (c) his national character. These are:

4.3.1 Inner Qualities of Manager

"The Manager can be compared to lungs of the human body. While the owners are like the heart and workers are like organs of the body. It is the manager who, like lungs, cleans the blood before it is pumped into the heart. What makes this cleaning possible? Qualities of Manager (*which become qualities of firm's management*) purify the blood circulation (*within firms and society*). What are the qualities of a Manager? He should have both 'Mind of Man' as well as Awareness of *Atma*. He should have Knowledge of 'Nature of Nations'. He should understand 'aspects of environment'. He should lay down and follow 'guidelines for goodness'. He should conduct 'enquiry into ethos' and should comprehend 'role of rules'...." Refer Diagram 4.0 for role of mind of man and awareness of *Atma*.

4.3.2 Broad Nature of Understanding of Man and Mankind

"A manager understands management as knowing mankind. Therefore, when he thinks he has the mind of a man it implies having a broad vision. Thinking of problems as 'his' and 'mine' i.e. thinking that 'his problem is his and my problem is mine' is the nature of animal mind. Thinking of others and their problems comes naturally to man and not to an animal. Hence, a Manager must have 'mind of man'. This is possible only if he has Awareness of *Atma*". Refer Diagram 4.0 which shows that these two control management

The realisation that *Atma tatwa* is the same in all, man does not voluntarily plan any harm – directly or indirectly – for others. This emerges from the awareness or holistic experience of *Atma*. However, "...awareness of the same *Atmic* principle in everybody can come only from 'enquiry into ethos'. Ethos helps one to know fundamental truths. Giving encouragement to others is an approach that emerges from ethos. The highest fundamental truth is about '*Atma-Tatwa*' or experience of man as Soul. High thinking through 'enquiry into ethos' generates high quality of output." Gandhiji, too, insists on high thinking.

4.3.3 National Character
"The Japanese have patriotic feelings and work for the development of their nation. This higher order feeling makes workers take lesser wages, work longer hours till a problem is solved or task completed. This has led to a 'spirit of work'... They were willing to indulge in self-sacrifice and experience self-satisfaction"... This "...Self-Satisfaction should be a pre-requisite for all who work in an organisation." True self satisfaction, however, will come when there is a search of excellence within oneself. This implicitly implies that "imitation or reducing quality is not true competition..." The focus is on higher order needs of man.

4.4 Basis of Strategy: 5 "Life forces of Business" in tune with "Nature of Nation"

Business has to be carried out in tune with the nature, traditions and culture of nations. Strategy encompasses all aspects of the business – including Porter's determinants. These include: home demand conditions, availability of raw material, suppliers and factor conditions, related and supporting industries, nature of firms rivalry, cooperation and cluster development, if any. Availability of finance with firm, working capital management, production, TQM, human resource management, market research, marketing strategy and Positioning, Distribution etc. is important. The business, in this tradition, however, depends upon 'Life Forces' which enable formulation of both Strategy and Structure. This enhances the life breaths and leads to their utilization in an optimum way. These 'Life Forces' are: "1. Production 2. Collection 3. Protection 4. Connection 5. Direction"

The Life forces are inexorably linked with each other and must be in tune with 'Nature of Nation'. This important concept includes: home demand conditions, local culture, factor conditions, nature of rivalry and cooperation, supporting industries etc. As usual, it can be related to the body of man. Diagram 4.0 gives a brief description of how five elements of nature (Space, Air, Fire, Water, Earth) become forces that give life to man. Ancient Indians believe that the element of Space gives birth to emotions, prejudices, apprehensions, shyness etc. Air Element gives movements like reflexes, walking, respiration etc. Hunger, thirst, sleep and fear are aspects of Fire. From Element of Water, blood, mucus and saliva appear. Skin, muscles, veins and bones represent Earth element. Together, the elements co-operate to give force of life to man. This understanding makes the body maintain good health and seek excellence. Similarly, an understanding of the Life Forces of Business makes the search of excellence possible in a healthy society.

As discussed earlier, Protection is related to physical protection, balance, working capital management etc. Protection also comes from many subtle forces like Character of manager and the firm. The nature of cooperation and national character displayed by raw material suppliers and industry is important. The nature of focussed concern, too, plays a critical role. An enquiry into ethos described above and appreciation of the role of rules, voluntarily adhered to – give protection. In the Indian context, there is a saying "*Dharmo rakshati rakshata*" i.e. for man; too, *Dharma* protects those who follow it. The best protection comes from following truth, morality and social responsibility. Coupled with this is the nature of cooperation. Cooperation with customers should be a continuous process. It should be backed up with cooperation with suppliers, supporting industries and good working capital management. Adherence to quality in production and right connection with the market and suppliers naturally gives protection to a business. Of course, physical protection of resources is the basis of protection but skills too need it. They are protected by usage that enhances them and training that increases them in others.

The life force of 'Production' has been discussed in TQM earlier. 'Collection' refers to collection of payments as well as all resources – mental and material. The co-operation between a firm and raw material suppliers has been discussed earlier. The inter-relation between 'Production' and other life forces is explored here. 'Production' cannot be sold if 'Direction' is not correct. So, customer needs should be properly understood, direction of thinking and company policies must be correct etc. Production is meaningless without 'Connection'– with customer, supplier, distributors, market, within workers and manager etc. Cooperation makes it possible. 'Connection' with customer through market research gives direction of both the optimum product mix and quantity to be produced. Similarly, if physical safety of human and non-human resources is not there through 'Protection', 'Production' will not be possible. Production needs a 'Collection' of skills, ideas, customer feedback, resources and payments for further production. For continuous and optimum production plan efficient working capital management is a must. Similarly, 'Production' has to be inexorably interlinked with 'Direction' or the strategy devised by a manager.

The interrelationship between the five "life forces" gives meaning and direction to the firm's strategy. The 'Just in time' strategy is useful in production management. It gives the parts on the right time thereby having efficient working capital management. Similarly, customers must get the right quantity 'Just in time' to lower working capital needs of distributors. The 'Connection' alternatives and cost should be worked out carefully to ensure product delivery even in extraordinary demand conditions. This Optimisation of circulation of capital among all constituents of business leads to Optimisation efforts for all. It gives value addition to the system. "One of the most important things in business is to calculate costs – especially cost of production accurately. Chanakya, an Indian thinker has clearly mentioned that one should take into account all expenses incurred before calculating profit. He also propounds that out of total income one fourth should be saved for the future and three-fourths should be used for the five life forces of business." Source.

4.5 Strategy: Firm's competitive response ('Direction', 'Connection'): '90s Theory

The firm's strategy is a flow. What is the nature of this flow? 'Direction' of a flow is important and is decided by the Strategy, national context as well as the cluster. For delivery of Strategy, a "Connection" is needed – between customer and raw material suppliers – through the firm, in the most efficient way. 'Production', some 'Collection' and 'Protection' are like the hardware of the firm. Its software is in 'Direction' and 'Connection' and collecting inputs for Strategy and Connection. The Connections are formed during the area of 'Focussed Concern' itself. These connections are similar to connection among different parts of a body which are formed in early stages of conception. The connection from 'customer needs' to 'product delivery' encompasses the entire TQM process. This is discussed in the previous chapter. **The unique 'direction' that a firm gives to its focussed concern is expressed through its Strategy and Value delivery.**

How do marketing & communication tasks flow from strategy? How and where do various tools of strategy contribute to this flow? Answers given in some marketing textbooks to these questions, (both in present and past theory – till late '90s), are recapitulated here.

4.5.1 The importance of national context ("Nature of Nation") & relevance of three communication & strategic processes:

Customers, today, can choose from products and services being offered by firms placed all over the world. However, the firm that has to offer them has to make strategic choices within its national context. Of course, it can set up production facilities in a different nation. Even at the new location it will be working within a national context.

Planning must recognise role of the national context. National environment plays a central role in the competitive success of firms. The home nation influences the ability of firms to succeed by building a national competitive advantage. The nature of this influence has been studied by Porter. He states that home nations competitiveness is not just a macroeconomic phenomenon of exchange rates, interest rates & deficits. For, nations have shown rapid growth despite budget deficits & high interest rates. Neither are low wages or abundance of national resources a explanation for national competitiveness. For, nations have succeeded despite high wages and lack of natural resources. Government policy, too, he concludes has not often played a decisive role. What, then, determines this national competitive advantage?

A nation's competitive advantage, in present theory, uses the 3C's as it is built on:
(i) Porter's realisation that no nation can be competitive in and be a net exporter of everything. Hence, in his analysis, the role of dependence is important both within the country & between countries. He shows that within the country the firm's dependence on factor conditions, related & supplier industries and demand conditions necessitates co-operation. Competitive advantage is built by firms excelling in an environment of mutual interdependence with suppliers, scientific community, related industries and even competitors. Society implies inter-dependence – like parts of a body.

Mutual inter-dependence requires co-operation. Developing co-operation, within the national context is conducive for competitive success. At the second stage, co-operation should percolate within the firms function as well as its style, staff, structure, skills etc. The increasing use of cross-functional teams for strategy building reflects this.

(ii) A focussed Concern on micro variables to understand determinants of productivity and rate of productivity growth. Porter understands determinants of national competitive advantage not with a focus on the economy but on specific industries and industry segments. This helps him find answers to key issue of why and how meaningful and commercially valuable skills and technology are created.

Competitive advantage results out of a process that is closely connected to competition in particular industries. The focussed concern of its human resource, in Porters approach, reacts to these competitive forces. This competitive pressure leads to a focussed concern on activities of the firm. This enables up-gradation of skills in an effort to perform these activities better or in a unique way. This process helps build a firms strategy.

In international competition the specialised skill of human resources is the most decisive factor. Communication enables it to first build channels of co-operation. Then, it helps express its creative potential through a competitive strategy. This emerges from a focussed concern to react to competitive forces.

(iii) Competitive response: Within a specific industry, competition plays a very important role. Porter shows that greater the degree of competition, better the ability of an individual firm to innovate. Hence delivery of better value added products depends on the degree of competition. It also depends on the ability of a firm to use competitive pressures to increase operational efficiency. This improves ability to combine activities in a manner that enhance value. The area of execution of firm's strategy will be elaborated later.

4.5.2 Three Generic Strategies and their 3 strategic fits: Theory till late '90s

To counter the competitive forces, Porter states that the firm's strategy can be built in 3 ways:

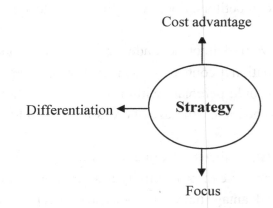

Porter's 3 strategic alternatives

Diagram 4.1

1. Overall cost leadership: Developing a focussed concern for & investing in cost-saving processes enables this. A high market share, economies of scale in production or favorable access to raw material also enables it.

2. Differentiation: This is the ability to create something that is perceived as unique. This could be in product design, brand image, technology, product features, customer service, dealer network or other dimensions.

3. Focus: Instead of targeting the complete market, a firm focuses on a particular buyer group or a geographic market. It chooses to serve it more effectively & efficiently.

Each of three generic strategies can be fulfilled if three 'fits' occur in all activities of the firm. These 'strategic fits' also are listed by Porter.

A successful strategy ensures these three things occur in activities as well as their interactive process within a firm. These three fits require unity of thought, word and deed. The firm, its suppliers and other life forces of business should have this unity. This enables reinforcement and simple consistency leading to an Optimisation effort.

(i) Simple consistency: There should be a consistency between each activity (function) and overall strategy. Identifying three C's of a firm's communication strategy enables this simple consistency. Co-operation between the functions of a firm, followed by a focussed concern for ensuring consistency, leads to delivery of the firm's competitive response.

(ii) Reinforcement: The various activities of the firm should reinforce each other. This is what identification of the 3C processes seeks to do.

(iii) Optimisation effort: The configuration of individual activities of firm and way they relate to each other should be an Optimisation effort. This, again, is the objective of identification of 3C processes.

The task of communication within a firm is, therefore, to ensure that its activities are consistent, reinforcing and optimizing in nature. Communication ensures this and enables a firm's competitive advantage and success. Communication strategy and firm's strategy building processes therefore flow with each other. The communication processes help build the strategic processes of a firm. This appreciation required having a relook at the role of communication, as it was popularly understood, then.

4.5.3 Delivering the 3 strategic fits implies using the 3Cs

Strategy building by the firm is not an event but a process. Understanding dynamics of this process helps a firm achieve competitive success. Every firm, irrespective of size, location or position in market is indulging in this process – formally or informally. By formally acknowledging the process due importance is given to key activities regarded as 'informal' and left out of plans. Lack of adequate feedback and data on these could lead to 'safe' or 'in-between' strategies. They can damage ability of the firm to take a winning differentiated position in the market place.

The strategy building and communication tasks need to be understood together. In a world based on communication, strategy building and execution depend on many things. These are: (a) knowing where to build communication channels, (b) ability to build them (c) their profitable use for inflow and outflow of desired information and response. Wherever communication channels need to be built, are built – and finally used, heart to heart communication, shown in 1.5 above, is needed. It creates natural trust through subtle, verbal and meta-verbal communication. The integration of ethic of 'Shared Value' of human 'Concern' and Selfless Love for others aids development of a strategy for the firm. Viewing strategy building through the eyes of heart to heart communication, we can divide it into 3 parts:

i. <u>What the customers and target audience see::</u> (4P's, Marketing Communication, Total Purchase experience etc.) : These include all activities of the firm visible to the outside world. It also includes the product, packaging etc. and all non verbal cues that the target audience is exposed to.

ii. <u>What the firm explicitly recognises</u> (the building of strategy, say: differentiation, cost advantage or focus) : The firm has a visible process for strategy building. The target audience views the firm based on what it communicates verbally and meta verbally. The firm recognises explicit strategy building activities accepted as the routine for taking strategic decisions. Perceptions about these activities may vary from detailed, bureaucratic, informal, unstructured etc.

iii. <u>The area of activities that communication theory needs to explicitly recognise</u> (a) Cooperation with cluster, industry, trade association, competitor, scientific community, other sources of information. (b) Need to 'process' information received for possible value addition. : These sets of activities are being informally or formally undertaken by every firm. It is their importance in strategy building that needs to be recognised not only by the firm, the industry but also by communication theory as critical for building competitive advantage.

The first two 'C's (co-operation and focussed concern), seen with a firm's eyes, are correctly judged by the 3rd C. If the firm's vision, to 'C', matches with customer needs, then the vision is correct. This can get it competitive success. However, whether it is good for long term balance of man, firm and society will be determined by the fourth 'C'. The ability to see the 4th 'C' as a guide to the other three is will be discussed later. This ability establishes true heart to heart communication amongst men, factors, firm, cluster, nation and nature.

Role of communication in building firm's strategy

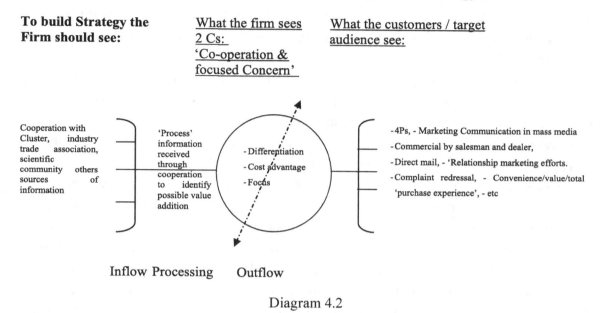

To build Strategy the Firm should see:

What the firm sees 2 Cs:
'Co-operation & focused Concern'

What the customers / target audience see:

Cooperation with Cluster, industry trade association, scientific community others sources of information

'Process' information received through cooperation to identify possible value addition

- Differentiation
- Cost advantage
- Focus

- 4Ps, - Marketing Communication in mass media
- Commercial by salesman and dealer,
- Direct mail, - 'Relationship marketing efforts.
- Complaint redressal, - Convenience/value/total 'purchase experience', - etc

Inflow   Processing   Outflow

Diagram 4.2

A firm's ability to deliver better value than competitors is determined by which activities it performs and how it configures them. It also depends on how these activities relate to each other. Porter states that Strategy implies having three order of 'fits' among activities of the firm. These 'fits' are not mutually exclusive.

Simple Consistency, Reinforcement, Optimisation effort of Chapter1: The first-order fit is **simple consistency**. This implies a simple consistency between each activity and overall strategy. The second-order fit occurs when activities **reinforce** each other. The third-order fits requires an **Optimisation** effort. It is not difficult to see that the three fits cannot occur without the 3Cs. Cooperation among the 'skills' of the 'staff' is essential for simple consistency, reinforcement and Optimisation. Focussed concern helps choose activities which will be consistent, reinforcing and optimise results. They will give greatest value added at least possible cost. The strategy or competitive response of firm is the three fits working in harmony with each other. They create differentiation, focus or cost advantage.

4.5.4 Positioning is 'Mark' plus 'Get' of Marketing

Positioning is identifying a point in a psychological space of customers' mind which delivers value & satisfies his need. It is like the archer getting the correct mark through single minded concentration after identifying the correct target. Three competitive response alternatives in terms of Positioning (identified by Porter) need to be considered here. The 3Cs are interlinked in execution of these strategic positions: Variety based, Need based & Access based Positioning

• Firstly, cooperation among firm's resources and a focussed concern identifies and brings together a distinctive set of activities. These are determined to best produce particular products or services. This implies that firm's product or services range need not be produced identically. There may be better ways of producing a subset of them through a unique activity or activities done in a unique way. This is Variety Based positioning.

• Secondly, where groups express Individuality through different needs, a focussed concern on a particular segment is possible. Cooperation or bringing together of firms activities can be done to serve Individuality of these needs best. This competitive response is Need-Based positioning.

• The third alternative is a variant of need based positioning. This refers to situations where needs may be same but customers need to be reached in different ways. This may be due to customer geography, customer scale or anything requiring a different set of activities. A focussed concern on ways of reaching and cooperation of activities to offer value gives a competitive response called Access-based positioning.

Building a strategy based on differentiation or focus or deciding among three positioning alternatives involves knowing the target audience as well as the marketing and communication objectives. These two tasks of marketing communication are done at an early stage of competitive response. The 3 fits are designed to deliver a firm's competitive response to meet marketing objectives. Execution of this process requires using the 3Cs.

4.5.5 Competitive communication response needs focussed concern on and co– operation of tools of strategy: Present/ Past Theory (till late '90s)

If any positioning alternative naturally unfolds from a process of focussed concern as above, a communication strategy can proceed with them. Otherwise, it may be useful to start with three questions instead:

a)   What should the firm do?   (b)   How to do it?   (c)   When to do what?

Answering these three questions by interlinking strategy with communication is addressed here. The flows of marketing strategy and communication decisions from tools of strategy are explored.

All the techniques / tools of planning are capable of answering these questions in a direct or indirect way. However, for convenience we could look at the following as a simplified way of understanding.

Flow of 'marketing strategy, communication' from 'tools of strategy'

Questions.of competitive response	Tools for competitive response	Strategic Decisions (The Competitive response)
What to do	SWOT, BCG Matrix	Build, Hold, Harvest, Divest.
How to do it	3 Generic Strategies	Differentiation, Cost leadership, Focus.
When to do what	Product Life Cycle, Competitor Response Profile etc.	When to expect Competition? What strategies will competitors adopt? When to react & how? Other such competitive responses.

Tools	Strategic Decisions	Customer communication decisions.
SWOT, BCG Matrix	Build, Hold, Harvest, Divest	Listing firms strategy alternatives Deciding marketing objectives after balancing firms product portfolio Deciding budget available (including communication budget).
3 strategic positions	Variety-based, need-based, access based positions	Deciding firms strategy Deciding target audience Determining marketing and communication objectives.
3 generic strategies	Differentiation, cost leadership Focus.	Communication message. Choice of communication channels depends on exposure & preferences of target audience
Product life cycle and competitor response profile	How will competitors react? When will there be maximum competition? Impact on 4Ps. When to react to competition & how?	Deciding the promotion mix. Marketing communication tasks are usually influenced by the stage of product life cycle.

Diagram 4.3

4.5.6 Strategy, Product Life Cycle (PLC) and implications for Promotion mix: '90s Theory

4.5.6a) Generic strategies and their ease of use in PLC stages

Generic strategies should last the firm through all stages of the product life cycle. However alert competitors may copy technology, make it better, and undertake cost saving or other means to make this task difficult.

Using Porter's logic, in certain stages of the product life cycle, certain strategies may be easier to achieve. For example differentiation may be easier to establish in *introduction and growth stage* of product life cycle. Cost advantage may not be critical for competitive success in these two stages. But, if the firm develops this advantage, its success in the *maturity and decline stage* becomes more assured. Focus strategy, by its very nature, implies sacrificing some market share. In the *introduction and growth stage* firms may not find this strategy attractive unless they have limited resources or specialised skills which can only cater to certain customers. However in the *maturity and decline stage* 'focus' is probably the most useful strategy to follow for all firms, irrespective of their size.

Generic Strategies / Stages of PLC	Differentiation	Cost Leadership	Focus	'Co-operation'	Focus concern	AIDA Process (A I D A)
Introduction	Easy to establish (Product benefit differentiation established here)	Low Criticality — Need of customer more important than cost of product	More useful strategy for smaller firms or	- Co-operation with 'other' industries to build processes, technology & product to satisfy customer	Business Process 'Engineering' and TQM critical	
Growth	(More focus on technical and performance differentiation)		those having specialized skills only	- Co-operation with industry to create enabling conditions to sustain growth. - Co-operation with supplier to delivery 'quality' and 'quantity'	Business Process Re Engineering critical for firm's survival. TQM Important.	
Maturity	(Market segmentation) Less product differentiation	Survival of firm	Most useful	- Co-operate with customer to identify Individuality and 'Creativity' that is not getting satisfied - Co-operate with 'other' or outsider source to discover products, process and technologies to satisfy needs	Business Process ReEngineering and TQM critical.	
Decline	Little product differentiation — Difficult To establish	May depend on low cost — High Criticality	Strategy for all firms	- Co-operate with industry to lower cost and delivery greater value	Business Process ReEngineering and TQM critical.	

Generic strategies and AIDA process - in stages of Product Life Cycle - PLC (as per '90s Theory) Diagram 4.4

Diagram 4.4

4.5.6b) Influences of product life cycle on product, marketing, distribution and overall strategy (Direction, Connection): '80's and '90s Theory

The marketing and overall strategy of the firm is often influenced by the stage of product life cycle. The implication on product design and development, distribution as well as marketing and overall strategy, as in standard textbooks of '80's and '90s, is listed below:

	INTRODUCTION	GROWTH	MATURITY	DECLINE
Products and product change	Product design & development is the key	Products have technical & performance differentiation. Competitive product improvements	Less product differentiation. Trade-ins become significant.	Little product differentiation.
Marketing	-Very high advertising / sales ratio -Creaming price strategy	High advertising but lower percentage of sales than introductory stage -Advertising & distribution key for non-technical products	Market segmentation Efforts to extend life cycle -Service & deals more prevalent. -Packaging important -Advertising competition -Lower advertising / sales percentage	Low advertising to Sales percentage & other marketing costs.
Distribution	-Specialized channels	-Scramble for distribution -Mass channels.	-Distribution channels pare down lines to improve margins. -High physical distribution costs due to broad lines. -Mass channels.	-Specialty channels
Overall strategy	-Best period to increase to market share. -R&D, engineering are key functions.	Practical to change price or quality image. -Marketing the key function	-Bad time to increase market share especially if it is low. -Competitive costs is the key -Bad time to change 'price' or 'quality image' -"Marketing effectiveness" is the key	-Cost control is the key

Source: Adapted from "Competitive Strategy: Techniques for analysing industries and competitors" Michael E. Porter

Diagram 4.5

4.6 The 4C Approach to 'Competitive Response'

The 4C Approach has a different understanding that reflects in implementation of the third 'C' i.e. Competitive Response. Management theory identified the 3rd C as outlined above in 1990's (when current decision makers were in business schools). However, this does not incorporate major concerns of Indian wisdom. So, such an approach is not found in its texts. What would be the impact of these concerns on a firm's Competitive Response?

The focus of the 4C Approach is on transformation of man. This leads to transformation of firm, society, nation and finally, family of nations. The transformation of man happens when he rises up in Maslow's Hierarchy of Needs. In ancient Indian tradition this rising is a three stage process from Self Preservation to Self Sacrifice to Self Realisation.

Academic Theory: Theory, discussed in 4.5 above, does not differentiate between actions based on understanding of the Truth about Man. The 4C Approach begins with this concept. Man, who is performing all actions, in 4C approach, begins by asking the Truth about himself. This enables him to rise up hierarchy of Maslow's needs faster.

Man's Understanding of Truth about himself: In the theory outlined above, man's understanding of Truth about himself can be on the construct: 'I am the body'. This makes Self Preservation the prime focus of his and firm's activity. In this approach, man is not clear about difference between human needs and desires. Only use of his Discrimination ability (which is the result of 'education') helps him in this task. Man has a right to fulfill his needs. However, the ability to restrain desires which harm others and society is created by the ancient Indian tradition. Hence 'sacrifice' of selfishness results from education. This 'transforms' him to reach the higher stage of Self Sacrifice. He, then, rises in Maslow's hierarchy, too.

Impact on Action: When desires are taken as basic needs, fulfilling them is understood as a 'right'. Then man believes it his duty to fulfill them. This leads to imbalance in society.

Role of Discrimination (esp. in Education): Without discrimination, which comes through education, individuals imagine rights without realising duties. Then, impact of action on others, society, environment etc is not given importance. Actions, therefore, become selfish in nature. This attitude harms balance in society or development of industry, cluster or home nation advantage. Whenever such co-operation does take place, its selfish nature does not allow long term benefits to be sustainable over centuries.

Combined impact of actions: When a majority in society acts, driven by selfishness, it leads to a fractured society, as pointed out in the Background, here.

4.7 The 4C Approach in economics, management and life: Control greed, prevent recession

The study of economics started with a simple definition. It stated that man had limited means and unlimited wants. So, he had to choose in an optimum manner. As economies became affluent, this definition did not seem relevant. For, man could satisfy many wants. When need is fulfilled, greed can come. It may lead to over exploitation of resources – both human and natural. The pace of this may have accelerated after the Industrial Revolution.

Thomas Piketty of Paris School of economics did research along with his colleagues that led to his book 'Capital in the Twenty – First Century'. He studied the history of income and wealth distribution over twenty countries since the Industrial Revolution. The study of equality and inequality in society was the focus of study.

The main equalising force, according to his research – both within and between countries is **diffusion of knowledge** and skills. This is the focus of this book also.

The most powerful force in the long run that pushes towards rising inequality is also identified. When rate of return on capital 'r' exceeds the rate of growth 'g', wealth disparities increase towards extreme – Piketty concludes. This view coincides with the ancient Indian view about Price and Optimisation effort as discussed below.

Price determines profit and profit determines return on capital. The unrestrained desire for profit leads to rising inequality in society. It is an expression of man's greed. This was the understanding of ancient Indian tradition also. Thus it taught self restraint. The voice of conscience was awakened and a natural ceiling on desires was ingrained in man – leading to restraint of greed. This not only constrained inequality in society but also prevented over exploitation of natural resources. When no such restraint on greed is self imposed through education there is exploitation of not only natural but human resources as well.

Thus the ancient Indian approach or the 4C Approach is not just an economic theory or a management theory. It teaches a way of life. Discipline, within a 'study of limits', ingrained by education leads to balance. This balance within man leads to seeking 'g' or growth to be greater than 'r' or return on capital! This leads to balance in society. When there is less inequality in society there is better balance. Lack of exploitation of man by man also leads to an attitude that does not over exploit natural resources, too. This leads to balance with nature, too. Awareness, inculcated by education, gives righteous self restraint.

Pikkety feels that the biggest equalisers were shocks that came in 1914 to 1945 through financial shock of Depression and world wars. The ancient Indian tradition avoided global conquests, was described as the 'Golden Sparrow', avoided a state of Decline in Porters stages of National Competitive Development, and contributed significantly to global GDP (as projected backwards by researchers) for thousands of years. How?

Its approach transforms man's life through education. For, in the ancient Indian tradition, just as Piketty postulates, education was the greatest equaliser as it created Excellence. It did not just impart information of tools and techniques or impart skills. In fact, imparting skills was done after transformation of man. Then, these skills could not be misutilised.

Hence morality and truth were the most important Best Practice of Management when excellence, not success, was a goal. If excellence was not implemented, all other practices did not even remain good practices! Untruth or immorality would make man cheat himself, first. If man cheats himself, he can cheat the firm, too. His success can make the firm cheat society. If cheating society, customers, suppliers etc. does not prick man's conscience, cheating nature would become a second nature. Then, the whole cycle of trust on which society balances itself is disturbed. Then, balance between man and nature, too, is shaken.

Thus its concept of economics or management started with man and how he lived life. Managing man's life was the first Best Practice of Management. The Strategy for managing man's life was the same as Strategy used for managing the firm. The simplicity of life was accentuated by the common concepts of strategy. This is how recession was prevented and a significant contribution made to global GDP.

Thus management flowed from life of man to the firm. It led to balance in man, balance in firm and balance in society. Such an approach made the civilisation survive.

Ancient Indian tradition did not indulge in war of 'isms' of Capitalism or Socialism. It did not deny that some inequalities will always exist. Efforts at removing them totally have led to fall of regimes in the long run. It made efforts to minimise them, always. Such an effort was an ongoing one through education and character building. It educated man to remove disparity in thinking. It taught that all should be loved equally – irrespective of social status. However, social status is relevant for social roles. Man should learn to perform his duty with equal Love for all. This removes feeling of inequality in society.

4.8 Beyond 3C Approach: Profit Optimisation not Profit maximisation!

Porter's Optimisation Effort is elevated to Profit Optimisation in the 4C Approach. It replaces Profit Maximisation strategies of capitalism, economic theories and competitive strategy. Optimisation Effort is explained as **changing speed of car to suit terrain**. Thus, **when growth slows, Optimisation effort implies business should adjust Piketty's 'r', too!** This implies two things:

(a) Business is not driven by greed which implies that man is able to control his desires when the situation demands. Such an understanding can only emerge from education.
(b) Business understands the concept that it is dependent on society and can not divorce itself from what is happening in society. Realising this interdependence is basis of *Vedas* in ancient Indian tradition. Man can no longer afford to remain selfish and seek high profits when society is suffering low growth. The responsibility of inculcating this attitude rested with education – in this tradition.

It may not be possible to fight cycles of business, but the ancient Indian approach did give a value system that can normalize them.

In Indian tradition the 3C Approach is designed to prepare for a 4C Approach. Till now, we have discussed only the 3C Approach. The *Vedas* help man to study Upanishads and, later, *Atma Vidya*. *Vedas* deal more explicitly with the first three *Purusharthas* or the first three 'C's'. *Upanishads* and *Atma Vidya* prepare man for 4th C or *Moksha*. However, a linkage between them is always there and above distinction is a simplification. It is impossible to follow *Upanishadic* teachings if selfishness instinctively appeals to an individual. This is the problem in explaining Competitive Response in 4C Approach here. Until a Background of Selfless Approach is ingrained, the text ahead would be meaningless.

How to understand Competitive Response correctly in 4C Approach?

Competition that breeds hatred (as can happen in 3C Approach) can never add value to man and society. Such competition is against the spirit of ancient Indian tradition. It must be avoided at all costs. For, it may lead to success, but does not promote excellence.

To get a correct understanding of Competitive Response in 4C Approach, it is best to revert to the Background of this book. If any idea is not clear there, the understanding will not be clear here.

The facts of the world are not denied in the 4C Approach. In fact, their study is considered necessary. Only man bases actions on a correct understanding about himself and purpose of life. There are 3 stages of wisdom in the Indian tradition. These stages relate to Maslow's hierarchy. They are: Self Preservation, Self Sacrifice and Self Realisation.

3 stages of Wisdom in Ancient Indian tradition

1. Knowledge gained by analysis of objective world is called *Jnana*.
2. When this knowledge is further studied and practiced to serve best interests of society it becomes *Sujnana* or Beneficial Wisdom.
3. The intentions and urges arising from a purified consciousness saturated with Divine qualities is *Vijnana* or Highest Wisdom.
In the stage of Self Preservation, knowledge is only gained by analysis of objective world. The ancient Indian tradition expounds that: "the use of discrimination leads to first Intelligence, then to Intellect and finally to Intuition". These three govern thoughts and actions of man.

One leads to another. Discrimination is used to raise intelligence of man to the level of intellect. Then, he analyses results of his actions on others and society. When "What a man can be, he must be" (Maslow words on Self Actualisation) then, man realises his full potential. This is referred to as Self Realisation. Then, intentions and urges arise from a purified consciousness and lead to *Vijnana*. Man's intelligence leads to awakening the intellect when he serves society. Finally, when he purifies intentions, he develops intuition. Thus man moves from selfishness or *Swartha* to *Parartha* and *Parmartha* (enlightened self interest and highest good of society). This transition is explained later.

The 4C Approach

The purpose of education, in this tradition, is to focus on intellect to transform the heart using 'intelligent discrimination'. This is understood as *Viveka*. While there are 4 goals of life, there are two types of education: lower (*Apara Vidya*) and higher (*Para Vidya*). Fulfilling first three goals of life requires lower learning. Fulfilling the last goal requires only the Highest learning. However, the last goal cannot be achieved until first three are fulfilled in a particular way. What is this way? How anyone judge from behaviour of man that he is ready for the Highest learning? This distinction becomes clear from the 'focus' of his 'concern' and his competitive response. Actions of man may differ as per changing situation and time. However, there are some norms of behaviour that enable a teacher or others to judge students. What are these norms?

Impact of Education of 4C Approach on Man's actions

a) Without 4C Approach: An 'uneducated' man's actions show greed for competitive luxury and conspicuous consumption. Wealth is important but **attitude** to wealth is critical.
b) With 4C Approach: Man's actions are signified by his behaviour. It shall be based on humility, morality, compassion and detachment. Wealth does not give a feeling of superiority.

Basic determinant of Demand in 4C Approach

The practice of life starts with righteous conduct or *Dharma*. Therefore, the basic determinant of demand also emerges by following *Swa-Dharma* boldly. **Dharma, as understood by ancient Indians, is something which makes the entire world prosperous.** This is the inspiration for and **purpose of Co-operation. It should bring prosperity to the whole world.** One dimension of *Swa-Dharma* is to exercise control over desires – not generate their senseless multiplication. By following this in performing duties, knowledge or experience of *Atma* slowly emerges. The purpose of practice (or *Sadhna*) is to help clarify Awareness of *Atma* or Soul.

Some differences between the two Approaches

Discrimination 'leads' (a function of Management) man to 'direct' and 'control' (both functions of Management) desires through daily practice (*Sadhna*). This (leading, directing, controlling) involves a study and practice of Man Management. It transforms the current 3C Approach (which does not focus on Discrimination) into a 4C Approach. The impact this transformation has on Man's understanding of Self, his 'actions in society' and 'purpose of life' are given in Diagram 4.6. Man stops bargaining for 'Income' with employers, society and others to perform his duty. Instead, he seeks merger of his self interest into highest good of all. The 'Out-come' of his actions becomes more important for him. This transforms duty into enlightened self interest. This makes man move from *Jnana* to *Sujana* to *Vijnana*. He serves the cluster, industry and society Selflessly. This unleashes the creative potential of man. Society protects those who protect society. Hence, with this confidence and conviction a man should serve the firm and society. His contribution, if it adds value, can not go unnoticed by those who receive its value. The ability to add value comes from self confidence which emerges from an ability of self sacrifice. Without sacrifice a greed for rewards demeans human effort. A hankering for rewards takes the focus away from work – leading to a decline in quality and productivity. This does not allow the potential of either man or the firm to be realised.

Discrimination transforms 3C Approach to 4C Approach

3C Approach without focus on Discrimination	4C Approach
Man's Actions in Society:	Man's Actions in Society:
Maximise Salary for Self. If this requires then Maximise profit for division and firm. So, firms give incentive for performance!	Maximise welfare of customer.
	From '*Jnana* to *SuJnana* to *Vijnana*' Merger of Self interest with highest Good of society.
Man's Understanding of Self:	Man's Understanding of Self:
I am the Body.	I am the *Atma* or Soul.
Man's Purpose of Life:	Man's Purpose of Life:
Purpose of Action is to seek and maximise personal pleasure and fulfill 'Selfish Desires'. Firms and nation should align their interests by integrating incentives for individual's selfish needs.	To seek the highest good of all Selflless for Cluster, industry, society

Diagram 4.6

View about wealth: Man's view on wealth also changes with 4C Approach. He considers wealth as that which cannot be stolen. Wisdom is the greatest wealth, for no thief can steal it! Money is a recent phenomenon after the barter system. Material wealth earned using wisdom is considered true wealth. Proper education or following *Purusharthas* only can lead to true wealth. Wealth should emerge from application of knowledge as wisdom. That wealth which is earned by selfish means or harming others is not considered as true wealth. For it cannot lead to balance in man and society.

In ancient Indian tradition there is a case study of an emperor whose kingdom was made of gold. He did a lot of repetition of God's name. Yet his kingdom faced a recession and was burnt. The King was killed. His name was *Ravana*. Even though he had wealth, there was one fault. His instincts worked from one assumption: "I am the body". He could harness a lot of material wealth and spiritual powers. However, none of them could help him in the end. The idea is that material wealth is not a sign of true wealth. It is important – but – the attitude to wealth is more important. This attitude develops only through education.

Education makes man 'Creative', changes 'Influencers', upgrades skills

The unleashing of creativity has a tremendous impact on productivity. It removes fear of failure, reduces self preservation instinct and spurs innovation. The diagram that analyses customer as an individual can also analyse the manager of firm, worker and all employees. The influencers that work on a customer also work on others in a similar manner.

'Creative' Man: The upgrading of Knowledge & Skill

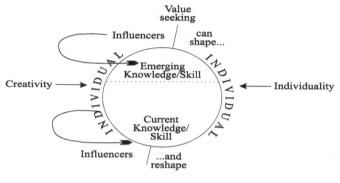

Diagram 4.7

Diagrams 4.7, 4.8 (similar to Diagrams 3.2 and 3.3 depicting Creative Market) illustrate man's creative nature, unleashed by Selflessness which directs his desire for excellence (Diagram 4.9).

'Creative' Man: The 'influencers' & Man – their inter-play

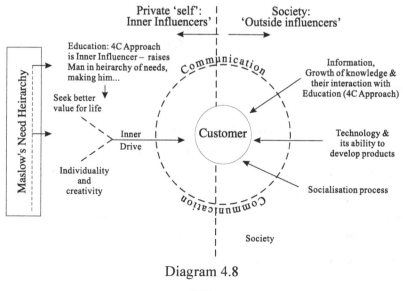

Diagram 4.8

What is the difference in the understanding of Excellence?

The desire to excel is an inborn trait. This desire for Excellence is fulfilled by achieving the best for society. Expression of this desire is different when behaviour of man is selfish i.e. when creativity unleashed by pursuing highest goal of life does not exist. 3C Approach shown below leads to success – but 4C Approach leads to excellence as depicted below:

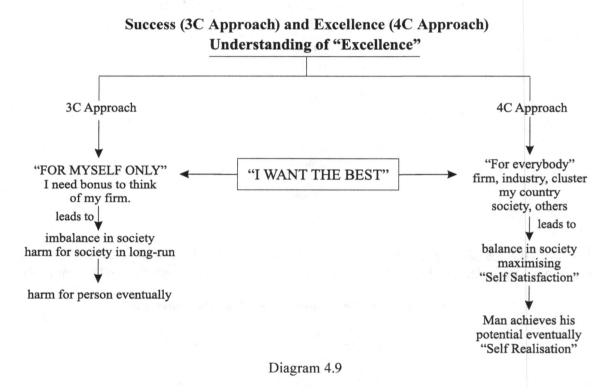

Diagram 4.9

The economic concept of society

In 4C Approach, economic concept of society is not just profit maximization but different. It is based on an understanding that earth's resources are enough for everybody's needs – not everybody's greed! Such conviction emerges from unleashed creativity of Selfless Love. Therefore, a rush for competitive consumption is not indulged in by firms or customers. Education moulds thoughts by inculcating a habit of 'control on unnecessary desires' in man. The firm and customers work from this common understanding. Firms do not try to promote competitive consumption either through promotion or product design.

View about Price

The firm, in ancient Indian tradition, should earn 10 to 15% profit according to the spiritual Source of this study. This approach creates balance in society, prevents recession etc and answers Piketty's concerns. When high profit margins are earned, it invites more competitors. Then, competitors may create production capacity leading to unbalanced allocation of resources towards one product. Finally, excess capacity may lead to discounts, schemes or maybe waste of resources to create temporary sale. The ancient approach of 'Limits', in their experience, gives value to customer, firm, society.

The different impact of 3C and 4C strategies on firms and society

Will supernormal profits help maintain balance through efficient use of scarce resources? Will this result in best price and product? Will consumer get value delivered in the most efficient way – and will products be promoted to heighten genuine usage and satisfaction? Excess capacity, unnecessary promotion and competitive price war imply waste of scarce resources of society. Price of product, thus, helps efficient allocation of society's resources. Determining the right price depends on attitude – which comes from education.

Promotion, an illustration of how imbalance can result in 3C Approach

Misusing promotion can increase competitive consumption in society. It can also set up high cost barriers for entry into an industry. Such intentions do not find favour in the 4C Approach. For, the ultimate cost is borne by the consumer. Setting up a barrier to entry by promotion budgets increases cost of the product – even if low profit margin is charged. Such a strategy is designed to eliminate small players. They cannot afford such campaigns and are squeezed out of business. Once the smaller competitors are out of market the producer is tempted to charge higher margins. These high margins, then, attract players with bigger and deeper pockets to enter the industry creating further capacity.

Non – generic products with shorter life cycle may also wish to have high promotion budgets. Due to fast changes in consumer preferences, producers may wish to keep higher margins. Waiting for consumers to develop a habit is too slow as fashions change fast. Quicker return on investment may need risk of high promotion budgets. Such strategies of high margins tempt new entrants who are attracted by margins. They may not have in-depth study of circumstances that have led to them. Hence new entrants with even bigger pockets and higher promotion budgets can enter the market. This leads to further capacity. Of course, oligarchic practices also limit competition and prevent entry into the marketplace. The cutting down of supply cost to below production cost level by giving distributors, dealers or customers special deals/ price when new competitor enters is another strategy. It can not only scare competition but also result in closures of factories. This leads to misallocation of resources of society. Many of these entrants use bank finances which are savings of common man. Any default due to too much capacity is at the cost of banks that have to service savings of common man. Higher Non-performing assets weaken banks and raise cost of capital. They lead banks to have bigger difference between interest paid to savers and interest rate charged from industry. This is not good for either savers or the industry in the long run.

Regulators and regulation cannot ensure efficient allocation nor can state planning. A common sense understanding of business and life is best ensured by education. Competitive consumption can be promoted by firm to ensure higher price and higher sales to use excess capacity. It can use symbols and visuals that have a direct impact on desire creation. The temptation to appeal to baser instincts of man is not far away. This usually results in sale, utilisation of larger capacities and, therefore, higher profitability. Higher profitability with lack of competition leads to less emphasis on creativity. New ideas to improve productivity do not arise. Firms with large profits may increase their overhead in an unsustainable manner. In a recession – or when faced with some competition – it may be forced to outsource some operations. Thus, it may lose old employees and facilities. This may happen with a suddenness that disrupts organisation morale and commitment. This does not create balance at workplace or sense of belonging that generates co-operation, innovation and productivity. How to prevent such recession pressures from occurring?

A continuous awareness of total quality management is needed to increase productivity. It recognises early signs of availability of low cost resources. It makes commitments to develop them in a manner suitable to organisation culture. This requires alertness, efficiency, creativity as well as proactive thinking and action. Awareness of higher self interest includes customers and society. It uses discrimination and does not restrict competition. Its actions prevent misallocation of society's resources. Monopolistic practices restrict flow of information. Competition encourages development of low cost resources leading to long term productivity and continuous innovation. Other customer unfriendly policies, too, harm society. For example discounts given to doctors to recommend laboratory tests/ drugs even though they may be unnecessary for patient etc harm the faith in the most trusted profession as well as in goodness itself. Industries following such practices can lead to inefficient allocation of resources in society. In the long run, the consumer boom that results may be sowing seeds of a recession.

What is competition, who is the competitor? – Compete only with your own self

Competition is necessary when self motivation needs an intervention from outside to activate itself to a higher level. In initial stage competition is necessary for it promotes humility by experiencing other's excellence. It improves skills of man and firm by using benchmark of competition. It helps develop team work in firms to generate a competitive response. This requires co-operation across all functions from design to production to suppliers to distribution. It helps develop new ideas. However, the prime motivation is outside or fear of survival. The locus of control, too, is outside. To counter the threat of outside doing better, co-operation of everybody inside is necessary. This develops humility and makes the team realise the value of everybody. Spirituality shifts man's locus of control within him. This leads to experience of his uniqueness giving him self confidence. Then, individual excellence and groups focussed concern lead to Value Creation that is valued by society.

Therefore, the next step after developing humility is to experience Individuality. The winning idea in a competitive response does not come through efficient imitation of market leader. It emerges from the Individuality of response that the firm can offer. Individuality, without developing humility may lead to great success. Long term balance and survival comes with co-operation of others who can contribute to this Individuality. Adding others Individuality and creativity to ones own helps develops society. Understanding competition becomes as important as understanding the customer when marketing strategies are reactive. Then, features, price, advertising, sales, promotion and distribution of others are the focus. The concept of 4C Approach is not to be reactive but proactive. There is a saying: 'imitation is human while creation is divine'. Effort towards Divinity creates balance – among all.

Divinity is taken as excellence in all dimensions. For, excellence comes through Love for work. When this Love is expanded to include everything it becomes Divinity. How does this emerge? Humility, as we discussed above, should lead to development of Individuality and not imitation. The goal of development of this Individuality within and by the firm is development of Nationality. When firm, industry and cluster work towards National Competitive development, then excellence in all dimensions can emerge. This can lead to the experience of Divinity. It cannot be based on imitation but creativity at all levels expresses the spirit of Unity. This spirit of Unity seeks unity among nations and people.

The development of excellence within man and firm is, thus, a 5 stage process (refer Introduction): a) Humility b) Individuality c) Nationality d) Divinity d) Unity

This 5 stage process has competition and competitive response only as an initial process. The development of excellence within man and firm helps express their Individuality. Their expression serves nationality to seek excellence in all dimensions. This enables them to experience the spirit of unity. How does this journey for excellence occur within man?

As detailed in three types of wisdom, man moves from intelligence to intellect to intuition. The customer, as noted earlier, is driven by creativity and Individuality. He seeks to satisfy demand for current and emerging needs in three ways:

a) Seeking better value delivery for current wants through current products.

This is the desire to satisfy present needs through present products in a better way.

b) Seeking better value delivery of current wants through alternate products.

Here, customer seeks alternate ways of satisfying present needs.

c) Seeking better value delivery of new wants through new products.

Here, products have to be designed for fulfilling new and emerging needs.

The use of intelligence helps in (a) above. The firm's resources and alternatives for action enable optimum allocation of resources for developing a firm's competitive response. The use of intellect, however, allows both (a) and (b) above. It rules out any scope for imitation in firm's competitive response. Intellect can formulate that which is beyond common understanding. However, intuition feels the customer's requirement 'as if it is my own'. Thus, it can satisfy it in a simple, new way. So, intuition enables (b) and (c) above. Intuition can become 'one with' churning of customers mind. It can feel the latent or emerging demand. The use of intellect raises a firm's capabilities above imitation of any nature. The firm, then, seeks to satisfy demand using same resources in new way. Intuition can add a new dimension to a firm's thinking and, therefore, to customer satisfaction.

The development of intuition requires Purity of thought, Patience and Perseverance. The Background diagrammatically represents how this, along with other factors, leads to emergence of Selfless Love within man. The five stage process above is the gradual progress of man and firm from selfishness to selflessness. Humility leads to destruction of ego ('I know it all' attitude). It prepares the ground for selflessness. Directing individuality towards nationality is a higher expression of selflessness. It leads to excellence within oneself. Finally, it helps man experience the highest truth of unity of creation.

Therefore, the real strategy for both individual and firm is to develop ability of Intuition. This process requires man to work on himself to achieve excellence within. When a group with similar commitment works together in a firm, they use skills of each other, through co-operation. Together they build a focussed concern for customer's needs. Total Quality Management expresses this focussed concern in all the firm's processes. It enables a competitive response that competes with only the firm's previous output. For, that is the only other benchmark of excellence in this dimension available. This is where secular and spiritual education comes together and the twain meets.

The 4C Approach uses Individuality and creativity of firm's human resources through co-operation to focus its concern on customer needs. The competitive response that results is a reflection of this individuality and creativity. This will be different for different firms and thus nature of output of each firm will be unique. The development of cluster comes from firms giving supporting inputs and resources to others. This enables competitors to develop their individuality and creativity in their own unique way. For, now, all understand that there is no real competition for individuality. The expression of all products is unique. All compete with themselves as they set higher and higher benchmarks of excellence.

Is 4C Approach a real situation – why study it?

If enough people are not following a path, why study it? If business does not find the 4C Approach relevant, why study it? Can we give examples of how many businesses are run by such thinking? This leads to a counter question: Just because everybody operates from selfishness, does it make a study of the opposite irrelevant? Is study of the Ideal to be abandoned just because nobody dare follow it? The reason of studying an Ideal is the Ideal itself. It seeks no justification for its study. Should *Atma Vidya*, or highest education, be denied just because there are not enough worthy recipients? This would lead to the counter question: In case you do not teach it, how will students develop an interest in it and some will finally follow it in daily life?

As explained in the Background, nature of Creation is ever changing. Time and circumstance are making situations change rapidly. In case excellence is found in management practice, theory should teach from it. If recession occurs, then practice should seek the Ideal of theory. Eternal truths and past experiences are signposts for writing a theory relevant to current times. All current theories are relevant – if they are followed within understanding of nature of Truth and man. Some questions may, however, be asked and we attempt a possible answer here:

Is the concept of Product Life Cycle relevant in 4C Approach?

The Product Life cycle expresses the changing nature of creation and will remain relevant. It may get elongated for the generic product as returns sought by industry are long term. However variants can flourish as customers follow 'limit to desires' but express individuality enabling output of each firm to be unique. The individuality and creativity of the firm would reward it with market share depending on the use of Intellect and Intuition.

The 4C Approach can treat the Product Life Cycle like the 4 stages or *Ashrams* of life cycle of man. Ancient Indians integrated management study with man's life. Just as the five life breaths of man apply to business, this idea, too, shows such integration. **We can apply four stages of life of man to four stages of life of product.** These are: *Brahmacharya* (student), *Grihasta* (householder), *Vanaprastha* (retired) *and Sanyaas* (renounced). The first stage of *Brahmacharya* signifies one who lives in the highest awareness of *'Brahman'*. This state is not *Tamsic* (dull) or *Rajasic* (activity). It is *Satwic* (pure) awareness – without greed, tricks or selfishness. Such **Awareness helps create value** – for all – man, firm, society. Thus, Awareness is the basis of not only man but also his output. The products he designs must also come from pure intentions which are basis of Awareness.

Education is imparted in the first stage of *Brahmacharya*. It seeks Unity of Thought, Word and Deed. It also seeks to remove selfishness from man's heart as he rotates on axis of Truth and morality. This enables man to 'C' interest of society first. When products are designed and Introduced from highest awareness, they serve society. Value creation will reflect individuality and creativity of the firm which has intuitive grasp of customer needs.

Growth stage of product delivers value to maximum numbers in society. Marriage of man's ideas and their implementation happens through products and services. They serve needs of marriage of man with society. Such marriage leads to balance in society. Marriage is, thus, a social institution designed to promote such balance. The *Grihasta* stage is of marriage, raising a family and looking after them. The family lives in unity. It seeks unity in neighbourhood which builds unity in society. This puts in practice the spirit of unity that results from education. This spirit of Unity is dealt with in Chapter 6. When there is unity in society, there can be unity in the nation and among nations, too. The growth stage of society is when the family expands – which happens when man enters *Grihasta*. In this stage, man has to live in awareness of other's needs – wife and children help him do it. Without that there can be no unity. Hence sacrifice of petty self interest is the basis of unity. Similarly, strategies of products – after Introduction – have to overarch petty self interest to deliver value to society. Only then they will get better market share.

The Background reveals that nature of creation is ever changing. Hence needs, too, are always evolving. Old ones fade out. *Vanaprastha* or Mature products spread knowledge freely – enabling design of new. Just as mature human beings become selfless as they retire. The example of a tree is given. When it is laden with fruit, it bends with humility. It gives freely to all who seek the fruit. The purpose of its life is to serve others. In the Decline stage, as the product renounces the market, its existence inspires all. Its life sets an example of how implementation of pure intuitive ideas can serve society selflessly. When men, too, seek *Sanyas*, they become sources of inspiration. **Both Maturity and Decline stage are not about quantity but about quality**. They help firm reach highest stage of Total Quality Management.

What is the difference between Maturity and Decline stage? It is the same as between *Vanaprastha* and *Sanyas*. In fact there is nothing known as Decline stage in ancient Indian tradition. A new term should be thought for it! Even for society, Porter talks about a Decline stage. This is not possible in the 4C Approach. However, we will use the word Decline here.

In Maturity stage, there can be much value addition through experience. This comes through new techniques of production, new processes to reduce cost or innovative use of materials etc. In ancient Indian tradition, the potter in maturity would start withdrawing after teaching his son. But, the trade continued. He used his experience to guide with ideas. Ideas on design, materials, techniques etc. can raise skills and standards of all. These new ideas help even new products and raise the productivity level of industry. Mature products search for doing the same thing in a better way. This raises level of skills, processes and techniques. These set new benchmarks for the industry. They may also innovatively use new materials to save cost or add value. The nature of material used may help raise industry standards. These new materials may be used for new product design. Hence their innovation adds value to society. Their desire for self satisfaction leads them to seek excellence in every aspect. This makes new benchmarks to guide new entrants. It also sets higher standards for excellence.

In Decline or *Sanyas* stage the fear of self preservation is replaced by a desire for self satisfaction. Hence, excellence is sought in all dimensions. The product is a limited dimension for expressing it. The Source of the book has given the example of a violin maker who spent his entire time perfecting just one violin. The desire for quality and perfection is the goal in itself. It leads to new standards for all. It is an example of excellence. If serving a few or limited customers with excellence is the goal, then it is not decline but the beginning of a new standard. Society gains by such excellence.

The *Sanyasi* or renunciant, in ancient Indian tradition, is sought by all. He seeks Absolute balance, now. The Introduction explains the difference between dynamic and Absolute balance. He generates peace where he sits. He inspires perfection and transforms hearts. His life is an example of selflessness. Even if He is not physically adding value, his value creation is like a mother's value creation for a child. It cannot be measured by money. He adds value to society by demonstrating morality and ethics. He teaches even through silence. His self sacrifice sets new standards for society. A retired Professor's past work continues to inspire search. The presence of sages ensures that values are followed in society. Similarly, products may reach decline stage, in terms of quantity, due to change in nature of demand. But, excellence with which they fulfill demand inspires the new generation – of men and products. They are examples of how to seek excellence selflessly and add value irrespective of reward. Their desire of self satisfaction sets benchmarks in values and value fulfilment for society. They help raise productivity, adding value to life.

The heart of man is the seat of desire that intellect seeks to fulfill. The purpose of education is to transform the heart. Hence, heart is the market. If needs and desires are transformed, society will be transformed. This is the Mark or target that marketing seeks to Get. Marketing, thus, is a difficult subject involving all human wishes and their transformation.

Mere hearing a lecture on marketing (without reflecting or responding) is 'sravanam' in this tradition. Such passive participation is 'tamasic' or dull brained. The individual's effort to turn thoughts over in his mind, while trying to assimilate, makes a person active or 'rajasic'. When man achieves experience of purity of intention this is 'sathwic'. Therefore, marketing is at three levels depending on qualities of the student. Its use is also at three levels. Dull students gain knowledge by analysing the objective world alone. Active Knowledge serves the best interests of society. Finally, purifying intention and urge of man is the goal. Action that arises from such pure intentions leads to the highest wisdom – It creates balance for all.

4.9 To sum up

This chapter shows cooperation of tools of strategy – integrating them with a focussed Concern of the firm to create value. This Cooperation and focussed Concern, then, enables delivery of a Competitive Response. The inter-linkage and interdependence of 3Cs, and their integrated effort to deliver value to customers are detailed. Inter-relationships between tools of strategy have been explored, too. The inter-relationship of three Generic Strategies with Product Life Cycle stage and the AIDA process reflects Simple Consistency, Reinforcement and Optimisation effort of Strategy. This chapter describes integration of 3Cs – an approach used to teach current managers (whose management skills were tested by the recession) in '90's. However, the 4C approach needs a larger definition of 'Competitive Response' which is elaborated above.

True competition is not with others but within oneself in a search for excellence. For this, understanding nature of nation and inner nature of man, customer, supplier, workers etc.

is important. This realisation can add value in a meaningful manner. Imitation or reducing quality to lower price or using "trick"nology to give appearance of adding value is not Competitive Response. Thus Competitive Response is:

- **In tune with 'nature of nation' which includes suppliers, customers etc.**
- **Is not copying by reducing quality.**
- **Is only competing within One Self and seeking excellence.** This should be in all aspects of value creation and delivery. It should emerge through co-operation and focussed concern for customer, society.
- **Is not based on a strategy of 'making money' alone.** It should identify genuine needs of customer and deliver value over a long period of time. Money is secondary, not a primary determinant in this Search for Excellence. Self Satisfaction is found when excellence is achieved. Then, profit is not the No.1 priority of business.

The Indian ethos requires scientific enquiry, explains role of manager and gives importance to understanding "life forces of business". It understands Competitive Response as a 4C approach. This study elevates competitive response – which by nature has an external locus of control – to an internal locus of control. This is achieved by becoming one with the customer and his need. It takes closeness to customer to its peak. Finally, there is no competitive response. There is just a Response. For, the only competitor is the past standard of excellence set by oneself. This makes the process of value addition and delivery merge with *Yoga* (understood as spiritual path and used in the title of each chapter of *Bhagavad Gita*) – discussed in Chapter 6 ahead.

"Cooperation vs Competition: Analysed thoughtfully one finds that modern thinking promotes comparison, competition and conflict. In contrast, in tradition, mutual cooperation and harmony are given priority. Modern civilisation is rooted in conflict and it is a natural law that conflict can never lead to a positive outcome. Two stones placed side by side can form a wall even a house, but if they collide with each other, they would either shatter or diminish. This is the fundamental difference in the vision of the modern and traditional civilisations." Prof Samdhong Rinpoche.

Thus, co-operation or *Yoga* leads to excellence seeking, not conflict. A firm's response must improve each man's previous performance by learning from others excellence: without conflict.

Chapter 5

COMPATIBILITY ADVANTAGE:
THE FOURTH 'C' OF MANAGEMENT

Pursuing Self Actualisation makes Man, Society and Nature benefit from the Fourth 'C' or goal of man, firm

WHEN MANAGEMENT PRACTICE LEADS TO RECESSION, A NEW THEORY IS NEEDED TO GUIDE PRACTICE: CHAPTER 5 PRESENTS SUCH A MODEL

• Use of 4C's positively impacts Man, the firm, industry, cluster, nation, family of nations and interaction with nature. These ideas are inspired by the ancient Indian tradition.

• Man's actions and firm's output should be compatible with the needs of society for benefit of Compatibility Advantage to be shared by all.

• Compatibility Advantage is the Shared Value of Maslow's Self Actualisation need at work in society. It is used by man in life to include his value addition process in the firm. Man is, thus, an evolving being – capable of self improvement. This desire of self improvement is guided by the education process in the 4C Approach.

• The current 3C Approach does not train and guide man for Self Actualisation. Such an approach which did not incorporate values in actions led to the global economic recession.

• The 4C Approach uses Shared Values in shaping and reshaping customer wants in Diagrams 5.3 and 5.4.

• The role of Shared Values, as outlined in McKinsey 7S model, is also recapitulated and used. Porter, too, has stressed the need for a shared value and feels theory about it is still emerging. This Chapter helps this formal theory emerge.

• Shared Values concept moves our understanding from 3C Approach to 4C Approach. Above all, it gives a framework of action. Its critical role is shown visually in Diagrams 5.6, 5.7 and 5.8.

• The 4th C is the Compatibility Advantage at work. It creates a model of balance within man, in the firm as well as society, nation and with nature. Simultaneously. This is depicted in Diagram 5.9 as the goal of academic endeavour of this book.

Does
theory guide practice or practice guides theory?

Theoretical models can never ensure good practices.
Bad practices can never create good theoretical models.

Society does, however, need guides for action – just as man does.

The car's example can guide – if man understands his (cars) nature;

Ancient Indian analogy:
The car of man's life drives society to work and towards balance.
This vehicle is drawn by the senses of man. It is driven by his intellect.
The two pairs of wheels are Time and Action – both rotate continuously.
Discrimination and detachment are the two reins (like a chariot) for them.
The spokes of the wheels are the rules of righteousness bound by the rim of Love.
The axle is Truth and the destination is Peace.

If the above understanding is the basis of practice,
the model shown in this Chapter works
...otherwise, it does not.

4THC

Actions of man, firm, cluster, industry and society should be

Compatible

with the dictates of one's

Conscience for man, firm, industry and society to enjoy the benefits of optimisation effort and

Compatibility Advantage. Equilibrium with nature is possible

by man's actions in a firm, industry, society and nation. The voice of Conscience focuses on what is 'right' and is not persuaded or dissuaded by results (non-attachment). Pursuit of righteous action (optimisation, not profit maximisation) prevents many social problems including recession. Non-attachment to fruit of action is man's goal as in the ancient Indian text of *Bhagavad Gita*. This **attitude** towards seeking excellence led to prosperity for thousands of years – using righteous restraint and non attachment. Optimality is a quest natural to man. It is visible in theoretical models since 1800s. Pareto's optimality influenced welfare economics and his idea of utility had moral, ethical dimensions.

No theoretical model ensures good practices. However, can current practices – which led to a recession – produce a good theory? Ancient practices that demonstrate compatibility of man and society's needs with nature for thousands of years can give a new theory. Can these ancient practices be used for a modern management model? A new theoretical model cannot ensure practice. However, it can visually demonstrate that balance among man, firm, society, cluster, industry, nations is achievable.

The search for excellence in serving customers must use co-operation of thought, word and deed by man. To serve a larger group – cluster, the industry or building a national competitive advantage, the ambit of co-operation must increase further.

Similarly, to serve society too (and achieve balance within man and society) the ambit of co-operation must keep increasing – from man to family to society to nation to family of nations. Let us begin with man...

When marriage partners become compatible with each other it creates balance.

The marriage between man and his mind, man and his work, between man, society and nature should be compatible to create balance. This is Compatibility Advantage at work.

It is best achieved when man pursues Self Actualisation as a goal.

Compatibility Advantage: The fourth 'C' of Management

THE FOURTH GOAL OF FIRM ALIGNED WITH GOAL OF MAN'S LIFE

Pursuing Self Actualisation makes man, society and nature benefit from the Fourth 'C' or goal of man, firm: a management model using ancient practices

Three aspects impact strategy of a firm, but are sometimes ignored. These are: "national interests, psychology of people & needs of people". Needs of people requires products to be designed for them, not transplanted from another culture. Nations, also, must realise the need to seek value based economic development. Firms & cluster should look after this national interest. Prof. Gunnar Mrydal thought nations should have mineral resources, perennial rivers and adequate forest coverage to look after their interest. However, Porter has argued otherwise. Psychology of people determines stage of development. For, when higher order need of Maslow's Self Actualisation guides man, his understanding of growth changes. Prosperity can then be guided by youth, who, through value based educare, become enlightened citizens. With purity of mind, ethics & morals they can harness potential of all resources in a unique way. The fourth 'C' of strategy i.e. 'Compatibility Advantage' emerges when such enlightened citizens work together.

5.1 Compatibility: Shared Value of Maslow's 'Self Actualisation' need at work in society

Strategy and its communication are powerful tools for transformation of actions undertaken by managers, society and nations. Society can communicate a strategy of life to transform children into value-seeking individuals through educare. This empowers them to seek their Self Actualisation potential. Values have an important role to play in influencing the nature of human needs. Strategy of a firm should emerge from man's strategy of life. Communication about these strategies can transform any inertia of mediocrity to dynamism of excellence-seeking. This enables using a nation's resources and capabilities into a competitive advantage and creates balance. A sub-optimal use of resources can make a firm, cluster or nation lose competitive advantage. Similarly, sub-optimal use of strategy and its communication (when strategy of firm does not emerge from a strategy of living life) can make society lose the advantage of compatibility. Society survives on interdependence. When this interdependence is based on a shared value of fulfilling Self Actualisation needs, there is compatibility among actions undertaken by man in society with earth's resources. This creates balance within man and society and with nature's resources, too.

5.2 Limits to current 3C Approach

The purpose of business is to add value. This chapter discusses the meaning and dimensions of value.

Man is a social being. Every individual depends on society for satisfaction of his needs. All value that he receives, therefore, is because of society. The way man seeks to define and enjoy value has an impact on society.

While proposing the societal marketing concept Kotler raises questions about philosophy of marketing. The previous chapter does the same and also offers a solution. He states: "In recent years, some have questioned whether the marketing concept is an appropriate philosophy in an age of environmental deterioration, resource shortages, explosive population growth, world hunger and poverty, and neglected social services. Are companies that do an excellent job of satisfying consumer wants necessarily acting in the best long-run interests of consumers and society? The marketing concept sidesteps the potential conflicts among consumer wants, consumer interests, and long-run societal welfare." How can societal marketing concept work? The answer is explored here.

Civilisations need to be built on a focussed concern that value received by a customer implies value added for society, too. Then, actions of man are guided by Selfless Love – understood as self actualisation need of men. Cooperation is the basis of a social structure and also its value creation and delivery structure. More so, when specialisation and division of labour form the basis of social systems, co-operation becomes an imperative. This cooperation should result in compatibility between creation and delivery of value for man and society – which is important for its long-term mutually supportive functioning. This approach will automatically build a focussed concern for environmental, ethical and other issues in creation and delivery of value. Then a firm's competitive response, within shared values of society, will add value for all. In absence of Selfless Love or a self actualisation need, many legal and ethical issues emerge. Kotler's list of major marketing decision areas that pose legal or ethical questions is presented in Diagram 5.1.

292

Major Marketing decision areas– posing legal or ethical questions

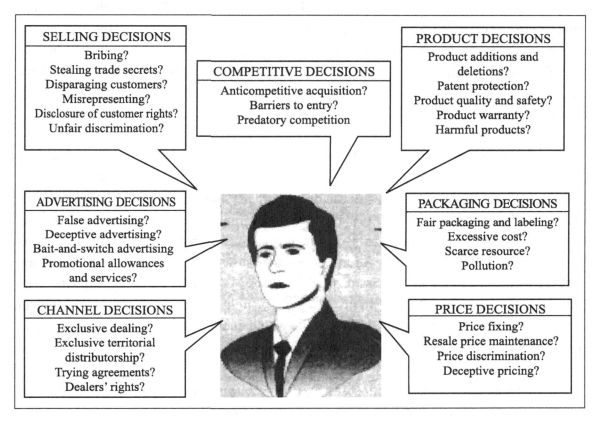

Diagram 5.1
Source: Philip Kotler "Marketing Management" Ninth Edition

There is a rising concern about ethical issues in research and development. The growth and use of knowledge for production of goods and services adds to concerns for the environment: natural, as well as social environment. Marketing and its communication (which stimulates needs) raises concerns for values and norms that are useful for society.

The above concerns can be met through communication of society's shared value of self actualisation. All participants in the value creation and delivery processes must share this. This shared value should form the basis of value creation and delivery. Communication, then, at the level of 4th C, can align different dimensions of self actualisation expressed by the firm, cluster, industry, nation and customer with shared values of society.

Information, in today's world, is considered to be power. The role of technology is going to make access to information much easier. However technology offers no solutions on the nature of use of the power. With rapid growth of information and knowledge the dimensions of use of power increase. For example, so much information on consumer likings is available that the dangers of intrusion into privacy of citizens become real. Self-restraint can only emerge from shared values. Only this can prevent misuse of such power in every area from genetic research to consumer research.

What is the necessary determinant of shared values? Broadly speaking, it can be identified as Selfless Love, a desire for wisdom realisation or self-realisation/actualisation. This desire addresses the highest order needs of individuals and takes a holistic view of man and society's interaction. Protecting society's long-term interests would naturally flow out of this. When this determinant is at work, the growth of information and knowledge gets both meaning and direction. The limitations of the knowledge society are then overcome with the respect, search and realisation of wisdom. How does this express in understanding the 'need of a nation'? India, for example, lives in its villages. So, value based development needs integrated rural development there. This would entail sacrifice, ceiling on desires to serve rural needs (not desires) first, a spirit of service, high level of ethics etc.

The knowledge society has to transform itself into a wisdom-driven/Selfless Love/ self actualised society. Such transformation ensures that sum of value additions by firms does not subtract value from society. Society is harmed by damaging of environment, violation of social values, ethics or government laws. Greed is wealth driven and motivates such behavior. Porter has observed that when a society becomes wealth-driven it enters a stage of decay. Greed knows no limit. This eventuality is unlikely to occur if Selfless Love becomes engine of growth – for excellence, too, is a limitless search: opposite in its nature to greed. The objective of growth of knowledge should be to work towards this stage.

5.3 The role of Shared Values: shaping & re-shaping customer wants

Communication has an important role to play in influencing creation and re-shaping of human needs. How human wants influence growth of knowledge, products it creates and socialisation process has been discussed earlier. Communication is the medium through which all influences travel. This process starts from early years of the life of every individual. Over a period of time, this individual evolves into a full-fledged customer. This customer should be 'values-driven' in expressing the 'value-seeking' nature of wants

For values to be shared, communication is necessary. Today concern for legal, environmental and ethical issues is expressed after harm has been done: i.e. knowledge has created products and they have been consumed. This is like wondering how to shut the stable door after a horse has fled. Society has to decide when to shut stable doors and how to execute this task. This task begins with an understanding that knowledge acquisition is different from self actualisation. The biggest question facing society is: will growth of knowledge be used for the end of realising wisdom? This challenge facing communication, society and strategy is addressed when man seeks excellence leading to self actualisation.

A study of flows of communication, as they occur today, is shown in Diagram 5.2 below:

The 'influencers' and the customer: their present inter-play
(An individual has little control over communication processes)

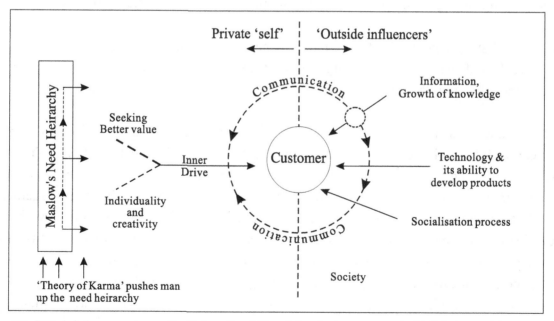

Dotted circle represents growth of information & Knowledge that is not tempered with 'Wisdom-Seeking'. When this becomes the major influencer for technology development, socialisation process and customers inner drive, the individuals influence over communication process diminishes.

Diagram 5.2

295

The growth of knowledge, aided by ease of its delivery, has become the dominant influence today. This growth of knowledge is not always tempered with wisdom emerging from Selfless Love. This influences individuals as well as firms exposed to such knowledge. The socialisation process further creates pressures on individuals to adapt quickly to this growth of knowledge. The individual, in this case, has no control over this process and emerges as a puppet or victim.

The seed of a new theoretical model:

Inculcating a desire for excellence reverses the above flow. This will happen in three steps: a) Shared values will be formulated before human wants & needs are fully created. This implies that before customers are fully formed (with fixed attitude), values are shared. The role of ethics and human values in family life and in education of children is the first step. b) The social impact of technology becomes more important than process of invention. c) Informal social mechanisms will monitor processes – and their impact on environment and society. When such mechanisms are purely self-driven and voluntary they do not become self serving for those who monitor them. Shared values guide process.

Shared values influence best when they emerge naturally in behaviour patterns of individuals and firms. Hence the suggestion of imbibing human values at the early stage of life and education through educare.

Shared values re-shape individual goals. They enable individuality and creativity of man to express itself by avoiding zero-sum situations. Diagram 5.3 makes such an attempt. It gives the seed from the tree of ancient Indian tradition. The implications of this attempt shall be elaborated upon in further Diagrams. These diagrams will expand into a management model that demonstrates the balance that Best Management practices, beginning with the transformation of man, ensures. It is the ideal of practice for man, society and nations. Just as soccer match needs a goal post for the game to be enjoyable, man and society's actions, too, need a goal towards which they can converge. The purpose of a model is to provide this. The goals of life culminate in the fourth *Purushartha* – as does the study of man and management.

The 'influencers' and the customer: their proposed inter-play

(The individual, empowered with wisdom, communicated within ambit of shared values, to determine direction of growth of Knowledge, technology and socialisation process)

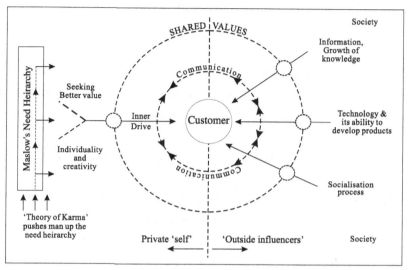

Dotted circles (in the area of 'outside influencers') represent individuals as influencers. Individuals now influence:
(a) knowledge creation
(b) product and value creation in firms
(c) the socialisation process.
The individuals are 'Wisdom seeking'. The dotted circle inside the 'private Self' represents the individual centred on the axis of Shared Values which shape his inner drive now.

Diagram 5.3

The importance of 'shared values', new 'influencers' on customer's wants

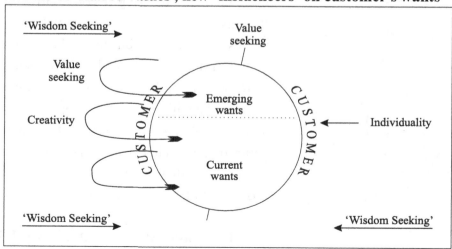

Diagram 5.4

297

The individual, in diagram 5.4, centered on shared values, seeks wisdom. This individual then becomes the dominant influence for growth of knowledge and the socialisation process. Again, an individual in the firm enables conversion of growth of knowledge into products. When this is tempered by wisdom, both – the socialisation process and growth of knowledge are given a meaningful direction.

Wisdom implies that an individual should always keep interests of society in mind. For, it is society that brings balance. Ancient wisdom states that when all members of a firm have good thoughts, see good, indulge only in good talk and good actions, it leads to balance.

4.4 The role of Shared Values: McKinsey 7S Model recapitulated

The McKinsey 7S model, shown in diagram 5.5, places shared values where they rightfully belong – at the heart of a firm's value creation process.

The hardware of 7S model is driven by the software. This software is individual-oriented. It deals with staff, their skills and style in which potential of skills is used to add value. Shared values transform individuals first and build strategies later. Educare allows individuals working in a firm to share values. This enables them to build common values of the firm. Value addition, when motivated by shared values, moves firms to excellence. Porter gave many examples of communities, firms and nations that shared values and used them for creating a competitive advantage. Italians had deep clusters which used shared values of extended families. The Japanese share values of a work culture. The Swiss shared values of respecting multiple cultures and languages and combined it with a social philosophy of compromise and accommodation. This reflects in their political neutrality, too. This became a competitive strength for the Swiss that enabled them to trade and transact business with many countries.

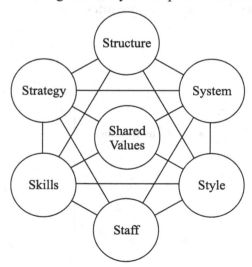

The Firm and Shared Values: Mc Kinsey 7S Model Diagram 5.5

This attitude also helped develop an image of trust for their banking community. When common human values are shared in process of education itself, the task of creating value through excellence becomes simpler for firms.

The McKinsey model in Diagram 5.5 demonstrates how shared values of the firm drive it towards excellence. They also enable higher as well as better value creation and delivery.

4.5 Shared Values move theory from the 3C to 4C model: A new theoretical management model which is the goal of management based on goals of man

The 3C model explored how communication is necessary for value to be added by the firm. Similarly, for values to be shared, communication is necessary. Kotler expresses concern of ethical, environmental, moral and legal issues. Unfortunately, it has been expressed after knowledge has created products and services and they have been consumed. The 3C model till now shows how customer wants become the driving force for firms. These firms operate in a national context to create competitive strategies. Customer wants are influenced not only by three factors but also by their drivers. These are (a) nature of changes in knowledge leading to (b) advances in technology and (c) social pressures. The emerging strategies give firms competitive success and create a competitive advantage for nations. Nations, again, work in an international environment of trade, exchange of knowledge and flow of information. This enables transfer of value as well as value creation. This value creation can build new social pressures. It gives new direction to growth of knowledge, information seeking and technology. However, the products, services, technology and value creation creates social concerns, ethical questions and legal issues. Kotler has raised them. There are instances where global aggregation of individual value additions by firms does not seem to be giving positive results.

The Earth summits reflect the need of eco-friendly approaches to growth of knowledge and development of science and technology. This can enable man to live in harmony within him and society and with resources of the planet, too. Communication has to integrate shared values of customers, firms, national influences and international context with shared values of society.

Strategy has three ingredients: Simple Consistency, Reinforcement and Optimisation effort. Shared values become core of processes within man, firm, cluster, industry, nation and family of nations. Then Simple Consistency of shared values helps value creation, value delivery and adds value to both – strategy of firm and strategy of life. The succeeding diagrams illustrate the balance that strategy of man, firm, society and nature create in the 4C Approach. Optimisation effort refers to configuration of individual activities and the way they relate to each other. Succeeding diagrams show strategy as an optimisation effort. They also show how man, firm, cluster, industry, society and nature relate to each other. This creates balance – which was the search of this book from its Synopsis onwards.

4C's: the customer, home nation, firm and society's compatible interaction (on basis of shared values) during process of value creation

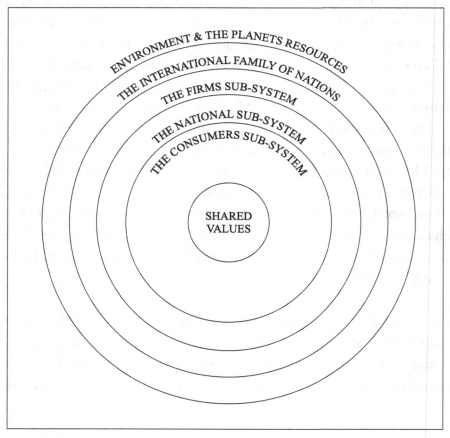

Diagram 5.6

PRESENTING A NEW MANAGEMENT MODEL THAT CAN GUIDE PRACTICE AWAY FROM RECESSION AND OTHER SOCIAL PROBLEMS:

The proper study of mankind is man. Goals of mankind will only work if they apply to man, first. Similarly any theoretical model for management of a large group (firm, cluster, industry, society, nation, family of nations) will only work if it works on man. Hence if goals of man are the basis of goals of society, there is not only a simple consistency but actions based on these lead to reinforcement. The strategy for life and work – for man, mankind and nature benefits from an optimization effort, then. This model will create balance within man, in society, among nations and with nature. The Diagrams that follow give a shape to this model.

The new model would look something like Diagram 5.6. The configuration of individual activities of Strategy and the way they relate to each other is demonstrated in Diagram 5.7. The customer is at the core of the process and the context (shown as outline of Diagram) is society. All concepts of earlier chapters are shown diagrammatically here to highlight how they relate to each other. Diagram 5.8 shows that the customer based view is part of/ leads to the Market based view. The area of each of the 4C's is marked and area of Competitive Response (building and delivery, separately) is shown. The area of Compatibility Advantage, too, is marked. Diagram 5.9 shows, finally, how balance is achieved.

These diagrams are described – but not in much detail – for the idea is to enable their experience by the reader. If the ideas are assimilated, words are not necessary beyond a point. Using this idea many diagrams in the book, too, are not explained beyond a point. Visible truth can be explained in words and can be seen by the eyes but the invisible Truth (*Adwaitha*) can not. However, *Vishisht Adwaitha* is a method of education – to enable the experience of the invisible Truth using some words and different modes of communication. Finally, such communication is complete when Truth emerges from 'within' a recipient. Any description of the Truth, even in glowing words, pales in comparison to its experience. Diagrams are given here as as a catalyst that helps the Truth to emerge within. The words used are pale. In case the Truth is not visible, there is a need for practice. When it becomes visible there is no need for Diagrams. However, till it becomes visible, diagrams are useful guides to convince man and mankind that what is shown and seen is an achievable target.

Activities of Strategy and the way they relate to each other

Diagram 5.7

The customer based view is part of/ leads to the Market based view

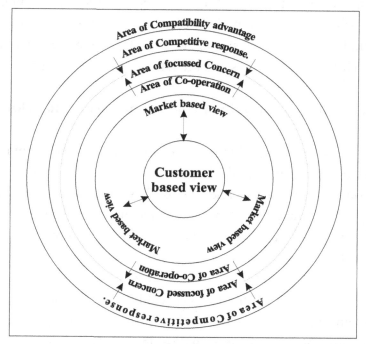

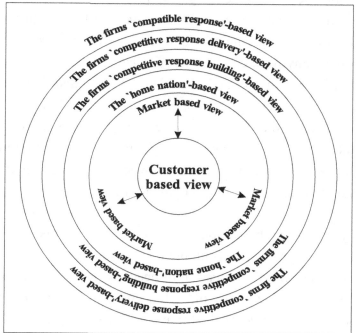

Diagram 5.8

Diagrams 5.7 and 5.8 that elaborate the 4C model show the integration of a focus on the customer and customer based view with the market based view. The home nation based view expands to include firm's competitive response 'building' & 'delivery' based view. The firms compatible response view shows the final stage of expansion of thought of man, firm and society. This makes the 4C's emerge naturally in Diagram 5.8.

5.6 The fourth 'C': The Compatibility Advantage at work – end of knowledge is Love

Values, when they drive value seeking desire of man, create a new environment. Firms, scientists and specialists can explore the impact of knowledge they create on society. This becomes as important as creating this knowledge. This is Wisdom – the practice of Selfless Love. The re-shaped individual goals have an impact on evolving nature of customer needs and firms functioning. After all, individuals work in firms and move the software of 7S model towards excellence.

Shared values are at the heart of interactions within a firm which produces excellence. Shared values, when guided by wisdom-seeking, can make a firm's output match with society's expectations. The wisdom-seeking described in this model is referred to by Jesus as Love, by ancient Indian tradition as Selfless Love and by Buddhists as Compassion. Wisdom implies this Love – of loving others interest as your own self interest. When this does not emerge in man, environmental, ethical and legal issues emerge in society. Guided by discrimination and 'wisdom-seeking', man drives knowledge creation in society, adds value within firm and helps create a new socialisation process. Diagram 5.5 recapitulates the role of shared values in the firm's processes. Diagram 5.6 shows shared values (of Selfless Love) as the core of the 4C process. Diagram 5.3 shows the interplay, as it should exist, between man, the influence of growth of knowledge and the socialisation process. It, therefore, clarifies role of forces that retard compatibility from occurring today.

Firms say that they are driven by customer wants. Thus, they take shelter of marketing ethic to justify creation of products unsuitable for natural and social environment. Social analysts and critics blame firms for creation of needs which are irrelevant, frivolous and may harm man and society. The nature of such accusations reveals the play of zero-sum games. The way out can be offered by the three possible steps suggested earlier. Society's long-term concerns create an environment where conversion of knowledge into products is not immediate. It is done on basis of study of their long term impact on society and environment. This is part of a wisdom seeking process of man in society. It reflects a commitment to the customer beyond borders of selfishness.

Individuals and firms express their knowledge through products. These products impact consumers, society, its culture or the environment. If this impact is adverse in the long term – while appearing beneficial initially – is a social concern. The recognition of profit to include the concept 'what is truly profitable for customer also' is an expression of Selfless Love. It signifies a mindset of business being 'realised' as a non-zero sum game – in thought, word and deed. Deeds emerging from such thoughts must be communicated. Communication, to fulfill its objective, must become a two-way process as shown in Diagram 5.3. Only then can potential of communication as a transformational process and tool be realised.

This model depicts how processes of communication in society can be used to their optimum potential to add value. They no longer become imposition based as represented in Diagram 5.1. Kotler lists the example of fast food industry which promotes products that are tasty but may not be very healthy. Their packaging may be convenient but leads to much waste. The process of satisfying human wants, here, maybe hurting consumer health and causing environmental problems. A similar example was given of detergent industry which catered to consumer's desire for whiter clothes by polluting rivers and streams, killing fish etc. Of course, these examples are of the '90s – but similar ones exist, today.

The one-way flow of information, from firm to consumer, concentrates only on firm's short-term objectives of market share and profitability. Such a one-way flow does not inform adequately of other consequences of fulfilling a need in a way this product promotes. Instead, it seeks to impose its communication in a manner that influences the consumer to purchase a product immediately. It encourages habit-formation to ensure repeat purchases. The transaction, then, becomes a zero-sum game with the firm gaining at the cost of the customer and society. Then, knowledge and value creation must give importance to social implications of technology – as they give to the process of invention. Informal social mechanisms, voluntarily respected by all, are needed to monitor them. Overtime these mechanisms must develop within man. When three steps suggested earlier have been undertaken, Diagram 5.3 can become a reality. The first step of inculcating human and Shared Values in early years of education ensures that following two steps occur as a natural corollary. This is depicted in this Diagram 5.3 as all communication in society is now taking place within the ambit of shared values.

When individuals, firms and society share values, a compatibility advantage (the fourth C) emerges. Enabling this is the challenge that communication faces. Diagram 5.9 shows how customer, firm and society can participate in compatible value enhancement for society on basis of shared values. The Indian tradition states that the 3rd C should be guided by the 4th C for balance in man and society. Then, desire fulfilment process of man, firm, cluster, industry, nation and family of nations is guided by Selfless Love. The desire to harm others is understood as detrimental for man, himself. What is detrimental for man is also detrimental for firm, cluster industry, nation and family of nations. The interconnectedness of man and society is, thus, deeply engrained by the ancient Indian education system. Diagram 5.9 demonstrates this theoretical understanding – using management concepts and theory.

Ancient Indian texts of *Purushasuktam* explained the same concept in a language and grammar that were suitable to that time. The text of *Rudram* demonstrates the two fold approach for fulfilling legitimate desires of man. It makes man seek prosperity in all righteous forms that are comprehensible. In this manner goals of life were understood as Duality or two pairs. The first pair makes righteous conduct guide creation of wealth. The second pair makes Selfless Love (Love for work with detachment towards result) guide wish fulfilment. It is fruitful for man and mankind to live in such duality. It ensures survival of civilisations.

When these concepts were forgotten, it led to decline – just as Porter postulates about the decline stage in national competitive development. To prevent a decline stage, the end of knowledge was recognised as wisdom. What does this wisdom enable man to see? The Highest Truth was envisioned through such wisdom. This is discussed in Chapter 6. The tests of Truth or validity of earlier chapters will be shown in Chapter 7. Education transforms the heart of man. The heart is known as *Hrudaya or Hrud+Daya* in ancient Indian tradition – implying that Love and Compassion should pervade Heart of Man. Education builds Character of man so as to unlock this potential.

To sum up: The future of business rests with recognizing the primacy of inculcating selfless shared values in man. This will create balance within man, firm, cluster, industry, society and with nature.

THE 4C MODEL EXPRESSING BALANCE:
MAN MANAGEMENT and 4C APPROACH – BALANCE in MAN, FIRM, SOCIETY
Simple Consistency of Four Shared Values of Man, firm and Society get
Reinforced in Optimisation effort to create balance among all.

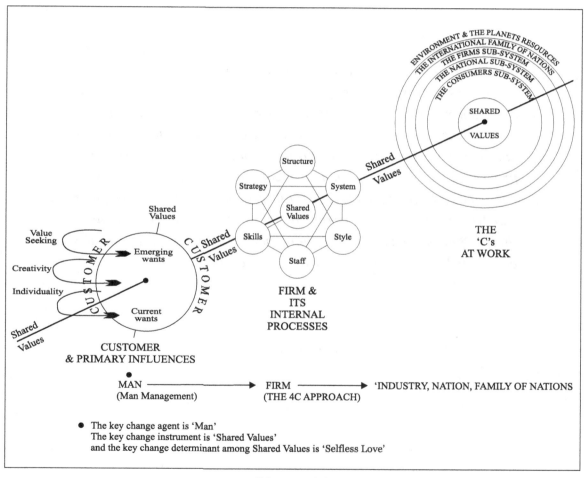

Diagram 5.9

What is the meaning of the Sanskrit sloka Tat Twam Asi *or
'That thou Art' and how to fulfill this realisation?*

"

*Today people are too immersed in the all-persavive delusion to take
advantage of the natural characteristics in the universe and elevate
themselves...The scriptures clearly teach: From which you are born,
by which you live, into which you dissolve – 'That' is Brahman....
(it) is 'That' from which the manifested emanated with its moving
and unmoving entities;* **'That' prompts, promotes and fosters your
progress.** *The cosmos is not one continuous flux. It progresses
persistently towards achieving totality in its evolution.* **Everyone
can transform themselves from their present status only through
their self effort and discrimination**. *The moral forces permeating the
cosmos will certainly promote your achievement.*

"

Spitiual Source of the book in Sutra Vahini, Chapter 2

Chapter 6
Many spiritual paths lead to
The Highest Truth

This chapter reveals that the expanding circles of diagrams in Chapter 5 say:

If the left hand hurts the right hand, the body feels the hurt.

Men are many, but the body of mankind is One.
'That' whom you hurt is 'You' only

So:
Help Ever, Hurt Never

CONCLUSION: The business of living life integrates the study of Man and Management through experiencing the HIGHEST TRUTH

Experience of Unity with customer, society comes by serving them with a heart devoid of selfishness or full of selfless LOVE. Expansion of the heart for others leads to experience of Uniy with larger groups – from family, firm to cluster, industry, society, nation. This expansion of the heart is directed by ancient wisdom towards an experience of UNITY OF CREATION. Then man and his inner nature feel a union with Nature too

Management Theory, starting from Peter Drucker, states that the 'purpose of business is to create and keep a customer'. Therefore, 'Customer is the purpose of business', 'Customer is King' etc. A Firm's Strategy, thus, seeks to maximise 'customer delight'.

Earlier Chapters have concluded that this is not a profit maximisation but an Optimisation effort. It follows Simple Consistency and Reinforcement – of Co-operation for and focus Concern on customer needs. When man co-operates within the firm, with suppliers and sources of information etc with a focus on the customer with a Concern for his needs, he creates value: for the firm, customer, society and himself. Humility makes him 'feel the needs, individuality and creativity' of the customer. Individuality makes him create and deliver value in the context of Nationality with an emphasis on excellence (or Divinity) with a feeling of Unity. Unity with the customer is the beginning and Unity with society and nature the end. Until this Unity with the customer is not 'experienced', value cannot be created or delivered with 'excellence'. Excellence achieved by serving others (with a feeling of Unity with them) when expanded to society becomes Spirituality.

Spirituality is not selfish. It helps man serve others – with soft Truth.

Spirituality = 'Business Of Life'

(Spirit of working selflessly)

A Strategy of Simple Consistency, Reinforcement and Optimisation effort by the firm can add value not only to man and the firm but also the cluster, industry and home nation giving it competitive advantage. Shared Values and moving up Maslow's need hierarchy (Chapter 5), transform Competitive to Compatibility Advantage – as Unity views society as Self.

Following Simple Consistency and Reinforcement by 'Unity of thought, word and deed', man creates balance. This occurs within himself, firm, industry, cluster, nation and family of nations. This is an Optimisation effort. Values imply Spirituality in action. This leads to selfless service of others i.e. society in the 'Business of Life'. Indian texts prove that this approach is not only modern – but ancient, too…

Ever since man has moved to settlements from nomadic state, he has been giving up his life just to protect his city or state – as part of the army.

The ability to protect the interest of others as if it is our own self interest creates balance in society. It is the goal of education. Then, ancient Indian Highest Truth *"Tat Twam Asi"* (That thou Art) guides man further. It enables him to 'C' Divinity or excellence in everybody/everything.

When this broad vision is expanded from city state to the universe, balance of man with nature emerges. Just as he does not over use his body, he does not over use nature, too. Man's Character guides him to use nature's resources – only in an optimal manner. The earlier Chapter of marketing teaches man to feel as if he is 'one with the customer'. Thus, man only helps, not hurts others. This Chapter expands the vision further preparing him to 'Help Ever, Hurt Never'.

Then, he can envision the unity of creation. For, Spirituality gives Divine powers, but **true** Divinity is only 'realised' in, and as, Unity.

C the Universe as a City

('Vasudeva Kutumbakam'): translates as 'The World/ Creation is one family'. If 'World is one family' - then, universe should be like a city

= University

(Learn from Nature, universe just as you do from the wise in your city)

Welcome to the University: Chapter 6. Ancient wisdom trains man to 'C' creation as a family where *Neeti* (morality) is more important than *Jaathi* (community). Thus the Sanskrit prayer: *Samastha loka sukhino bhavantu.*

To achieve the goal of education, man fulfills the four *Purusharthas* – the goals of life or 4Cs. Man achieves the goal of education by a change in perception – or ability to 'C'. This relates to the concept of human body, how to live life (4Cs) in society, purpose of life and how to achieve it, economic concept of society and their integration with spirituality.

What does man have to envision about business and life? What makes individual and the highest good of society merge? How can man 'C' it? When man (after being 'good' and doing 'good') sees the good of society, effortlessly, he is ready to 'C' further. The 'Great Truth' of ancient Indian sages: 'That Thou Art' becomes clear to his inner eye. This removes selfish attachments or *Moha,* preparing him for *Moksha,* actualising his potential.

Validation of merger of 4C Approach back in Ancient Indian Tradition

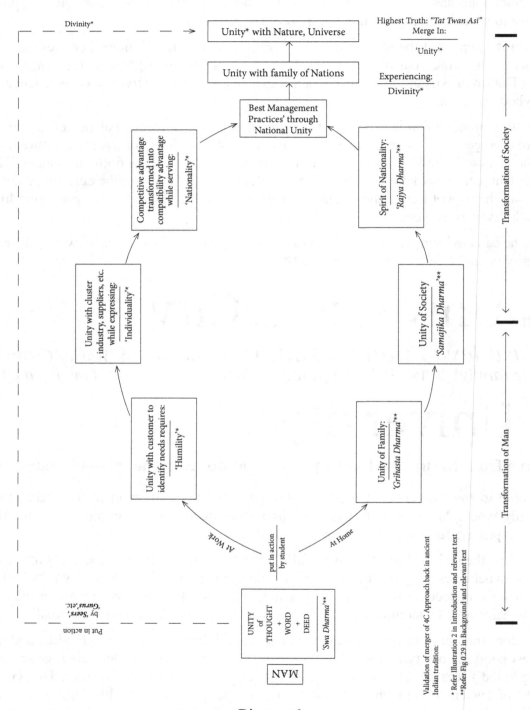

Diagram 6

MAN MANAGEMENT: Integration of business and life through HIGHEST TRUTH

Highlights of contents of Chapter 6: The same Truth can be seen using many routes

The Chapter states that Management is meant for man to enable him to serve society: The study of Management is meant for Man. As stated earlier, Man can be a pun on the word *MUN* (in Hindi) – or mind of man. So, what does the mind of man have to be trained to 'C' or see by the 4C Approach? The mind of man should be trained to experience the Unity of Creation. This trains man to help ever, not harm. When actions of ancient Indians did not hurt society, prosperity and wisdom resulted – making its civilisation outlast.

Diagram 6 shows how **Best Management Practices** create balance in society while the idea of Man Management integrates business and Highest Truth with Life – in this manner: There are **three concepts** that emerge from ancient Indian tradition: They are: (1) An economic concept of society that differs from the present understanding. (2) An absorption of the idea that 'if we wait for society to reform, we will have to wait forever'. (3) A realisation that an Attitude of 'change yourself to change the world' is the only way.

The **four fold validation of 4C** Approach is done in four ways; i.e.: **how to** – **D**iscover the purpose of life, – how to **L**ive it, – **U**nderstand its business and – **R**ealise the excellence within man. Based on this understanding the 4C Approach emerges with Co-operation. *Yoga* depicts this union or 'coming together'. What do its various forms imply for our study? Diagram 6.1 shows the 'gestalt'– from co-operation to compatibility.

Part A or Awareness led to Part B of this book. In this chapter, a different approach of Part B leads to the same Awareness of Part A. Diagrams 6.6 and 6.10 validate that Awareness is same through all routes. So, Part A and B validate their inseparable nature. Sections 6.1 to 6.3 study Limits from different route – Sections 6.3 to 6.6 lead all routes to Awareness: **6.1** Importance of human body, **6.2** Six Lessons for using human body, **6.3** Three things to remember about man and society, **6.4** Integration of 4C's with ideas of Yoga, meditation **6.5** The Integration or merger of Education with Life: ancient Indian approach in 4 parts. **6.6** Spiritual means lead to the four ends. This merges 4C Approach back into Awareness. – The ancient Indian tradition believes that ego and anger hide the excellence in all dimensions (called Divinity) hidden in man. Desires lead to attachment. *Japa, Dhyana, Yoga* (meditation, repetition of name, spiritual path) may give temporary peace. To get permanent Peace man has to unlock Awareness of Selfless Love in the heart – the desire of Fig 0.9 of Background. Directing this love in selfish directions leads to many problems. The wave that emerges from the ocean of knowledge (Background) merges back here – as Diagram 6.11 shows 4Cs in action and Diagram 6.12 integrates flow of education and life. – This chapter integrates theory and practice. Individual good merges with the highest good (*Swartha* leads to *Parartha* which is used for *Parmartha*). Its understanding and practice unfolds the excellence within man. It merges this view with the management framework of Chapter 5 in Diagram 6.13. A dynamic balance for man and society emerges.

– Finally section 6.11 shows how balance in society occurs as man proceeds to non duality. Awareness of nature of the Great Truth: 'That Thou Art!' emerges through Selfless Love.

Though Truth is the same irrespective of the route to it – misunderstanding it is easy: *Tat Twam Asi* is interpreted casually to imply *You are God*. Without Awareness this leads to misunderstandings. It needs to be remembered that if the explanation or realisation was so simplistic, it could be given in two minutes. Why would students spend about a decade of their youth living a spartan life and indulging in spiritual practices (given in Chapter 7)? Why would they spend the remaining years of their life following some of these practices? Also, why would they be taught humility as the first principle? Following any simplistic prescription of man being a supreme power should have resulted in ego maniacal society – convinced of its superiority. The ancient Indians, on the other hand, looked forward to receiving other religions interpretation of Divinity and giving them a place of respect. This implies that the realisation of this Great Truth is deeper and its explanation may lie elsewhere. The Great Truths of ancient Indian tradition emerge from *Adwaita*. The book gives interpretations that prepare man for the understanding of *Adwaita*. The final goal is that Unity with creation idea is like imagining and feeling the Love God has for creation.

The book approaches the understanding of this Great Truth as follows:
• Excellence in all dimensions that is viualised outside man is there 'within' man. This affirmation gives self confidence to ahieve it.
• The task of education is to unravel this excellence through spiritual practices and a proper study of Truth as well as Truth about man and the world.
• Skills of a trade or profession help unravel it in in one dimension.
• The application of knowledge to serve others selflessly is the way to unravel this excellence further. This comes through transformation of man.
• When selfishness is overarched, the increasing dimensions of excellence start unfolding – within man – for the benefit of society. Education enables this.
• Man and society are deeply interlinked. When man can see others as himself and serve others as he serves himself – this is the interpretation that enables both man and society to achieve dynamic balance. It enables a civilisation to survive.

Tat Twam Asi is a Great Truth that is used as an instrument for transformation of man – for the benefit of society. Man rises in Maslow's hierarchy, learns that life is a non zero sum game. Seeking the highest good of society brings out the highest good in man – which is excellence. When man strives for highest good of all – in all dimensions, it leads to excellence in all dimensions. Then, man has both – goodness and excellence. The book starts with God being defined as having both goodness and excellence in all dimensions, simultaneously. The Great Truth, thus, becomes clear. In this manner the ancient Indian tradition defines the goal and path to achieving it – through selfless service to society.

INTEGRATING STUDY OF MAN WITH MANAGEMENT IDEAS
Integration of business and life by experiencing the Highest Truth of ancient wisdom

"It is a miracle that curiosity survives formal education."
Albert Einstein

The basic curiosity: **'can man's capacity to think come from matter?'** is not adequately addressed by formal education. Education studies matter forgetting that it impossible to prove that capacity to think grows out of physical matter. Yet, who seriously pursues an answer? Curiosity, thus, dies – and man does not awaken to his true potential. Awareness of man's potential always comes through some questions:

The animal acts as if it is a physical body. What will be the difference if man, too, gets educated believing he is only the body? Finally, when he behaves in a manner that expresses this belief, does it not harm all? The beginning of curiosity about **nature of man** leads to exploration of **nature of Truth**. This encourages a curiosity for (and awe about) **nature of creation**. The exploration of nature of man, truth and creation prepares the background for education of man. This has already been discussed in the Background here.

This Chapter addresses the lack of curiosity, lamented earlier. The previous chapters (2 to 5) integrate ancient Indian tradition's idea of managing life with modern management concepts of strategy and business. The 4C approach emerges from it like a wave from the ocean of knowledge of this tradition. This Chapter seeks to validate that the wave and ocean remain the same irrespective of the route to Awareness, thus satisfying our curiosity.

How is this validation done?
The roadmap from section 6.1 to 6.11: 4Cs and other spiritual ideas of ancient Indian tradition merge as education integrates with life in four ways – other spiritual means also lead to four ends for a four fold validation – integrating with the Highest Truth

This chapter uses curiosity of man to discover 'what is the importance of a human body and the technique of using it – to fulfill the purpose of life?' It also seeks an answer to: 'What should man remember about himself and society to Realise the highest Truth or highest state of Awareness?' These questions relate to the use of physical body of man – and are, therefore, within a Study of Limits. The answers lead to Awareness (that Chapters 2 to 5 generate). This validates that the wave of Chapters 2 to 5 belongs to the same ocean.

The Awareness is an understanding that the purpose of business is to help man 'Realise' the business of life. The business of life creates balance, within man and society – together. To achieve this goal, education and life should integrate. The significance of a four-fold study through *Purusharthas* is validated here. This is done through education about other spiritual means too, that lead to four ends. Based on this four fold validation of other spiritual means, how does the 4C knowledge merge back in this ocean? This is tested here. Such a search takes man to the knowledge (wisdom) of *Atma Vidya* or Awareness of Self. This Chapter, therefore, merges the study and practice of management with achieving the goal of life of man. Awareness, created by absorbing these ideas, enables such a merger:

6.1 Importance of human body

6.2 Six Lessons for using human body

6.3 Three things to remember about man and society

6.4 Integration of 4C's with spiritual ideas of ancient Indian tradition (Yoga, meditaion)

6.5 The Integration/ merger of Education with Life; ancient Indian approach in 4 parts

6.6 Spiritual means lead to the 4 ends: Merger of 4C Approach back into spirituality

….and many other means of validation ending with

6.11 The 4C Approach prepares man for *Advaita*: the Highest Awareness of *Tat Twam Asi*

Finally, **three concepts merge** (between sections 6.6 to 6.11) in the Awareness they generate:
First, how does this new 4C knowledge merge back into life – giving simple guidelines for each stage of 4C process?
Secondly, what is the understanding of Highest Truth for man and what is it for society?
Finally, how does the Highest Truth merge into one; applicable for both man and society?
Such a merger prepares man's vision in four ways through which he can 'C' – helping him understand his role and how to perform it in society.
This helps envision the 'Great Truth' or *Mahvakya* of this tradition: *Tat Twam Asi* or 'That Thou Art' – dealt in section 6.11 that follows.

In the ancient Indian spiritual tradition, philosophy is called *Darshana* or sight. It gives a way of seeing things that help experience of Truth (*Vedanta Darshan* or *Shad Darshana*). *Dharma* and *Moksha* are inner eyes and *Kama* and *Artha* are eyes that experience the outside world. Each of these 'outer vision' eyes has to be married to an 'inner vision' eye. For, only then emerges meaning for man (*Purush – artha*) – or meaning (another possible interpretation of the word '*Artha*') in what man or '*Purusha*' does. This ability to 'C' Truth through the four ways of *Purusharthas* should merge in the sum up (section 6.9).

The wave of 4C Approach has emerged from the ocean of ancient Indian tradition in two ways. Firstly, it emerges through Awareness of Self and secondly by a Study of Limits of the body. It is appropriate that each section of this chapter reveals how this wave merges back. To enable this, the **first three sections deal with the Study of Limits of the body and the last three with Awareness of the Self.** Finally, Awareness of the 'One-ness' with *Purusha* (or excellence in all dimensions, simultaneously) emerges in section 6.11.

The seeming complexity of this Paper is reduced to simplicity in the final analysis. This simplicity is shown by Diagram 6.11 as the Structure of the Paper. This also leads up to the merger of Highest Truth of man and society (section 6.7), enabling a sum-up (section 6.9).

6.1 Importance of human body

The ancient Indians allowed a curiosity about importance of body and its changing nature to overwhelm them. Then, they came to conclusions about how man should lead his life. The six lessons for using it, given below are the end product of their search and education. Surely, there is need for some concern about physical comforts. The ancient Indian scriptures state clearly that "The body is essential for realisation of *Dharma*". Demands of the body need to be satisfied. Family responsibilities have to be fulfilled. In a similar fashion society has to be served – for it, too, is the extended family of man. The physical body enables fulfilment of these tasks. When these tasks are inspired by a higher learning and higher goal, their fulfilment leads to fulfilling the purpose of life. The recommended Path for man is based on discovery of knowledge that leads to wisdom. For, it helps fulfill the responsibilities towards the body – and the body of society – using some simple lessons:

6.2 Six lessons for using human body

Lesson 1 Understand the True/False nature of the world and try to experience that Truth which does not change. The first sign of True/False world is man himself. He appears as the body (which itself is ever changing) but his reality is different (an invisible mind and something that is never-changing or eternal). Discovering the Truth about man is a process in which the understanding increases with passage of time. The application of this increasing experience of Truth in daily life is the preparation for life through education.

Lesson 2 Understand that each action of man will have an unavoidable reaction. Hence, indulge in actions of excellence based on righteousness, truth and morality (Theory of *Karma*). This Theory lays the basis of interdependence of man, society, nation, world etc.

Lesson 3 Fix a path or field of excellence as per inner urge or nature. Adam Smith calls it specialisation. Ancient Indians called it the caste system. Here castes were **originally** formed to use the *natural skills each individual was endowed with for benefit of society.*

Lesson 4 Follow this path sincerely and with a heart filled with selflessness, tirelessly with no desire for fruit of action. This can also be the path 'four *Purusharthas*' – even without them this ideal is relevant in today's context of management of business and of life of man.

Lesson 5 While following the Path, do not hurt others – for hurting others is like hurting yourself. Therefore, there is an integration of man and management (now called Man Management). Man has to first manage that which is *within* him (thought, word and deed). For, hurting others through thought, word or deed is like hurting one self. Man Management seeks to impart the experience of Unity of all creation within man. In case this is not experienced, the least it enables is an inability to hurt others. This inability is the greatest of all abilities. It can only come if the human heart is filled with the same Love for others as for one self. Education, thus, begins with transformation of the individual. Transformation of society cannot be achieved if each individual is not transformed through education, first. This is discussed in detail below.

Lesson 6 The human body and its senses recognise and live in the diversity of creation. The Highest Truth is that there is a Unity behind the diversity. This is not in realm of theory but in realm of experience. Man Management is the study of man by man to enable the experience of this Highest Truth. Different people are endowed with different natural skills. The task of dedicating this diversity of skills to achieve excellence within man leads to different paths for realising this Truth. Therefore, the declaration in ancient Indian tradition: *ekam Sath vipra bahuda vadanti.* Truth is one – different people express it differently depending upon the path they have travelled. This recognition of Individuality emerges from the Humility of realising diversity of skills. It is directed towards Nationality (where all those who seek the same goal – even though from different paths – share a nationality). This leads to the realisation of Divinity or Excellence within One Self. The realisation of excellence led to the experience of Unity behind diversity for ancient Seers

The understanding and experience of excellence gradually increases, with experience of each individual following this path. As the individual moves from truth to Higher truth, his productivity for society and progress towards realisation of Self occur simultaneously.

The study of limits in three ancient Indian texts leads to Awareness:

This Paper is in two parts. The first part deals with The Awareness and the second with the Study of Limits. From the ocean of knowledge of ancient Indian tradition (Background) – how does the emerging wave of 4C's merge back into this ocean? Though all its texts can be used for both – yet, for Awareness three books are useful: *Upanishads*, *Brahma Sutras*, and *Bhagvada Gita*. We have demonstrated use of their concepts. The Study of Limits deals with the gross body. The task is to understand the gross in such a way that the subtle becomes obvious, overtime. This guides man how to live life in the human body. Jesus used parables for this. The ancient Indian tradition also has three famous **epics whose Study of Limits is used for generating Awareness** in all human beings. These are: *Ramayana*, *Mahabharat* and *Bhagvata*. It is desirable to study them independently before the subtle Truth encased in the gross body of two of these tales is elaborated upon here.

The story of *Ramayan* signifies the story of every man who has the body which is *Jada* (Inert physical body). The resident in the body is *Chaitanya* (Awareness). *Rama* is the *Atma* or Soul. He has assumed the role of *Jivi* or man wearing the dress of the body. The role is His play because He is beyond joy and sorrow. This role play is taking place in every heart with *Atma* Rama or Soul being the witness. The Awareness or *Chaitanya* is born with the name *Seeta*. The *Jada– Chaitanya* become one and is called 'SeetaRam'. So long as the *Jada* and *Chaitanya* are One, there is no suffering. Therefore where Role of Limits and Awareness (the two sections of this Paper) are One, there is perfect bliss. It is only when they get separated that all problems arise. When man loses Awareness (*Seeta*) or *Brahmajnana* he goes away from the *Atma* or Soul. Falling into the darkness of the jungle is inevitable. *Lakshmana* signifies the 'mind of man'. One should always have the mind on one's side to find the way out. *Sugriva* represents discrimination which has to defeat the brother *Vali* who represents despair. *Hanuman* represents courage. This is required to build a bridge over the ocean of delusion. Crossing this ocean of *Moha* or illusion is necessary for the *Jivi* has to slay *Rajoguna* and *Tamoguna* (represented by the two brothers *Ravana* and *Kumbhakaran*). Only then coronation of *Sathwa Guna* (represented by the third brother *Vibhishana*) can happen. The reunion of *Rama* and *Seeta* is the reunion of *Jada* and *Chaitanya* (the 2 sections of this Paper). This gives *Ananda* or Salvation to the Soul. This is the subtle form of *Ramayan* that is occurring in everybody's life. Understanding the epics Study of Limits in this manner creates Awareness and merges the 4C wave of Management of business and life back in the ocean of ancient wisdom.

6.3 Three things to remember about man and society

(i) The economic concept of society: Education gives context of interrelationship with man

In the 4C Approach, the economic concept of society implements a firm belief that earth's resources are enough for everybody's needs, not greed! Current practices differ from this.

The rush to increase competitive consumption is not indulged in by firms or customers. For, it is frowned upon by society. This idea is incorporated in the **education process** through the concept of ceiling on desires. This concept is the *first building block*. It makes man implement the realisation that he is not the body. Thus he learns to exercise restraint on the senses. Such attitude allows man to discover his true nature by curtailing distractions of sense objects. Finally, it prepares man for social action. For, when he acts in this manner, firms and customers, too, work from this understanding. Firms do not try to promote competitive consumption either through promotion or product design. And, society frowns upon wastage of resources or their unnecessary exploitation.

Thus man and society are ready for balance as their harmony is not disturbed by social pressures of competitive consumption. The latter promotes individual vices like ego, jealousy, anger, greed etc that disturb harmony among men and, finally, in society.

It may be useful to understand the concept of *vyapara* or 'busy-ness' in ancient Indian tradition. The process of change, renewal, regeneration is associated with both the change and exchange process of life. A good example of this is the story of seed and tree. The tree is a manifested form of the seed in the soil. The change from seed to tree and from tree to seed shows that *Shakti* or power in seed has *Vyapara* or principle of 'busy-ness'. Creation results from interaction between *Akasa* and *Prana*, as in Background. There is a *sthula Akasa* or gross form of *Akasa* and we see it with our senses. But there is a *shukshama Akasa* or subtle form of *Akasa* too. This is the subtle firmament of the heart. The *Buddhi* is the Sun in this subtle firmament and *Prema* or Selfless Love is like the moon with cooling rays.

What is the implication of this understanding for society and for preventing social strife today? The epic of *Mahabharat* shows us the application of this concept within man and in today's society.

In its subtle form *Mahabharat* is being raged, within man, even today. Just like the *Ramayan*. In this epic, *Sathya, Dharma, Shanti, Prema* and *Ahimsa* are the five *Pandava* brothers. The evil qualities are *Kauravas*. Both fight over kingship of man's heart. The millions of thoughts and feelings are soldiers and citizens of kingdoms. The *Atma* or Soul, as Lord Krishna, is the witness but also the charioteer of the *Jiva*. The fight is over Hastinapura city. This body's skeleton is *Asthinapura*. Both have nine gates. Both, *Kauravas* and *Pandavas* are born within. The wars happen because Kings have confidence in their subjects and these subjects, too, encourage the rulers. The subject of delusions pushes an individual into battle. When delusion, illusion and 'I' and 'mine' feelings or body attachments are dropped, the war will never happen. This is the 'inner meaning' of the *Mahabharat*. A study of Study of Limits in the epic in this way creates Awareness.

The principle behind the 'seen' is termed as *Prakriti* (Creation). The principle behind the 'see-er' is *Purusha* (eternal, Soul, never changing). The tradition concludes that the union is the result of delusion; prompted by delusion, it produces delusion again. This is the law of seed and the tree. For a realised Soul, all that is seen outside is a delusion and is a projection of what is within man! So, man is the basis of society. If he attains the Highest stage of Self Realisation, there is nothing else but the Self. So, starting with the individual is not only the beginning but the very end of education where it merges with life. Attaining experience of One Self is the end. Education helps us see through the delusion by grasping the inner meaning of all epics – example of *Ramayan* and *Mahabharat* is used here.

The idea of allowing Selfless Love to sprout and spread its branches in the heart of man is that it will sow the seed of Selfless Love in all. When his heart has nothing but Selfless Love inside it, there will be nothing but the same outside him. The 4C Approach merges back in the ocean, then. This is the experience of the Seers of ancient Indian tradition. Having not experienced this state, the author can only state this. Hoping that it becomes the experience of the reader, the author wishes to draw inspiration from such a reader, one day.

(ii) If you wait for society to reform, you will wait forever

Understanding the nature of man, nature of creation and nature of Truth have implications for education. What are these implications?

Education seeks the Truth and makes man realise the Truth about himself. **Living in creation, or 'universe', respecting rules like we do in a 'city' we live in, fulfills the purpose of education in this 'universe – city'.**

Creation is a continuous process without beginning or end. This realisation tells man that there will never be a time when everything is perfect as per his perception. Waiting for such a time is a perpetual wait. The nature of creation is ever evolving, ever changing. This is an eternal process whose dynamics does not allow a state of pause. **The only way out is to change man's own perception or way of 'C'ing things.** The only perfection possible is within control of man, i.e. Perfection in unity of his own thought, word and deed. This is the first duty and first righteous conduct or *Swa – Dharma* of man. Taking this first step begins the journey of a thousand miles. However, the experience of Indian sages' states that taking the first step is important. The rest simply follows, though slowly – but surely. This unity of thought word and deed is referred to as Purity or *Trikaarana Shuddhi*. Such purity is needed in following four goals of life. Then, with patience and perseverance, the flow of life can change. This gives benefits of balance through enjoyment of both worldly and spiritual life. The emergence of Selfless Love within man enables him to reach realm of Highest Truth. This has already been depicted in Fig 0.29 in the Background.

Education, as this tradition concludes, is individual. There is no mass conversion or conveyor belt approach. Each individual has unique mix of inclination for *Karma, Bhakti* and *Jnana*. Education uses concepts given here to help man to act. The purpose of education is transformation of man. Only as a result of this transformation can society be transformed. It is impossible to transform society without starting with each individual. This attention to the individual can only be given by parents and teachers through education. Therefore, the flow of education, or *Vidya Vahini*, is the life breath of society.

iii) Change yourself to change the world

Understanding the nature of creation teaches us that the world will be ever changing and this nature is never changing. The only thing in the world that can change is man himself. So, the ancient Seers say, start the process not today, but now!

This leads to the question: 'How'?

It can be done simply by sharpening the distinction between man and rest of creation. Discrimination is the distinction between man and the animal world. Acquiring this discrimination can be done in either of two ways:

(a) Through education – The path of *Satya, Dharma (Satyam Vada, Dharmam Chara), Shanti, Prema*. Please refer Figure 0.5 shown earlier ('How to acquire Discrimination') **OR**

(b) By honourably earning wealth with effort though various means (Four *Purusharthas*).

Both these approaches are discussed in earlier chapters. Some may not understand fully the importance of discussing ancient Indian texts like *Vedas* in this context. The *Vedas* give the background of fulfilling the three goals of life to attain the highest wisdom. The foundation of transforming man is built on unity of thought, word and deed which transforms the heart. The Figure on how to acquire Discrimination, given in the Background of this Paper, refers to the *Vedas* preparing man for the Highest Truth. One common question needs an answer here: How do the *Vedic* rituals help? The rituals are not important, their significance dawns through constant repetition and education. The significance of rituals in *Vedas* is explained in the following way:

"The heart is the ceremonial altar. Your body is the fire place. Your hair is the holy grass *Darbha*. Wishes are the fuel-sticks with which the fire is fed. Desire is the ghee (clarified butter) that is poured in the fire to make it burst into flame. Anger is the sacrificial animal. The fire is the tapas (penance) you accomplish. People sometimes interpret penance as ascetic practices like standing on one leg, and so on. No, *tapas* is not physical contortion.

It is the complete and correct co-ordination of thought word and deed. When all words emanating from you are sweet, your breath becomes Rig Veda. When you restrict what you listen to and prefer only sweet speech, all that you hear becomes *Saama gaana*. When you do only sweet deeds, all that you do is *Yajur homa* (sacrificial ritual). Thus, you will be performing every day the *Vedapurusha Yajna*, the *yajna* that propitiates the Supreme Vedic Being."

The inner meaning of the ancient Indian rituals relates to living practical day to day life. They are designed to change man to sharpen distinction between man and animal. Thus, they enable man to achieve the purpose of life.

Gestalt of Ancient Indian tradition with management theory

Michael Porter's three ingredients of strategy for firms: simple consistency, reinforcement and Optimisation effort also apply to strategy of man – for living life. This strategy starts when man shows consistency in thought, word and deed. He should also Reinforce thought by word and deed to indulge in an Optimisation effort. The latter is achieved by removing the waste of disharmony that comes through difference between thought, word and deed. These three ingredients are Meant for man in this Age to incorporate ethics in the business of life. In this manner, the business of life itself emerges from education. It is expressed through integration of Man with Management within and without. Thus, the true study of management is the study of Man.

The education in Man Management or Self Management is expressed in personal and professional life as a Gestalt. When man operates on the axis of Truth and Morality in his personal and professional life, there is harmony among all. Then family and firm, society, cluster, industry, nations are all in balance. The management of national competitive advantage of nation and finally harmony among the family of nations occurs. This Union of minds and actions or *Yoga* lead to the Source of Highest Peace in this Universe-city.

This is depicted in Diagram 6.1.

Yoga – from co-operation within man to co-operation between men

Yoga – from co-operation within man to co-operation between men

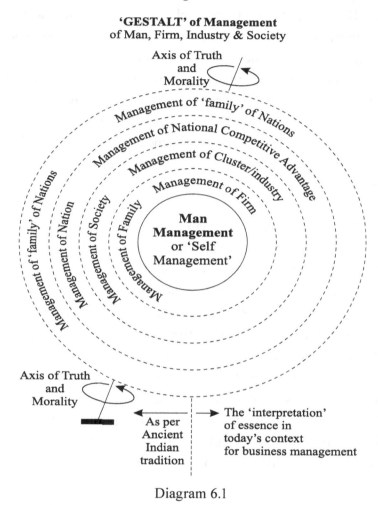

Diagram 6.1

6.4 Integration of 4C's with spiritual concepts of Indian Tradition (Yoga, meditation)

(a) How is Co-operation understood in Indian texts?

Bhagvad Gita refers to its chapters as *Yoga*. This is union of Self with its Source. The various spiritual paths teach co-operation of thought, word and deed to enable this union i.e. co-operation of man with spirituality or the spirit of working selflessly to discover Self.

The Indian spiritual tradition believes that knowledge is partial when it is without a harmonious co-mingling with other points of view to comprehend the Truth. *Yoga* means 'coming together' in India. The path of *Yoga* is designated differently in Sanskrit under different contexts. However, those who are able to conceive and execute the Union are revered as Yogis. The harmonious co-existence of many faiths and beliefs has come through a union of ideas. Where *Yoga* is the basis of learning, one's excellence is enhanced by adding to it the excellence of others. This togetherness or union, when established between outer and inner nature of man leads to purity. This is the hallmark of progress in both spiritual and material world. This faith does not leave any room for fanaticism. Its practical application makes individuals and society experience 'together-ness' (Co-operation) with Compatibility – which is experienced when all paths merge to reach the final destination within man and in society.

The understanding of *Yoga* unfolds with man's inner evolution. It begins with Chapter 1 (Co-operation) and leads to Unity (Chapter 6) and merger. It is also the union of this inner journey and outer journey of man. It is the union of man's action with the higher good of all (society). It is also man's experience of the Unity of creation which guides him to Love all Serve all and Help ever, Hurt never. Thus *Yoga* is not just co-operation. It is that understanding of co-operation that emerges from pure intentions of the heart. It leads to the highest good of man and society. It encompasses all points of view by directing them to the highest goal. It learns to co-operate with opposing viewpoints also if they have pure intentions. Thus its thesis co-operates with an anti thesis to produce a synthesis – in the Hegelian dialectic or co-operates with its prothesis. The progress of mankind is from one synthesis to another – shown in Background as the ever changing nature of creation. *Yoga* is expressed differently as per different inner urges of man to get the experience of Unity. These include:

Karma Yoga: Those who try through activities and achievements this Union are *Karma* Yogis. Many men seem to be born just to accomplish one mission or project. Their intellect is not satisfied with just planning or imagination. For such men a guide book (or *Sastra*) helps them along the most beneficial path. This guide book is *Karma Yoga* which leads man to get the maximum result out of their activity. This *Yoga* teaches man how to deal with despair when desired action from *Karma* or activity is not occurring. It teaches man to undertake activity for the sake of excellence – without getting attached to the fruits of the effort. There is no bargain for results or calculation – except the pleasure of doing work for the sake of work – to achieve excellence. Then, grief becomes a stranger as there was no hidden motive or benefit that was sought. Excellence in work, guided by Truth and morality, is a pleasure that comes naturally for man. It enables him to be in harmony with himself. In this manner when others follow such actions, harmony in society results.

Bhakti Yoga: This path, some believe, is fit for those whose nature is emotionally oriented. Some are inclined to remark that this is not the way to achieving Excellence or Divinity. Infact, when one is emotionally involved in excellence work becomes worship or *Bhakti*. History of the world shows that many great Seers, sages, teachers and guides achieve excellence or Divinity through this path. They have exercised great influence on the mind of man across time. The conquest of mind has brought fame to them and to the land where they were born. They continue to give inspiration for following the path of Truth and Righteous Conduct. Both these attributes lead to harmony within man, between men and in society. This path leads men to expand their hearts to the suffering of others (using their inner emotions) which is a validation that the path is being truly trodden upon by adherent.

Jnana Yoga: Those who stick to logical analysis and rational interpretations and attain intuitive perception are the *Jnana*-yogis. The disciplining of the mind leads to control over senses which gives intuitive perception that can go beyond *Satyam* also. These intuitive perceptions are validation of the path which needs to be followed with Truth and morality.

Raja Yoga: This is the process of establishing mastery over the mind. It requires testing, through one's own intellect and experiences, everything. Surrendering blindly one's intellect to any untested religious leader is not this path. Every being has three instruments of acquiring knowledge and through that knowledge, wisdom: First is: The visible fact – knowledge relaing to these facts is 'instinctive' and very strong, active and advanced in animals. It is the lowest and least beneficial instrument and operates only in a limited field of sensory experience. The second instrument is 'rational'. It seeks cause and effect. This is most evident in man. The sensory is subordinated to the rational in man whose limits are large unlike sensory perceptions. Yet, logic has its limits as its road is often circular. It cannot experience the third instrument of 'Consciousness' which pervades the cosmos from the single cell to transcendental fullness – its realisation is: Selfless Love for society.

The 'coming together' of thought, word and deed within man or Yoga begins the journey. When expressed through any of the above Yogas, it leads to an experience of Consciousness within man. Thus, it makes man compatible with the needs of society – enabling Compatibility advantage in society.

(b) The path of focussed Concern *within* for man's spiritual progress

The ability to focus is the ability to concentrate. It requires discipline. This is done by man and by firms in society to execute daily tasks. What is the underlying concern behind this focus? The Indian tradition judges the intention behind the action more than the action itself (both doctor and thief use a knife with different intentions). Therefore, the nature of concern is the determinant of the fruit of action. A concern for maximising wealth for the individual and firm without concern for others is harmful. Customers, society, nation and environment suffer. Knowledge is not a bag of tricks to be used to misguide, mislead or force customers through cues of competitive consumption to buy a firms output. Education works on the concerns which man has. However, this, too, should start with focusing first.

The path of focusing that occurs *within* man, in the ancient Indian spiritual tradition is a threefold path:

(i) *Concentration*

Concentration is the unwavering determination that man applies in his daily activities to achieve goals and fulfill tasks. It involves the realms of the senses, feelings and intellect of man. Concentration deals mainly with Truth experienced as *Nijam*. Concentration used for fulfilling selfish goals through selfish means occurs when man believes he is the body. He believes his duty to his body is to fulfill all desires the mind can have. The impact of such thinking or education is shown in Fig 0.28 in the Background. Through humility and co-operation and right concern, man is given an experience above concentration. The use of concentration should be related to '*Jnana*' or knowledge gained by analysing the objective world. This was pointed out when differentiating between 3C and 4C Approach.

ii) *Contemplation*

Contemplation is a stage when the senses withdraw for some time. This emerges from attachment for worldly objects slackening. This process gives insights and leads to the experience of *Satyam*. Selflessness emerges here. The experience of Selfless Love gives insights leading to expression of Individuality in a creative way. It also gives skills for performing tasks which are extraordinary. The possibility of tremendous value addition is opened. However, a focus on right concern is still needed so that experience of *Satyam* is not overwhelmed by *Nijam*. The gradual extension of experience of *Satyam* is the direction that education gives man. The beginning of the experience of Selfless Love leads to application of '*Jnana*' or knowledge. This is acquired through concentration for analysing the objective world. Knowledge is further subjected to contemplation so as to apply it for the best interest of society. This leads to *Sujnana* as elaborated in 4.6 above.

iii) *Meditation*

When man breaks away from all attachment and becomes completely Selfless, this stage is called meditation. This stage is not easily understood. In fact, it is described as continuous like rain – and a day long process with eyes open. It is merging with the excellence in all dimensions or Divinity or God. Like milk and water cannot be separated, similarly the mind once merged with Divinity cannot be separated. Selfless Love blossoms and it opens the true Individuality, creativity and productivity of man. The actions of man in this state can never be a zero sum game. They only promote the highest good of society. The **constant integrated awareness** of this experience is *Ritam* or Highest Truth. When man is not divorced from his meditation, *Ritam* is realised. The realisation of *Ritam* is expressed as the Compatibility Advantage at work in this Paper. This state of awareness has to be realised *within* man. When intentions and urges emerge from a purified Consciousness saturated with excellence, '*Vijnana*' results (4.6 above). Then tasks are executed by man as *Nishkama Karma* (propounded by the ancient Indian text of *Bhagavad Gita*). This state of Awareness of man involves experiencing Truth first as *Satyam*, later as *Ritam*.

Dharma or righteousness is basis of all activities of man. Cooperation with others gives the discipline of humility to withdraw from the senses. Co-operation within man, of thought word and deed, expresses Individuality through focussed concern for customer and society. This expresses as a desire to excel and increase one's capacities (*Dakshata*). The withdrawing from senses makes man seek a higher goal of nationality. Here, the concept is that all hearts that beat as one – seeking same goal of excellence – are one nationality. The competitive response is the expression of competing within one self to improve one self further. Such progress within man leads to meditation or complete withdrawal from senses and attachment to indulge in *Nishkama Karma* only.

(c)The understanding of Competitive Response in 4C Approach

How do we understand the development of Competitive Response within man? Is this response necessarily a zero sum game? How can Indian tradition's understanding be translated through using terminology of Benchmarking? This is attempted here in 5 steps:

Step 1. *Benchmarking*
Benchmarking superior performance of others is only the first step of competitive response. Its purpose is to develop humility within man and to generate co-operation to gather resources to develop a response. It is the first step in the search for excellence. The excellence outside man gives the initial inspiration to search for excellence *within*.

Step 2. *Focussed Concern*
The ability to focus one's concern is the first expression of Individuality. This becomes productive after humility of learning from others initiates excellence seeking. This focussed Concern is at three levels within man. These are Concentration, Contemplation and Meditation. These generate different levels of response.

Step 3. *Competitive Response first stage – competition is the Benchmark*
Competitive Response in this stage emerges from simple concentration and answers the competitors. Current study of marketing is limited to this area. Often inability to ensure adequate competitive response leads to trickery, unfairness and misuse of human mind. Grabbing market share instead of commitment to add value to self and society may be the focus. The tools of marketing can be used to exploit customers, competitors, society etc for short term gain. This may even involve manipulating environment of government, natural resources, labour, structural inefficiencies and laws. The first competitive response is the lowest level of response and not the purpose of education. It fulfills only physical needs of man and firm. If not directed properly, it can harm all, ultimately. Can men who indulge in these practices be called educated? Do their college degrees bring repute to their college or do they bring repute to their parents? Ancient Indian society pondered over such questions. It made transformation of man as the purpose of education. By simply giving information about use of tools and techniques of doing business, transformation is not ensured. The purpose of this Paper is only to highlight this small point.

Step 4. *Competitive Response second stage*

Shifting benchmark within man: The meaning of *Artha* is declaration of distinction. It is the way man declares his distinction from others in creation. It is the expression of Individuality guided by Truth and morality. If this is directed by immorality, low goals of trickery and cheating or misleading it hurta man, society and nature. Swami Vivekananda has said: "Man is man so long as he is trying to rise above his nature and this nature is both internal and external...". *Artha* is the expression of distinction of man who is following the definition of man given by Swami Vivekananda. This understanding of man about himself can only come through education. For, it generates the experience of Truth within man. It does not restrict itself to bookish knowledge. Then, desire or *Kama* emerging in him is to express this distinction in a unique way. Creativity and Individuality then become the hallmarks of output. This emerges through Contemplation. The ancient Indian Seers have experience that this state leads to insights or *Satyam*. These insights into nature of things lead to capacity for tremendous value addition to man and society. They are the basis of a civilisation that outlasts. Ancient Indians, as some state, dominated global GDP for thousands of years because of this capacity of Contemplation. Their focussed concern expressed itself in desire fulfilment for man and society. Angus Maddison is quoted in Harvard Business Review (2011) as stating that India and China contributed 50% of Global GDP in 1800's. The benchmark, for ancient Indians is no more the outside world. For, that is realised as only a beginning for the search of excellence within man.

Step 5. *Competitive Response third stage*

The only benchmark is within the Self: This stage of competitive response is a pure expression of Individuality of the highest order. It comes from inspired thought that is based on the collective good of all. It leads to good of each individual in the value chain, simultaneously. It is a theoretical concept till it is experienced within man. The only evidence that supports this possibility is the value addition Indian economy has done to global economy since time immemorial. The deteriorating standards of education overtime have led to lack of enough material to validate these claims in a theoretical way. Chapter 7 validates use of this idea by Source to benefit society in a practical way.

d) Compatibility: when *Karma* merges into *Bhakti* and both merge into *Jnana*

When man's actions are suffused with a spirit of service, Selfless Love inspires his actions.

His actions represent True Knowledge *(Jnana)*, for, *Karma, Bhakti* and *Jnana* merge. At that time the unseen reality behind all that is seen becomes obvious. In the ancient Indian tradition this is known as *Purushottam Yoga*. It is that which is put into practice not just put in words – by writing or speaking! That is why *Jnana* is not just knowledge but *'Sadguna'* – that which is expressed through all human senses and organs. This shows how well the knowledge is absorbed in thoughts and behaviour of man. When all work is executed as an offering to excellence (titled Divinity in ancient texts) then merger occurs. The good of the person performing such action, the higher good and the highest good become one. This is the merging of *Swartha* (self interest), *Parartha* and *Parmartha* (highest good of all) and leads to Compatibility advantage for man, firm and society.

So long as man is in the physical body he experiences Duality. For those who live in Duality, this tradition states, the concept of God or excellence in all spheres can be very useful. When recognition of the one outside the body is taken as God (He), then, in the first stage I and you become 'We'. Next, 'We' and 'He' are identified. The *Jiva* (man) becomes identified with *Prakriti* or creation (You) and then with Supreme Consciousness of excellence or 'He' which is referred to as 'That'. This, the ancient texts state, is signified in the mantra *'Om Tat Sat'* ('That' is Truth). Section 6.11 explains this.

The process that leads to Compatibility Advantage begins within man. First, there is unity of Thought, Word and Deed. This follows Porter's Strategy of Simple Consistency and Optimisation Effort within man. This unity is expressed by man through 4C's or four *Purusharthas* as given here. Then, Strategies of Simple Consistency and Optimisation Effort are applied in execution of business and the business of life, simultaneously. Their repeated practice leads to the Strategy of Simple Consistency and Optimisation Effort becoming operant condition for Gross, Subtle and Causal body.

The journey of man, as he moves from maximisation of Selfish gains to Selflessness has been traced above. Simple consistency of selfishness is replaced by optimal benefit of man and society.

The alignment of Body, Mind and Soul leads to Compatibility Advantage *within* and *without* simultaneously. The ancient Indian texts state that *Swartha, Parartha* and *Parmartha* merge in this stage. The Self interest of man and the enlightened Self interest of society become One. That stage is the Compatibility Advantage at work.

Within & 'by' man
Alignment of 'Inner World', 'Outer World' leads to Highest Truth

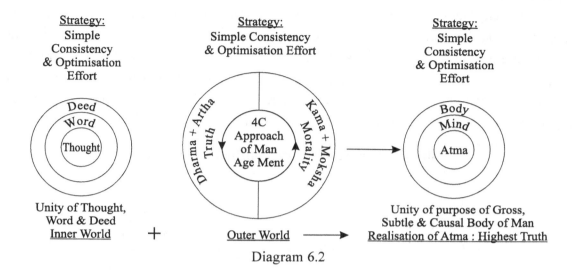

Strategy:
Simple Consistency & Optimisation Effort

Strategy:
Simple Consistency & Optimisation Effort

Strategy:
Simple Consistency & Optimisation Effort

Deed
Word
Thought

Dharma + Artha Truth
4C Approach of Man Age Ment
Kama + Moksha Morality

Body
Mind
Atma

Unity of Thought, Word & Deed
Inner World

+

Outer World

Unity of purpose of Gross, Subtle & Causal Body of Man
Realisation of Atma : Highest Truth

Diagram 6.2

The coming together of self interest of man and the enlightened self interest of society is shown in Diagram 6.3.

The Unity within Man
Leads to Unity with All

Realisation	Resultant Action
Atma can never consider any one as different from Oneself "Bhava Adwaitha"	Help Ever Hurt Never Just as you would to your own physical body
Mind sees the Atma or the Self everywhere as Part of "oneself"	,,
Body follows the mind & the Atma but within "Study of Limit": "No Karma Adwaitha"	,,

Diagram 6.3

333

Their union has a simple logic: The Soul is the Universal Consciousness and can not consider any other entity or person as different from One Self. This Awareness automatically results in actions that 'Help Ever Hurt Never'. This is the summary of the ancient Indian texts of *Puranas*, *Vedas* and *Upanishads*. The human mind, when it sees the *Atma* or Soul everywhere, visualises everything and everybody as part of One Self. It can not think of doing any action to hurt himself. The physical body follows dictates of the mind and acts exactly as the mind sees and experiences. Therefore, man becomes incapable of hurting anybody. The Unity within man leads to Unity with All.

Unity of purpose of Gross, Subtle & Causal Body

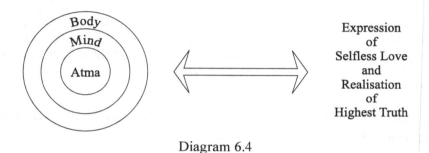

Diagram 6.4

Therefore, the natural expression of unity of purpose of the gross, subtle and causal body of man is Selfless Love. The realisation of this Highest Truth comes through the natural expression of man's True nature.

Fig 0.29 in the Background details the process of emergence of Selfless Love in Man. The wave of knowledge of man merges back into the ocean through social action. This is the reverse of the same coin as shown in Diagram 6.5.

**Reverse & obverse
of same coin**

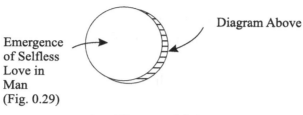

Emergence
of Selfless
Love in
Man
(Fig. 0.29)

Diagram Above

Diagram 6.5

There are three chief instruments in the ancient Indian tradition that help attain this state. They are;

a) A mind unsullied by attachment and hatred.

b) A speech unsullied by falsehood and

c) A body unsullied by violence.

The complexity of intellectual search is reduced to simplicity in action in this manner. This is the process of integration of education with Life. To see the four parts of this integration is the next task.

6.5 How does Education integrate with Life: Four parts of the Approach?

Integrating management with ancient Indian education can come easily by understanding the ancient Indian *Sanatana Dharma.* Then, integrating it with management of business and life can be done. This Paper follows the same approach. Therefore, we first understand this tradition and its texts. Then, we see if there is a validity of a four fold approach. Not necessarily of four *Purusharthas,* but of other concepts, too, that lead to excellence within man. Once a four fourfold understanding is validated, we see how the wave of the structure of this Paper merges back in life.

The process of integration of education with life is shown here in four parts;

i) **Discovering the Purpose of Life**

ii) **How to live life**

iii) **The business of living**

iv) **Realisation of Excellence within One Self**

Part 1 Discovering the Purpose of Life

The purpose of life is analysed in the context of Truth and the level man has achieved. Therefore the matrix summarises for each level of Truth:

- Texts relied upon for education at each level of Truth
- What do these texts represent
- The Path of Progress at this level of Truth

Diagram 6.6 depicts how man moves from Higher to Highest Truth. At each level of Truth some texts are found more useful for instruction. These texts represent different things and lead to a path of progress *within* man that enables progress to higher Truth. *Vidya Vahini* is the journey from Truth to Higher Truth *within* man. The Diagram 6.6 is self explanatory and any elaboration would require maybe more than one textbook for each sub-section. The purpose, here, is to summarise the subtle essence of this tradition. Then, it validates the 4C Approach with this subtle aspect. The subtle Truth permeates all levels of Truth. Each level of Truth helps man reach the final goal. In fact, each and every text has, within itself, the route to reach the highest Truth. It depends on the ability to interpret the text. Such texts that are told as stories are easily understood by everybody. Hence, stories are the beginning of education. How the stories of *Ramayan* and *Mahabharat* are to be interpreted to reveal the Highest Truth has been demonstrated earlier in this chapter. The highest interpretation of *Sri Rudram* and *Purushasuktam* from the *Vedas* has also been demonstrated in the Introduction.

Despite being Aware of the above limitation, the classification given below is used for ease of communication in education – and partial understanding is expanded overtime. In fact, all texts are inextricably linked and inseparable. Finally, it must be remembered, the same stream of bliss or *Ananda* (that emerges from Selfless Love) flows through all texts.

The call for action – irrespective of text – is only one: Help Ever, Hurt Never! The end result they seek to achieve is to make non – attachment to fruit of action emerge from 'within' man. This is the goal of education in ancient Indian tradition. Chapter 7 shows the importance of this conclusion.

Integration of Education with Life:
Ancient Indian Approach in 4 parts
Part 1: 'Discovering Purpose of Life'
Ancient Indian Education : Moves from Higher to Highest Truth

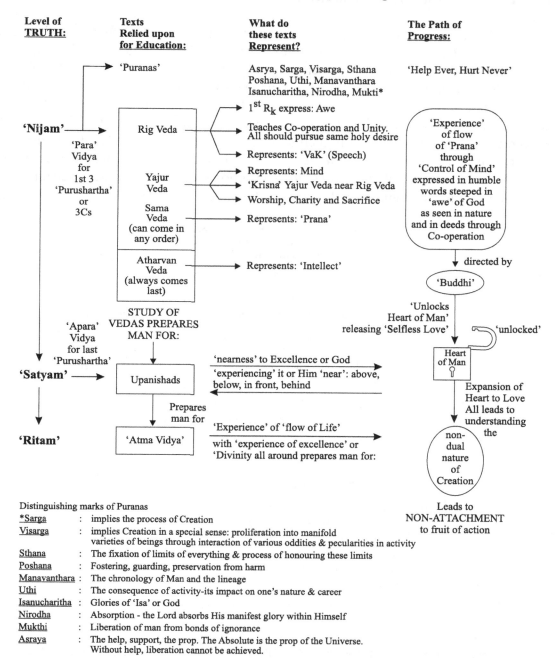

Level of TRUTH:

Texts Relied upon for Education:

What do these texts Represent?

The Path of Progress:

'Puranas'

Asrya, Sarga, Visarga, Sthana Poshana, Uthi, Manavanthara Isanucharitha, Nirodha, Mukti*

'Help Ever, Hurt Never'

'Nijam'

'Para' Vidya for 1st 3 'Purushartha' or 3Cs

Rig Veda

1st R$_k$ express: Awe

Teaches Co-operation and Unity. All should pursue same holy desire

Represents: 'VaK' (Speech)

Yajur Veda

Represents: Mind

'Krisna' Yajur Veda near Rig Veda

Worship, Charity and Sacrifice

Sama Veda (can come in any order)

Represents: 'Prana'

Atharvan Veda (always comes last)

Represents: 'Intellect'

'Experience' of flow of 'Prana' through 'Control of Mind' expressed in humble words steeped in 'awe' of God as seen in nature and in deeds through Co-operation

directed by

'Buddhi'

'Unlocks Heart of Man' releasing 'Selfless Love'

'unlocked'

STUDY OF VEDAS PREPARES MAN FOR:

'Apara' Vidya for last 'Purushartha'

'Satyam'

Upanishads

'nearness' to Excellence or God 'experiencing' it or Him 'near': above, below, in front, behind

Heart of Man

Expansion of Heart to Love All leads to understanding the non-dual nature of Creation

Prepares man for

'Ritam'

'Atma Vidya'

'Experience' of 'flow of Life' with 'experience of excellence' or 'Divinity all around prepares man for:

Leads to
NON-ATTACHMENT
to fruit of action

Distinguishing marks of Puranas
*Sarga	:	implies the process of Creation
Visarga	:	implies Creation in a special sense: proliferation into manifold varieties of beings through interaction of various oddities & pecularities in activity
Sthana	:	The fixation of limits of everything & process of honouring these limits
Poshana	:	Fostering, guarding, preservation from harm
Manavanthara	:	The chronology of Man and the lineage
Uthi	:	The consequence of activity-its impact on one's nature & career
Isanucharitha	:	Glories of 'Isa' or God
Nirodha	:	Absorption - the Lord absorbs His manifest glory within Himself
Mukthi	:	Liberation of man from bonds of ignorance
Asraya	:	The help, support, the prop. The Absolute is the prop of the Universe. Without help, liberation cannot be achieved.

Diagram 6.6

After discovering the purpose of life – of helping not hurting others, the next task becomes:

Part 2 How to live life – Action and Result

Diagram 6.7 below gives guidelines of daily living that emerge from the essence of ancient Indian tradition. The ability to magnify your own fault and see the fault of others as very minor is the starting point of experiencing Truth within man. This leads to the Highest concept of Surrender to excellence visualised in the form of God for ease of understanding. Surrender is not running away from action – instead it performs duty surrendering fruits of action. If *Dharma* requires killing the enemy when all alternatives have failed, it is done. However, it is without any trace of ill feeling – only as a duty performed by the body. The inner nature is detached from the fruit of the action. Jesus, too, says: Hate the sin, not the sinner. This is the essence of *Bhagvad Gita*. The action recommended is the definition of 'Gentle'man in English language and concepts of 'gentleman soldier' etc emerges from it.

Part 2: 'How to Live Life': Action & Result
Ancient Indian Education: Integrating with Daily Life
(Guidelines for daily living)

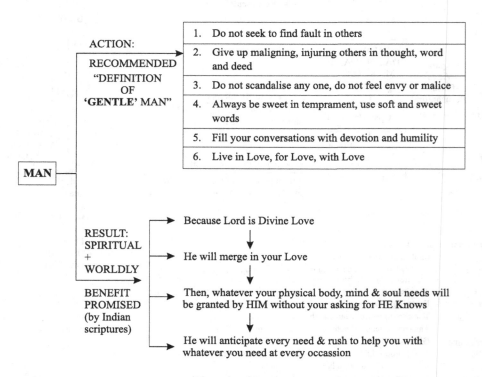

To Sum up: Love all, serve all; Love the world and the world will Love you and take care of you.

Diagram 6.7

338

A final test: When the 4C Approach merges back, does meaning of the ultimate promise given by Lord Krishna in *Bhagavad Gita* become clear with the logic used here? If this ultimate test of validation, too, can be attempted – then this wave belongs to the ocean.

Bhagvad Gita states in Chapter 18: "***Sarva Dharma parityajya mamekam sharnam vraja...***"

Ancient Indian tradition **transforms Attitude of man** guiding it towards Surrender of fruit of action to excellence. Then all actions are done as if they are being done for the Divine and not for selfish end. Surrender of ego removes selfishness. Along with a desire to excel in performing the work – as it is to be given to the beloved object of devotion – it promotes excellence. This makes the work beneficial to society. It enables realisation of the interdependence of man and society. Any actions done will automatically be adding value to society. Actions are the basis of life, in the Indian spiritual tradition. So, purification of action by surrender of the ego automatically adds value to man and society. Fig 0.29 shows that *Dharma* is a progression of giving up selfishness – from self preservation to self sacrifice – *Vyakti Dharma* to *Rajya Dharma* etc. to reach self satisfaction (the highest stage). This *sloka* asks for surrender to Highest Dharma of Excellence in all dimensions. The peak of co-operation or *Dharma* happens when man surrenders the ego. Then, "*Dharmo Rakshati Rakshatah...*" applies, for, *Dharma* protects man. Ego is selfish. Selfless work for society, surrendering to the experience of excellence is the goal. It is natural that the output will be excellence in the dimension chosen as per inner urge. Those whose inner urge is devotion or *Bhakti* will propagate love for excellence within man differently – not discussed here. They spread the message of righteous conduct and *Thithiksha*. This is more than forbearance – for it implies a capacity to retaliate yet the decision not to do it. They are teachers and no society which calls its teachers unproductive can survive in the long run. Of course, society that respects false teachers will suffer. So, 'Help Ever, Hurt Never' and 'Surrender to Excellence' leading to non –attachment are the **first two** steps. Keeping the above in mind, what is the understanding of life and 'business' or 'busy-ness' of living?

Part 3 The 'Business' of living through '*Bhakti*', '*Karma*' and '*Jnana*'

Diagram 6.8 takes the logic of Part 2 further. Each Man has a different inner nature. The individual path towards excellence is thus determined. For those emotional, the *Bhakti* path gives fulfilment. For others the path of action or *Karma* and for those intellectually inclined the path of *Jnana*. Chapter1 Diagram 1.4 etc show these paths have the same goal.

Irrespective of the path, Part2 has clarified the next step for all paths. Business is about give and take. The law of the seed and tree shows how the seed takes from the elements. Through co-operation within itself, it expresses its value addition in a manner that fulfills its need for expansion (as per the nature of creation). It benefits all, simultaneously. The merging of *Swartha*, *Parartha* and *Parmartha* is demonstrated by this law of seed and tree. Similarly, give and take of life emerges from Part2. Here, man gives to all as per actions recommended for him and takes from excellence within him all that is offered. Just as the seed can give to all what they desire by unfolding the excellence within itself. The seed first expresses its *Swartha* by co-operation with elements for its own prosperity and growth. Later, by selflessly sharing its oxygen, shadow and fruit with man its selfishness merges with higher good nature and highest good of all. Through completing many useful cycles of nature, it keeps nature in balance. This is beneficial to itself, nature as well as man – thus serving higher levels of good to the highest good of all. The tree signifies sacrifice, co-operation and sharing. When this becomes the social norm, compatibility advantage promotes balance in society. The tree has within it the seed and the seed contains within itself the tree. This is the secret of creation. If we take the full from the full, the full remains still – so an ancient *sloka* or verse states. The full tree can be taken out of the tree through the seed without disturbing the tree. Full benefit of nature and society can similarly be taken by man without in any way reducing the bounty they offer. This is the law of the seed and the tree for nature and man, both. The seed's desires are fulfilled in the tree and the tree's are fulfilled through the seed.

The merger of the three states happens within man in his spiritual quest, too. When every activity is done as an offering to excellence the merger of *Karma* or work occurs with the devotion or *Bhakti* as work becomes like worship. Knowledge or *Jnana* that is required to ahieve excellence, then emerges. The three paths not only seek but lead to and also merge into excellence. The final destination is a state of Awareness which does not differentiate between the paths taken to achieve it. The paths are thus One just as the seed and the tree.

There is another way of understanding the concept. The ancient Indian tradition states that Divinity cannot be grasped either by the brain or senses of man. It has unfolded itself through the concepts of Creation, Sustenance and Dissolution. This tradition further states that man can penetrate the inner meaning of Creation by performing Duty as Worship (*Karma Yoga*). Similarly, he can grasp the significance of Sustenance through Devotion to the Lord or Excellence (*Bhakti Yoga*). The experience of Union with Divine is Dissolution of the ego which happens with attainment of Wisdom (*Jnana Yoga*). When the **unity of creation** is experienced the ego dissolves automatically – as tree realises its unity with the seed. Then, everybody or everything is seen as the Self or Divine. Devotion to the Divine or excellence makes work a worship enabling *Jnana* of excellence. Thus, the paths merge.

Part 3: The 'Business' of Living through Bhakti/Karma/Jnana 'Business is Give & Take'

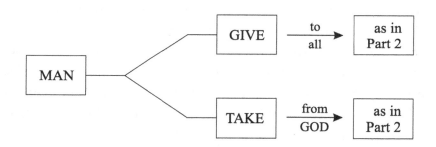

Part 4: Realisation of 'Excellence' within 'One Self'

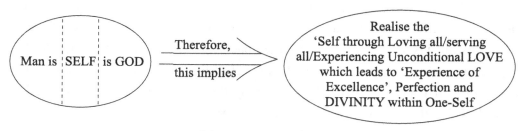

Diagrams 6.8 and 6.9

Part 4 Realisation of 'Excellence' within 'One Self': *Advaita* or non– Dualism

Diagram 6.9 is the last stage for man where he discovers Himself as expressing excellence in all actions in all dimensions similar to ideas man has about Divinity. Duality, then, dissolves. How does this stage, promised by the ancient Indian texts, occur?

Through the process of serving others with humility man experiences the unconditional Love that is the basis of excellence within man. Such an experience of true self leads him to the higher experience of Perfection or Divinity that is his true nature. The author has no experience in this and, thus, cannot comment further – only can restate texts here. The validation of their Truth in ancient India was the balance in man and society. It was demonstrated by personal life of Seers. They taught Truths selflessly without desire of even a fee. Yet their needs were looked after by society. Kings bowed as they guided them.

6.6 Spiritual means lead to four ends: Merger of 4C Approach back into Awareness

Having tested that wave of the Paper and ocean of Indian tradition are same, now we go to the next test. The four-fold classification of the Paper is tested with a check if such four-fold classification applies to other spiritual means in this tradition. This is done In Diagram 6.10 below. Again, detailed explanations are not given but a dip stick test is taken just to verify the validity. Is use of a four fold classification and its applicability to life valid? Therefore, can it be applied to business as well? The spirit of living life should emerge as same – irrespective of the route. That tests the validity of its conclusions. While Diagram 6.6 proves that the conclusion 'Help Ever. Hurt Never' guides action in daily life validating that irrespective of the route the call of action is the same. The same non– attachment to fruit of action that guides a competitive response is the second call of action, too. Diagram 6.10, then, concludes that irrespective of which Vidya (Knowledge leading to wisdom), virtue or devotion (*Bhakti*) we study or practice, its essence merges into the four *Purusharthas* or goals of life. This validates that whichever wave we pull from the ocean of knowledge (that contains all wisdom within it) it merges back into the same ocean. Infact all waves have the same ingredient and the same water. All of these can be interpreted through the *Purusharthas* – irrespective of whether we study the wave first or ocean first. **All of the *Vidyas*, *Bhakti* and virtues lead to the same Awareness.**

Many Spiritual means lead to four ends

A) 4 TYPES OF VIDYAS:

Aanveekshaki	→	The Vidya by which one can discriminate between Atma & Anaatma	] MOKSHA

Relate to cycle of birth & death

Thrayee	→	Vidya by which Swarga/Heaven attained through appropriate rituals/Karma	] KAMA
Vaartha	→	Agriculture & other productive efforts	] ARTHA
Dandaneethi	→	Rulers & guardians of society rule & guard according to this Vidya - ESSENTIAL for enjoying RICHES & CROPS	] DHARMA

B) MASTERY OF MIND LEADS TO SPIRITUAL VICTORY: (MOKSHA) TO PURGE MIND OF EVIL → 4 CHIEF VIRTUES NEEED:

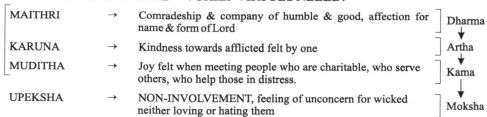

MAITHRI	→	Comradeship & company of humble & good, affection for name & form of Lord	] Dharma ↓
KARUNA	→	Kindness towards afflicted felt by one	] Artha ↓
MUDITHA	→	Joy felt when meeting people who are charitable, who serve others, who help those in distress.	] Kama ↓
UPEKSHA	→	NON-INVOLVEMENT, feeling of unconcern for wicked neither loving or hating them	] Moksha

C) FOUR TYPES OF BHAKTAS:

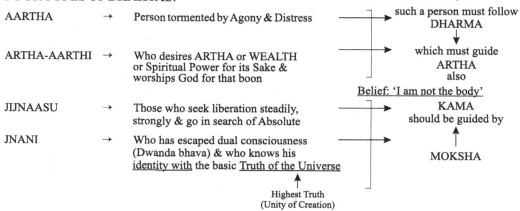

AARTHA	→	Person tormented by Agony & Distress
ARTHA-AARTHI	→	Who desires ARTHA or WEALTH or Spiritual Power for its Sake & worships God for that boon
JIJNAASU	→	Those who seek liberation steadily, strongly & go in search of Absolute
JNANI	→	Who has escaped dual consciousness (Dwanda bhava) & who knows his identity with the basic Truth of the Universe

Belief: 'I am the body'
such a person must follow
DHARMA
↓
which must guide
ARTHA
also

Belief: 'I am not the body'
KAMA
should be guided by
↑
MOKSHA

Highest Truth
(Unity of Creation)

Diagram 6.10

6.7 The Structure of the Paper: going back to the beginning

The Background of the Paper in Fig 0.30 gives the basis of emergence of the 4C Approach from ancient Indian tradition. This section deals with merger of this concept back in this tradition. Fig 0.30 starts wit Truth. Search for Truth has been the starting point of education across civilisations. It is also the starting point of the 4C Approach to business and life. This approach emerges from this concept and culminates in *Prema* or Selfless Love on one hand and Compatibility Advantage on the other. Their coming together signifies balance within man and society.

Diagram 6.11 below installs this *'Prema'* (Selfless Love) of Fig 0.30 as the heart of 4C Approach. It depicts the 4Cs as revolving on the axis of Truth and morality. The guidelines of understanding of 4Cs in simple words – applicable to business and life are stated. With this, both business and life merge back in this tradition. In this manner the wave and the ocean of knowledge from which it emerges are One. A drop is tasted here to validate it.

Structure of the Paper

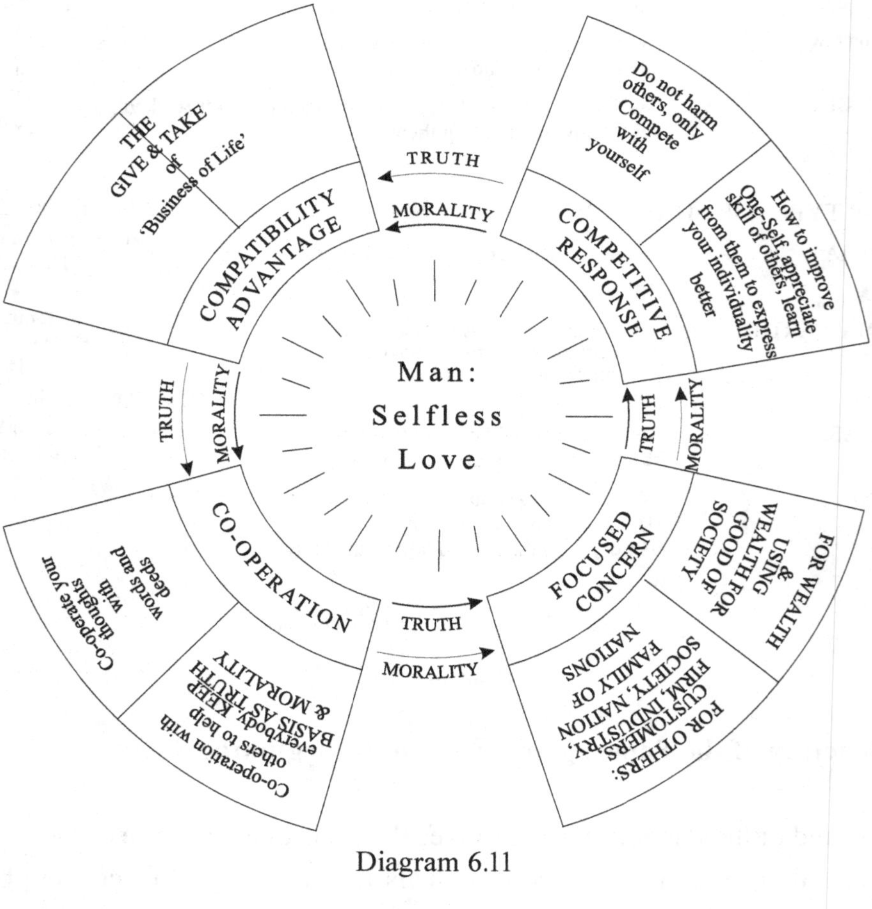

Diagram 6.11

6.8 The Highest state for man and Society: Their integration

The Highest state in man and society occurs when they are in harmony within themselves and with each other. This harmony when extended to the world and nature restores the natural balance of creation. The fact that process of creation has no pause leads to assumption of a natural balance. For, that must be so to ensure a continuity of the process. When man Realises this balance within himself, the process of balance of society, nation, family of nations, world with nature and universe begins.

When people live in harmony with each other, it leads to society and nations achieving this harmony. The expression of this harmony is peaceful co-existence or Peace. When this peace extends to all of Creation, it leads to the Highest Peace which is called *Prashanthi*. This *Prashanthi* is the result of experiencing the Unity of Creation. It is the ocean in which the flow of *Vidya Vahini* or education merges.

However, achieving this Highest state begins with the first step of co-operation within man and between men. Finally, this co-operation is co-operation between thought, word and deed *within* man. For, the world outside is a projection of the world inside man.

6.9 For those who say "This Paper does not make sense"

Even if there is a forecast of rain, the piece of paper declaring such a forecast does not yield even a drop of water despite all attempts at squeezing it. The purpose of a paper declaring forecast of rain is not to give rain but only to give information about it.

This Paper is the forecast of rain *within* man. Meditation on any subject, or all, is described as continuous rain. A study, alone, can never give the experience of Truth. Its application in daily life is the only source of experience. The author started writing this Paper as a guide for himself – that shares the direction and goal as he 'C's them.

The Paper is about Integration of Education with Life. To illustrate this concept Diagram 6.12 is broken up into two parts. Part (a) is to live in the Awareness that life is a 'flow'. It is dynamic and not static. The process of ageing of man makes this statement self-evident. Therefore, to integrate in life, education, too, must be a flow. Part A of the Paper deals with the Awareness that should be instilled in man before education. This is Awareness of true nature of man. It should lead to man experiencing this nature. This experience can only result after man develops Character – that education helps build.

Part (b) of Diagram 6.12 shows that only a man enriched with above experience can integrate flow of education with flow of life. Part (a) of the Diagram shows how Awareness of *Atma* leads to discrimination and control over mind by man. This enables man to direct his mind to right goal. This further enables him to use his physical body to perform daily tasks and duties in a Selfless way. When man does the above, he automatically starts living life according to the four *Purusharthas*. For, when he acts Selflessly, he is following *Dharma* or righteous conduct. By such behaviour man can declare his distinction from animals. He can fulfill his need for progress and prosperity or *Artha* – seeking only one desire or *Kama*. The only desire is for excellence or perfection in execution of his duties. This behaviour of man continues till he realises the potential of excellence within Him Self. This is the final integration of education and life.

Education teaches man to Love, co-operate, bravely follow Truth and to be helpful, sympathetic and grateful. Parents, elders and teachers (who also practice Selfless Love) are revered and approached with humility. When these virtues are practiced with humility and detachment or non – attachment, the experience of Selfless Love will begin to make sense. Even for those who feel this Paper does not make sense.

A usual source of confusion is 'How to deal with people or situations which are totally unfair and based on cheating me? How can concepts of Selfless Love apply in such situations?' Thus, the arguments of the book may be dismissed. This is where reading the book can help. The book clearly states: "Live in the Awareness that hurting others is like hurting oneself – *Bhava Adwaitha* – or non duality in thought". It also states equally clearly: "do not indulge in non duality in action" i.e. act as per demands of the situation with detachment towards fruit of action. If it does not give adequate material to change the heart of the reader, reading *Mahabharata* can help. About this epic it is said: all that can happen to man is told here. It has case studies for all problems! Here, even war is indulged in with non attachment to fruit of action (as the essence of the story)! Hence, there must not be *Karma Adwaitha*. Act as per *Dharma* or Righteous Conduct, detached from the fruit of action – following the principle of Jesus. For He has Selfless Love for all: Hate the sin and not the sinner! *Krishna* and *Jesus*, both guide man towards the same path of action – to remove all confusion in thought and deed of man. Spirituality is the essence of religion. It seeks to avoid confusion in life of man.

Integrating Education with Life

Part (a)
The concept:

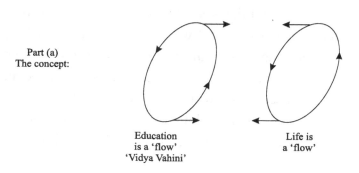

Education
is a 'flow'
'Vidya Vahini'

Life is
a 'flow'

Part (b) How it happens?

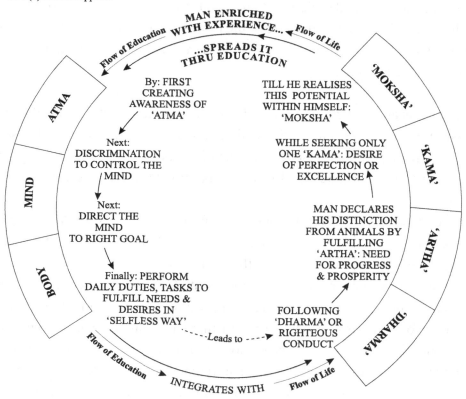

Diagram 6.12

6.10 To sum-up

Everything (all feelings, emotions and actions) of man should emerge from a heart transformed by education. Heartfelt communication and action, with Selfless Love at its core, can drive the world. It will help bind the world to formulate strategies of man and firms. Only new technology that benefits mankind will then be used. It will also enable nations to create competitive advantage and foster international trade and wealth creation. However, the first challenge is to enable consumers, firms and nations to cooperate and/or compete (if that is the incorrect word used today) with each other using strategies that have a common context of shared values. These are basic human values – of which Selfless Love or 'caring for customers and society as we care for one's own self' is the core.

Diagrams 6.11 and 6.12 complete the cycle of this Paper by demonstrating how the 4C Approach emerges from ancient Indian tradition and merges back in it. The final application of this Approach for man and society is demonstrated in Diagram 6.13 below. It installs the shared value of Selfless Love at the core of the process shown in Compatibility Advantage chapter (Chapter 5) from Diagrams 5.6 to 5.9. This impacts all that is Meant for man in this Age and the socialisation process.

When above ideas are applied to the firm during value creation, it impacts the nation, the optimal use/allocation of resources, national diamond etc. Such an approach also impacts the industry. This approach to resource utilisation (not exploitation) is based on concepts of co-operation and a new understanding of competition for delivering value in a new way.

The impact of such enlightened thinking has an impact on society – which spreads to the family of nations, finally. Diagram 6.13 shows area of Man Management as core of this process. 4C Approach emerges from it – through dotted circles and shaded area in these Diagrams. These Diagrams only try to demonstrate how the three concepts of *Swartha*, *Parartha* and *Parmartha* become one. They show how self interest merges in the highest good when performed with Selfless Love. In this case, balance *within* man and *within* society becomes the same. How is this possible at the physical level? Can the world change with just one individual changing? The ancient Indian tradition states that though millions of men are there, each person lives in his own world. The world is different for each man depending upon his experience of it. When the quality of individual experience is elevated, his experience of the world changes accordingly. In this manner the change happens within man and in society simultaneously. Thus states the ancient Indian tradition.

Man Management & 4C approach: integrated framework of Selfless Love

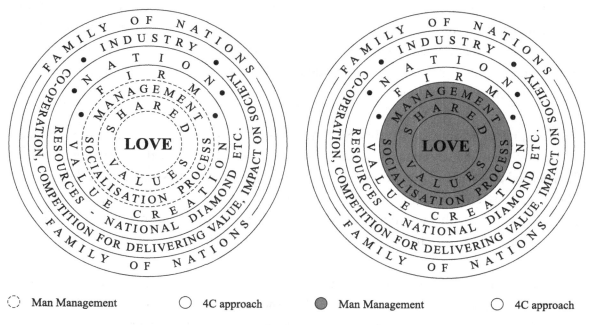

Diagram 6.13

The final merger of 4C Approach back in the ancient Indian tradition will recap all its ideas: just as an ocean will have the same taste as the wave that emerges out – only to come back to it

The final merger occurs when man 'realises' that the studying of this Paper, the drawing or understanding of Diagrams will not help man. Even if God comes, it is for man to change. This is the main teaching of ancient Indian education. **Each man lives in his own world**. So, 'the only way to change the world is to change oneself'. This *Adwaithic* vision is not easily comprehensible especially in a *Dwaithic* context of man. Hence the *Vishisht Adwaithic* approach of 4C Approach was explained in this Paper. Its subtle version is also detailed. The Paper started, like the ancient Indian tradition, with a sole focus on man. It ends with the same focus again. This focus expanded from man to guidelines of action, through the four *Purusharthas* or 4Cs. This has unfolded from the introduction to the conclusion of this Paper. It now merges back to the point where education started. The wave, thus, merges back in the ocean of wisdom.

Is this method of learning restricted to the ancient Indian tradition? Can the current system of education offer no meeting point? To travel from the popular education system to this Paper, there are some points where we can travel together. Organismic theorist Kurt Goldstein introduced the term Self Actualisation to describe the motive to realise One's full potential. This is not different from the term Educare which in Latin means 'bringing out that which is within 'One Self''.

Maslow and Goldstein imply that Self Actualisation implies a "general transcendence of the environment" by man. Self Actualised persons are 'focussed on problems outside themselves' and without prejudice accept others in a similar way as they accept themselves. There is no difference in the definitions of Maslow, Goldstein and the 4C approach. Here, caring for others with same depth as one cares for oneself is described along with non – attachment. Help Ever, Hurt Never reflects this approach in man's actions.

The two major obstacles for implementing this are selfishness and self-interest. The simple most important enabling factor is Love – like the natural expression of a mother for her child. When this Love is experienced in a Constant Integrated Awareness, it expresses itself in human values. These are the shared values referred to. This Love leads to value based economic development for the nation. For, it is based on the spirit of sacrifice within the boundary of protection. Protection comes from balance which comes from non – attachment to fruit of action. The Love that forms the core of individuals, firms, industry, suppliers and cluster expands to create national competitive advantage. Finally, it benefits the family of nations. Such an expansion of love from individual to society to mankind in a Constant Integrated Awareness achieves man's purpose. All spheres of human endeavour – economic, personal and social interactions – benefit from it. The Source states "One should become Love itself so that we can Love the whole world without any discrimination".

At the end, there is a need to restate that end of education is in one word: Character. The purpose of education or educare is character building. The process of building character starts when adherence to Truth (*Sathya*) becomes man's resolve. This naturally leads to following righteousness or *Dharma*. When *Dharma* is adhered to, there is Peace because natural justice is being done. When there is Peace, natural love man experiences for himself can be shared with larger groups. This four stage ladder of '*Sathya', Dharma, Shanti'* and '*Prema'* is the essence of balance in society. Fig 0.30 in Background of the Paper gives the 'basis of emergence of 4C Approach'. It diagrammatically depicts how balance in man and society can be achieved when the four *Purusharthas* are followed by man. Society is, then, in balance using the four stage ladder of '*Sathya', Dharma, Shanti'* and '*Prema'*.

Therefore, any curriculum, whether in Management or any other subject, should have one beginning and focus – to build character. Tools, techniques and ability to analyse things can be misused by recipients. Without individual character as well as 'national' character society will remain in danger. The beginning and end of education is the focus on man. The world it seeks to change is the world experienced *within* each individual. This *Adwaithic* vision is not easy to comprehend esp. when man emerges from Duality or *Dwaitha*. The *Vishisht Adwaithic* approach proves useful to proceed with, then. Therefore, the purpose of writing a Paper is to expand the set of receivers of educare in society. This is in tune with expansion that is natural to creation. When this expansion tunes itself with the expansion of the heart within man to include Love for all in creation, there is harmony *within* man and so in his world, society and universe.

In other words, the purpose of writing a Paper is to give a common context for an Ideal 'world' – for education to open within us. This education style recognises that different paths exist for each individual. The fact that every man lives in his own world is recognised here. Mass dissemination of information is, thus, never understood as education. The Paper is written to enable a firm resolve in individuals leading to co-operation within man first and then between men. A firm resolve will add value through morality guided Individuality and creativity. The new measure of profit discussed should create clusters of excellence seeking value generating entities. Nationality is the coming together of all individual forces that share the same goal of excellence through such value addition. The cluster, then, guides its industry towards Nationality. This unleashes the hidden potential of excellence within man giving him insights or revealing *Satyam* or the higher Truth to him. Higher Truth is, then, expressed through a firm resolve using the cluster of excellence based on co-operation guided towards the concept of Nationality.

When this occurs, *Swartha, Parartha* and *Parmartha* become one. Compatibility Advantage is achieved as the individual good and highest good merge. This is the subtle aspect of 4C Approach. It prepares man for *Advaithic* understanding just as demonstrated in the subtle aspect of *Ramayan* and *Mahabharat*. Hence this approach merges the wave back into the ocean even more strongly to the beginning i.e. transformation of man.

The essence of all Indian spiritual texts and epics is summarized in four words "help ever, hurt never" as Diagrams 6.3 and 6.6 conclude above. Translated into an action plan it reads: "love all, serve all". These are personality traits of a 'gentle'man who expresses non – attachment.

When students are transformed into gentlemen, the purpose of education and the purpose of life converge. This individual ethic, when shared with others, promotes excellence in society. When gentlemen operate in society, collectively, they are in balance within themselves and society is also in balance. The balance between man and nature is also preserved. The focus in Indian cultural ethos is on man and not technique. Therefore, this ancient tradition believes that the right understanding of Management is Man Management. Man can also be punned upon as mind in Hindi (if the 'a' is pronounced like a 'u'). Man is nothing but the mind. If the mind is managed then man, society and nature will also be in balance. This is not a conclusion but a beginning, as the wave merges in Chapter1.

6.11 The 4C Approach prepares man for *Adwaita*: The Highest Truth *Tat Twam Asi*

Ancient Indian tradition enhanced productivity for thousands of years. It significantly added to global GDP. What did it 'see' that enabled this? What did its education teach that was different? What did its students 'C' as a result of their education that enhanced their productivity in ever changing scenarios? It **trained** the mind through education to see the interest of society as if it is the students own self interest. Chapter1's Diagram 1.5, 1.6 and 1.7 and text set the goal which later chapters achieved.

When man protects the interests of others as if it is his own self interest, he cannot harm society. Also, his output enjoys a credibility and natural trust with customers – adding genuine value to their life. The educated man, through his Study of Limits, also knows the limits of everything – including the use of his body. If he over uses his body, there is imbalance. When he views nature as part of his expanded vision, he cannot over use natural resources. Then, balance between man and nature naturally occurs. And, man, firm, society and nature are viewed as part of the same balance. The ability to see what is outside him as part of himself – leads to serving others with excellence. This leads to excellence in all dimensions. When all actions are excellence driven, overtime, the Great Utterenace or *Mahavakya*: *Tat Twam Asi* (That Thou Art) is experienced. Crossing Limits, in any activity, is like hurting One-Self. The mantra *Om Tat Sat* ('That' is Truth), too, creates Awareness as realisation of 'That' leads to identification of 'That' with Self. Such Awareness, by a Study of Limits, creates balance within man, in society and with nature.

How does this theory apply to life of man, how will it prevent recession?

Diagram 6.13 gives the theoretical background to convince man to experience Selfless Love – for all. By opening the human heart to others man can gain the wealth he seeks – by serving society. Selfishness depletes Self Confidence, restricts the heart and pulls man and society into recession. Unity prevents recession. How? Selfishness leads to tricking the customer, seeking profit only – even at great social cost, not being commited to quality of process, product or life, copying instead of expressing Individuality – leading to waste of resources. The products are copied with cosmetic changes to trick without offering real benefit to society. Then, to sell such copied products demand is pumped up through suggestive advertising and product obsolescence. Old models are dumped. No thought is given about how will such waste – that harms the environment – be managed?

What is the feeling in the heart which makes an individual experience the Unity of Creation?

It is:
"Human beings may be many – but humanity is one."

How to check if this feeling is true in science, spirituality and can it work if used and lived by in the world of today?Is there any example of its application? How have spiritual ideas that capture the spirit of life been used to transform man and benefit society in a continuing manner? Is there any evidence that can be seen?

Chapter 7

Validation is the ethics of research

"Vaishnava jana to tene kahiye je peed parai jaane re…"
(The above is the daily prayer at public meetings of Mohandas Karamchand Gandhi. He could motivate a mass movement for personal and social reform using such an idea.)
The achievement of individual and social change validates impact of an idea.

This prayer can be translated as:
"Only those who feel other's pain as their own and help them without any trace of ego can have Divine qualities (quality of expressing excellence)"

In the language of this book this prayer can be read as:

Excellence is expressed by those who live in the Awareness of Help Ever Hurt Never. They follow social and ethical norms (which ensure no pain is given to others) while expressing their Individuality emerging from Humility (by elimination of the ego or a false sense of self importance – this is achieved by a feeling of oneness with creation).
Excellence transforms man and society. Expression of this excellence can lead to individual and social reform – thus validating management ideas of ancient wisdom

Any argument is valid only if you can conclusively prove it.

How is the Validity of a relationship exhibited?

If an unknown young person gets sick, it may not make one undertake much serious effort for a cure. However, if one gets married to the same person later – and the illness occurs again, one will be very worried and will make much effort. A compatible marriage brings people together with a spirit of unity. It removes the feeling that the other person does not belong to you. The idea of education is to evoke such a feeling of unity with society and with nature, too. Then, hurting them is like hurting yourself! 'That', which was earlier treated as far away, now becomes part of 'You'.

Similarly, that excellence which you felt is outside yourself is found at no other place but within you. In fact, that excellence is you yourself –
'Tat Twam Asi'.

TEST OF VALIDITY OF CHAPTERS 1 TO 6

In this chapter Exhibit 4 gives tests to validate that ancient wisdom is being used in daily behaviour. The validity of chapters 1 to 6 is given in section (a) and (b) below.

Exhibit 4 – <u>Validity of Ancient Wisdom</u>: This is **not** tested by reading this book but by man's behaviour in society. The Background gives rise to Awareness in Chapter 1. This enables both man and firm to fulfil goals from Chapter 2 to 5. Chapter 6, then, helps man discover purpose of his activity, how to live life and discover the excellence 'within'. It gives a view about life for harnessing Selfless Love (which enables non attachment to fruit of action). It, then, merges this view with the management framework given in Chapter 5.

How to test that man's actions in society validate ancient wisdom? There are **Two tests** of man's Self Actualisation or *Moksha* – reflected through his actions. When human behaviour passes these tests, it leads to balance (within man, society and with nature), generates growth and prevents recession. Diagram 6.6 has already validated how ancient Indian texts prepare man's path of progress – preparing him to meet these two test criteria in daily life.

<u>Validity of earlier chapters</u> is shown by applying it to research. Finally their Truth is tested

7(a) Application of ideas of the Paper to current Academic writing
7(b) Tests of 'Truth' of Study – in Spirituality, Science and World

To test the validity of a concept, a check is needed: 'Does it correspond accurately to the real world?' If it does, then, it is accepted as well founded. Validity can also be understood as the degree to which evidence and theory (or hypothesis formed) supports the interpretations given. Even scientific validity addresses the nature of reality and is an issue of epistemology and philosophy as much as it is an issue of measurement. When this term is used in logic it relates to Truth of inferences made from premises. Validity is, thus, like ethics of research and a true measurement of the construct or idea in question.

In the case of Chapters 1 to 6, validity would imply that the construct, hypothesis or theory is able to address concerns of other researchers. This is best tested when applied to work of those who may seem to disagree with basic assumptions of another. The ability to integrate differing viewpoints with a similar appraoch validates wisdom. Chapter 7(a) does this.

Another way of testing validity is to see if conclusions of the research converge with not only a reality in the real world but also with some conclusions in diverse fields. Often, spirituality and science are understood as having opposing or dissimilar views. Can research about this new construct, hypothesis or theory find some of its conclusions merging with theirs? That would test validity of its application – across disciplines, too. Chapter 7 (b) does this.

Moksha is not something to die for: it is to be lived for and achieved

An old saying:

"Men fight for religion,
Kill for it
Die for it
... anything but live for it."

Excellence can only be achieved by living to work for it and
then living to exhibit it in daily life and work...

HOW TO PREVENT RECESSION?* - Two Tests of human action

VALIDATION of APPLICATION of CONTENTS OF BOOK

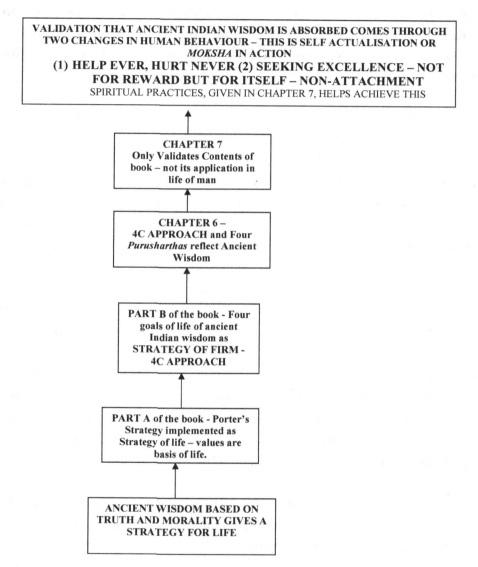

VALIDATION THAT ANCIENT INDIAN WISDOM IS ABSORBED COMES THROUGH TWO CHANGES IN HUMAN BEHAVIOUR – THIS IS SELF ACTUALISATION OR *MOKSHA* IN ACTION
(1) HELP EVER, HURT NEVER (2) SEEKING EXCELLENCE – NOT FOR REWARD BUT FOR ITSELF – NON-ATTACHMENT
SPIRITUAL PRACTICES, GIVEN IN CHAPTER 7, HELPS ACHIEVE THIS

CHAPTER 7
Only Validates Contents of book – not its application in life of man

CHAPTER 6 –
4C APPROACH and Four *Purusharthas* reflect Ancient Wisdom

PART B of the book - Four goals of life of ancient Indian wisdom as **STRATEGY OF FIRM - 4C APPROACH**

PART A of the book - Porter's Strategy implemented as Strategy of life – values are basis of life.

ANCIENT WISDOM BASED ON TRUTH AND MORALITY GIVES A STRATEGY FOR LIFE

Exhibit 4

*Recession is prevented by transformation of Attitude through Education. Ancient Indians use Spiritual Practices (Chapter 7) and Four *Purusharthas* to enable it. Man validates wisdom through actions that meet two criteria given above. Non attachment in man's actions reflects absence of greed. It prevents recession. Help Ever, Hurt Never promotes 'balance' and growth.

Exhibit 4: An Explanatory Note

The ancient Indian tradition of education believes in practice. Any understanding of its transformational philosophy is considered a 'full loss' if not practiced in daily life. Part A details this philosophy – which can only be 'experienced'– not understood. This 'experience' emerges from spiritual practices that create Awareness. These are detailed later in this chapter.

Ancient Indian tradition has three spiritual paths: *Karma, Bhakti* and *Jnana.* They begin with *Karma.* Actions or *Karma* must be continuous. Even taking breath is action. So, *Karma* is the life breath of man. If action is stopped, there are harmful repercussions. The Source gives the example of *Karma* as a bus driving through the dust track of a village road. A cloud of dust follows it. As every action has a reaction, the dust of reaction will settle down on the bus if it stops. Hence, it must do action dedicated to excellence which becomes *Bhakti.* This is like the town road where there is less dust. However, when the bus moves on the royal highway of *Jnana,* there is no dust there. When man visualises and 'experiences' the Unity of creation he cannot harm others as it is the same as harming himself. This is the royal path where action and reaction does not apply. There is no dust that will settle on the moving bus here. Without practice of *Karma,* action dedicated to excellence in all dimensions (understood as Divinity – refer *sloka* of Bhagavad Gita which promises that dedicating all actions to God enables Him to take responsibility) is not possible. For this action must be Selfless and without attachment. When this emotion of dedication (emerging from transformation of the human heart – through education) is put into practice this path transforms into the royal highway of *Jnana.* Hence *Karma* or action puts theory into practice. Also the different paths finally merge through the highest Truth.

Part A of the book describes how ancient Indian tradition of education creates purity of intention. Part B describes how such purity translates into action to benefit society. Together, Part A and Part B convince man that the highest stage is achievable through goal directed human action (path of four *Purusharthas*). The last column of Diagram 6.6 shows how texts of this tradition pave the path of progress of man towards this goal – preparing him to 'C' higher levels of Truth. Finally, human action that:

(a) Seeks good of society (everybody) to demonstrate the Unity that man sees between him and others. Such action emerges from the understanding "Help Ever, Hurt Never"
and
(b) that seeks excellence for its own sake – not to achieve any selfish goal (is detached from fruit of action). Non– attachment enables it. This creates dynamic balance in society, makes man achieve Self Actualisation.

Seven steps for achieving the goal of education and life, together:
1. Self Actalisation and *Moksha* are achievable through goal directed human action: An explanation about the point of convergence of Maslow and ancient Indian tradition may need clarity for some. When Self Actualisation is interpreted as *Moksha* – it becomes something to live for and achieve. It is not a state after death. The idea of learning about lives of *Avathars*, Buddha, *Tirthankars*, Jesus, Guru Nanak and realised Souls like Sages, Ramana Maharshi, Parmahans Yogananda etc. is to visualise the demonstration of Self Actualisation in action – in different contexts and settings at various time periods of human history. However, the situation today is not the same as during their lifetime. But, the ideas that guide education remain the same. In previous periods of time Profit may not have been the only or no.1 priority of business – or the business of life – in a manner it is today. Does this imply that there is no hope for society? If ideas of education have remained constant across time, their application should have desired impact – in today's times and circumstance, too.

Is it possible to attain the state of *Moksha* while earning wealth? *Sanatana Dharma* (or ancient Indian tradition – whose philosophy pre dates formal religion) believes that all paths of Truth and righteous conduct lead to Self Actualisation. Irrespective of the task allocated in society or the role man chooses to perform therein, he can achieve the desired state. Also, irrespective of the time in history or circumstance of society, goal directed human behavior enables the highest state in man and creates a dynamic balance in society.

2. Means are more important than ends: Previous chapters have pointed out that the idea of earning money may not lay emphasis on means used. In ancient Indian tradition wealth is that which cannot be stolen. The important role of wisdom as wealth was the core of education. Ancient Indian history demonstrates this. Their use of wisdom shows how, despite foreign invasions, productivity was not dampened – to earn wealth, once again.

3. Shaping human intention is the purpose of education: The task of education, in ancient Indian tradition, was not just to give skills of a trade, vocation or information about how to conduct a set of activities. It was primarily to shape human intention. Therefore, it began education with a search for Truth. The repeated practice of searching for Truth, when applied to daily activities of a student, led to the idea of *Dharma* or righteous conduct. Spiritual practices enabled the student to 'experience' the impact his actions will have on society. This tradition trained the student to judge himself by his intention. Such repetitive training led to purity of thought and intention. This also taught patience as the easy and rewarding way, sometimes, had to be shunned. Perseverance in purity of intention enabled action that did not harm others or society at large. Ancient Indian philosophical ideas enabled this. Socrates and other traditions, too, have similar teachings.

4. The importance of human action: The spirit of ancient texts implies that *Moksha* is a state to achieve through action or *Karma*. Diagram 6.0 shows that but for Seers and saints all go through the path of *Purusharthas* and moving from family to larger family of society and nation. The guide to righteous conduct at each stage enables man to see others as an extension of his family or himself. Just as he would not hurt himself or his family he cannot think of hurting society. This is the spiritual path of this tradition – when practiced in daily life. In ancient Indian tradition, the Seers agree that for human beings more than luck, it is dedicated human action which fulfills the purpose of human life. Dedicated human activity emerges from right intention and helps man to actualise his potential.

5. Intention behind actions – the path to Self Actualisation: To help shape man's intentions many ancient texts were written. The purpose was to give meaning and purpose to man's actions. The Theory of *Karma* is an important guide for action. For, it teaches that actions undertaken with wrong intentions or those that harm others will make the doer a recipient of similar actions later. This enables a strong urge to protect oneself from harm by having pure intentions and actions. With pure intention when action is performed, it is not guided by selfishness. Then, efficiency in implementing selfishness is replaced by *Dharma* becoming a guide to seeking excellence in action. When activity (*Kriya*) is performed as an offering to God (excellence in all dimensions, simultaneously) individual good, good of others (society) and highest good (*Swartha, Parartha, Parmartha*) all merge. Then the individual Soul identifies itself with Creation (*Prakriti*) and then with the Supreme (excellence in all dimensions, simultaneously). This is the essence of the *mantra 'Om*

Tat Sat', as explained earlier. The path to achieving such excellence begins with purity of intention which makes an individual prefer choosing *Dharma* or righteous conduct to selfishness.

6. Wisdom of ancient Indian texts – Help Ever Hurt Never: Theory of *Karma* makes it simple to teach the first, but most important guide for human action: Help Ever, Hurt Never. As each individual has a different 'inner nature', this most important teaching is taught in different ways so that it appeals to each one. Hence many stories, routes to explain and theoretical constructs are used – but the goal is the same. Wisdom and detachment, together, lead to *Moksha*. This spiritual idea emanates from the wordly fact that man has to give up all that is dear to him when he leaves the body and dies. The sense of 'mine' leads to attachment. When this sense is lost, all becomes 'mine'. Then Help Ever Hurt Never emerges naturally in thought, word and deed. Wisdom implies becoming aware of the eternal Truth (*Ritam*) and immortal virtues that *Atma* represents. This Truth and these virtues can be understood by any other name apart from *Atma* (in any other tradition). The sense of renunciation is as important as wisdom – for they are like two wings of a bird.

7. Bhagavad Gita's guide for human action (Nishkama *Karma*) – seek excellence for its own sake not for result of action: Finally, the process of transformation of man is complete when he is ready to practice *Nishkama Karma* – the central teaching or the crown jewel of the Bhagavad Gita. The teaching is simple in theory but needs a lot of self observation, self discipline and self discovery before it can be practiced effectively. Practices that enable it are detailed later in this chapter. Man is trained to undertake righteous conduct. While undertaking such action, he should not be tempted to compromise just a little because of some benefit he might receive. Hence man is trained not to look at the result of action (called 'fruit of action') but undertake all actions with a sense of detachment from their result. This ensures that all actions of man are righteous. When such actions help ever, hurt never – they lead to Self Actualisation or the 'experience' of *Moksha*. As explained earlier the *kshaya* of *Moha* or end of delusion of false attachment is the highest stage.

Academic research will benefit from the diversity of its thought if each resarcher is able to experience a unity with others search for excellence.

(a)

Application of ideas of the Paper to current Academic writing:

A Sample:

<u>Harvard Business Review June 2013 Cover Story</u>

"Transient Advantage"
Rita Gunther McGrath

"Achieving a sustainable competitive edge is nearly impossible these days –
A playbook for Strategy in a high velocity world"

The above article and its supporting book may seem to invalidate this book's idea.

This book has chosen Prof. Porter's work on Strategy and building sustainable competitive advantage for integration with ancient Indian tradition. Its ideas of strategy formulated are never changing (hence sustainable) – but perfectly adaptable and applicable to an ever changing world.

McGrath proves how the idea of sustainable competitive advantage, itself, is no longer sustainable in today's world. So, where does it leave the basic hypothesis of the book – which it seeks to integrate with ancient wisdom?

A true test of validity would be if concerns of 'Transient Advantage' can be addressed by sustainable ideas formulated and given in Chapter 1 to 6, earlier.

In the following pages the book integrates McGrath's ideas and concerns, too, with its approach. A broad understanding of Strategy from the point of view of ancient Indian tradition is recreated in the context she has written in. This gives perspective of ancient wisdom to today's problems – facing managers, firms, customers and society. Then the outward differences resolve and some points of similarity emerge.

Ancient Indian tradition states:

The world is a 'reflection, reaction, resound' principle.
So, never criticise others – build on their excellence, instead.

Broad approach of many articles in academic journals:

Rightly, many articles in academic journals point out how theories of '90s or 2000 are not applicable in 2010 or 2013. The nature of things is to change. So, is this book relevant (which is based on the writings till 2000) that, too, of an author whose propositions may not seem sustainable? Not so, if we learn to extract the sustainable Truth from observations about the everchanging world of business.

The purpose of this book is to demonstrate how academic theory can be integrated with ancient wisdom. If this is so, then opposing concerns, too, should find solutions from this book. How? This is demonstrated here.

But first, a question: "If academic theory of 1999 is not applicable in 2013, what is the guarantee that what we teach in classrooms in 2015 will be applicable in 2025?" The book is written to answer this question, too. The ability to extract a sustainable Truth helps here.

This book seeks ideas of Strategy that will remain constant or sustainable overtime. They only need to be adapted to new situations in an ever changing world. If the basic ideas are strong, strategy will be on firm ground. To help us, the book begins with an understanding of the basic idea of ancient tradition – that education is about searching for the Truth.

– Ideas about the constantly changing nature of world are integrated with an understanding of Truth here: This tradition shows that Truth is at many levels. One level is the Gross Truth that senses experience – common for animals and man. The higher level is subtle Truth. Understanding of phenomenon of gravity is one example of a subtle Truth – that emerges 'within' man through disciplined observation and thought. Ancient Indian wisdom based its education ideas on subtle Truth or *Satyam*. Even the body of man changes overtime – hence the world, too, is always changing. Wisdom involved imparting education that gives constant concepts that have to be adapted to ever changing current situation by a mind disciplined by wisdom. Its discipline and ideas make the subtle Truth or *Satyam* arise from 'within' a manager.

We will view the application of ideas of this book to McGrath's concerns about Strategy to test their applicability.

Here are some ideas of Mc Grath:

Idea 1: McGrath agrees with the hypothesis of the book about the relevance of Strategy. So, where is the difference? Instead of restricting the idea of Strategy to sustainable or transient advantage, this book broadens the idea of strategy. It states that man should follow a strategy of life – based on excellence. Education should train man to seek excellence – in all his actions. Then, this strategy of life will flow into the firm, too. How this excellence can be achieved is not a study of theory alone. It depends on practice and training – above all, it is training the mind to follow righteous self restraint. Without these education and strategy, both, lose meaning. They will, then, not add value to society – in fact, they will harm society. Recession and other social problems occur when the first lesson of education is not implemented by students: in life. The methodology of imparting this training has been explained in this book along with the tools used for practicing it (at end of book). Then, management ideas are fitted into the ancient Indian strategy of life. This strategy is based on human values being put into action by man – through goals of life. It is, therefore, not surprising that ideas of both – sustainable and transient advantage fit into such a framework.

Idea 2: McGrath gives the examples of Cognizant and Brambles who abandoned the assumption that stability in business is the norm.

McGrath states that having a sustainable competitive advantage is the exception while having a transient advantage is the new norm. So, she states, that "the dominant idea of strategy of establishing a unique competitive position sustained for long periods of time is no longer relevant for most businesses." The ancient Indian tradition never had such a dominant idea of strategy. In fact, its idea of Strategy of life is based on the opposite assumption. It states that the nature of *Prakriti* or Nature is to be ever changing. Man's body, too, is part of this Nature and, therefore, keeps changing – falling and graying hair, falling teeth, wrinkles and other such visible examples demonstrate this. How to deal with this changing nature of things in the world is the strategy of life – which has remained constant for thousands of years. It is based on concepts which have been put into action and have led to prosperity. The attempt, in this book, is to translate these ideas into a language, format and grammar that modern management is used to – and can, therefore, practice. Such practice may lead to sustainable advantage for some who keep changing, and transient for others – who do not adapt to change.

Idea 3: McGrath's transparently states: "If a firm is <u>fortunate</u>, it begins a period of <u>exploitation</u>, in which it captures profits and share…"

She has further stated that "For sensible reasons companies with any degree of maturity tend to be oriented towards the exploitative phase of the life cycle" McGrath, when talking further about success states "Often the very success of the initiative spawns competition, weakening the advantage". Two things capture our immediate attention here. First is the use of word 'fortunate' when cause of success is explained. Second, that 'exploitation' signifies sensible and mature behaviour. Use of such words captures the 'Attitude' of business and its theory today. This book is designed to change this attitude. Success can come through many factors – some of them external to man. Hence the use of word 'fortune' is understandable when related to success. However, excellence emerges from 'within' man through rigorous training, self discipline and feeling of unity – with the customer, society etc. Success, therefore, can be a random event. Can a study that only chases successes and tries to find their cause be stable? It is like finding stability in an ever changing random variable. Thus theories based on such a study of randomness may get redundant. Wisdom lies in seeking excellence through control of senses, behaviour, attitudes – developing empathy with customer, colleagues, suppliers, cluster, industry, society etc. With such an attitude knowledge of a particular subject or skill is practiced with sincerity. Only then, excellence in action can result. The idea of the book is to collate the work of academic thinkers in the format of strategy of life. It is not surprising that while developing such 'Attitude' exploitation is the last thing on a man's mind. In fact, the purpose of ancient wisdom is to transform the attitude of exploitation to the attitude of service. The 4C Approach enables man to 'C' this Truth. A chapter of this book explains the importance of Attitude – from costing to other aspects of business. Business is done on basis of an Attitude. A customers Attitude decides what features are important for him. Take a pen and a gold tipped pen, for example. The first product is designed to fulfill the need to write while the second is designed to fulfill the same need of a customer with a different Attitude. Quality, too, is an Attitude. So is costing. Is cost to environment to be included in costing depends on Attitude of manager. 'Can the product be used in a way that harms the customer?' – asking such a question depends on the Attitude of a firm's management. In ancient Indian tradition 'Attitude of Exploitation' harms society and, finally, business. The 'exploitation' period can instead be looked upon with an Attitude of further value addition/ expansion of creativity in an individual way etc.

Idea 4: McGrath deals with stating the way business is.

If excellence is evident in society, then, academics must follow practice. Recession shows that academics must guide practice. This book understands why it happens and states the way practice can be – to avoid recession and other social problems. It seeks a study of excellence to achieve this goal. How can understanding of strategy lead to sub optimal solutions, within man, firm and society? McGrath observes that "In a world that values exploitation, people on front lines are rarely rewarded for telling…that a competitive advantage is fading away". This shows that Chapter 1 and 2 of this book (the beginning of understanding of strategy) is neither understood nor implemented. Chapter 1 and 2 ('Awareness' of how excellence emerges from 'within', communication and co-operation) prepare man and firm for social action. Greed, when accompanied by lack of mutual trust and heart to heart communication is dangerous. McGrath's analysis of the fatal impact on a firm demonstrates the need for this book. The purpose of value based education is to help minimise these within man. This is the foundation of building character in ancient Indian tradition, too. The failure of businesses is due to lack of conviction about this aspect.

Idea 5: McGrath concludes that "Competitors and customers have become too unpredictable and industries too amorphous."

Forces that enable it, according to her are "the digital revolution, a 'flat world', fewer barriers to entry, globalization." Her solution of "creating a pipeline of competitive advantages" she concedes implies a "challenge (that is) even more complex because they (firms) will have to orchestrate many activities that are inconsistent with one another". Chapter 3 of the book gives a study of man as a customer in Diagram 3.2. Then, Diagram 3.3 shows how the customer seeks better value as information and growth of knowledge, technology, rapidly changing products and socialisation process shape and reshape customer wants – as the customer is influenced by where he emerges in Maslow's hierarchy of needs. Diagram 3.4 shows how shaping and reshaping of customers needs happens through three primary influences leading to change in present products, new products and alternate products. These Diagrams are not just a theoretical tool – but should be an 'experience'. If a firm cannot experience the emerging needs, Individuality and creativity of the customer through a feeling of 'oneness' with him – then, many complex problems will arise. The customer, too, should get the 'experience' of how the firm fulfills its emerging and current needs using its own Individuality and creativity. This experience should be fulfilling for both. Then, there is a relationship between the customer and the firm. Otherwise, success in fulfilling customer needs will be another random event. When 'exploitation' and not empathy or 'oneness' with customer is the rule, advantages will be fleeting. If pure selfishness is the guide to economic behaviour, a feeling of 'exploitation' is natural and empathy cannot be achieved. The transformation of selfishness to enlightened self interest and, then, to highest interest of man and society is the journey of man using education. This removal of selfishness, as an attitude, should be witnessed even towards workers, suppliers etc. Then, even if the whole industry shifts to another location (USA to Asia, for instance, in case of textile manufacturing for the firm Milliken), McGrath found that they did not shut all their plants in 1980 but continued some till 2009! In this time, while closing slowly, they made every possible effort to relocate the workers. Such empathy and lack of selfishness (with excellence of action – expansion at new locations, in new technologies, new markets and arenas – using its competitive and other abilities) helped the firm survive and emerge as a leader in specialty materials and high IP – specialty chemicals. Such empathy gets expressed with firm's customers, too. This may enable the firm to use talents in a way that expresses its individuality and creativity to add value. Humility expressed through a desire to learn more about new customers, markets and techniques with a feeling of 'oneness' with customers needs (along with the strong desire to seek excellence in all dimensions possible) enable a tenacity to overcome odds. This is usually enabled by the firm's managers and workers sharing a commitment to these cardinal principles – not in words – but as an 'experience' of the way life is to be lived. McGrath is a great advocate of avoiding cruel downsizing and gives example of work culture at Infosys, too.

McGrath's 7 dangerous misconceptions and 4C Approach:

McGrath discovers seven traps that high velocity businesses fall into. The same view is echoed in ancient Indian tradition, too – for all businesses – maybe using a little different terminology.

1. The first– mover trap: While ancient Indian tradition stands for excellence which is synonymous with efficiency, effectiveness and speed, yet it states clearly 'Haste makes waste'. Ancient wisdom, too, trains man for life by advising man: 'act in haste, repent at leisure'. Excellence is expressed as fulfilling the desire of self satisfaction. It is a race of

self improvement more than a race to be the first to introduce something. McGrath's point of view is same here. Even in some slow moving industries speed maybe critical but haste is always dangerous – as it is the anti-thesis of excellence.

2. The superiority trap: The book's idea of excellence begins with humility as the first expression of attitude of man. Then the firm, too, can not suffer from a feeling of superiority. Such an approach along with a feeling of 'oneness' with the customer enables the experience of inability to satisfy the customer – avoiding superiority traps. If an attitude is based on exploitation of customer, then success is a destination. Excellence, however, is a continuous journey from higher to higher levels of satisfaction. Thus there is no room for lethargy or 'dullness' or *tamsic* qualities – for the training of the mind and body in the ancient Indian tradition is the opposite.

3. Quality Trap: The ancient Indian tradition treats Quality as an Attitude. The Attitude is mixed with an attitude of service to customers and society. Closeness and 'oneness' with the customer enables a good idea of the desired quality that is appropriate for needs of customer. The concept of Attitude based costing of Chapter 3 is designed to prevent such a trap!

4. Hostage Resources Trap: Individuals and firms not exposed to Chapter 1 and Chapter 2 of this book can fall into such a trap. But any degree of awareness and an experience of heart to heart communication with customer and within a firm should prevent the Nokia example of McGrath from being replicated by practitioners of the 4C Approach. The idea of the book is to sensitise readers that the mass market, too, is filled with individuals wishing to express their individuality and creativity.

5. White Space Trap: This is a trap for firms that do not implement co-operation as 'Dharma'. The purpose of *Dharma* is to create prosperity by serving customers and society. Firms 'experience' such a joint commitment (instilled by education) enabling prosperity and excellence in society. The book shows how…

6. Empire Building Trap: The emphasis of education in ancient Indian tradition is to transform man from an orientation of greed for power to a need to serve society. When such a transformation does not occur, McGrath rightly points out that this trap leads to decline of firms. History proves that it leads to decline of empires too.

7. Sporadic Innovation Trap: This is a trap that companies that do not understand dimensions of excellence can fall into. Excellence is a compulsive innovator – not a lethargic enjoyer of past achievements. It seeks Self Satisfaction not by becoming an exploiter but by serving in better and newer ways – on a continuing basis. As the nature of things is to change – there

can be no room for lethargy in a firm that realises this truth. Empathy with the customer gives meaning and direction to innovation.

Thus, McGrath's concerns are addressed by the 4C Approach.

McGrath's Playbook for Strategy for achieving Transient Advantage:

McGrath points out eight major shifts needed for companies that wish to enjoy benefits of Transient Advantage.

1, 2, 3, 4, 5, 7, 8 Points: The first point of McGrath is the theme of this book, too. Its very definition of competitive response states clearly that competition is only an initial starting point. The destination is decided by the firm's individuality and creativity while seeking Self Satisfaction through serving the customer. Understanding the uniqueness of the customer expressed through his individuality is implemented using attitude of humility. The creativity of the customer is tickled with the firm's expression of its individuality in a creative way. This book does not, therefore, study Porter's 5Forces Model. Kaaren Hansen's quote of "fall in love with the problem you are trying to solve" can be expanded. The solution to the problem, Drucker has advised long ago, can only emerge from asking the right question. Hence the right questions that lead to the right understanding of man and customer are the starting points of ancient Indian tradition. Self confidence in man and firm's individuality is directed towards satisfying current and emerging needs of customer in creative ways. This is the 'spirit' of business. When anything is done in the right 'spirit' – it becomes spiritual. This spiritual experience of doing business comes through building trust of the customer first and is expanded upon by the mutual trust and respect man and firm share among themselves, with suppliers and other resource groups.

McGrath's Point 6: Promoting removal of myopic selfishness as the goal of education has already been commented upon. Such an approach helps avoid brutal disengagement.

The book shares McGrath's concern about the importance of leadership. Ancient Indian tradition's idea of leadership and its role has been dealt with in extensively – including in Diagram 1.3a.

Other ideas of McGrath:

1. McGrath discovers that only 5% of publicly listed companies in USA were able to increase their net income by at least 5% per annum for ten years in a row. Such companies, she discovers, were probably able to do this because "they maintain a core of stability in leadership, strategy and values". The emphasis on qualities of leadership, values and strategy of life are the highlights of this book, too.

2. McGrath's 'Insightful Market Segmentation' is based on developing hierarchy of needs of different customer segments. This book, too, emphasizes importance of understanding individuality of customer by experiencing where the customer emerges from in Maslow's hierarchy of needs. Education helps man rise up Maslow's hierarchy and the book mirrors this rise – following techniques and approach recommended by ancient Indian tradition. Thus 'transformation', not just imparting information, is the task that the book addresses simultaneously.

3. The Kite Framework: While McGrath states that 'if elements comprising an organization's core systems do not align and support each other, the organization will not deliver high performance". In short, the Kite will not fly…This book seeks to prevent such an occurrence in the firm. It starts with the core system of man. Porter's ingredients of simple consistency, reinforcement and Optimisation effort are used for this. They are first implemented 'within' man – through thoughts, words and deeds. Chapter 1 details it. When such men operate in a firm they experience alignment and work towards achieving it. Chapter 2 builds on this alignment from within man to between members of a firm. Thereafter, the other ingredients of strategy come into action. As mentioned earlier, McGrath is describing phenomenon which stem from the inability of firms to implement contents of Chapter 1 and 2 of this book. This is because these concepts are left to self learning, parental instruction etc. Their vital importance in character building and the link of character to balance within man and in firm, society is not verbalised.

4. McGrath understands and highlights the importance of the role of Culture of an organization. This book, too, is dedicated to developing a culture (called *samskara* in ancient Indian tradition – refer ending line of Preface – *Samyak kriti iti samskara*) and core values that are shared by man, firm and society through education.

(b)

Tests of 'Truth' of Study: in Spirituality, Science, Finance, World

The wave of management study (that emerges in this book – from the ocean of knowledge and wisdom) merges back in Indian tradition. Do the contents make sense in the real world, the world of science, finance and other spiritual traditions? Do they relate to a world that cannot be captured in words? This chapter verifies it.

The reader should, first, be aware of the limitation of a book. This will help a focus on seeking experience. Truth is an experience beyond words. Explore it.

- **What a book can never teach** (sub section 1)

Does the taste of the drop of the ocean change if the ocean of knowledge is called by a different name? Buddhism and Jainism do not prescribe to the ancient Indian text of *Vedas*. They do not have the same understanding of a God. Yet, the end result of spirituality, spiritual practices and rules leads to man transforming into a Good human being. This tests the validity of this Study. The drop of ocean has the same taste as in the 4C Approach. A detailed study will, of course, be needed in all traditions by more learned ones. But, if conclusions are similar, such studies may use different terminology to teach similar concepts.

- **Truth of the Study across traditions** (sub section 2)
  Truth across traditions: Teachings of H.H. The Dalai Lama.
  Truth of the Study: from the point of view of Jainism.

The world of science and finance is important and some believe its conclusions vary from spirituality. Hence, an application of this study in these worlds is briefly presented here.

- **Truth of the Study: Echoes from the world of Science** (sub section 3)
- **Financial theory: Cost of debt – Charvaka and Chanakya** (sub section 4)

Are concepts of this book theoretical constructs of ancient texts? Have they been **practiced** for a considerable length of time – in today's world? If so, what results have been recorded and has society benefitted? How? This is shared in sub section 5.

- **Validity and Source of Paper in Real World** (sub section 5)
- **Practices that aid transformation of man and lead to Awareness** (sub section 6)

The validity of this study, finally, occurs when it is applied to an individual's life – and – the author makes no claim of having done so...

- **A Confession** (sub section 7)

Truth is an experience beyond words.

What a book can never teach

The ancient Indian tradition is about Experiencing the Truth. Experience is personal and cannot be taught through the written word. This tradition is, therefore, based on two concepts: *Shruti* and *Smriti*. Hearing the inner voice of Conscience is *Shruti*. Remembering or memorizing it is *Smriti*. The written word comes later. The search for excellence starts within man with a search for Truth. It can relate to any aspect of or object in nature, man or universe. The purity of search leads to an inner inspiration or inner voice from the Conscience guiding towards the Truth. The Seers, as also many seekers and scientists in recent times, have experienced it. The route of learning and, therefore, teaching catalyses this process within man. However, only **a** teacher who has experienced Truth can catalyse its emergence in a student. Students were, therefore, sent to live with Seers to enable catalysis through continuous observation. Personal ethics was essential for the teacher to experience Truth about man. Imbibing this value system in daily behaviour of student was the first step of education. This invisible part of education proceeded simultaneously with the visible transferring of skills or techniques as in popular education.

Where does the commitment to ethics emerge from? Ethics is not visible, cannot be experienced by sense organs of man and yet is the basis of man and society. Ancient Indian education ingrained this concept by enabling a realisation that the invisible is as important as the visible. This was expounded as *Vishishst Adwaita* or the true-false nature of the world. The experience of senses alone is animal nature. It can lead to selfishness that harms others. For, selfishness gives immediate visible benefits while the loss for society and, therefore, man maybe invisible. The True nature of things is revealed when man understands himself as part of society. If something harms society, it harms man also. Ingraining this understanding as the purpose of human life is education.

However, ancient Indian education may appear strange to some minds as it states that values (which are not visible) are more important than the visible. Popular education concentrates more on visible tools or techniques and information. Ancient Indian approach views education as a tool for transformation of man and society. A diagram below depicts how education has to move man from the experience of Duality or *Dwaita* to *Vishist Adwaitha*. This journey prepares him for the final experience of the non dual nature of creation or *Adwaitha*.

Popular, Ancient Indian Education and Self Realisation

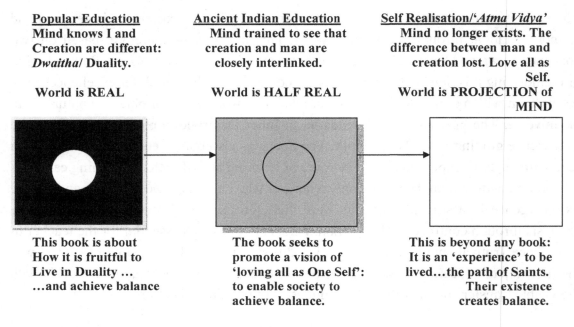

Popular Education	**Ancient Indian Education**	**Self Realisation/'Atma Vidya'**
Mind knows I and Creation are different: *Dwaitha/* Duality.	Mind trained to see that creation and man are closely interlinked.	Mind no longer exists. The difference between man and creation lost. Love all as Self.
World is REAL	**World is HALF REAL**	**World is PROJECTION of MIND**

This book is about How it is fruitful to Live in Duality … …and achieve balance	**The book seeks to promote a vision of 'loving all as One Self': to enable society to achieve balance.**	**This is beyond any book: It is an 'experience' to be lived…the path of Saints. Their existence creates balance.**

Diagram 7.0

If what senses recognise as the world is taken as the only reality, the perceiver and what is seen are two different entities. Self interest can clash with greater good. However, when man and creation are perceived as closely interlinked harming others is not possible. In the grey area of Diagram7.0 above, man sees society as he sees himself. So, harming others is similar to harming oneself. Then, any study of management will be beneficial for all: man, society and nature. One question still seeks an answer. If the transition from duality, *Dwaita*, to viewing world as *Vishisht Adwaita* or true-false creates balance, then what does transition from true-false nature of world to *Adwaita* lead to?

The answer is simple. The balance created within man and society is a dynamic balance in first case. While society can be moved to a state of dynamic balance in the perception of man, Absolute balance is a different experience. The movement, in both cases, is within man. Education enables the first stage. For the second stage, higher education is needed. Following the nature of creation, man enters Absolute balance in the *Adwaitic* state. For, then, the difference between him and society is lost – for him. Hence the movement of man and his understanding of society is from imbalance to dynamic balance. The further movement of man – from dynamic balance to Absolute balance is an experience beyond words. This book is only about *Vishisht Adwaita.* Hence, all concepts deal with dynamic balance. A different book needs to be written to move from dynamic to Absolute balance. The author does not possess the experience and, therefore, the skill to write it.

Truth across traditions: Teachings of H.H. Dalai Lama

Buddhism's merger with this book is demonstrated as follows: Buddha realised that physical activity is a means to the goal of *Nirvana* or liberation, *Moksha* or Self Actualisation. He realised that the practices of Vedas and other spiritual texts do not give it. *Japa, Dhayana, Yoga, Yajna* etc. are mere physical activities. They are needed for those who think that they are the physical body. Awareness is beyond physical activities (Part A of the book). This Awareness should be the undercurrent of all physical activities. When Awareness has led to Self Realisation, these physical activities become irrelevant. *Nirvana* lies in making use of the five senses of speech, touch, vision, taste and smell in a sacred manner. So, *Nirvana* is best attained by a simpler route. He urges developing *Samyak Drishti* (vision). Sense control by man enables it.

Samyak Drishti to 'C' is first step. *Samyak Vak, Sravanam, Bhavam, Kriya* (sacred speech listening, feeling, action) follow. Buddha could 'C' beyond diversity in unity. He experienced the underlying unity of creation. Experience of Oneness or *Atmic* principle leads to total transformation. So, how to control body and its senses to achieve it?

The 4'C' Approach of Management guides man how to use the physical body by following the four *Purusharthas.* These convey the same idea as the **Eight Fold path** of Buddhism. They are meant for man so long as he feels that he is the physical body.

The important teachings of His Holiness Dalai Lama are given below. Their similarity with ancient Indian tradition and understanding of modern management demonstrates unity of spiritual principles.

This proves that the same spiritual concepts apply to man's life – irrespective of religion! After all, Truth and morality are basis of life!

Buddhism talks of three fold refuge. First, surrender to excellence in all dimensions (*Buddham Saranam Gacchami*) or Buddha principle. Excellence is attained through physical activity guided by Morality (*Dhamman Sarnam Gacchami*). Working for benefit of society (*Sangham Saranam Gacchami)* spiritualises it – leading to *Moksha or Nirvana.*

1. *"ALL MAJOR RELIGIOUS TRADITIONS CARRY THE SAME MESSAGE – LOVE, COMPASSION AND FORGIVENESS. The important thing is that they should be part of our daily lives."* – The Dalai Lama

The basic idea of the book is to integrate human values as per ancient Indian tradition into mainstream academics. This will enable inculcation of ethics as an integral part of both – academics and living 'life'. This will enable ease of implementation and application in a common framework. As there is documentation of ancient Indian thought – both in management and education – integration is academically possible. However, it is assumed that all major religious traditions carry the same message. Hence, there is universal applicability of conclusions of the book and its call for action.

The above quotation of H.H. The Dalai Lama validates this assumption.

2. *"Education is the way to achieve far-reaching results; it is the proper way to promote compassion and tolerance in society."*

The proper way to prevent a crisis in society is through education. This hypothesis of the book, which emerges from ancient Indian tradition, is validated by H.H. The Dalai Lama. Thus, the same view about importance of education in curing the ills *within* man and society is likely to exist across all ancient traditions and faiths.

3. *"It is vital that when educating our children's brains, we do not neglect to educate their hearts by nurturing their compassionate nature."*

The ancient Indian tradition integrates teaching of 'management with values' in this book. *Vidya Vahini* states clearly that the use of the brain is to develop *discrimination* – so as to transform the heart of the student.

This approach is the same as outlined by H.H. The Dalai Lama above.

4. *"The challenge today is to convince people of the value of truth, honesty, compassion and a concern for others."*

"We live in a world in which we are dependent on others; we cannot expect to fulfill our goals while disregarding others' needs."

"Placing all our hope on material development is clearly mistaken; the ultimate source of happiness is within us."

The challenge pointed out above by H.H. The Dalai Lama is sought to be met through education. Crisis *within* man and *within* society are the cause of misery. Part A of the book deals with essence of 'Four noble Truths' and recommends essence of 'Eight fold Path' for man to follow.

Vidya Vahini is based on the understanding that so long as man considers himself as the body or mind he will keep suffering. When he overcomes this attachment, the way out of suffering becomes clear. This was shown by Lord Krishna to Arjuna in the Bhagavad Gita. With this Awareness, man should do *Purushartha* and there are four *Purusharthas* to show him the way out of cycle of misery. These four *Purusharthas* contain within themselves the essence of the 'Eight fold Path'. And, the 'Eightfold Path' contains the essence of the 'Four *Purusharthas*'.

Part B translates this path into action – integrating their application with current Management Theory.

The 'Right Livelihood' (called the *Purushartha* of *Artha* and second 'C' of this theory) is achieved through this 'Right Understanding' and 'Right Aspiration'. It emerges from Part A with unity of thought, word and deed (Right Mindfulness, Right Speech, Right Conduct). This 'Right Concentration' or 'focus' is mixed with 'Right Effort' that is full of 'Concern' for everything and everybody (The second 'C' of the book – 'Focussed Concern').

This gives management theory and the management of life the advantage of putting the Three Jewels into action by taking refuge in them.

The refuge in Buddha is the focussed Concern that all sentient beings should have. Seeking Buddha – Dhatu or Buddha Principle allows them to become Buddhas. The fourth 'C' and sixth Chapter of book address this issue. *Moksha* or *Nirvana* should guide action or desire fulfilment. It removes the selfish instinct in action filling it instead with Selfless Love. Such action enables man's self interest or *Swa-Dharma* to merge in the highest good of society and universe. These actions are to help all sentient beings – just like the Law of the seed and tree in *Upanishads*. This makes man's actions Compatible with the needs of others, society and nature. This gives the benefit of the fourth 'C' (fourth *Purushartha* of *Moksha* or Nirvana) or Compatibility Advantage.

The refuge in *Dharma* or Righteous Conduct is merged with the refuge in Sangham or society to achieve the first 'C' or Co-operation. The application of *Dharma within* man is when there is Co-operation of thought word and deed on the axis of Truth and Morality. The application of Co-operation in a human body is exhibited every moment as all parts of the body co-operate fully for daily tasks. Similarly, men, like different parts of society, perform different roles. They must co-operate fully so that society can achieve optimal output. This emerges when welfare of all sentient beings is uppermost in the mind of man and in society. Thus refuge in *Dharma* merges with the refuge in society.

What is the correct pairing of *Purusharthas*? When the refuge in *Sangham* and refuge in *Dharma* become the guide of economic activity this is the correct pairing. Similarly, when desire for Buddha Principle becomes the guide to wish fulfilment, it is the second correct pairing. In this manner the nature of desires is transformed. Chapter 4 demonstrates the two approaches to the third 'C' of Competitive Response. For, this is the basis of desire fulfilment in corporate world and in society. The understanding of competition and 'who is the competitor?' changes significantly when essence of these principles is applied by man. Of course, he should be transformed by education, first. Man naturally practices Compassion after this transformation.

5. *"We naturally have self-interest, but it should be wise rather than foolish self-interest by taking others' needs into account as well as ours."*

"It is important to consider others at least as important as ourselves. This is the essence of spirituality."

"If you want others to be happy, practice compassion...

...If you want to be happy, practice compassion."

"Love and compassion are necessities, not luxuries. Without them, humanity cannot survive."

"This is my simple religion. There is no need for temples; no need for complicated philosophy. Our own brain, our own heart, is our temple. The philosophy is kindness."

"If we can cultivate a concern for others, keeping in mind the oneness of humanity, we can build a more compassionate world."

The above statements of His Holiness are the basis of understanding of norms of human behaviour. They are the essence of spirituality in the tradition of *Vidya Vahini* also. Heart is *Hrud* plus *Daya*. Thus, heart is where compassion resides.

Man has a right to his actions so long as his actions do not harm others and society.

The 4C Approach to Management, outlined in this book, is based on this construct.

As discussed above, man has a right to Self Preservation so long he is not hurting others. This practice of *Swa – Dharma* will lead to highest interest of society and creation if the essence of *Dharma* is followed. This is called the merging of *Swartha* with *Parartha* and with *Parmartha*.

Diagram 5.9 demonstrates this balance and a higher understanding is demonstrated in Diagrams of Chapter 6 – Diagrams 6.1 to 6.13.

The One-ness of humanity, in last quote of H.H. The Dalai Lama above, is a state of Awareness. It is the essence of *Adwaita* which *Vidya Vahini* prepares man for – through *Vishisht Adwaita*. Chapter 6 can be studied in detail for a fuller understanding of this transition.

As shown in Point 5 above, the result of the transformation is practice of Selfless Love and Compassion by man. This is a natural form of behaviour – this is the essence of all teachings of His Holiness as well as *Vidya Vahini*.

****

Buddha taught man not to get angry, find fault with others or harm them in any manner. For, all are embodiments of the same principle called *Atma* in the ancient Indian tradition.

Compassion is the natural expression when the above is adhered to. All are endowed with natural wealth of Love from heart, *Hrud + Daya* or *Hrudaya*. This wealth is expressed as compassion. As all have the same wealth and the same loving heart, all are one in this Love. Hence, all are one and man should be alike to everyone. This is the same teaching as *Bhava Adwaitha* (be alike to everyone in thought). However, keeping the outer worldly requirements duties should recognise outer differences. Hence there should **not** be *Karma Adwaitha*. This book begins and ends with this understanding of education.

Truth across traditions: Jainism

How it prepares man for life in society

What are the principles of Jainism? There are 3 metaphysical and five ethical principles. This two-fold classification echoes in the translation and commentary by J.L. Jaini in the Jain work titled *Samaysara* (loosely translated as 'Crux of Time'). It refers to a 'pure standpoint' and a 'practical standpoint'. "The practical standpoint does not yield the real meaning. But the pure (or real) standpoint has been said to give the real meaning. The soul dependent on the real standpoint verily is a right-believer."

Socrates also states that man is not just the body but the Soul. Living in the Awareness of man as Soul gives the 'Pure' standpoint. Living in the world requires a 'practical' standpoint.

These two standpoints synchronise with the tendencies of man: an 'internal' tendency and an 'external' tendency.

The merger of the internal and external paths is shown by the 3 Jewels and 5 commandments. Right Knowledge, right faith and right conduct are 'internal' tendencies that must be promoted *within* man for his transformation. They help conquer the mind and, consequently, the senses. These are, then, expressed in society through action of man (or *Karma*). These actions must be executed within Limits of the five cardinal principles.

The 3 metaphysical principles or 3 Jewels of Jainism are Right faith, Right Knowledge and Right conduct. These pave the way to achieve the goal of life or 'Nirvana'. This is the same goal as in Buddhism, while Hinduism understands this concept through the word *Moksha*. Right faith gives right 'thought'. Right Knowledge gives it right 'word' and Right conduct expresses this in right 'action'. When there is unity in 'thought, word and deed' man is on the path of Realising the Soul. He is ready for merger of the internal and external paths through action in society.

The path can only be adhered to by those who are able to exercise self control. This requires conquering the mind – the Sanskrit root of the word Jainism is *Ji* which means conquest. So, to live in the world man should follow the 'Practical' standpoint. For this there are five commandments of non-injury, truthfulness, non-stealing, 'Brahmacharya' or Chastity or Celibate behaviour and non-covetousness (emerging from non-attachment).

How does 'spiritual' knowledge become 'practical' for society?:

Prof L.C. Jain in his work 'Mathematicoscientific Ideas in Jaina *Karma* Theory' states that whatever happens absolutely in nature (fire moving up, water moving down, wind moving horizontally etc.) is called celebate or nature. He concludes that the "...nature of Bios is to transform in form of love, etc., and the nature of *Karma* is to generate or create love, etc. However, without fault of interdependence, the nature of bios and *Karma*s has been said to be ab aeterno. Moreover, the bios is non material and the *Karma* is material, still their relation exists as such..."

The use of pure Awareness of Right Knowledge for practical daily behaviour must follow certain Limits. Character gives the limits of behaviour and ensures survival of society and the civilisation.

The survival of Jain faith for thousands of years shows belief in Right Knowledge transforms man so that society sustains. Hence, right Knowledge is inextricably linked to survival of man and a civilisation.

The link between man and society, too, is inextricable. Man is born in society to achieve Awareness of his potential for perfection (i.e. of 'Nirvana'). This is an individual goal achieved through conduct in society. The path to 'Nirvana' – or 'Purity or Perfection' or 'excellence in all dimensions simultaneously'– is attained only by following the Triple Jewels. This highest path has its boundaries or Limits defined by norms of behaviour comprising of the 5 commandments of 'Practical' standpoint.

The 'practical standpoint', place Limits on daily behaviour of man. This starts with the principle of 'treating others as you would treat yourself'. This is the *Dharma* of man and leads to perfect 'co-operation' and unity in society. When put into practice, it leads to 'Ahimsa'. This is not only the *Dharma* but the '*Paramo Dharma*' or eternal righteous conduct which leads to survival of the civilisation.

The commandment of Truthfulness gives meaning or *Artha* to life. The pursuit of adding value should be true. The process of adding value to life and society should also be true. There should be no element of cheating or untruthfulness. In this way meaning is added to the 'internal' and 'external' tendency of man simultaneously.

When non-stealing is the basis of value creation and delivery of man in society, his response to competition is not based on hurting others. He protects interest of suppliers, workforce, contractors and society. Neither will man steal from customers by compromising quality or 'appear' to give value without doing so.

Then, Competitive response follows the principles of Chastity. When this competitive response is guided by the principle of non-covetousness (which emerges from non-attachment), the highest good of man and society is achieved.

The ability to perform with excellence and perfection incorporates purity of intention. With a non-attachment to the fruit of action, it adds value to man and society. It translates into action the dictum of play of life: 'It does not matter whether you win or lose – it's how you play the game'!

Thus the 'internal tendency' is directed by Awareness to transform into Selfless Love. The 'external tendency', expressed as action (loosely understood as *Karma*) in society, generates or creates Selfless Love. In this manner balance is created within man and within society simultaneously.

Sikhism, other ancient Indian religions:

Sikhism emerges from the word *Sikhi* whose meaning is 'to learn'. Thus, it is an education process – which is the heart of assimilating ancient wisdom. *Khalsa* stands for purity – in thought, word deed. Such wisdom does not need further detailed comment.

It shares all its ideas with ancient wisdom and the understanding of earlier Chapters. For example, the idea of *Bhava Adwaitha* or working with the feeling that all are same or one or like 'me' is there in *Guru Granth Sahib ji* (349), the sacred holy book. This sacred text also states the same ideas of humility, restraint of desires, praise of the Lord (simultaneous excellence in all dimensions), contentment, keeping desires under restraint etc (1084). The idea of Love all is expressed as being a friend of all (1299) while the theory of *Karma* is deduced from 'Man himself sows and himself eats (reaps)' (4).

It draws upon the best of ancient Indian tradition and others. It promoted group singing of *bhajans* just as group prayer is done in Islam and Christianity.

Chapter 6 defines the peak of sacrifice – when man sacrifices all – to serve others. The Gurus of Sikhs are examples of this. Their sacrifice inspires all. Sacrifice, based on Truth and morality, validates basic tenets of ancient Indian tradition. Religion, it believes, is a way of expressing Truth and morality through action. For, this tradition is demonstrated not by words but by life. It states that wherever Truth and morality is followed, a common nationality is shared. This is its concept of *Vasudeva Kutumbakam* or unity of world. Sacrifice of petty selfishness is sought from all. Eternal Leaders sacrifice everything for Truth – and to teach or help others. This Ideal leads to unity and prosperity in society and world. Ancient traditions teach how to **first deserve, then desire**. This Ideal promotes balance within man and in society.

Jain *Tirthankars* sacrificed personal needs – to seek Truth. This Truth was spread to all. Buddha's life, too, sacrificed to search for and spread Truth. Jesus' life demonstrates sacrifice to help others. Hence, it is unlikely that His teachings would be different from ancient Indian traditions.

'Speak the Truth, follow Righteous Conduct' is how education begins in ancient Indian tradition. It should be no different in all traditions. This commonality is the basis of merger of morality with education and life.

The ability to see unity in diversity is the main teaching of this tradition. This is why various faiths, modes of worship, rituals and ways of interpretation are given equal respect. The only pre requisite is that they promote Truth and morality. They should also be based on one premise – Help Ever, Hurt Never. Man has rights but these are limited by a duty not to hurt others. By helping others he can help himself in the most optimum fashion.

Truth of the Study: Echoes from the world of Science

The difference between eternal Truths and scientific theories is simple. The former do not change across generations, centuries, millennium or 'Yugas' of ancient Indian tradition. Scientific theories, on the other hand, have not been able to demonstrate such consistency. Therefore validation of the study from scientific determination is not considered as a sufficient condition. Some may, still, feel it is a necessary one.

The August 2013 issue of the journal **Nature Communications** has published the work of two Michigan State University evolutionary biologists.

The Michigan State University website covered this study in August 2013. It stated: "Much of the last 30 years of research has focussed **on how cooperation came to be,** since it's found in many forms of life, from single-cell organisms to people….". Scientific research, thus, validates our study of Co-operation as *Dharma* or righteous conduct.

The same website also covered the research of Layne Cameron and Christoph Adami under the title: "Evolution **will punish you if you are selfish and mean".** This theory disproves earlier theories that selfish players can beat players who follow co-operation (by following "Zero Determinant or ZD" Strategy). The researchers concluded that the selfish players can win for a short period of time and against a 'specific' set of opponents. However, they concluded that selfishness is not evolutionary sustainable.

Further remarks on the MS University website, in August 2013, are also noteworthy. "… they used high-powered computing to run hundreds of thousands of games and found ZD strategies can never be the product of evolution. While ZD strategies offer advantages when they're used against non-ZD opponents, they don't work well against other ZD opponents."

The above findings validate the basic hypothesis of the book that Selflessness (that results in co-operation) creates balance within man and society.

Financial Theory: Handling Cost of Debt – Charvaka & Chanakya

This book has covered production (through TQM), marketing and strategy. Now about finance: Three generalisations need to be avoided. Firstly that accounting is practical and has no role of spirituality. The second is about cost of debt. The third is: an idea that policy freedom to set interest rate for cost of debt exists – Freedom may not be so free!

1. The three accounting principles capture the 'spirit' of life. Debit the receiver – credit the giver, debit what comes in – credit what goes out and debit all expenses/losses – credit all income/gain: these appear to be spiritual accounting or *Karma* theory. Now about debt:

2. A study of Modgliani and Miller's arguments about capital structure of a firm can sensitise us to impact of debt on risk cost of equity. How much risk to take? This is a question that is no longer relevant to a firm alone. It is also relevant to individuals as well as nations. The global economic crisis occurred because individuals in United States took too much risk on housing. They considered debt as low risk. Nations, too, in today's context, need to understand the impact on society of high levels of national debt. Man's Attitude towards debt was reformed by ancient Indians by harnessing greed.

What perception leads man to increase the limit of risk taking? What determines level of responsibility? What strategy of life, philosophy, education and value system impact people, firms and nations belief about limits to debt? Low cost of debt may not lead to financial bubble if there is internal control by man. There are different schools of thought in ancient Indian tradition – Chanakya and another identified as Charavaka. They have totally different strategies for life which impact strategy of man and even of the firm. The latter believes in the philosophy of *"Yaavam jeevete sukham jeevete, rinam krutva ghritam peevete, bhasmi bhutasya dehasya..."* This is a philosophy that focuses on the individual and his selfish needs. Individual comes first – society last. Such an approach gives primacy to that which is observed above that which can be inferred. So, hedonistic pleasures are recommended. They are to be pursued to live so as to enjoy all material pleasures. So, **take as much debt as you can**.

Education should sensitise man to the importance of inference about nature of world over that which is observed and experienced by senses. Else, it is difficult to counter hedonistic arguments in real life situations. The ancient Indian civilisation survived because some people who could counter materialistic arguments, even though they seem so compellingly right and lead man to the path of unlimited debt for current pleasures. While one makes social perception of debt as low cost, Chanakya's concept is different. When men lead self disciplined lives, the perception of risk and responsibility is different. Society comes first in this value system, individual considers himself last. Projects that add to society's welfare paid interest after the project became successful. The cost of debt became zero till a project is successful. Social behaviour was not guided by individual greed but by Selfless Love, society's need and mutual trust about each other's commitment to it.

When all men believe that society comes first, individual character and national character impact society and even the cost of debt. Then, there is Peace in society. Many current concepts of financing policy may, then, become irrelevant. Social responsibility was the basis of how Indians understood strategy for life. Righteous conduct made Truth an important determinant when men, firms and nations drew up their balance sheets. Ancient Indians lived not to take debt – but to repay their three eternal debts. Then, even when cost of debt is zero, there is no financial bubble that threatens the world.

3. There maybe a false understanding that freedom to set interest rates is total. Can interest rates be taken to extremes using it? Interest rates balance rewards given to savers and risk takers. Both have a role in society. With the formers sacrifice, the latter takes risk for growth. The reward for both should be balanced, unless the risk is worthwhile for society. If trust exists that profits are used for society, the cost of debt can be zero. Only a recession in thought rewards self centered risk takers by misusing long sacrifices of savers interest.

Validity and Source of Paper in the real world – Part 1

Any work of academic importance derives value and validity from its source. The ancient Indian tradition and wisdom has *Vedas* as its primary source. These lead to understanding of the triad of *Upanishads*, *Brahma Sutras* and *Bhagavad Gita*. It is well known that Indian civilisation is among the oldest. Its advanced education system led to economic prosperity and social well being, simultaneously. As detailed in the Introduction, the requirements for action change with the change of circumstances in each '*Yuga*' or time cycle. However, the goals of life remain the same. How do we interpret the Ideal of education in today's time and age? How does this Ideal exhibit itself as an Ideal for 'living life'? These questions remained unanswered leading to confusion. This Paper has listed a theory and its implications of practice. It draws inspiration from the Source as mentioned in the Introduction of this Paper.

The ancient Indian tradition depends upon the triad of Upanishads, *Brahma Sutras* and *Bhagvad Gita* for the Ideal in education as a guide to living life. This Paper expounds the validity of a 4C Approach to managing life and business. It draws its value and validity from a practical demonstration of this Ideal or 'Compatibility Advantage' at work. These projects are giving free healthcare, drinking water and education in a village in India – Puttaparthi. They validate the Study. The free of cost model has proved to be sustainable even after the lifetime of the physical body of the Source of this Study. The inspiration of His teachings continues to inspire funding of these endeavours till date. They also inspire those offering services here at low cost.

A Doctoral thesis on quality aspects in management of healthcare sector in India has interesting findings. It researched satisfaction level of both in patients and out patients, as well as the value they receive. It discovered that in the super specialty hospital in Puttaparthi this was far higher than hospitals in the government or private sector. Hence, the concept of providing free healthcare is achieved with giving highest quality of service leading with highest level of patient satisfaction. This is the Ideal that education prepares man for. Similarly, the drinking water projects were executed by the Trust and handed over to the Government of Andhra Pradesh. This is again the Ideal of detachment that pervades spirit of service emerging from Ideal in education. It is demonstrated by primary school and also colleges that are a part of the Deemed University of Puttaparthi.

The basic difference between the two systems of education is simple. The current system measures success by mean salary offered to graduating class. The ancient Indian tradition, on the other hand, seeks to promote self reliance, self confidence and the ability of self sacrifice. To test the strength of these in the graduating student the Puttaparthi Deemed University did not permit student placement on campus. Instead, it exhorted students to go back and serve their parents for some time before seeking a job. For, it believed that if the graduating student forgets to serve his parents, he will not be fit to serve society too. The attitude of gratitude must be developed to serve society.

How do we measure the commitment of the graduating students? In other universities, bright students are remembered by their salary levels. In Puttaparthi, the author has observed a different culture also. Some of the bright students refused to leave the campus. They waited for an opportunity to be assigned some social work by the Source of this Study. Sometimes the waiting period ran into half a decade also. It is not surprising that some students who passed the 'test' of a seemingly endless waiting period are today involved in service activities. They continue to work at salaries that are just enough for their material needs. Many ex-students are involved in activities of the Trust, the University (in both teaching and administrative positions), in the Hospital etc. Many others, after serving have joined the corporate sector also.

A final question remains: "If this Deemed University is already implementing these concepts, then, what is the need of this Paper"? In the author's limited understanding, the answer is simple. The university implemented, three decades ago, what it sought to teach its students. 'Do not try to change everything in the company or firm that you join. First, assimilate yourself in the culture of the firm. Keep implementing the values you have learnt. Slowly, these will give strength to the firm and to society. The **change that is gradual will last forever**'. Therefore, the syllabus of the deemed university is the same as other universities in India. It did not try to revolutionise education in one day. It allowed itself to be like all other universities with only one difference. While the syllabus remained the same, it concentrated on transformation of the student into a good human being. For, a good human being will be a good employee, a good citizen, a good son or daughter! After three decades of demonstration, this concept of education can be shared as the necessary validation has been done – over decades.

Therefore, the demonstration of 'Compatability Advantage' at work is taken as the source of this Paper. It is not necessary that those practicing or teaching these teachings of the Source of this Study agree to the analysis here. Their analysis and explanation of their Truth is valid from their point of view. For: *"ekam sath vipra bahuda vadanti"* – Truth is One, the wise describe it in many ways – is valid and True.

For those who can relate to this Paper, it is the Truth. For those who understand things differently, that is their Truth. So long as the Goal is the same, the different Paths will meet – sooner or later.

Education and Life are inextricably linked just as Values and Strategy are in any study of Management. Values merge into Strategy and Strategy emerges from Value. Just as

Education merges into Life and practice of Life emerges from Education or *Vidya*. Thus, Life is a flow or *Vahini* – of the practice of the Highest learning or *Vidya*. It merges in the ocean of Selfless Love. From this ocean, water vapours arise to feed streams and rivers, once again. The Source of this Study demonstrated that the practice of Selfless Love is the foundation of Human Values. This is evidenced by His projects and His actions.

Some of His teachings to His students are listed as they validate the Ideal of education in the ancient Indian tradition – and its practice in daily life.

A few teachings for Management Students:

– **"The main cause for confusion, fear and turmoil in society today is selfishness... which should be eschewed for overall progress of society."**
– "...So, if one questions: '**What is the panacea of financial problems**?' there is no readymade, permanent solution. Hence a bid to search for an everlasting solution will be futile. **The only way out** to overcome such an imbroglio is: '**Ceiling on Desires**'.... "Gunar Myrdal...realised towards the end that people should not transgress the laws of nature, so as to retain balance in society".
– "**BALANCE**, which is highlighted by Bhagavad Gita, **plays an important role**, the **strength of which depends upon fostering human values in society**." ... "As Finance is God, it should be put to use very carefully... Students should develop lofty ideals and objectives..."
– **"The lasting solutions to economic problems can be found only in Spirituality."**

1. Education is for Life and not living:

"Wherever you work, you must be responsible and feel the factory is yours. Never feel that you are working only for money. Work is worship and duty is God. Education must be for life and not for living. This should be imprinted in your hearts." "The sole aim of education is not to make money by taking a job in some organisation. The goal of education is reconstruction of nation...one should....control the mind". "In this world there are lakhs of officials, political leaders, business people and educated people. All these people are endeavouring only for their family and not for society. This is the reason for the present unrest in the country... Every person should keep the society in view. He should realise that he cannot live without society. If you want to feed your family, society is the basis…Instead of asking the question 'What will I or my family get by doing this task?' he should ask questions about what society gets by the task…by losing morality man is losing his strength. To overcome all this hurdle, spirituality is essential." ……"Animals, beasts and birds are also living. To which University have they gone? Which education did they get? If it is for the sake of livelihood alone, then education is not necessary. This education must become useful to others in society and life must become an ideal life"… Feel that: "My well being is in the society's well being. I should have sacrificial feelings that I should use my strength for the good of society." "Self improvement is the starting point of all social revolutions. Self development begins with Self enquiry, the ultimate query being: 'Who am I?' This results in transformation of the individual." "..People engaging in rural development work should not regard their work as philanthropy but consider it as service to themselves…". "Every individual largely depends on society for his needs…even the simplest human needs are met only with the help of society." So: "An individual should always keep the interests of society in mind. He is born in society, lives in society and dies in society, and hence he must live for society…It is but the society that brings about a BALANCE.". "People should… subordinate individual interests before national interests."

2. Salary commensurate with work:

"Happiness does not depend on worldly possessions or affluence but it depends on control of desires". "…Education is necessary to secure livelihood but one should not become a slave to anybody. The secular knowledge that gives worldly knowledge cannot give happiness. Spiritual knowledge, on the contrary is capable of giving happiness."… "Today, the world remains divided on various counts because of people…who are over-obsessed with wealth and its acquisition." "Each one has to question himself whether he is working equal to the worth of his salary or not…In factories (where) expenses are increasing…the reason is that because of decline in morality the spirit of work is lost in man……This is a very sacred, pious and Divine age….Students should not desire fat salaries and cause trouble to people for it….Conduct that is filled with Discriminatory Knowledge is Morality. So, man has to develop good principles". "Man's happiness does not depend on amount of one's earnings but it depends on his regulated and disciplined life and his expenditure pattern"…. "So, in everything man should aim at 'Purity of Purpose' which results in Wisdom."

3. How to conduct yourself at work:

"Never keep changing jobs. Stick to a job for at least five years. Due to this, one will gain experience…." "Conduct yourself with humility and obedience…do not bring arrogance and other bad feelings in your speech…What you study today is different. What you apply on the job is different….Undesirable qualities and thoughts will not gain entry into us if we keep the feeling of God in our heart. Then only can we put our studies to good use. To put our studies to good use, we have to develop spirituality…In a factory you should not come late and sit in an air conditioned room…You must go around the factory. You should find out if…water supply is enough or not, whether raw material stock is sufficient or not, if labour is available for the day, if there is proper production or not…If a worker is working at a machine you should learn from him…you should respect his Knowledge and competence. In a factory you should be a student and continue to learn…" Also, when needed: "….Teach workers with love. People who teach are of three types: those who inspire, those who explain, those who complain. Managers should become role models who will inspire. Remove dissatisfaction among workers and create enthusiasm among them. You must never give room for strikes. Guide them to follow the right path. For whom are we working? This is our country. Are we taking the salary commensurate with our work? Are we doing the right amount of work? Teach and explain in the right way….Only then will patience and courage automatically increase in you. Develop self confidence. Then you will have self satisfaction, self sacrifice and finally, self realisation. These are the foundation, wall and roof of life. We must understand the inner relationship of these."

4. Serve parents first, only then can you serve society:

"After you complete your education go to your house and serve your parents till you get a job. Throughout your period of study, your parents have helped you, and therefore after your studies you should help them…If you cannot satisfy your parents, how can you manage a factory? If today you satisfy your parents, tomorrow your children will satisfy you. This is resound and reflection…" "The most important thing that one should understand is gratitude. You must always express this to the firm that gives you the job. Gratitude must first be learnt at home…An exemplary life is essential. One should earn a good name for his parents and his job. This is the opportunity given to you for further progress. I bless you all to put these into practice."

5. Avoid Imitation:

"There is no meaning for one country to naively imitate or copy management practices of another...leads to wastage of resources and undesirable results". "The culture and values of India are different from others. These different situations cannot be treated alike. The artificial integration of different sets of values may result in erosion of values of a less developed country".
Etc....

These and other such teachings were given to students along with practices that aid transformation and lead to Awareness – which are detailed in the next section.

Validity of the Study in real world – Part 2
Excerpts from an interview with a corporate leader

Many academicians may wonder why theory is trying to include ideas of Humility, everchanging nature of creation, loyalty to firm etc. in a course material.

Given below is an excerpt from an interview of Vice Chairman John Rice of GE to Vinod Mahanta of an Indian newspaper, Economic Times, published online on 9th January, 2015.

The title of the article is: "**Vice Chairman John Rice on how GE stayed on top for 100 years**" Some quotes from this interview:
1. Importance of Humility
"You have to listen and learn...Effective leaders are **humble** and open to learning from anybody they interact with – might be a senior member of the team, might be a person on the shop floor who is running a machine tool..."
2. GE's Mantras reflects a deep understanding of everchaning nature of creation:
"– Don't hesitate to throw out yesterday's great ideas because it's not going to work tomorrow"

"...One of Jeff's (Jeff Immelt Chairman GE) great strengths was to recognise that we had to change...it didn't make sense to have half our earnings come from financial services; it made a lot of sense for us to concentrate our resources in infrastructure".

3. Importance on being focused with a concern for others and not personal promotion

"If they (your team) think you are a leader who just wants to get to the next job or wants to make a name in the current role so that you can move to another senior role; chances are that it won't work out for you (in GE). You have to be willing to be committed to the team that you are leading for whatever time it takes. You can not worry about what your next job is, you have to be **focused** on what your job is right then."

4. Importance of loyalty to firm as pointed out by Source of the book:

Response to question: "Why are GE leaders so much in demand?"

"...Its hard for me to answer that question because I have never worked anywhere else."

Etc.

If I know who I am, I will know what to do.

CREATING 'AWARENESS' IN MAN:
SPIRITUAL PRACTICES THAT LEAD TO IT –
IN THE 'EXPERIENCE' OF ANCIENT INDIANS

What is the point of knowing about a hierarchy of needs if there is no known way to rise up in the heirarchy...?

HOW TO MAKE MAN RISE IN MASLOW'S NEED HEIRARCHY?

1. Instruments of man and their interrelationship

"People have three chief instruments for uplifting themselves: INTELLIGENCE, MIND and SENSES.

When the mind gets enslaved by the senses you get entangled and bound.

The same mind, when regulated by the intellect, can make one aware of one's reality (*Atma*)." – Spiritual Source of this book.

2. How to use mental power emanating from spiritual practices?

"The mental power gained from spiritual practice must be directed to turn the mind away from wrong paths.

Direct your senses using the principle of intelligence (buddhi) and release them from the hold the mind has on them." – Spiritual Source of the book.

3. Executing the task of rising up in Maslow's need hierarchy

"The mind *(manas)* is a bundle of thoughts, a complex of wants and wishes.

As soon as a thought, desire or wish raises its head from the mind, the intellect (buddhi) must probe its value or validity – is it good or bad, will it help or hinder, where will it lead or end.

If the mind does not submit itself to this probe, it will land itself in deep trouble. If your mind obeys your intelligence, your spiritual progress will be accelerated." – Spiritual Source of the book

These practices make man Aware of impact of his actions on others: society, nation, nature – leading to actions being compatible with them. This actualises potential of man or 'Self'.

Practice makes a man perfect.

Practices for transformation of man leading to Awareness, *Moksha*

To understand Indian tradition, the aspirant must 'culture' the mind just as farmer prepares a field. The thorns and weeds of egoism, pride and greed are to be removed before ploughing. Truth, Meditation and focus on excellence are like ploughing and leveling the field. The water of Selfless Love makes the field of the human heart fertile, soft and rich. The 'excellence in all dimensions' is the seed that has to sprout. Ancient Indian tradition calls it God's name. Non-stop repetition of the focus on excellence leads to sprouting of the full potential of man. This sprouting plant is protected from the cattle signified by desire and anger using the fence of discipline. This enables man to reap the harvest of bliss. The traditional concept is of the eight-fold path or *'Ashtanga Yoga'*. There can be detailed explanations of the idea. The Wikipedia, however, gives a generally correct listing and explanation. For easy verification and understanding of the reader, this is described below as:

Yama: moral codes, *Niyam*: self purification and study, *Asana*: posture, *Pranayam*: breath control, *Pratyahara*: withdrawing the mind from the senses, *Dharana*: concentration, *Dhayan*: deep meditation, *Samadhi*: Union with the object of meditation.

The end result of these practices is control of mind and reduction of desires. Hence, the first and most important spiritual practice is reduction of desires – for that gives proof of control over mind. If you really need something only then buy it or desire it – above all do not waste it. This is against the grain of consumerist economy that over exploits resources and is driven by unrestricted greed taking it into cycles of inflation and depression.

Much has been written on the above topic and does not need elaboration here – for that can result in another book. The purpose of this book is to avoid debate, simplify and integrate ideas that purify and control the mind with popular education. Chapter 1 gives a good background for this. However, in addition to the text there, practices listed below enable Awareness. These are only indicative, not exhaustive. Serious practice is needed and the idea is to encourage the reader to follow practices of his tradition. Few practices, which are secular in nature, are listed here. For details of more secular practices, it is recommended that the Source of this study is referred to, independently, for a more exhaustive list.

Self Observation:

Chapter 1 has listed watching your thoughts, which is part of a 5-fold WATCH acronym consisting of:
Watch your Words
Watch your Actions
Watch your thoughts
Watch your Character
Watch your Heart

Self discovery:

The journey of self discovery through meditation is found useful. The Source recommends 'Jyoti' Meditation (or meditation on Light). This technique focuses on a flame and then uses imagination to make it travel inside the body (after half closing the eyes) to open the lotus of the heart *chakra*. The flame is the flame of the light of Selfless Love and the meditation ends with one experiencing being enveloped by Light as well as experiencing it within oneself till the Light and the 'meditator' become one. This is filling oneself with the light of Selfless Love, being enveloped in Love and becoming Selfless Love itself. The light of Love is spread from the heart to others, society, nation, world, nature, universe in ever expanding circles. This implements the idea of the book through inner visualisation to transform the 'inner urge' from selfish to selfless. The visualisation of everything as light and being part of this light helps visualise (ability to 'C') Unity which is the subject of Chapter 6 – that implements the earlier 5 chapters.

Self discipline (starting with control of unnecessary desires):

There are many techniques of self discipline that can be chosen.
These include:
• 'doing one good act a day'
• Maintaining a daily dairy to record achievement of various desired/ target activities. For example: 'did I speak the Truth, did I obey my parents, did I help somebody, did I have any bad thoughts, **did I get angry**, did I speak loudly or harshly, did I waste food, water, time, energy – physical and mental, money'?

- Practice of the dictum 'See no evil, hear no evil, do no evil' always. Keep good company. Respect parents and elders. Avoid cruelty to animals and all living beings. Serve the needy, whenever possible. A daily study of spiritual literature, silent sitting and a disciplined daily schedule are important. Cleanliness including personal hygiene and of surroundings is emphasised.

- Remembering a name or form that one identifies with excellence and repeating it in the mind or through writing or through visualisation. This focus on excellence has been found to have a 'transformative' ability. Here the seeker inculcates the qualities of excellence he is focusing upon – overtime. This has many forms and names in ancient Indian tradition. Some of them are: *Deva Yagna* (daily prayer), *Likhit Japa* (Writing repeatedly the name or concept that appeals to the seeker as representing an 'excellence in all dimensions'), Recitation of holy verses or *Bhajan* (devotional singing), etc.

- Self help, lack of dependence on others for ones needs – Speaking less, speaking softly. – Social work – Charity etc.

- Noting before sleeping at night whether there was harmony in thought, word and deed every day. Resolve to ensure harmony among them next day.

- Noting before sleeping at night whether undesirable or bad thoughts crossed the mind and how often. Resolve to redirect them correctly next day.

- Answering the question every night, before sleeping: "Have I done anything wrong today?" Resolve not to repeat the same ever.

- Self Audit every night: "Did my good thoughts result in good deeds"? If not, resolve to do the same the next day.

The Awareness of potential for excellence is an experience. It enriches man and his actions in society. It brings man close to the Truth about himself. The experience of Truth about Self emerges only when mind is conquered. As discussed in Chapter 1, suppressing the mind is a futile exercise. The ancient Indian tradition of education or *Vidya Vahini* uses many practices including those listed above to overarch suppressing the mind and help conquer it. These practices should not come through use of force but come from the 'source' – i.e. the desire to follow them should emerge from within man.

These practices give more result if done with abstentation from alcohol, tobacco and non vegetarian food – as per ancient texts and 'experience' of practitioners. For students, vows of *Brahmacharya* (the first *asrama* of life – meaning of the word is *acharan* in *Brahman* – or living in a state of Awareness) are followed. These include not living in a manner that creates an inability to live without sense pleasures in later life. In the thinking of ancient Indians, and in their experience, this is important. For, in later life when pleasures are to be enjoyed man should not be their slave – but master. The mind is responsible for pleasure and pain. It is also responsible for freedom and slavery. When it is trained to visualise pleasure and pain with the same detachment – this is equal mindedness – that is considered as freedom. Business, too, will be successful if gain and loss is viewed with equal detachment while doing the right thing always. The capacity of forbearance is inculcated in the early years of youth. In ancient Indian education the intermingling of students of both sexes was also avoided till education was complete – to enable mature interaction based on balance and to create it.

The end of journey of Self discipline, Self observation and Self discovery is Self Realisation. This book seeks to lead the author and reader towards it. The ancient Indian tradition, finally, seeks to lead to the realisation that God does not exist in a special form with special powers etc. That which is contained in each heart as clean thought and Supreme Consciousness is God. This sacred part of the heart is present in every human being in the world. As this sacred heart is within man, spiritual practices will unravel it – they will lead to the 'experience' of God (or goodness with excellence in all dimensions) within. Then, there is no need to search for Him outside. This tradition states that this sacred heart is in everybody, hence it seeks to convince that this God is equally present in everyone at all times. When there is supreme faith in oneself and purity of intention and action, then, without attachement to results all actions that result are the essence of man. Such actions will not harm others and create balance within man and in society.

A Confession

The Paper presented above is not a claim by the author of having achieved any state of Awareness. It is only an attempt to share what has already been seen by the ancient Indian 'see'rs. A wave is pulled out of their ocean of knowledge, here. This enables us to 'C' Truth through eyes of Management of business and life. That too, in today's age and context.

For those who wish to learn from this Paper, it would be useful to remember the ancient Indian *mantra*: *"Om sahna vavtu, sahna bhunattu saha viryam karwavahi tejasvinaditamastu ma vidvishavahai Om Shanti Shanti Shanti Om"*.

This is a prayer where entity teaching and taught pray together – to excellence (or Divinity) that both seek. The teacher learns through questions of a true seeker. The student learns from appreciation of texts by his Teacher – and the 'experience' their application has given in daily life. This is shared as both learn together. In this way the ocean of Knowledge expands. This Paper needs to expand with questions and answers of true seekers. First, management theory and finally, theory of all other subjects needs to be integrated here.

Proceeding in this way, both this Paper and its future contributors will discover Individuality. This will contribute to development of balance. Simultaneously, it should lead to balance in and development of society. Of course, in ancient times, teachers were Self Realised and filled with experience. Finding such a worthy *Guru* or Seer-Teacher would enable grasp of knowledge without reading a book. From authors personal experience he can only say that a *Guru* would Reinforce and teach. He would take students slowly through concepts, repeating them in different ways. This will ensure that knowledge is absorbed through Reinforcement. This Paper tries to do the same: repetition in different ways. The pain in the process is of giving up the ego of 'I know it all'. The fault, if any, is in the receiver when the *Guru* is perfect. The process of absorption of knowledge for the author was slow. This must have been due to many subtle faults. Therefore, even after writing this, it is difficult to claim that he is implementing it. He can only claim to have collected it.

The text above is a beginning of process of author's self discovery. The sharing of this process is only a recording of what the author has just begun to 'C'. If the author was in a state of *Adwaita*, he would not need to write. Yet, ancient texts have been written to benefit those who are in *Dwaita* or Duality. It is worth repeating that Duality is when the *Purusharthas* are understood as **two or dual** pairs. Then, Righteous Conduct guides economic behaviour and desires are guided by non-attachment to fruit of action. Only such Duality can be transformed to a higher state. Then a journey to *Vishisht Adwaitha* and from there to *Adwaitha* or non dual experience of the world is possible.

What would the journey from *Vishisht Adwaitha* to *Adwaitha* be like? The author can only speculate. LBNL (USA government laboratory referred in Background) has concluded that three fourth of creation is dark matter. This dark matter makes the universe ever expanding. Similarly, three fourth of man's potential is in darkness. This makes his universe of desires ever expanding. Ancient India's technique of meditating on light involves expanding it in ever widening circles (just like creation) to cover the universe. This must be to remove the dark matter within. The idea is to see everything as light and be the light. Just as Jesus taught in simple words: 'I am the light of the world...' Swami Sivananda of Divine Life Society has written an experience when a stranger came to attack him during a public meeting. He visualised him as light and this calmed the attacker. Phyllis Krystal, a psychotherapist, has recorded her experience of sending Divine Love through her heart to hijackers of her plane. They let the passengers free. However, reading about a subject is different from practice. And the author has some distance to travel...

Bibliography

This Paper uses the triad of: 'All writings and speeches of Sri Sathya Sai Baba (public and private)', 'Michael Porter's work till 2000', and management textbooks of '90's including Philip Kotler's, 'Marketing Management 9th Edition'. The last two were reading material used by top managers and CEOs when they were in college. It also uses standard textbook concepts like Maslow's hierarchy of needs, 7S Model of McKinsey etc. The Bibliography, therefore, is limited as the focus has been on integrating some modern management concepts with the ancient Indian tradition of business & life as revealed by the writings and teachings of Sri Sathya Sai Baba (who has written/ spoken on all the subjects covered in this Paper). If integration of some concepts can be successfully demonstrated, then, hopefully, all concepts can be integrated for a holistic learning and teaching experience of Management. This is the idea behind this Paper. Also, many ideas are presented in a new way here. Much research may have been done. However, for ease of reader, bibiliography includes publications which help verify these ideas through easily accessible public sources. The Bibliography of this Paper, therefore, includes:

1. Man Management: Discourses of Sri Sathya Sai Baba on Management (Compiled and published by His students of The School of Business Management, Accounting and Finance, Prasanthi Nilayam) and Printed by Gunasundari Modern Art Printers, Chennai. **Also 'Vahini's written by Him personally** including *Vidya Vahini*, Upanishad Vahini, *Sutra* Vahini, Sathya Sai Vahini, *Sandeha Nivarini*, Prema Vahini, *Prasnottara* Vahini, Prashanti Vahini, *Jnana* Vahini, Gita Vahini, *Dhyana* Vahini, *Dharma* Vahini etc. All His public and private discourses – some of them compiled as 'Summer Showers in Brindavan' May/June 1974 etc... They are Published by Sri Sathya Sai Books and Publications Trust, (Now Sri Sathya Sai Sadhana Trust, Publications Division), Prasanthi Nilayam, India.

2. Michael Porter: Complete work till around 2000 (the time current top managers and CEO's attended classes in Business School).

3. Philip Kotler: Marketing Management 9th edition

4. Al Ries and Jack Trout: Bottom up Marketing

5. Standard Textbooks for Management Students prescribed in '80's and '90s.

6. H.H. Dalai Lama His comments of on 'The Nalanda origins of Tibetan Buddhism' were reported in Hindustan Times-interview with Shishir Gupta, Nov3, 2012. 50 thoughts from Dalai Lama– published in Times of India in 2013: http://timesofindia.speakingtree. in/spiritual-slideshow/seekers/wellness/fifty-thoughts-from-dalai-lama/19228

7. Wikipedia, Encyclopedia Britannica, Online Dictionaries: Though background reading from different sources may have been done, the 'Simple to search for' quotes enable the reader to test the validity of what is written as the focus of the Paper may not allow more details of the subject. Ideas verified by research can use a Wikipedia source.

8. India Today, Special Volume 2012 Sri Sathya Sai Baba, S. Gurumurthy: Data of His public service is from this source. Pg113 lists village uplift activity undertaken by devotees (not included in Paper).

Shankracharya Sri Chandrashekhar Saraswati: Though he has written extensively, http://www.kamakoti.org/hindudharma/part10/chap3.htm gives readers a quick update and may motivate further search.

Michigan State University website: The research by Layne Cameron and Christoph Adami was easily accessible on this link in August 2013: http://msutoday.msu.edu/news/2013/evolution-will-punish-you-if-youre-selfish-and-mean/

11. Jainism: http://en.wikipedia.org/wiki/Mahavira. In addition, the researcher may use the following reading material– useful to begin with: http://www.jainworld.com/science/mathephysics1.asp Mathematicoscientific ideas in the Jaina *Karma* Theory: Abstract by Prof. L C Jain, http://www.jainworld.com/scriptures/samayasara.asp Digambar philosophical work "Samaysara" esp. Point 7.

12. Harvard Business Review June 2013 Cover Story: "Transient Advantage – Rita Gunther McGrath

13. Sikhism: http://www.speakingtree.in/spiritual-slideshow/seekers/god-and-i/10-lessons-from-guru-granth-sahib/235118

All unacknowledged quotations are from public and private speeches of SRI SATHYA SAI BABA whose date, time or occasion are difficult to trace and acknowledge individually. The concepts of "5 Life Breaths of Business", 5 "Life Forces of Business" and almost all explanations of Indian spiritual texts and economic thinking as given in the Introduction, Background, Part A have been replicated from His teachings (Please refer Introduction – Choice of Sources). The definition of the role of Manager and qualities required to become one (given in Section 4.3) are quotes from Him. Section 4.4 also concludes with His quotation about Chanakya's view of business so does the section on Financial Theory in Chapter 7 use His discourse about Chanakya. In fact, Sections 4.1, 4.2, 4.3, 4.4 and 4.6 are all derived from His views on Management. Each individual quote is difficult to trace. The Paper shares insights given by Him (in public or in private) and inspired by the study of His interpretation of the practice of Management of Life to seek excellence or Self Realisation.

Acknowledgements

There is no excuse for placing acknowledgements at end of the book. It should always be in the beginning. However, the end is the most important place – after the beginning. Two things influenced the author in making this choice. The first question the author asked himself was: who is the book written for? Secondly, what is the purpose of the contribution of those acknowledged here?

The answer of both questions point to the reader. The purpose of effort of those acknowledged is to make the book more readable – for the reader. So… readability decided. The message of book started from the dedicatory page and an Acknowledgements page there may have disturbed this flow. So it seemed to the author. Also, how many readers would read serious acknowledgements there? – They want to read the book, first! Only those who find such a book interesting would be interested in knowing who contributed to it. Also, an author wants to keep acknowledgements short at the beginning of the book – while at the end he can elaborate. In this way those acknowledged get their due.

The primary Sources of Study are acknowledged in Introduction. These are also acknowledged throughout the book. The logic that other acknowledgements relate mostly to contributions made after the book was written, and, are acknowledged at the end is unacceptable. Assuming this to be a new beginning…we start.

Eternal Acknowledgements (in first person – author's words):

"The first acknowledgement is towards my mother and father. I am still to fathom the depth of their spirituality. I, then, acknowledge the debt of the Seers who were recipients of the knowledge shared here. I also acknowledge the debt of the beneficial cycles of nature (understood as Gods) which create balance enabling comfort in which we can seek answers to questions. Similarly, I bow to all elders of my family. But for their DNA – both biological and spiritual, my understanding would have been different. My maternal grandmother and maternal uncle encouraged me on my spiritual journey. As did many others – who remain unnamed. The family members' experiences and moral life of India's freedom fighters left an indelible impression on my young mind. My interactions with political and spiritual leaders led to imbibing ancient Indian spiritual tradition from an early age. It made me write a '*Rupak*' (in prose and poetry) based on India's freedom struggle while I was in Class 8 of school. I produced and directed it on stage, when in Class 9. I am grateful to all who inspired me – then and thereafter. Finally and, also, the first – in all ways, there is 'One' who has enabled this experience of spirituality. Acknowledgement is a trifle for Him. He does not need or encourage it. For, remaining unnamed only adds to His natural state. He seeks the difficult – that I live by what is written here. If only I could give Him that bliss!"

Acknowledged – but not sufficiently:

The ancient Indian tradition depends upon a triad of sources. The acknowledgements of this book, too, depend upon a triad: The **two Sources of Research** (mentioned in the Introduction) and **Circumstances**. These can ever be adequately acknowledged: irrespective of where we place this page. Had the latter not created adverse conditions – an 'inner search' may not have started. This book may not have been written. Lest persons involved in these unfortunate events feel otherwise, the author's gratitude is expressed here.

Acknowledgements:

After the recession, the author was dissatisfied. He felt predicting recession it is not enough. How to prevent recession is a bigger contribution. The circumstances and the dissatisfaction that led to the book are acknowledged with gratitude.

Prof P.N. Sharma's contribution needs acknowledgement. He is a scholar and Member of Governing Body of Library of Tibetan Works and Archives. He has translated many books as also 9th century classics for His Holiness The Dalai Lama. Jawaharlal Nehru, India's first Prime Minister, has written the Foreword to one book authored by him. He looks like a 65 or 70 year old but is 91 years of age! He reviewed this work in great detail to help discover a typographical error in the word *Nijam*. This word is not found in texts but used by the Source of the Paper. The Source uses it to describe Truth as visible in the world experienced by sense organs – common to both man and animal. The word is commonly used in *Telgu* language – mother tongue of the Source. As almost all discourses of the Source were delivered in *Telgu*, no alternate word is used here. Prof Sharma also corrected a mix up between two Sanskrit *slokas*. Such diligence is unparalleled. This made receiving his final comments most rewarding: "Excellent work…Brilliant in its integration of ancient Indian Truths with the concepts of management. Congratulations on your unique effort…" Asked, separately, after amendments, about changes needed in manuscript, he graciously commented "I think the accompanying draft is admirable as far as it goes…". He introduced the author to His Holiness The Dalai Lama and also Prof Samdhong Rinpoche. His lifelong service to spirituality was evident in the way he was received by His Holiness.

Grateful thanks to His Holiness The Dalai Lama for giving so much of His valuable time to the author and writing the Foreword of the book. Prof Samdhong Rinpoche took a deep interest in the book after He began reading it. His quotation on co-operation and competition has been used at the end of Chapter 4. Practice of Awareness section was triggered by some of His observations on right livelihood, right speech, right action and, above all, right intention put on His Facebook page by admirers. This section, then, sought to fulfill Prof Sharma's desire to include the valedictory *sloka* of Upanishads, too, in the text.

The contribution of Mr Lakshmi Narsimhan the then Registrar of Sri Sathya Sai Institute of Higher Learning is acknowledged. After briefly reading some portions of Part A – even before even reading the early draft on four *Purusharthas* section – he presented his personal copy of the book 'Man Management' to the author. This gift is the Primary Source of research and is gratefully acknowledged.

Prof Pradip Khandwalla, former Director of Indian Institute of Management, Ahmedabad is acknowledged. He took time from his busy schedule for the book and gave a review.

The contribution of Ms Aarti Nagraj and Ms Archana Jain is duly acknowledged. Ms Aarti Nagraj edited 187 pages. Ms Archana, in doing the proof reading, pointed out the importance of Contents page. They also refused to accept any compensation for their untiring effort. Ms Archana's 13 pages of mistakes in publishers proof are proof of her commitment to ensuring high quality. Prof Gautam Datt is acknowledged for introducing Ms Archana to the author. Ms Rupali Bhagoria's contribution is acknowledged. She worked on the Glossary despite a hectic teaching schedule but could not complete it due to health problems. Mr Ashish Bhagoria, too, gave very freely of his resources and time and was a genuine well wisher of the project. He took time from his business to always help. Mr T.C.

Bhagoria gave a copy of the manuscript to Prof Sharma for review, co-ordinated with him and made his time available for this book.

Prof Kumar Bhaskar of Sri Sathya Sai Institute of Higher Learning (SSSIHL) is also acknowledged. He compiled the later edition of the book 'Man Management'. The earlier version of this book, prepared by students of SSSIHL, is the Primary Source, used here. He commented that the manuscript was "A very good effort". He humbly stated that his opinions have "limited application". His inputs are incorporated here and if not, reasons shared with him. Dr Dhiraj Sembhi read the book in detail and gave some useful inputs. One input, he received from Source of this book, has led to a Diagram. His doctoral thesis is referred to in Chapter 7. Dr Kshama Aggarwal of University of Rajasthan shared her inspiration of incorporating the four 'ashrams' of life in management study. The author elaborates it in Awareness and this idea fits into the concept of Product Life Cycle, too.

Mr Satpal patiently made and remade diagrams of the book since mid '80s. His patience and availability were a source of strength for the author. Educationist Dr Punam Datt's assertion about real worth of Manuscript and marking words for Glossary helped.

Prof Abhinandan Jain of IIM A was supportive of the book's idea and felt that 'goal' is an important aspect of strategy. Prof Arvind Sahay of IIM A and Prof Sunil Gupta of Harvard Business School updated the author with developments in management thought. Prof V.L. Mote graciously came for the presentation to Phd (FPM) students at IIM A and exchanged ideas with the author on ethics for a couple of decades. Batch mate from IIM A, Mr. Nayan Parikh gave of his time. Ms. Madhavi Murthy and Rashmi Malik, too, read the manuscript. Prof Amitava Chattopadhyaya of INSEAD Singapore was supportive towards the book. Profs Nanda (Director), Piyush Sinha, M.R. Dixit & BP Area of IIMA are also acknowledged.

The helpfulness of Shelly Edmunds and her team at Partridge is acknowledged.

Unacknowledged:

The occurrence of ideas and their flow often left the author amazed. A strong suspicion of a hidden inner source inspiring them grew overtime. Unable to claim authorship, he uses the title 'scribe' – on inner page as Part A of the book starts. This phenomenon has no name – nor can it be ignored. A final unacknowledged source of strength needs to be recorded. The contribution of wife and children usually remains unacknowledged. For, only they know the family cost of writing a manuscript. They became aware of its existence only in the last two years before publication! So, for many years they never knew why they suffered. However, once they discovered, they were full of concern with a willingness to participate. Vivekananda's conversation with secular teacher was the wife's contribution as also cover copy polish idea. Sai Priya volunteered to edit the book from Page 187 onwards. Swabhanu, too, helped in some editing as also using MS Word to make Sketch 1a,b,c. Aditiyaa and Swabhanu helped in Diagram 4.0. Aditiyaa also helped draw Illustration 1. Swabhanu made Figure 1.1b while Sai Priya fitted it in the book. Swabhanu usually stopped every activity to listen when the author spoke at home. He came back with questions, asking about progress of the book. The author feels blessed to have such a thoughtful family. He has, indeed, learnt much from them. Their affection and support – extended without ulterior motive – adds meaning to life.

Final Acknowledgement:

Finally, the author acknowledges that all faults in the manuscript are his sole responsibility. Despite having such strong Sources of research, if errors have slipped in, it is only due to his lack of Awareness. In case contents of the book are not clear, it is, again, due to his inability to communicate. For, the same spiritual material has guided Indian civilisation for thousands of years – leading to economic prosperity with spiritual balance. The same Management texts are used in all universities. If a *Guru* or reincarnation can interpret them for the benefit of man and society through transformation of each student – the author will be grateful. That such a possibility exists or is likely to happen soon, is a hope. This hope inspires the author – for our civilisation.

Many authors and many words may remain unacknowledged –
but their contribution is acknowledged in the ancient Indian tradition
by a debt called 'Rishi Rin' (*debt to the preceptors*).
He who has come to know about the experience of the process of transformation
is supposed to repay this debt by trying to disseminate knowledge about it.
Then, lack of acknowledgement in Bibliography or Glossary may be forgiven.

Forgiveness is sought for words or authors missed out, here.

Glossary

Ab aeterno:	From the ancient past
Adwaita:	It is a school of Vedanta popularized by Adi Shankaracharya. *Advaita* means non dual or not two. It teaches that everything is part of the same non dual consciousness.
Atma:	The true Self of man, *Atma,* is pure consciousness – which is same as *Brahman,* the Highest Reality.
Akasa:	means ether in both elemental and metaphysical sense in ancient Indian tradition, Space etc.
Angapaka:	It is a branch of mathematics mentioned in *Sastras* or ancient Indian texts.
Apaana Shakti:	Here it is referred to as force of Gravity. *Apaana* as breath is also the downward moving breath.
Apara Vidya, Para Vidya:	There are two types of education: lower (*Apara Vidya*) and higher (*Para Vidya*) for fulfilling the four goals of life. Fulfilling goals of *Artha* and *Kama*, some feel, requires lower learning. However, fulfilling them appropriately requires the Highest learning which gives an understanding of *Dharma* and *Moksha* – both of which guide *Artha* and *Kama*, respectively.
Apastamba sulba sutras:	They are sources of mathematics and ` geometry in Indian Mathematics form Vedic Period.
Artha:	Sanskrit term meaning "purpose, cause, motive, meaning, notion, wealth, economy or gain". Ancient Indian tradition, however, understands it as 'declaration of distinction' of man from rest of creation. Hence, such activity that gives meaning to human life can be considered as *Artha*. Another meaning of *Artha* in Hindi language is 'meaning'.
Atma Vidya:	The science and art of knowledge of Self.
Atma:	Soul.

Balance:	Balance occurs when implications of Truths are 'realised' and acted upon by man – it is a state where everything is in correct proportion and leads to equilibrium. There is a Dynamic Balance (dealt by the book) and Absolute Balance (outside the scope of this book). (The Source states that Knowledge should lead to Skill. Both, together, should lead to Balance. When knowledge is not applied in a manner that helps others it leads to imbalance within man and society. Hence application of Knowledge using Skill to help others leads to Balance. Balance within man leads to Insights that enable man to express Individuality and are a result of Focussed Concern for others or Self – which, again, leads to concern for all. The book is about creating Balance. At the end of the book an example of Insight is given – in the author's prediction of the global economic recession).
Baser instinct:	baser instincts imply the lowest order needs in need hierarchy – shared with animals.
Bhagavad Gita:	Ancient Indian tradition depends upon a triad of spiritual texts. *Bhagavad Gita* is one of them. It is a dialogue between *Pandava* prince Arjun and his guide Lord Krishna on the battlefield signifying every battle in life – within and outside man.
Bhakti:	Devotional worship directed to a supreme deity.
Bhava Adwaitha:	*'Bhava'* implies feeling in the heart. This implies having same Attitude of equal Love for all – as all are part of same consciousness. This is recommended in ancient Indian tradition.
Bhu sastra:	Sacred Text about the earth.
Bhugola sastra:	Sacred Text about the earth – which is a sphere.
Brahma Sutras:	The Brahma sūtras are part of the triad of texts that form basis of ancient Indian tradition. They are early exposition of the Vedanta-interpretation of the *Upanishads*

Brahmajnana:	Awareness / total understanding of Self.
Buddhi:	Intellect.
'C'eers:	Seers. In ancient Indian tradition, the Seers did not take authorship of their sacred formulae or 'mantras' but 'saw' them unfold in their mind. Hence the Seers are called 'mantra drashtas'.
Chaitanya:	Awareness / consciousness.
Darbha:	Coarse grass that is honoured by the Hindus and is used by the *Brahmans* in their religious rituals and practices. It is also referred to as *Kusa*.
Dharma:	*Dharma* encompasses ideas such as duty, rights, character, vocation, religion, customs and all behaviour considered appropriate, correct or morally upright.
Dharmic:	Righteous.
Dipstick test:	Dipsticks are dipped into a liquid to perform a chemical test or to provide a measure of quantity of the liquid.
Dwaita:	A school of Vedanta founded by Shri Madhvacharya: a strict distinction between God — the Supreme-Soul and the individual Soul – *Atma*. They are two – not one!
Educare:	To bring out what is within man: the best!
Ethos:	A Greek word signifying 'character', used to signify guiding beliefs or ideals of community, sect, nation etc.
Gestalt:	A physical, biological, psychological, or symbolic configuration or pattern of elements so unified as a whole that its properties cannot be derived from a simple summation of its parts.
Gola:	A sphere.
Guru:	Master.
Hamurabi:	The sixth king of Babylon from 1792 BC to 1750 BC middle chronology. He became the first king of the Babylon Empire. He followed idea of reciprocal justice among social equals known as code of Hamurabi: life for life, eye for eye, tooth for tooth etc. Jesus in His Sermon on the Mount is said to have opposed this.

	This opposition has been interpreted by some to imply that such reciprocity encourages excessive retaliation rather than restricting crime.
Hedonistic:	Self indulgent – indulging in pursuit of sensual pleasure.
Hellenistic Period:	The Hellenistic age is a period in history defined as the time between the Alexander the Great and the rise of Roman domination. During this time, Greek culture was dominant throughout the Mediterranean, thus the name Hellenistic, which is derived from the Greek "Hellas" means Greece.
Heretic:	Non conformist thinker, capable of dissenting with popular opinion, practicing religious heresy etc.
Hiranykashipu:	*Hiranyakashipu* was the king of the *Daityas*.
Hypothesis:	A tentative explanation for an observation.
Jada:	Non living, not Self.
Jnana, Sujnana, Vijnana:	A rising hierarchy of Truth leading to higher Truth and, then, Highest Truth through knowledge. Man, through education, moves from *Jnana* or Knowledge to *Sujnana* – the higher knowledge that seeks the best interests of society. *Vijnana* is the Highest Knowledge leading to Highest Truth and emerges when intentions, urges of man become totally Pure. When experience of Selfless Love begins, it leads to application of '*Jnana*' or knowledge. This is acquired through concentration for analysing the objective world. Knowledge is further subjected to contemplation so as to apply it for the best interest of society. This leads to *Sujnana.* When intentions and urges emerge from man's purified Consciousness saturated with excellence, '*Vijnana*' results.
Jyotisa:	Study of Mathematics in ancient Indian tradition. It is called the eye of Knowledge. As the Universe is interlinked (Chapter 6), the movement of stars impacts each other and also the earth and people living on earth.

Astrology is thus the popular understanding of *Jyotisa*. However, it is not just knowledge of interconnectedness, but the other sections of Chapter 6 which are more relevant.

Ancient Indian centers of learning, thus, have a Planetarium to learn about the interconnectedness of the Universe. They also teach Self Awareness (Part A of this book) along with. This gives 'Jyoti' or Light. This Light of *Vedas* shows the way to man and mankind. Knowledge of mathematics has led this tradition to calculate accurately the distance between the earth and Sun and many other sophisticated equations detailed in Background.

Kama:	Desire. It is the Third *Purushartha*.
Karma:	Activity, work, action.
Karma Adwaitha:	This means having same attitude of equal Love for All being put in action without recognising the physical differences in the world. This is not recommended in ancient Indian tradition which states that give a King respect that his status requires while having equal Love for him and a farmer.
Kuttaka:	Indian method of solving Linear Intermediate equations for Integral Solutions – This is title of book published by Rashtriya Sanskrit Vidyapeeth, Tirupati
Lakshmana:	In ancient Indian *Sastra* of Ramayan, he was brother and close companion of Lord Rama.
Lila:	No English translation is possible but loosely it can be understood as 'play' or 'divine play'. The Wikipedia states a generally agreed upon notion that it has different connotations in *Dwaita* and *Adwaita*. It states "Within non– dualism, Lila is a way of describing all reality, including the cosmos, as the outcome of creative play by the divine absolute (Brahman). In the dualistic schools of Vaishnavism,

	Lila refers to the activities of God and his devotee, as well as the macrocosmic actions of the manifest universe, as seen in the Vaishnava scripture *Srimad Bhagvatam*, verse 3.26.4"
Locus of control:	idea from personality psychology – internal locus of control implies man believes he can control events affecting him while external locus of control implies that man believes he is controlled by outside world.
Mahabharata:	A Sanskrit epic. It is one of the oldest case studies in the world. It is said that whatever happens in the real world is included in this epic. It details the dynastic struggle and war between cousins *Pandavas* and *Kauravas* – with *Pandavas* winning by following *Dharma* and Lord Krishna despite having smaller size of army.
Mahasamadhi:	Is the act of consciously and intentionally leaving one's body by enlightened Souls.
Mahatma:	Great Soul.
Maslow:	Was an American psychologist who was best known for a theory of psychological health predicated on fulfilling innate human needs in priority, culminating in non-attachment.
Moksha:	It is understood in ancient Indian tradition as *Moha-Ksheya* or end of delusion of delusion of attachment. It is also understood as liberation.
Nalanda:	Was an ancient center of higher learning in Bihar, India.
Nijam:	This word is not found in texts but used by the Source of the Paper. He uses it to describe Truth as it is visible in the world as experienced by sense organs (or *Maya*) – common to both man and animal. The word is from *Telgu* language – mother tongue of the Source. As almost all discourses of the Source were delivered in *Telgu*, no alternate word is used here.
Nirvana:	Final goal for man in Buddhism. Liberation is from sorrow, desire and cycle of birth and death.

Nishkama Karma:	Action undertaken without attachment to fruit of action.
Om Tat Sat:	A Sanskrit *Mantra* implying – What is everlasting and unchanging is Excellence in all dimensions simultaneously or God, whose infinite Existence – Consciousness Bliss is denoted by Om. This is understood as primordial sound and consists of letters *A, U* and *M.* These three letters have tremendous meaning in Islam and Christianity, too, it is believed by some. For the words 'Ameen' and 'Amen' share common letters. Hence ancient Indians believe that within Om is everything. Om contains all. Om is all. Om is present everywhere, like light.
Oligopoly:	A state of limited competition where the market is shared by few producers.
Panch Pranas:	*Prana, Apaana, Udana, Samana, Vyana* 'forward moving air', 'air that moves away', 'Upward moving air', 'balancing air', 'outward moving air' respectively. *Prana*, some say, brings in the fuel. *Samana*, they say, converts the fuel to energy. *Vyana* circulates the energy to various places. *Apana* moves the waste materials. *Udana* governs the positive energy and governs the work the body does. Key to health is to keep *Pranas* in harmony.
Param Atma:	Supreme Soul or Spirit, called the Primordial Self who is spiritually identical with the Absolute or *Brahman.*
Parmahansa Yogananda:	Indian Yogi and *Guru* who founded the Self Realisation Fellowship. Author of book: 'Autobiography of a Yogi. This book has many instances of what is not possible according to modern science but spirituality makes man achieve that. It introduced millions of westerners to meditation and *Kriya Yoga.* This book seeks to fulfill His last wish. He gave hope for a united world combining the best qualities of efficient America and spiritual India.

Porter:	Professor of Business Administration at the Harvard Business School. He is author of Competitive Strategy and Competitive Advantage of Nations.
Prahalad:	*Prahlada* is the saintly son of *Hiranyakashipu* from the *Puranas* – known for his piety and bhakti to *Vishnu*.
Prakriti:	Nature or Creation as distinct from the Creator or God – while God is eternal, *Prakriti* is ever changing.
Prana:	Primal Energy.
Prema:	Selfless Love.
Puranas:	Ancient Indian texts with stories about the Divine.
Purushartha:	A goal, end or aim of human existence. Another possible explanation: The word consists of '*Purusha*' and '*Artha*'. '*Purusha*' is the Creator. '*Artha*', according to the Source of book, is the 'declaration of distinction'. In common Hindi language, '*Artha*' is understood as meaning. *Purushartha* is only for man and not for the rest of creation. Hence, firstly, *Purushartha* can be understood as that which gives meaning to man's actions. Or, it is the declaration of distinction for man, designed for him, by the Creator. Or, it is about understanding meaning of Creator – for man!
Purushasuktam:	*Purusha suktam* is a hymn of the *Rigveda*. It reveals the Source of all and is considered to be the essence of all 'Sruthis' or Divine revelations.
Rajasic, Sathwic, Tamsic:	The Supreme Consciousness, in ancient Indian tradition, projects itself as living beings projecting 'Rajo Guna'. Mere reading of the book (without reflecting or responding) is passive, not active learning. Such passive participation is '*tamasic*' or associated with dull brains. The individual's effort to turn the thought over in his mind, trying to assimilate it makes a person active or '*rajasic*'. When man achieves the experience of purity of intention this is '*sathwic*'.

Ravana and Kumbhakaran:	*Ravana* was the demon or *Rakshasa* king of Sri Lanka and *Kumbhkarana* was his brother. *Ravana* had learnt 64 types of knowledge while Lord Rama, even though He had not learnt so many types of Knowledge in this physical incarnation, was able to defeat *Ravana*. This is because He adhered to Truth, Humility and Righteousness and embodied all ideas of ancient Indian tradition in His behaviour.
Rekha Ganita:	Geometry.
Rig Veda:	First among the *Vedas*. Its text shows awe of creation, among other declarations.
Ritam:	Highest Truth which does not change across Space and Time and is based on the experience of the Universe as One Soul. Even *Upanishads* use *Satyam* and *Ritam* interchangeably but the Source reveals that *Ritam* is that which does not Change across Space, too.
Sacrifice:	The word sacrifice is used in context of sacrificing ignorance and other activities of man. The spiritual Source has given both dimensions in *Prema Vahini* authored by Him as follows: "All action (*Karma*) done for the sake of three goals viz. to leverage the Universe for the worship of the Lord, to establish peace and justice in society and to control and co-ordinate the functions of the body, is sacrifice. The first is called a holy sacrificial ritual (*Yajna*); the second, charity (*Dana*); the third penance (*Tapas*). All human acts must subserve these three needs and an ethical life is the foundation for attaining that stage. This ethical life is based on the discrimination between truth and falsehood. Just as the pearl is retained while the shell is discarded, the essence that is Truth must be accepted and the non-essential rejected.

For this, individual exertion and divine grace, both should be present. One should also practice the great lesson that the body and the Atma are separate. This is a highly beneficial exercise. Such discrimination is necessary for secular as well as spiritual life."

Sadhana: Practice something as a discipline, in order to learn from it, and make it a regular life habit. It is understood as a Spiritual practice.

Salaat: Devotion in Islam.

Samikarna: mathematical exercise in ancient Indian mathematics which is same as equation in modern mathematics.

Samyak Drishti, Samyak Vak, Samyak Bhavam, Samyak Kriya: Sacred speech, listening, feeling, action in Buddhism.

Sanatana Dharma: The original name of what is now popularly called Hinduism or Hindu *Dharma*. It is referred to as Ancient Indian wisdom and tradition, here.

Sangham: Group/Community Together. Buddhism talks of taking refuge in *Sangham*. This is a group of virtuous, kind, compassionate and generous – for without such qualities any group is doomed – ultimately.

Sastra: a word used in ancient Indian tradition to describe a sacred scripture.

Sathwa Guna: Pure and good quality of everything in nature.

Satyam: That Truth that does not change across time unlike *Nijam* which changes with time. This Truth emerges from within man through discipline, enquiry and sincere application of unity of thought, word and deed.

Self Actualiston: The realisation or fulfillment of one's potential and talents. This need motivates man to become the best person he possibly can in service of both himself and others.

Selfless Love: Love that is noble, pure and free from desire or egoism

Shanti: Peace.

Shruti:	Hearing the inner voice of Conscience or revealed word of Divine – depending on how one interprets the revelation.
Shukshama Akasa:	Subtle form of *Akasa*.
Siddhanta-skandha:	Ancient Indian text that is the source for Arithmetic, trigonometry, geometry and algebra.
Siddhi:	The higher stage of experience where Wisdom is won.
Smriti:	Remembering or memorizing the 'Shruti'.
SQC:	Statistical Quality Control.
Sthithi:	The stage of experience. Education, in ancient Indian tradition, gives a higher state of experience of Truth.
Sthula Akasa:	Gross firmament. The gross *Akasa* experienced by sense organs of man.
Sugriva:	In the Hindu epic Ramayana, Sugriva was the younger brother of Vali, whom he succeeded as ruler of the *vanara* or monkey kingdom Kishkindha.
Swami Vivekanada:	A Hindu monk. He introduced Hinduism at the Parliament of World's Religions in Chicago in 1893 and Vedanta, Yoga to western world.
Swartha, Parartha Parmartha:	Self interest, enlightened self interest which looks after interest of others, highest interest of society and universe.
Tamasic, Tamoguna:	It implies Darkness/ Ignorance or inactivity. It is the principle of inertia or dullness.
Tapas:	Penance. It is not physical contortion but complete and correct co-ordination of thought, word and deed.
Taxila:	Taxila is considered to be amongst the earliest universities in the world.
TQM:	Total Quality Management.
Trikaarana Shudhhi:	Unity and purity of thought, word and action.
Upanishads:	They are part of the triad of texts that form basis of ancient Indian tradition. They give 'Atma Vidya' or Knowledge of the Self. They are also referred to as Vedanta or end of *Vedas*.

Vali:	Was king of *Kishkindha*, a son of *Indra* and the elder brother of *Sugriva*.
Vedapurusha Yajna:	*Yajna* is sacrifice. Society exists only on basis of sacrifice. Mother sacrifices for child, friend for another, individual for the group, man for society, nation etc. Such sacrifice should be conscious, voluntary, without desire of reward – and, therefore, spiritual. The inner significance of offerings to the fire is sacrifice of faults, failings, temptations, transgressions. This ritual, with such significance, was performed by the Source of the book for seven days during the festival of *Dasara* for the promotion of the material and spiritual well-being of mankind. *Vishnu, Siva* and *Brahma* are all worshipped during this *Yajna*.
Vedas:	Ancient Hindu scriptures revealed solely by inner hearing to seers. These are divine revelations. They are later classified by Sage *Veda Vyasa* as four *Vedas*: *Rig, Yajur, Sama* and *Atharva*.
Vibhishana:	A king who was given the rule of Sri Lanka in the ancient Indian historical epic Ramayana. He was the younger half brother of the *Rakshasa* (demon) king *Ravana* of *Lanka*. Lord Rama chose not to rule Himself and gave the crown to *Vibhishana*.
Vidya Vahini:	The flow of highest education. Water is life giving – like education. Water, when still, gathers moss, insects and disease. Flow of water ensures purity. Education that gives life to society is, thus, a flow in ancient Indian tradition. It is the life breath of society. It is a journey from Truth to Higher Truth within man. This flow of education flows into the ocean of *Prashanti* or Highest Peace.

Vishisht Adwaita:	Qualified non dualism. It states that *Brahman* or Supreme Consciousness as defined in *Adwaitha*, alone, exists. However, it is characterised by multiplicity. It shows that all diversity subsumes to the underlying unity. The triad of *Brahma Sutras, Upanishads* and *Bhagavad Gita* are interpreted in a way that shows unity in diversity – for any other way would violate their consistency.
Viveka:	To focus on intellect to transform the heart using 'intelligent discrimination'. This is understood as *Viveka.*
Vyakta-ganita:	Arithmetic was called by this name in ancient Indian tradition. It included addition, subtraction, multiplication and division.
Yajur homa:	Sacrificial ritual signifying sacrifice of faults, failings, temptations, transgressions. Fire purifies gold. Sacrifice of these in the inner fire purifies man and makes him fit to act in society while achieving the highest goal within.
Yajur Veda:	One of the *Vedas*. It is a collection of sacrificial formulas and prayers.
Yugas:	There are four Ages or Yugas (*Krita, Treta, Dwapara* and the present day *Kali*). They follow each other in ancient Indian tradition. They can be understood as time cycles.
Zaakat:	Charity in Islam.
Zeno of Citium:	Was a Greek philosopher from Cyprus. He founded the Stoic school of philosophy. This school of philosophy dominated thought from Hellenistic to Roman period. It was based on moral ideas, on goodness and peace of mind. These are gained by man through living a virtuous life in tune with nature.

When there is sincerity in the search for excellence – without the veil of selfishness, many Truths emerge from within. There is always a sea of data available, but to the sincere researcher only that data will appeal which can add value to society. In the author's experience there is a reality hidden in the quotation given before Chapter 6 which states: "...'That' prompts, promotes and fosters your progress".

This has been the authors experience about 'That'.

This book and the enclosed article are examples of this experience.

What is the point of predicting the future if you cannot give a way of changing it for the better?

The book begins with an understanding that education is about seeking the Truth. It ends with a demonstration of how this Truth is reflected in action. Awareness about Truth makes values emerge from 'within' man. Truth in action is *Dharma* or righteous conduct. That which is done with the good of society in mind is righteous conduct. Four *Purusharthas* or 4C's are the limits within which this Truth is implemented.

Case studies can only give Truth as at any one point of time. As the nature of world is ever changing, each situation is unique. What is the right conduct in a unique situation? This should emerge from 'within' man as *Satyam* or Truth.

An example of Truth emerging from 'within' man:

Truth that is not obvious to all may become obvious to some. For thousands of years apples have been falling and water rising on entering a tub of water. However, Newton and Archimedes happened to be thinking of this phenomenon. Is this a coincidence that they applied their mind to it when the physical event happened? If so, why did these coincidences not happen earlier to thinkers in formal education of the West? Truth or *Satyam* emerges from 'within' man on observing phenomenon that maybe 'outside'. When this happens fear of ridicule may not deter the braver ones. When some proclaimed that the earth is round – when all thought that it is flat – they were burnt at stake. How to transmit that which is not obvious to all? Jesus used parables. They appeared as stories but for those who had ears, they could hear. For, is it not said 'none as blind as those who have eyes?' Opening the eye of man, enabling him to 'C' the Truth is the task that each spiritual tradition entrusts to itself – to save man.

A financial parable was published seven trading days before the first down tick in S&P 500 (an index of USA equity markets) in Business Times, Singapore. Maybe this is an example of Truth emerging from 'within'. Its timing, probably, makes it the most accurate prediction of the recession. *Satyam* is not a phenomenon of an ancient past restricted to a chosen few. It can happen to ordinary mortals addressing mundane concerns. It does not require special skills – only a sincerity of purpose. It is experienced by many individuals in their daily life. In fact, its non occurrence should be a source of surprise for an educated man.

Why a story of Goldilocks?

Since time immemorial stories have been used to explain difficult ideas.
Jesus used parables and they were easily understood. This financial parable
tries to explain an idea – which otherwise was difficult to believe, for many.

The Prediction about Goldilocks growth:
"__When in late '07 the interest rates are adjusted upwards, severe pain is likely to be__
__felt__ (an estimated $ 1 trillion on ARMs i.e. adjustable rate mortgage, will be reset)."

Roald Dahl, a childrens author, was not charitable about Goldilocks.
He felt that Goldilocks was a 'brazen little crook'who stole porridge,
broke a chair and slept in a borrowed home. Cinderella, another child
fiction character, on the other hand, was a hard working young girl.
This is another matter that Cinderella's talent was not recognised.
Surprisingly a poverty of ideas is a step sister considered beautiful
by some. However, it took a prince to recognise her inner beauty – which
finally did get rewarded around midnight – just when all was at its darkest.
The ideas of hard work, no needless product obsolescence, value delivery
at a fair price will never get outdated. Common sense ethics like truth,
too, will always command a premium – despite an apparent discount.

Truth is just as relevant to the balance sheet of an individual
as it is to that of a firm or a nation. It prevents a recession.

Prediction of economic recession published on October4, 2007*

The Story of Goldilocks in the house of 'Bears'
Will cheap credit and hedges make her lead the world markets into the house of 'Bears'?

Goldilocks has strayed away from home once again. Deep in the forest of the global economy, Goldilocks has found a "safe" resting place – Where porridge and lodging is free. Just like credit (well, almost-in Yen carry trades). The 3 bears of "twin deficits", liability of retiring "baby boomers" and "excess liquidity, cheap credit" turn out to be friends after all.

Like Papa Bears porridge, some issues (like twin deficits) are too hot to handle and, therefore, irrelevant. Some others, like Mama Bears porridge (fate of retiring "baby boomers"), leave Goldilocks stone cold and, therefore, can be ignored. What Goldilocks loves is the porridge of Baby Bear full of cheap credit & uncontrolled spending. This she can lap up till she falls asleep (sadly, after breaking the very chair on which she eats).

The three bears do not return Goldilocks favour of gobbling up the porridge by doing the same to her. Instead, they call out to a fleeing Goldilocks and invite her to keep supping with them whenever she likes. Goldilocks has been doing so for some time now.
This "true" story of global growth is referred to as a "Goldilocks" situation by economists today.

The Story of US housing

Goldilocks prefers the borrowed house of bears to sleep and eat her porridge. Sleeping in a borrowed house is dangerous when the bears mood changes.

From 2001-2005 outstanding mortgage debt in US had risen 68% to 8888 billion $: an unparalleled debt expansion. Borrowing to own a house is easy when interest rates are low and "easy" cash is chasing borrowers. Repaying the same loan when interest rates are high may imply a liability much larger than what the buyer can afford. This is more so if the loan was a little beyond the means of the buyer to begin with and / or his subsequent

433

income stream does not increase to match the new liabilities. When rates increase from 5% to 7% that implies: a 40% increase in amount of interest to be paid. US Fed fund rates have risen from 1% to 5.25% in last few years.

Why should a loan be given to a buyer who can barely afford it? There are reasons. Firstly, if the lending bank can push the risk of default (by selling these loans) to Fannie Mae (ultimately, US taxpayers) or to buyers of Mortgage backed securities then the risk of default is not on the banks books – Even though it remains in the system. Secondly, the extreme competition among lenders to capture the same "prime" target audience of homebuyers forces them to expand to "sub prime" borrowers who have dubious or no credit record.

Consequently, home prices in the US today are not in any known relationship with either rents or salaries. Many homeowners complain that rents are less than half of mortgage payments. Salaries, for many, cover only short-run repayment using adjustable interest rates. When in late '07 the interest rates are adjusted upwards, severe pain is likely to be felt (an estimated $ 1 trillion on ARMs i.e. adjustable rate mortgage, will be reset). According to a typical "exploding" ARM sub-prime loan, buyers are considered qualified for loan if the original ("teaser") monthly payment is not higher than 61% of their post-tax income. The scheme works out such that in 2 years, without interest rate increase, the repayments become 96% of purchaser's income.

Goldilocks lost in "Hedges"

The Goldilocks economy has witnessed an explosive growth in derivatives. The housing loans, in a low credit risk environment, like many other transactions, were converted into derivatives. The size of these derivative transactions, used to "hedge" risks of Goldilocks growth, is many times larger than the jungle of global growth itself. Financial innovation has replaced technological innovation as the support system to global growth today.
The outstanding volume of derivative transactions is growing annually at 54%, while global nominal GDP is growing at less an 8% in dollar terms. If this rate of growth continues till end '08 the total outstanding derivates would cross 1,000,000 billion USD. Some estimate that the total volume of derivatives is over 60 times global M1, more than 12 times M2 and about 8 times global GDP.

In Goldilocks world every $ of GDP is being hedged 8 times or every demand deposit 60 times. Most of these hedges are done at historically low volatilities. Crisis occurs at high volatilities. We have seen what volatility in Mid-August did to equity prices the world over. Surprisingly 90% of these derivate transactions are on the books of a dozen global banks.

Nobody knows the collective impact of these derivative transactions in a financial crisis. Just as nobody knows what will happen to Goldilocks when the bears mood changes. The last time this impact was tested in 1998, outstanding derivatives were less than quarter of the current volume. The New York Fed had to undertake a dramatic rescue, supported by the same major banks that hold almost all the derivative paper today.

Of course, the objective behind most of the hedging transactions would have been to mitigate unnecessary risk or seek return. However, where the growth of derivatives is so much larger than the growth of global GDP, there is a high probability of some derivative transactions that are not funded by adequate capital. These pose a risk to the global financial system in a period where consistent & continuous volatility upsurge happens. While liquidity has generated asset bubbles, the risk of these bubbles has been "hedged" with derivatives and financial innovation. When will a pinprick burst a bubble? This is always difficult to forecast.

Financial innovation sometimes presents weakness as strength. Initially, excessive global liquidity allows the less credit-worthy to borrow more than they earlier could and now should. The big banks add fuel to the fire of credit expansion when they don't hold this debt but sell it to others through securitization. Sadly, each bank believes that risk 'removal' is taking place by distributing debts 'far & wide so that no single holder has significant exposure'. In reality, risk has spread for while derivatives do insure 'a holder against losses', but the sale of this risk to many small buyers spreads it in a manner that almost everybody will now be impacted.

"It is only a story…."

It is true that Goldilocks is a story meant only for children. Also, using parables was relevant only during the time of Jesus. While the risk of Goldilocks growth being unable to extricate itself from the "hedges" threatens to become real, one question inevitably arises:

"Will the porridge of "cheap credit" and the shade of 'Hedges' make Goldilocks lead the world markets into the house of 'Bears'?"

*Contents of the above article were published in Business Times, Singapore on October 7, 2007. Please refer front page title 'A Financial Parable' and editorial page.

The USA equity markets started falling around 14– 15 October 2007. It was thought to be a healthy correction, at that time...till it cascaded. In 2008 this down movement of the stock markets was recognised as a recession.

Printed in the United States
By Bookmasters